*Apparitions in Late Medieval
and Renaissance Spain*

Apparitions in Late Medieval and Renaissance Spain

by William A. Christian Jr.

Princeton University Press
Princeton, New Jersey

Library of Congress Cataloging in Publication Data will be
found on the last printed page of this book

This book has been composed in Linotron Aldus

Clothbound editions of Princeton University Press books
are printed on acid-free paper, and binding materials are
chosen for strength and durability

Printed in the United States of America by Princeton
University Press, Princeton, New Jersey

Contents

List of Figures

Maps

Acknowledgments

The Tinker Foundation of New York City provided a two-year fellowship for a broader study of which this is a part.

I am grateful to the following persons for reading and commenting on some or all of the manuscript: J. Arrom, S. Arrom, L. W. Bonbrake, P. Brown, R. Burns, R. Christian, W. Christian, G. Filion, C. Gibson, J. Gimeno, S. Harding, T. Kaplan, J. Lang, M. O'Neil, G. Ringel, S. Sharbrough, J. Sobre, K. Stewart, and C. Tilly.

I am grateful to a number of other persons for facilitating my research or suggesting ideas: Q. Aldea, M. Arnau i Guerola, C. Baraut, G. Calvo Moralejo, J. Dittes, W. Fackovec, J. Fort i Gaudí, B. Friedmann, I. Gallego Peñalver, M. A. García, M. Jiménez Monteserín, T. Koehler, M. Kross, C. Lisón Tolosana, E. Luque Baena, T. Marín, F. Marquez Villanueva, D. Martínez, D. Pérez Ramírez, C. Staehlin, B. Storchovsky, G. Todini, and M. B. Young; the parish priests of Albalate de Zorita, Griñón, Escalona, Jaén (San Ildefonso), Navalagamella, Navas de San Antonio, and Valverde del Majano; the Franciscan community of Santa María de la Cruz, Cubas; and the Instituto Enrique Flórez de Historia Eclesiástica of the Consejo Superior de Investigaciones Científicas, Madrid.

Illustrations were provided by Archivo Mas of Barcelona, Cristina García Rodero, and the Marian Library of the University of Dayton, Ohio.

*Apparitions in Late Medieval
and Renaissance Spain*

INTRODUCTION
When People Meet God

Like most other peoples, Spaniards have long wondered about God and the saints—what they want from mortals, how they affect human affairs, even what they look like. The most direct evidence has come from face to face meetings with the holy ones. These meetings are the subject of this book.

In the past 150 years, divine apparitions to Catholics have been given worldwide publicity. In nineteenth-century France, a number of local visions played a part in the reestablishment of abandoned shrines and a revival of devotional Catholicism.[1] The two most famous were at La Salette in 1846, where the Virgin threatened famine and chastisement unless the world repented, and at Lourdes in 1858, where the Virgin confirmed the dogma of the Immaculate Conception proclaimed four years earlier by Pius IX. In 1917 appearances of the Virgin to three children at Fatima stiffened popular resistance to the first lay government in Portuguese history and became the symbol of the Church's opposition to Bolshevism. These visions in turn inspired others in Spain. Since 1900 there have been over thirty episodes of public apparitions, largely of Mary. Most of them, like the ones occurring at the time of this writing (the fall of 1979) are at rural sites and have received scant international attention.

Others, especially three cases in northern Spain, were famous in their time: the Christ of Limpias (Santander), whose eyes appeared to move beginning in 1919, attracting pilgrims from France, Belgium, Switzerland, and Austria (they still come); Our Lady of Ezquioga (Guipúzcoa), 1931-1934, from France and Belgium; and Our Lady of Garabandal (Santander), where the Virgin was seen almost nightly from 1961 to 1965 by three girls. Garabandal has become known on a worldwide basis as a warning of the coming end of times by a conservative portion of Catholic laity.

It was during a long stay in Garabandal in 1968 that my curiosity about apparitions deepened. I learned that the phenomenon is not limited to Spain in modern times. There have been hundreds of such episodes throughout Europe (particularly in Italy) since 1930.[2] Furthermore, this kind of public lay vision is attested by documents for at least six centuries in the West. I have studied about one hundred cases of Spanish apparitions from 1399 to the present. My sources are notarized investigations, largely made by Church and village authorities, still extant in manuscript form in parish, diocesan, or national archives; published versions of these investigations; and for apparitions of the twentieth century, newspaper accounts and the direct testimony of seers or witnesses. I have visited most of the villages discussed in the study and have been present at a number of contemporary visions.

The apparitions I examine here, although they generally occur to only one or two seers, are eminently social visions. They attract immediate public attention and call for some sort of verification. If believed, they provoke public devotion, often very emotional. Indeed, these visions are high drama, sacred plays in which everyday persons are suddenly elevated out of the normal round and granted ambassadorships to heaven, a foretaste of eternity. The village (for these are predominantly rural events) is the chorus, doubtful of why one of their number should be so chosen, but in the cases we learn about, feeling the pride of a chosen people. Villagers remembered actions and words, telling and retelling the stories so often that others can repeat them through following generations. The story of an apparition that occurred in a Segovian village around 1490 was quite fresh when recounted to an ecclesiastical investigator over 120 years later.

By consecrating places or images as special sources of grace, energy, and consolation, apparitions can create new shrines. They also provide critical instructions for coping with actual or imminent disaster, such as plague and war. In recent times they seem to confirm faith itself in the face of unbelief. What people hear the saints say, or the way they see the saints, reveals their deepest preoccupations. The changing faces of divine figures over the last six hundred years lead us to changes in the societies that meet them.[3]

People have direct contact with the supernatural in many ways. I have chosen to study those cases of direct sensory contact, whether apparitions proper or signs such as statues weeping, that are publicly known and have significance for a community or the wider society—the antecedents and successors, if you will, of La Salette, Lourdes, and Fatima. Hence exclusively personal visions, such as those to supplicants praying for cures at shrines or to members of religious orders with spiritual counsel and consolation, fall outside the scope of this study. Apparitions in the context of miraculous cures generally occur after a shrine is already in existence; they are usually not investigated, but merely recorded in the shrine's miracle book. Visions or revelations to nuns and monks turn up in biographies or hagiographies with little evidence, and their significance is usually limited to the person, convent, or order involved. Rarely does either kind of vision leave its mark in a new shrine or have an immediate social resonance. They could be termed secondary visions, because their social importance is secondary, in the first case, to the miracles and, in the second case, to the sanctity of the seers.

In the religious lore of the twelfth and thirteenth centuries, these stories of personal visions had a privileged place; their themes and motifs were repeated in the later, more public visions that established or revived shrines. Visions that played a part in miracles entered a Europe-wide pool of legends that circulated in legend collections. In the twelfth century, in the manner of miracle books of the shrines of saints' bodies, like that of Martin of Tours, these legends were collected about a particular Marian shrine, like those of Chartres, Soissons, Laon, and Rocamadour. But by the thirteenth century, these in turn were compiled into anthologies of legends, like the *Speculum Historiale* of Vincent of Beauvais and the *Miracles de la Sainte Vierge* of Gualtier de Coincy. These anthologies in turn were used in part by the Spanish poets Gonzalo de Berceo (c. 1250) and Alfonso el Sabio (c. 1275), who added local Spanish miracles. Visions occurring during miracles at Spanish shrines were also mentioned in the exclusively Spanish collections—those of the great shrines of Our Lady of Guadalupe, Our Lady of Montserrat, Saint James of Compostela, the Christ of Burgos, and those of the lesser regional shrines.

The frequency of visions among members of religious orders can be gauged from the *Dialogue on Miracles* of a German Cistercian, Caesarius of Heisterbach, written about 1223.[4] Caesarius was master of novices at his monastery, and his work is essentially a collection of miracles and visions that happened to his fellow monks and their acquaintances. The visions occurred largely around Cologne, but since monks circulated among the monasteries of the order, some of the visions reported took place in France and Spain. The visions were largely of the Virgin Mary, who was especially dear to the followers of Saint Bernard. They were seen by clerics, monks, or nuns who were especially virtuous. It is not difficult to see how this kind of familiarity with divine spirits, which first grew in Christian culture among the desert saints, could pass from monastic over to lay culture. With it came a series of techniques for distinguishing good spirits from bad, and true seers from false ones.

There is also a kind of theological vision, ranging from the Virgin nodding her head in approval of a mystical poem of Adam of Saint Victor to detailed eschatological revelations about the end of times. The visionary interpretations of the Apocalypse by Rupert, Joachim di Fiore, Bridget of Sweden, and others affected the lay visions we study. From the twelfth century on, they identified the lady clothed with light in Revelation 12 as Mary. Our seers often describe Mary as "brighter than the sun." While pre-Christian seers also saw heroes and gods with blinding auras, our seers' formulation must derive in part from a Marian interpretation of the passage in Revelation. As Mary in these visions also brings warning of impending punishment, the Apocalyptic parallels are all the more evident.[5]

Yet another kind of vision is that of souls in purgatory or ghosts. Such figures are still occasionally seen in Spain and are interpreted as unquiet souls seeking passage to heaven from their relatives (who should have responses or anniversary masses said) or as signs of displeasure at the dispersal of a patrimony. Medieval theologians accepted that souls could visit the earth in visible form, and these souls seem to have been regarded as good, rather than bad, spirits. Occasionally the information they communicated was used for a wider purpose, but generally the ghostly messages and appearances were of significance only to the families involved.

Visions to members of religious orders, theological visions, those of ghosts, and miracles at major shrines were all included in collections of exempla, or sermon illustrations. Caesarius of Heisterbach's compendium doubtless served this purpose, and there were such collections in use in Spain at the time of the visions studied here. Sermon stories must have been important vehicles for the diffusion of church and monastic lore among the rural laity. The striking anecdotes were powerful, long-lasting encapsulations of moral, theological, and mystical messages. Even in the early 1970s women in the villages of Santander illustrated their theological conversations with me by exempla I subsequently read in Clemente Sánchez's *El Libro de los exenplos por a.b.c.*, compiled from 1400-1420.[6] While the exempla collections did not generally include local Spanish miracles or village apparitions, they did provide preachers and their audiences with patterns and motifs that seem to have been incorporated into the plots of local visions.

In the cases I have studied of public, socially significant visions, there is a substantial probability that the vision took place. By that I do not mean that a divine figure really materialized or that a statue really wept or bled, but merely that people present thought or said so. These "real" apparitions must be distinguished from more legendary apparitions, stories for which there is no contemporary report. One would class as legendary, for instance, the story of Our Lady of Pilar in Zaragoza. The first written version of the apparition is dated about 800 years after the supposed event. Or Our Lady of Guadalupe in Mexico, for which there is also a considerable gap between apparition and documentation. Such legends were created to justify, illustrate, or dignify a preexisting devotion. But legends in turn can have a dramatic impact, and may even stimulate "real" apparitions of an imitative nature. They must therefore be taken into account as part of the cultural repertoire of a given

era. The people of the time rarely made the distinction that I
draw here between real and legendary cases.

Apparitions documented for Spain fall into two categories.
The first is the kind common in the twentieth century—one or
more divine figures who appear to one or more seers "in the
flesh," as it were. They usually speak, sometimes touch the
seers; often they walk with them and show them things; and
sometimes they leave sacred objects for the seers. These are
apparitions proper. Those I know about in Spain occurred
mainly in two periods: from around 1400 to about 1525 (the
subject of this book); and from 1900 to the present. Apparently
because of the activities of the Inquisition, only a handful of
cases occurred in the years between 1525 and 1900.

Signs, the second category (*signum, señal, senyal*) are phenomena that can be independently verified by the senses. They
can be seen by anyone who looks, felt by anyone who touches.
Most late medieval apparitions are "confirmed" by signs, and
in Spain in the early modern period, signs alone become the
main attraction. These were characteristically the weeping,
sweating, or bleeding of images, and group visions of saints in
the form of clouds in the sky. In Spain they are concentrated
in the sixteenth, seventeenth, and eighteenth centuries, with
four or five cases in the twentieth century. I hope to write about
them, like the twentieth-century apparitions, elsewhere.[7] I do
not treat in this study other marvelous phenomena more difficult to document, whether locutions (in which only a voice is
heard), celestial music, the smelling of divine aromas, or revelations that bypass the senses altogether.

A third type, not really a true vision, is the finding of statues
or paintings. The people of the time often considered these
events miraculous. Indeed, the notarized accounts of such discoveries generally include testimony of accompanying signs.
The chronology of the findings of paintings and statues coincides
with that of signs. While the apparitions are overwhelmingly
of Mary, the signs and discoveries are overwhelmingly of the
Cross or the crucifix, probably a function of the different periods
in which they occurred.

Agne Beijer, after talking about the relation between theater sets and paintings in the late Middle Ages and the Renaissance, defined the point of view taken in this book:

> What is most important, after all, is not the question of the influence of one art on another; it is the existence of a world of images—biblical, legendary, or purely poetic, in which poets, artists, and dramatists equally participated, and which all, in their way, sought to represent.[8]

This book investigates the world of images in the minds of the people of rural Castile and Catalonia in the fifteenth century. For this purpose, it comprises a series of verbatim reports of celestial visions of common people, children, farmers, shepherd's wives, servants. They, too, sought to represent the world of images, what they saw and heard, in words, like the poets; at times they seemed characters in a public sacred play; and their descriptions became the basis for paintings and statues. Rather than explaining away the visions, or even explaining them, I have tried to learn from them how people experienced both the world they knew and the world they had to imagine. These were extraordinary moments when the two intersected, and Mary and the saints were with them.

I have included complete texts whenever feasible, and have placed them in the forefront with a minimum of introduction for each, so readers can form their own opinions and make their own discoveries before reading my glosses. I hope you will experience in some measure the excitement felt by the villagers and townspeople of Castile and Catalonia when these epiphanies took place.

ONE

Late Medieval Apparitions in Castile

INTRODUCTION: RURAL LIFE AND RELIGION

In the eighth century, Moslems from Africa rapidly conquered most of Iberia. Over the succeeding seven hundred years, the Christian monarchies of Castile, Navarre, and Aragon slowly regained sovereignty over the peninsula, and by 1400 only the kingdom of Granada was under Moslem control. Castile's overall prosperity in the fifteenth century can be measured by the kingdom's expansion southward and overseas. For all but the front-line populations of central Andalusia, then, life in Castile was securely Christian. But it was not altogether peaceful. In the first half of the fifteenth century, the king of Navarre, allied with dissident Castilian nobles, made regular raids into New Castile, operating from forts near Guadalajara.

Individual Castilian monarchs had gained power and wealth in the twelfth and thirteenth centuries and built royal fiefs governed by military orders in New Castile. Royal power was limited, however, by a small number of noble families who controlled vast, fragmented domains in the north and central parts of the kingdom. Other centers of wealth and authority included cities such as Segovia, under whose jurisdictions fell numerous surrounding villages; dioceses such as Toledo with substantial patrimonies; and certain monasteries such as Guadalupe with extensive landholdings and large flocks of sheep.

Wool was Castile's chief export, and its large transhumant flocks were administered by an association of herdsmen under royal protection. Some of the wool from the Mesta flocks was woven in Spain for local use, as was almost all of the wool from village flocks. Woolen cloth production in fifteenth-century Castile was widespread and decentralized. In almost all of the towns and villages where apparitions took place, there were sheep, shepherds, carders, and weavers.

The settlement type can still be seen in Castile's densely packed nuclear villages and towns. From figures in sixteenth-century records it would appear that in the fifteenth century most settlements north of Toledo and south of the Cantabrian mountains ranged from ten to sixty households. Those on the plains of New Castile, south of the Tagus River, were substantially larger, some of them essentially rural settlements with what for the time were urban-sized populations of 500-1,000 households.

The modern distinction between city and country is difficult to apply to fifteenth-century Castile. There were towns of 5,000 inhabitants that were farming communities; and there were smaller communities with large contingents of artisans that were much less agricultural. In many of the hamlets around Toledo, Segovia, and Cuenca, cloth production predominated; others specialized in tanning and carting. Certain rural towns served as headquarters for the large feudal families, with a small court, bureaucracy and archives, and perhaps a family-supported convent. It was in this kind of mini-city—Escalona (Toledo), Pastrana (Guadalajara)—that some of the unorthodox religious movements at the beginning of the sixteenth century were nurtured. The towns from which the military orders administered their territories, Uclés (Cuenca), Alcázar de San Juan (Toledo) and Daimiel (Ciudad Real), had a similar structure.

The most socially complex were the diocesan seats. Toledo, Valladolid, Segovia, and Burgos were the largest towns of central Castile, rich in industry and convents. On a second level would be the smaller commercial centers, also diocesan seats or vicarates, of León, Avila, Alcalá, Talavera, Cuenca, and Jaén, all with populations of from 10,000 to 15,000 persons.

The visions studied here took place in settlements representative of the region. Some occurred in the poorer hamlets in mountainous regions where sheepherding was a prime occupation (Navalagamella) or was combined with cloth production (Navas de San Antonio). Most of them, however, took place in the mixed economy of the richer farmlands, where livestock raising was combined with vineyards and grain fields. These ranged in size from small villages in the north (Santa Gadea, Escalona in Segovia, Cubas) to larger agro-towns in La Mancha (Quintanar de la Orden, Santa María de los Llanos, El

Toboso) where significant numbers of the population may have been engaged in cloth production, and two small diocesan cities—Jaén and León.

Although Jews are nowhere mentioned in the vision episodes, and certainly there is no hint that any of the seers were *conversos*, our view and interpretation of the visions are inevitably colored by the persecutions that were going on in the region. Antisemitic sentiment had slowly increased from the mid-thirteenth century on, and the Jewish quarters of Castile were assaulted in 1391. In the following years, Saint Vincent Ferrer and other mendicant preachers were responsible for the coercive conversion of Jews in Castile as well as Catalonia, but many were converts in name only. When some monarchs protected the converts, these privileges were resented. There was a popular movement against converso merchants in Toledo in 1449, and brutal persecution of crypto-Jews began in the 1470s, first with diocesan investigations, then in 1483 with the new Spanish Inquisition. Unconverted Jews were formally expelled in 1492, but persecution of converts continued through the eighteenth century.

From the documents referring to visions, we get glimpses of what the ordinary, sacramental, religious life of country people was like. Villages were generally coterminous with parishes. In some there were a number of clergy, in others simply a substitute placed by the titular priest, who lived in the city. In general the farther north on the central meseta, the more clergy relative to population. This rule of thumb applies today, in the sixteenth century, and probably held in the fifteenth century as well.[1] Some of the largest towns of La Mancha had only one parish.

Formal religious practice of laypersons was probably similar to that today. The wife of a carder in Quintanar de la Orden in 1523, Francisca la Brava, was considered to be of average devoutness by her neighbors. She normally attended mass, except in bad weather or when she had to care for her children; she fasted half of the days of Lent (this may be above average), the vigils of feast days, and a few of the *tempora* (the days at the beginning of the four seasons). She confessed and received communion once a year, and knew three prayers well: the Ave Maria, the Pater Noster, and her own bedtime prayer. All of the seers who were asked what prayers they knew, including not especially devout eight- and nine-year-old boys in Catalonia, knew the Ave and the Pater, but even a girl known for her devoutness knew little else.

Sacramental religion attracted only part of the people's religious attention. As in all of Christendom, Iberian villages and towns had their special places, times, and techniques for getting in touch with the saints. Each had a set of particular saints they were accustomed to call on for help, and who sometimes called on them.

This set of saints was usually a combination of specific local saints, who served as general protectors for the community, and specialized saints who were venerated widely because of their special expertise. The general protector might be a specific image of Mary or Saint Anne (like Our Lady of Batres) or the body or relic of a saint (like Saint Macarius, of Boadilla del Monte). Only rarely would it be the titular saint of the parish church. The specialized saints might include, in fifteenth-century Castile, Sebastian (for the plague), Quiteria (for rabies), Anthony the Abbot or Anthony of Padua (for livestock), and Blaise (for sickness). But each town would experiment with different helpers and different specialties, coming up with its own unique, provisional, pantheon.

If they were identified through images, the most powerful protector saints would most likely be venerated in shrines in the countryside. If they were identified through bodies or relics, they would be kept safe from theft in parish churches or monasteries. The rural shrines, most of which survive today, were situated in particularly striking locations: near holy springs; on the sites of old castles; in parish churches of abandoned towns; or at fords in rivers.

Mary was the most important saint in terms of the number of images and district or regional shrines. As the use of images spread through the West in the twelfth and thirteenth centuries, Mary's popularity as a helping saint gradually eclipsed most of the great healing shrines based on the bodies and relics of mar-

tyrs, hermits, and holy bishops. First in cathedrals and monasteries, then in rural chapels, Marian shrines became the centers of practical religious devotion based on vows. The network
of Marian shrines popular in present-day Spain was by and
large in place by the end of the fifteenth century, except in
Galicia, where the cult of other saints held out the longest and
is still strong today.

Communities contacted their saints most in times of crisis.
But the relations in crisis, if effective, would be transformed
into annual, calendrical devotion.[2] For example, when a town
feared the approach of the plague, it might vow to a saint that
if the town was spared it would observe the saint's day. In 1575
most towns and villages in New Castile observed at least three
or four of these specially vowed days. The vows were made
solemnly by the government of the village, usually in public
assembly, and often transcribed by notaries as a formal contract.
Penalties for households who did not send a member to the
saint's procession or persons who worked on the day, would be
specified. By canon law such vows were binding on the village
in perpetuity, unless dispensed by the bishop. In fact, from the
early sixteenth century, if not before, the bishops of Castile
dispensed these vows, but the villagers, responding to a higher
law, generally observed them anyway, sometimes at the expense
of the holy days ordered by Rome or the diocese.

Village relations with saints, then, were a series of obligations,
many of them explicit and contractual, not unlike their obligations to secular lords. They involved the villagers' sacrifice
of work time and offerings. They also involved the religious
regulation of eating, often a combination of fasting on the saint's
vigil and consumption of animal protein in public feasts, called
caridades, on the saint's day or the day the saint helped them.
These laws of consumption seem to be an extrapolation from
Lenten fasting and Easter feasting, the honoring of a chosen
saint's death and glorification.

Apparitions were one of the ways that new saints were
brought into this system or devotions to old saints were revived.
Community pantheons were always in a state of flux, with

saints losing or gaining popularity according to their efficacy and national and international fashion. Saints were brought in in other ways. The most common was probably trial and error: saints were asked for help serially and the one that worked gained in devotion. Another way was the propagation of devotion to a given saint by local holy people, whether hermits or preachers.

Some kinds of initiatives seemed to come from the saints themselves. Even without appearing, saints constantly communicated their availability and benevolent interest through the obscure language of signs. This language might involve what some people call coincidence: a striking portent on a given saint's day. Or it might be a striking miracle worked by a saint to whom no one was paying attention. Or the signs might be provoked, in the form of lotteries—seeing which saint's candle burned longest or which saint's name was drawn three times from a bag.

To the villagers, then, both communities and saints were reaching out to communicate with one another. By use of assorted petitionary procedures and the alert observation of the correspondences and conjunctions of abnormal events, times, and places, villagers continually contacted and identified their celestial advocates. Apparitions, of course, were an unequivocal solution to this problem. Frequently they not only showed who the saint was but also solved the difficult riddle of exactly what the saint wanted. For communities involved in a relentless series of epidemics and crop failures, this was a matter of life and death.

Around the most venerated images and places in the countryside oral traditions formed that explained why a given image or place was powerful and helpful. These local traditions or legends would have been known by village visionaries. The local legends of Catalonia and Castile shared a basic pattern and are most easily discussed together. Unfortunately they were not recorded systematically until the seventeenth century in Catalonia and the sixteenth century in New Castile.

From 1651 to 1653 a Dominican from Girona, Narciso Camós,

personally visited all of the major Marian shrines in Catalonia. In addition to describing each shrine image in detail and listing the towns that annually visited the shrine, he carefully noted the story told about each shrine's origin. His book devotes separate chapters to each of 182 different shrines, largely located in isolated chapels and convents. In addition he listed 420 parish churches, 83 additional convents, and 333 additional chapels dedicated to Mary. His survey was published in 1657; its most recent edition was in 1949.[3]

What were the shrine legends when Camós made his survey? First of all (and this encourages trust in his reporting) about a quarter of the shrines (45 out of 182) had no legends. Pious Camós "supposed" that the origin of these shrines was miraculous, but unlike some of the chroniclers of Castile, he did not make up legends. For the 137 shrines for which he gave legends, all but twelve of the stories fall into one of two categories—the miraculous discovery of images (111 cases); and apparitions (14 cases). In six hybrid cases, an apparition led to the discovery of the statue.

The Catalan discovery legends essentially follow the Monte Gargano pattern. Through the mediation of male domestic animals, especially oxen or bulls, a herdsman is alerted to the presence of an image in a wild location: underground or in a cave, in a tree or some wild plant, or in a spring. The herdsman or the priest and townspeople try to take the image to the parish church, but it returns by itself to its hiding place, and eventually a chapel is built for it there. The accompanying tabulation indicates the frequency of each step in this process, among the 117 finding legends.

Statistics compiled from legends reported by Narciso Camós in *Jardín de María*, a survey of 182 shrines made 1651-1653 in the dioceses of Tarragona (22), Barcelona (30), Girona (19), Tortosa (9), Lleida (12), Urgell (33), Vic (15), Elna (15), Solsona (15), and the Priories of Ager and Meya (7). There is little significant difference in the distribution of legend types or motifs among the different dioceses.

LEGEND TYPES OF THE 182 SHRINES

  117 Discovery of image
   14 Apparition without discovery of an image
    6 Other origin
   45 No legend given

OF THE 117 IMAGES DISCOVERED

   95 Human intermediary indicated
   22 Human intermediary not indicated

   62 Animal indicated location
   15 Other signs
   40 No signs given

OF THE 95 HUMAN INTERMEDIARIES

67 Male herders		1 charcoaler
10 Female herders		1 hermit
4 plowmen		1 slave
4 noble hunters		1 villager
2 female woodcutters		1 peasant couple
1 male woodcutter		1 noble couple
1 carter		

	young	old	total
male	8	73	81
female	10	2	12
couples	—	2	2
	18	77	95

IN THE 62 LEGENDS IN WHICH ANIMALS
INDICATED THE STATUE LOCATION

50 Male animals		57 Domestic animals
2 Female animals		2 Wild animals
10 Sex not indicated		3 "Animals"

34 Oxen	3 Dogs and prey
15 Bulls	2 Crows
1 Bull and cow	3 "Animals"
1 Bull and ram	
1 Sheep	
1 Lamb	
1 Goat	

OF THE 88 OF THE 117 DISCOVERY LEGENDS
IN WHICH THE IMAGE LOCATION WAS SPECIFIED

Natural sites: 80

32 Cave or underground
17 Tree
13 Spring
7 Plant
4 Hilltop
3 Other

Quasi-societal sites: 8

2 Buried in vineyard	1 Well
1 In buried chapel	1 Well in field
1 Grave in church	1 Garden
1 Fallen house	

(but note: 6 of these are underground,
and the house was abandoned)

IN 36 OF THE DISCOVERIES OF IMAGES
THE HOLY SITE WAS RECONFIRMED

32 By the image returning to the site
3 By the image becoming too heavy to move
1 By an alternate chapel collapsing

When one considers that these images mediate between the
local society and the forces of nature (both in terms of weather,
insect devastation, and disease, and the world behind the real
world, the world of birth and death), then the legends of their

discoveries are explicable. The images of the mother with child, symbol of the creative power of nature within the human body itself, are embedded in the countryside. But not just anywhere. They are located at entry points in nature for matter from other worlds. Trees and mountain tops are connections to the sky; caves and springs connections to an underworld. The shrine images, which serve to transmit the human energy of love, prayer, promise, and gift, and return the energy of nature or God in the form of consolation, grace, and miracle, are discovered in the wild world at logical places for supplication and propitiation of the outside forces.

The intermediaries that locate the images and inform the society are themselves half-wild and half-domestic. Most of the statues are found by animals. But in only five of sixty cases is the animal wild. Three of those five exceptions are wild animals (rabbits and deer) that are followed by domestic animals (dogs), which are in turn leading hunters. Domestic animals that frequent the wilds are a part of nature built into culture. Bulls are perhaps the wildest and least controllable of domestic animals. In households without bulls, oxen, used for plowing, would be the wildest.

Stephen Sharbrough has analyzed the symbolic meaning of bulls in the cult of mother goddesses, particularly the Matronae, in pre-Christian Europe, and believes these Catalan legends hark back to the earlier beliefs. The special relationship that Christian culture created for the bull (at the manger) as in the Apocryphal Gospel of Saint Matthew, he points out, "would be recognized when Christianity moved into regions where the bull held a traditional symbolic role."[4]

The bull is an appropriate intermediary between culture and nature; so too is the herdsman. Uncultivated *monte* abounds in all but the richest areas of Spain. It bears a heavy cognitive charge as wilderness, a kind of spatial equivalent to darkness and night. Few people have occasion to enter it—woodcutters, hermits, hunters, charcoal burners, and, most of all, the herders. The herders are the society's interface with nature and know its ways best. They are the most "wild" of the people.

Why are the animals that find the statues, and the people

who find the animals, males? While the image that actually works the transformations of culture and nature is female, we cannot forget that it represents divinity. It is not a woman. The intermediary between it and the culture is male, down to the animals, as are most intermediaries between societies in Mediterranean culture.[5] Only twelve of the many finders are women, and of these, ten are girls, not women. The proportion is reversed for men—overwhelmingly adult, not boys. The less "womanly" the seers, the more they are likely to be accepted as intermediaries with the sacred. Hence girls more than women, boys more than girls, and men more than boys.

Once the image has been found, the society tries to appropriate it, as if it were a relic that needed to be protected in the parish church. The image refuses. From the shepherd's pouch, from locked chests, from the village church, the image returns to its site in the countryside. Generally if the villagers try to build its shrine away from the difficult place where it was found, it rejects that also. On the Cantabrian coast, from Guipúzcoa to Asturias, this rejection takes the form of the nocturnal moving of construction materials to the discovery site. In France the construction collapses overnight (of this there is one case in Catalonia, in French Cerdegna). The dominant pattern in Catalonia and central Spain is the return of the image.

These returns implicitly instruct the people that in order to deal with nature they must go to it. I believe what was partly involved was a paganization (from *pagus*, country) of Christianity—a kind of encoded recapitulation of the process by which rural pre-Christian notions of a sacred landscape reasserted themselves over an initially cathedral- and parish-church-centered religion.

Consider the difference between the scenarios of the discovery of saints' bodies and the discovery of holy statues. Both were ways communities obtained protectors. But the relics were usually found in settled areas, often urban graveyards, or perhaps removed from other churches or monasteries. And that, sociologically, is where they stayed. Because relics were mobile, they could be kept at hand, in society. The physical presence of once-human saints provides a society with links to its own moral heritage. In the first centuries of Christianity, as Peter Brown has shown, the cult of saints' bodies was a radical break from pre-Christian religion, whose heroes, once dead, peopled another world.[6]

The legends of discoveries of statues, although in some ways they resemble the earlier *inventio* of saints, perform an altogether different task, one appropriate for rural society.[7] They serve to explicate, not the society's relation to its history and the Christian world, but rather its relations with nature, and provide a valid intermediary or ambassador. The return of the image to its natural setting is the image saying, "No. I am not a relic; think again. Holy people you can move; I am showing you a holy place. You must face me there."

The preponderance of underground locations for these Marian statues, in particular, supports the notion of Mary's role as successor to mother goddesses dealing with fertility. In the thirteenth century when this transformation was taking place, Alfonso el Sabio, or the theologians around him, made this point at some length in Law 43 of the *Setenario*—"About how those who worshipped the earth, really meant to worship Saint Mary, if they understood it well." He draws the parallel between the earth that bears fruit and Mary who bore Jesus. His focus was on the fruit, Jesus, just as the Romanesque images Camós described show Mary presenting Jesus, and Jesus with the power. In that theology Mary was the ground from which the good things and the power sprung. The emphasis on the child-God on Mary's lap did not last for long. Mary became the central figure in these shrines. The legends of the discovery of statues in the earth and their worship in caves was a concrete connection between Mary and the earth that matched the symbolic connection made by the author of the *Setenario*.[8]

With few exceptions the stories of discoveries of images were reported by Camós as taking place in a remote and unidentified past. Eduard Junyent, canon-archivist of Vic, believed the legends were formed in the thirteenth to fifteenth centuries, although there is little real proof.[9] The legends of Montserrat and Nuria, which include episodes of the discovery of images, existed in the fifteenth century at least. There is a good chance that the legends in Camós already existed when the first documented apparitions took place.

A few of the Catalan discovery legends are combinations of findings and apparitions. Except for the fact that they ultimately involve finding images, they are very similar to the apparitions we can document. Most occurred to single shepherd girls, others to a carter whose wagon became mired and to charcoal burners. The signs that made them believable were the curing of crippled hands, three cases of hands fixed to cheeks, and the talking of a mute girl. The fact that these apparitions involve the finding of statues indicates that they, like the other discoveries, are probably legendary and not historical episodes. If they were "real" findings, there would not have to be an elaborate physical proof, as in an apparition; and if they were "real" apparitions, there would be no statue to be found.

The hybrid legends of apparition-findings suggest that "real" apparitions both in Castile and Catalonia ultimately served the same purpose as the finding legends; they were charters for relations between the village and the natural world. The seers, like the legendary discoverers of statues, were privileged inter-mediaries who introduced a people to its God, its holy place, and its holy times.

Camós reported fourteen cases of apparitions proper. Three were apparitions to people in battle against the Moors, a motif common in reconquest and Crusade chronicles; three were ap-paritions of preexisting images in the course of miracles (1348 and 1598, both plague years, and 1620). Two of the others, apparently legendary, were heavenly matins processions similar to the cases of Santa Gadea and Jaén (Our Lady of the Cinta, Tortosa, and Our Lady of Puiglagulla, Villaleóns); and the re-maining six, studied below in Chapter Two, were historical apparitions.

Castilian shrine legends were similar to those of Catalonia. Unfortunately in Castile a systematic survey of legends was never taken. The earliest collective source, and the only one uncontaminated by the forgeries of false chroniclers in the sev-enteenth century, is the responses sent by villages to royal historians in the 1570s. This survey of historical, social, and geographical information covered only New Castile, the area of south-central Spain between the Sierra de Guadarrama and the Sierra Morena.[10] About 500 villages from this region replied, and about twenty-five of them sent in legends, which were not specifically asked for.

About half of the stories the villages sent in described the discovery of images. As in Catalonia, the discoverers (when mentioned) were men (shepherds, knights, plowmen). Although no oxen or bulls were mentioned, other domestic animals (a dog, horses) played a role. The sites, like those of Catalonia, were outside villages in the realm of nature—underground, in caves, by springs, or in trees. In several legends the image returned to the place where it was found. This pattern applied to other female saints—Anne, Bridget, and Mary the Egyptian, as well as to Mary.

Fifteen apparitions or apparition-discoveries were mentioned in the village reports.[11] Mary appeared in most of the visions, and Saints Blaise, Gregory, Lucy, and Vincent each appeared in one village. In several cases the legend was only vestigial:

> They say that Our Lady appeared there [San Pablo, Toledo; Iniesta, Cuenca; etc.]

> They say that Our Lady appeared to a shepherd [Almonacid de Toledo]

> It is believed that [Saint Gregory] appeared to a good woman [Fuenlabrada, Madrid]

In others the vision was given in condensed form:

> . . . when a man was plowing on the site Saint Blaise appeared to him; and they say that he told him to plow no more, but rather that they should build a chapel there dedicated to him. [Cubas, Madrid]

> The Virgin herself appeared there and ordered the priest and the people of Hontova to build her a chapel where it is now and call it Santa María de los Llanos. [Hontova, Guadalajara]

And, in a few, the story was given in detail.

. . . and there is also a chapel to Lady Saint Lucy, about which there is a notarized document which says that the glorious saint appeared some time ago to a woman twice and told her to inform and affirm to the town authorities to go to a certain place that she pointed out and dig there, and that they would find a spring, and on the site they should build a chapel called Saint Lucy. The woman reported it to the authorities, and they went where she said and dug down and soon found a spring, and built the chapel there. [Ventas con Peña Aguilera, Toledo]

The town of Daimiel (Ciudad Real) sent in a long story in verse about a boy from Moral de Calatrava in 1465, whose horse fell down with a load of wheat on the way to the mill. The boy called on Mary for help, and she appeared to him, telling him his wheat was already ground and he should return home and tell his father to tell the town of Daimiel to build a shrine called the Crosses on the spot she appeared. The youth complained he would not be believed, and the Virgin said there would be candles burning on the site as a sign.

The boy and his father went to the chancellery (of the diocese of Toledo?) in Ciudad Real and told the story. But when the authorities went to the site, they found nothing, and so they beat the boy and hung him from a tree. The Virgin saw his plight "from the sky" and quickly came down to release him. The boy called the authorities back and pointed out to them both the candles and the footprints left by the Virgin. They believed him and built the chapel. The boy became a priest and was eventually buried in the shrine.

The people of Daimiel gave a vision as the origin of another chapel as well.

It is said as a certainty that the chapel of Our Lady of Peace was built in the years that there was a great plague in this town, so that by 1507 [e.g. the last great plague year before the questionnaire] it was already built. It was founded in the following manner. A girl named Ana Hernández (later the wife of a citizen of this town named

Pero Sánchez Mohino) was watching some of her father's grain on Saint Barnabas's day, while they were running bulls in town. Our Lady appeared to her to say in town that they should build a chapel there and call it Our Lady of Peace, for then the people would stop dying. The girl replied that they would not believe her; and Our Lady told her that they should dig a well there and they would find a colored tile inside, and by those signs they would believe. The girl told it in town, and the well was dug that is near the shrine at the Puerta del Sol, and they did find the tile. And so the chapel was built, and all this is general knowledge.

Each of the two stories from Daimiel (which I have not been able to confirm with documents) has themes in common with visions we can document—the conjunction of visions and the plague, the Virgin helping with mundane tasks, and saints leaving footprints. Whether or not they actually happened, stories such as these would have been known to the Castilian seers in the fifteenth century. In Castile as well as Catalonia, the idea of a villager having a vision of this kind was not unheard of.

On the other hand, I would hesitate to say that "real" visions were common. Most of the apparition stories both in Castile and Catalonia were given as mere traditions ("se dice . . . ") without mention of date or documentation. Their numbers are small to begin with, and doubtless many of them, like the discoveries of statues, were myths. My guess is that real apparitional episodes that led to ongoing devotions occurred in the historical memory of one in a hundred villages in both regions.

The cases presented below, thus, are accounts of unusual phenomena for the seers and for the towns in which the apparitions took place. Scholars have been misled, I think by monastic literature, into seeing the late Middle Ages as a period in which the divine presence was so common it was banal. An analyst of French Christmas plays written by priests, in which shepherds react to the apparition of the Angel Gabriel "simply filled with great joy" extrapolates to the culture at large—"there is no emotion, or at least no doubt when confronted with the supernatural"—to confirm Lucien Febvre's dictum, "for the men of the sixteenth century there was no mystery."[12] Shepherds in a play are one thing. Real shepherds face to face in the fields with the supernatural were something else. For the people who had these visions, they were not at all banal. They experienced terror and awe as well as joy, and doubt as well.

Legends become banal by repetition and replication. But when they suddenly become incarnate in real events, when they are experienced by neighbors or countrymen, the well-known mythic referents heighten rather than dampen emotion. This happens to even casual participants in rituals and dramas. How much more so when persons are surprised by a real epiphany.

Precisely because these visions were so out of the ordinary— something on the order of an earthquake or a volcanic eruption—they were documented, and the documents were preserved and recopied over the years.

MARY OF LIGHT WITH MATINS PROCESSIONS

Santa Gadea (Burgos), 1399

The two oldest apparitions for which documents are known are more similar to each other than to any of the later cases. The first supposedly took place in 1399, the second in 1430. Santa Gadea del Cid is a small village near the border of Alava in the present-day province of Burgos. There a shepherd boy claimed before priests, village authorities, townspeople, and notaries that he and his companion saw the Virgin Mary. The earliest extant transcription is a large parchment in the National Historical Archive in Madrid made sometime after 1471. Since of all the cases I have studied, it is the most allegorical, and since it may have served at some time to buttress the shrine's claims on and independence from the monastery of San Millán de la Cogolla, one must entertain the possibility that the apparition story was concocted years after it supposedly took place. On balance I tend to think not, but readers can form their own opinions by reading it in its entirety.

☆

Chronology

*seers: Pedro, son of Yñigo García de Arbe
Juan, son of Juan de Enzinas
place: Santa Gadea del Cid (Burgos)*

1) *Tuesday, March 25, 1399 Pedro and Juan found a honey tree while tending sheep.*
2) *Wednesday [March 26], they returned late at night to gather the honey and wax, and saw a bright lady and a procession.*
3) *Thursday [March 27], Pedro alone saw Mary, who explained the previous vision and gave him instructions for the town.*
4) *Sunday night [Easter, March 30], Mary appeared with monks and had Pedro beaten for not delivering her message. The neighbors were aroused by Pedro's cries, and he asked to have a town meeting convened, where he told his story.*

The notarized version of his testimony was made Monday, April 20, 1399.

In my translations of documents I have divided them into sentences and paragraphs, modernized the spelling of proper names and added quotation marks. I have also attempted to mitigate the legalese, cutting back on repetitions and transforming the adjective *dicho* ("said") into "that," "the," or omitting it entirely. For the sake of clarity I have occasionally capitalized pronouns referring to Mary, and for the sake of brevity I have sometimes omitted preliminary and final matter of a legal nature, which can be read in the Spanish texts in the appendices.

TRANSCRIPT OF VISION DOCUMENT, SANTA GADEA DEL CID (BURGOS)[13]

This is a copy of testimony taken in the town of Santa Gadea as written on parchment and signed by a notary public.

In Santa Gadea, Sunday, April 20, in the year of the
birth of our saviour Jesus Christ 1399.[14] This day in the
church of Saint Peter of the town of Santa Gadea in the
presence of Ruy Martínes and Juan Pérez de Río, parish
priests of the church; the other clergy and cabildo; the alcalde Diego García de Arbolancha; the procurador; the
governors; the council of the town gathered by ringing the
bell; in my presence, Juan Martínes of Santa Gadea, scrivener and notary public for our lord the King; and the witnesses whose names are written at the end of this testimony; there appeared a youth from this town named
Pedro, the son of Yñigo García de Arbe, a citizen of this
town.

He said that on the day of Saint Mary of March of this
present year he was watching his father's sheep with Juan,
the son of Juan de Enzinas, in the jurisdiction of this town
near a church called Sant Millán. In an oak tree in the
cemetery of the church they found a hive of bees, and
through an opening in the trunk they saw much honey
and wax. They agreed that on Wednesday of Holy Week,
once their flock was stabled in town and their parents had
gone to the matins ceremony, they would come to gather
the honey and wax from the tree.

When the day came they set out to do it. When they
went to the oak and began to take out the honey and wax,
they saw many people with white garments gathered
around a very big hawthorn tree, holding three lights that
lit up everyone quite clearly. And they saw a lady on top
of the hawthorn tree who shone brighter than the sun, so
they could not look at her without being blinded. And then
they heard a voice from the people there calling out,
"Come to matins (*Venit a la tiniebras*)"; and at this call
there appeared from the direction of Santa María de Guinicio a great number of people as if in a procession in white
garments; and most of them wore red garments with white
stripes on top, and many other colors. They carried in
their hands branches like palms and two torches that lit up
the entire procession as if it were daytime. This procession

came to join the people around the lady; and the brightness went up as far as the sky; and around her were three
torches like big candles, so powerful they lit up all of the
landscape; and it seemed that they went up as far as the
sky. And they heard singing, like priests chanting the
hours, and frightened by the voices they stopped gathering
their honey and fled toward town. When they reached the
flat place that is halfway, they looked back and saw all the
lights join in one; and the singing went up to the heavens,
so much that they did not dare go back.

The following Thursday Pedro was keeping the sheep of
his father, Yñigo García de Arbe, near the same spot in the
village territory. Suddenly there appeared to him a lady so
resplendent that he could not look at her directly, but only
in parts. She told him he should tell of his vision to the
parish priests, clergy, and council of Santa Gadea. And that
people everywhere should know that she whom he had
seen on the hawthorn tree was the Virgin Mary glorified
in person; and the people he had seen around her were the
angels of heaven, that very pure company. And that they
should know that her coming was willed by her precious
son, the redeemer of the human race. And that at the time
of the destruction of Spain there had been a town at that
place called Montañana la Yerma and a church in my name
in which, and in whose cemetery, refugees from said town
of Montañana la Yerma were forced to take shelter from a
great onslaught of infidels. In the church and cemetery
they were surrounded and taken by force of arms; and because they would not convert to their religion, they were
all martyred by beheading, and the entire church and cemetery and its surroundings were bathed in the blood of the
glorious martyrs.

And since the memory of this mystery was dying, at the
constant and assiduous urging of the martyrs and virgins
who perished there long ago and at their supplication, my
glorious son, redeemer of the human race, had to give in
to their prayers. It was his will that I come glorified in
person with the angels to celebrate the office of matins of

Holy Week and that those glorious souls be present with
me to visit the bodies that on a day like this one they had
left behind.

Just as God the Father came to Moses in the briarbush,
which was not consumed by fire for the good of his people,
so I was sent in the hawthorn for the good of the souls and
bodies of the faithful of the human race. You will find that
the hawthorn is not burned or damaged in any way; it will
serve as medicine for the diseases that people have here[?].
The voice you heard calling to matins was that of the Angel Saint Michael. Just as he was present in that place to
receive the souls of the glorious martyrs and take them to
glory at the time of their martyrdom, so his was the voice
that called them into being to celebrate that solemn office,
and our lord saw fit that they should respond quickly in
the form of a very glorious procession, as you saw. One of
the two torches they carried signified the crown of holy
martyrdom, and the other the virginity of the many virgin
girls who had perished there. The other three torches you
saw around me signified the three persons of the father,
the son, and the holy spirit. The voices you heard were the
sweet voices of the angels who performed the office. And
when at the end of the ceremony the torches were consumed in one it signified the unity with which we all went
up to glory, each to his established seat and place.

I order you to explain that this place is holy and occu-
pied by the many relics of the bodies that perished here by
martyrdom. I also order you to say that it is the will of
my glorious son that a monastery and church of the order
of Saint Benedict be built to revive the memory of this secret. You must say that all the people who come or send
their help or alms to build the church and monastery and
support the monks who will live in it will have remission
of their sins. Their souls will be in the company of the said
martyrs, and their bodies and property will be helped and
protected whenever they commend themselves with great
devotion to me. In memory of my apparition in this hawthorn tree [whoever] carries a depiction of my apparition

on his person will be freed from the power of the devil, and the devil will be powerless to harm him when he sees my emblem. Also, if carried with great devotion, it will ward off pestilence and all disease. I also order you to tell the parish priests, clergy, alcalde, procurador, and governors of the town of Santa Gadea gathered in council that, if they want their town and its people to prosper and their souls to grow in grace, they should immediately clean out the weeds and brush in and around the church where you had the apparition. Let them know that just as the harshness and wildness of the place has led to anger and thefts, so it will become a place of refreshment for the body and health for the soul. If they want to have their just desires met, they should begin to build the church and the monastery. As long as they do so, and they put their devotion into practice, things will improve for them and for all the towns and people wherever they are from.

I order you to keep on declaring this publicly to the parish priests, clergy, alcaldes, and governors of the council of the town of Santa Gadea and to all the districts and regions for the remainder of the short time you have to live. You must take as your name Pedro de Buena Ventura (Peter of Good Fortune), for truly you deserve it. And you must tell your companion Juan that he should soon take up the arms of the knights of the blessed virgin Saint Catherine, for he will die in them. His end will come nine days after he arrives at the grave of Saint Catherine from Jerusalem. I order you to make this known at once. Do not delay out of timidity, or else in my presence you will be punished as you will see. And with this she disappeared.

Out of timidity and fear he would not be believed, Pedro did not mention the apparition to anybody. The following Sunday night at the hour of the second cock crow, when Pedro was in bed near that of his father, the Virgin Mary came to it in the form that he had seen her the previous Thursday, and she brought with her two torches and two men dressed as monks. One of them took him by the arm and pulled him out of bed, and the other took his belt and struck him many blows and wounds. Neighbors heard his loud cries and got up, especially the alcalde Diego García de Arbolancha and his household. With others of the neighborhood they called out loudly at the doors of Yñigo García's house. No one answered them, and because of Pedro's cries, they knocked down the doors of Yñigo García's house. When they went up the stairs, they saw the house was as bright as at noonday, but the brightness ended when they got to the top. With the candles that the women carried they found Pedro lying in shock (*muy fatigado*) with many whip marks on the floor of a room.

At this point Yñigo García, his wife, and the other people in the house were roused. [Yñigo] angrily demanded what they wanted in his house at such an hour and in such a way. Diego García de Arbolancha replied that they had come to help the youth because he had been treated with great cruelty. The father replied that nothing of the kind had ever taken place in his house. Then Pedro spoke up and said that neither his father nor anyone else in the house was responsible and asked them, and in particular Diego García de Arbolancha in his capacity as alcalde, to order the parish priests and clergy and governors and council to gather in the church, and that he himself be carried there so he could declare what had happened. When the sun came up the mayor did this, and after the entire town had gathered Pedro was brought in. They all saw the welts and injuries, and he himself told them all that has been told above.

I the scrivener bear witness that I have seen the marks and wounds on Pedro and heard from his own mouth all the testimony given.

Witnesses named at the end of this document included two parish priests, two other clergymen, the alcalde, and five other citizens, one of whom was a scrivener, Ferrán Martínes.

A bull of indulgences obtained in 1404 from the Avignon pope, Benedict XIII, implicitly supports the apparition story, for it states that pilgrims were especially numerous on what would have been the anniversaries of the visions; "... it is believed by the faithful that many noteworthy miracles are being performed, and every year a multitude of faithful Christians gather out of devotion on Wednesday, Thursday, and Friday of Holy Week."[15]

The Virgin had not merely asked for a shrine; she wanted a Benedictine monastery. The chief promoter of a monastery was a priest, Ruy Martínes, listed as present when Pedro gave his testimony. In 1406 he secured an agreement with the prior of the powerful Benedictine monastery of San Millán de la Cogolla, located about seventy km. to the south. San Millán would cede property in villages surrounding Santa Gadea to the new monastery, and the prior of Santa Gadea would sit in the San Millán chapter. The Santa Gadea priests then secured papal permission to found the monastery. Benedict XIII's bull, dated 1406, mentions the *"maravillas"* and *"virtudes"* that have already taken place at the chapel, and grants indulgences to those who help build the monastery and maintain the monks.[16]

When the priests came back to San Millán with papal approval, the San Millán prior went back on his word; the dispute was arbitrated in 1410 by the prior of another monastery, San Juan de Obarenes, in favor of the Santa Gadea priests. In the documents of this dispute, there is no mention of an apparition, although the chapel is described as "recently founded." If the apparition did, in fact, take place, it was not considered something that would sway the prior of San Millán in a legal dispute.

In sum, a monastery was set up within a few years of the supposed apparition after marvels and miracles had taken place on the site, by a priest listed as present at the telling of the vision. Pilgrims were coming especially on the anniversaries of the apparition days. The earliest extant version of the apparition document was made some time after 1471.

Whether it is a true vision or a pious forgery, the apparition story is rich in mythic references. There is the obvious parallel to the drama of Holy Week. The shepherds are named Pedro and Juan, Peter and John, the two most beloved apostles. Pedro, by not telling his story, denies his lord, and after the second rooster crow on Sunday morning, which is Easter, he is forced to confess. But this is a revised version of the Passion, one appropriate to late medieval Europe. It is Mary, not Christ, whom Peter denies. The drama of rejecting and then accepting the epiphany of Mary and the martyrs is played out over Holy Week. The establishment of a new shrine with local protectors is a kind of replication of Christ's rejection and his eventual triumph on the Cross.

This kind of modified replication is found in many of the earlier shrine legends. Statues were supposedly found by oxen or shepherds after strange lights and music showed the way. All of these items parallel the story of the birth of Christ; and, indeed, these are generally statues of Mary holding the Christ-child. But it is Mary herself who is referred to as being found, at least as the stories were told from the sixteenth century on. The gospel was replayed in local mythology with Mary, not Christ, at the center. Each village becomes a Nazareth.

Allegorically, Pedro is not only one of the shepherds to whom the angels announced the birth of Christ and Peter the Apostle who denies his God, he is also Moses, to whom God appeared in the burning bush.

Mary tells Pedro that his friend Juan should take up the arms of Saint Catherine, and that he would die within nine days of arriving at her grave from Jerusalem. The alleged relics of Saint Catherine in the Sinai desert are in a monastery built by the Emperor Justinian on the site of the burning bush, at the foot of the mountain where Moses received the tablets of the law. This monastery was dedicated to Mary until the early fourteenth century, when it became known as Saint Catherine's. In the fifteenth century the memory of the previous Marian dedication was still alive to the pilgrims who came from Western Europe.[17]

A ninth- or tenth-century icon at the shrine appears to show Mary surrounded by the burning bush holding the Christ-child, who presumably represents the God speaking to Moses in the verses of Exodus.[18] By the fourteenth century, there was also a legend of a separate apparition of Mary to the monks.[19] The apparition at Santa Gadea borrows aspects of the apparition of Mary, and the reference to the burning bush of the shrine in the Sinai.

Again, as with the Passion and the Nativity, there has been a transformation. In the burning bush God speaks to Moses; and in the earliest iconographic representations Mary merely presents the Christ-child, who presumably speaks. But our apparition text makes no mention of a child. Mary refers to her son as the one who makes decisions, but she speaks for him, and she alone appears to Pedro and Juan, another instance of the Marianization of biblical patterns.

The symbolism of the hawthorn (the earliest blooming tree) as the burning bush, and the use of the biblical story as a pattern for medieval legends of apparitions of Mary was common in France. The great Gothic church of Notre Dame de l'Épine, outside of Châlons-sur-Marne, is one of the most prominent shrines of France. It was built at the same time that the shrine of Santa Gadea came into being—the first decade of the fifteenth century. E. Misset has shown that the French shrine was constructed by Canons Regular of Saint Augustine of Saint Victor, possibly because their foundation was ratified there. Hugh of Saint Victor, Richard of Saint Victor, and Adam of Saint Victor all devoted attention to the symbolism of the hawthorn in relation to Mary. For Hugh of Saint Victor she was the flower blooming out of the thorns of the Jewish race; in a later formulation the bush that burns but is not consumed is the perpetual virginity of Mary before, during, and after giving birth to Jesus.[20]

Notre Dame de l'Épine has a legend remarkably similar to that of Santa María del Espino. On March 24, 1400 (virtually the same day, a year later), two shepherd boys saw Mary on a brightly lit tree. They fainted; when they awoke they found a statue in the tree. Villagers, drawn by the light, came in procession. Misset speculates convincingly that the legend, first mentioned in 1633, arose from a misinterpretation of an engraving and a stained glass window, which showed Moses in two poses before the burning bush. The misinterpretation was that it was not Moses twice, but two shepherds.[21] As recent iconographic evidence from the Sinai suggests, the image of Mary in the hawthorn or burning bush may not be a metaphorical invention of twelfth-century theologians, but rather an emblem of Marian devotion at the shrine to the burning bush in the Sinai, which the theologians later explicated. The Santa Gadea story, although it is late, points that way.

The Spanish story existed at least a century before the French legend of Notre Dame de l'Épine was published and may have informed it. Could the Spanish story also be a misinterpretation of iconography? Obviously not. If the apparition document is untrue, then it was a deliberate forgery, one in which care was taken to have the visions coincide with the dates on which pilgrims arrived as early as 1404, and to include the name of the shrine's chief promoter as a witness. The Santa Gadea document with its explicit reference to the shrine of Saint Catherine indicates at the very least that there was more conscious use of imitative apparitions in the fourteenth or fifteenth centuries, possibly based on travelers' reports from the Sinai. One wonders whether a shepherd boy could have been so well informed about what was a very remote shrine. But the replication of apparitions such as those of Fatima and Lourdes today by children 8 to 13 years of age should alert us to the possibility of imaginative assimilation of legends by children in earlier times.

Another source for the Espino story is the kind of vision that led to the founding of monasteries. One of the earliest of the genre is the vision of Mary with handmaidens seen by a shepherd on the site of Evesham Abbey. The shepherd informed Bishop Egwin, who prayed, went and looked, and was blessed by the Virgin. The apparitions supposedly took place in 709, and the story was probably written sometime in the same century.[22] In the thirteenth and fourteenth centuries, the monks of Saint Catherine's told pilgrims of an apparition of Mary there. When a chapel (not the main monastery) was going to be moved from one spot on the mountain to another where there would be more food and fewer fleas and lice, Mary appeared to assure the monks there would be no more pests and send them two camel-loads of food.[23] Stories such as these were part of the culture of fourteenth-century Europe and would have been heard as exempla in sermons.

The Santa Gadea apparition is a creative combination of two kinds of legends—the Marian apparition, in this case ultimately derived from the apparition of God to Moses in the burning bush, and the invention of the bodies of saints. Although the former takes precedence, the latter—the "invention" of the martyrs of the abandoned parish church—is also very much present in Pedro's story, and points us back to the forerunner of the Spanish Marian legends and apparitions.

The invention of the bodies of saints is best exemplified in Spain by that of Saint James of Compostela in the ninth century. Such discoveries, which answered the need of bishoprics and towns for sacred relics and local sacred protectors, and which channeled peasants' promises and devotions into urban coffers, were frequent in Spain as late as the thirteenth century. (There was a new outbreak in Andalusia in the late sixteenth and early seventeenth centuries.) The inventions were often preceded by some of the same signs that occur in the Santa Gadea vision and which continue in the later, purely Marian apparitions, such as lights and celestial music.

According to the *Siete Partidas,* a comprehensive codification of civil and canon law compiled under the direction of Alfonso X of Castile around 1248, miraculous shrines based on discoveries of relics were being founded then, also.[24]

> Some men fraudulently discover or build altars in fields or in towns, saying that there are relics of certain saints in those places and pretending that they perform miracles, and, for this reason, people from many places are induced to go there as on a pilgrimage, in order to take something away from them; and there are others who influenced by dreams or empty phantoms which appear to them, erect altars and pretend to discover them in the above named localities.

Three kinds of "inventions" are distinguished here: fraudulent ones, ones based on dreams, and ones based on phantoms (*antoianças*). The Santa Gadea case, should it have to be classed in this way, would be an invention based upon the apparition of a phantom, fraudulently or not. In his *Setenario,* Alfonso el Sabio defines an *antoiança.* He goes through the different ways that people come to have mistaken beliefs: sect, opinion, fantasy (as in deliria), dream, and hallucination. His series goes from the more believable to the less, and he classes antoiança between opinion and fantasy. "Antoiança is something that stops before the eyes and then disappears, as one sees or hears it in a trance, and so is without substance."[25]

From the invention of relics based on visions to the Santa Gadea story, the founding of a Marian devotion on the site of relics based on a vision, is a very short step.

If relics could be located by visions or dreams, so could statues and crucifixes. As we will see, this kind of legend was part of the common culture of the late medieval period. The miraculous finding of statues, as at Montserrat, Guadalupe, Peña de Francia, Nuria, virtually all of the great Marian shrines of late medieval Spain, are based on a simple switch in the previous scenario from the finding of saints' bodies to the finding of images. If these stories were legendary, they in turn inspired or informed the way other statues were "discovered."

Such a case, near Nieva (Segovia), may have occurred shortly before the Santa Gadea visions, for there are certain disquieting resemblances. In these early visions it is difficult to tell legends from real episodes. For Santa Gadea there is a document that may or may not be legitimate. For the apparition/discovery of Mary near Nieva, no document exists. There, a shepherd named Pedro supposedly had a revelation around 1390 to tell the bishop of Segovia to look for a statue of Mary hidden underground. When the statue was eventually found, the shepherd was known, like the Pedro of Santa Gadea, as Pedro de Buenaventura. Which story came first?

The shrine of Santa María la Real de Nieva definitely existed first. The original bulls of the Avignon pope Clement VII that permitted its founding and granted indulgences for persons contributing to it are dated February 25, 1393. Like the 1404 bull for Santa Gadea of Benedict XIII, they mention an influx of pilgrims to the site, in this case because of miracles worked not only by the Virgin Mary but also by Saint Anne. The site was donated by Queen Catalina to the Dominicans in 1399, and they administered it as a monastery shrine and parish until the nineteenth century.[26]

Alonso de Venero, writing around 1550, said the church was

built "at the intercession of the image of the Virgin Mary that was found in the same place."[27] The apparition story may have been considerably elaborated after 1564, when the body of the lucky shepherd was rediscovered intact in the church. So it is impossible to say which Pedro de Buenaventura existed (as a person or as a legendary invention) first. Both were supposed to have ended their lives in service to the shrine they were instrumental in founding.

The shrine of Santa María del Espino of Santa Gadea is supposed to have started with an apparition, pure and simple. The story for Nieva includes in addition the finding of a statue and thus is much closer to the archetypal Castilian legend of the time, that of Guadalupe.

In 1399 Santa Gadea del Cid was no longer threatened by Moors. They had not been there for 300 years. It was, however, harrassed by bandits precisely from isolated buildings like the abandoned church in the countryside that was the site of the apparition. Doubtless it had also been threatened by the plague. The apparitions of Mary addressed these needs. The hawthorn would cure illnesses; a depiction of the apparition would be protection from the devil. But there was a condition. The abandoned church in the countryside was messy symbolically and spiritually as well as overgrown with brush and a social nuisance. In more ways than one, it had to be cleaned up.

Churches were places where pieces of saints were kept. The villagers, spiritual as well as physical heirs of abandoned communities in their jurisdiction, were responsible for spiritual obligations such as corporately contracted promises. A church that was once sacred had been desecrated. Were there also any obligations the living did not know about? What of obligations to the dead, masses for their souls. A parish church is also the site of a graveyard. Abandon a parish church and one abandons the dead.

The extent to which people in Spanish villages observed obligations to abandoned parish churches is evident in the 1575-1580 *relaciones topográficas* of Philip II; village after village reports processions to isolated churches in the countryside that were once the parish churches of villages abandoned because of

plague or drought. Even today, many isolated shrines are remembered as having once been parish churches, although by
and large there is much less sense of corporate duty to distant
ancestors and heavenly helpers.

Whether or not the village of Montañana la Yerma was over-
run by Moors, thus, such a story had a clear physical and
spiritual referent in the minds of the people of Santa Gadea:
the abandoned church of San Millán. If the village council
cleaned out the weeds and brush from the church their town
would prosper and their souls grow in grace.

If the devil was the enemy once the Moors were far away,
the Moors remained as an historic "other." They were perhaps
a present enemy as well, for men from all over Castile were
periodically called south to do battle until 1492. Santa Gadea
itself came to bear the name of Castile's most famous warrior,
El Cid.

Jaén, 1430

The threat of the Moors was a live one in Jaén, 650 km. to
the south of Santa Gadea in northern Andalusia. There, on the
night of June 10-11, 1430, two men and two women saw a
ghostly procession, similar to that of Santa Gadea. Two days
later they recounted what they saw to the vicar general of the
diocese, and the original document of their testimony that he
had drawn up is in the archive of the parish church of San
Ildefonso. The text was first published in 1639, when new marvels in nearby Arjona and Baeza seemed to threaten Jaén's
supremacy in miracles.[28]

In 1430 Jaén was near enough to the Moslem-Christian frontier that Moorish raids occasionally came up to the walls of the
city.[29] The residents who did not live within the inner walls of
the city lived in constant fear of attack. The vision took place
in a suburb, and was related to those fears. As with the apparition of Santa Gadea, the procession of Jaén was dense with
symbolism; but in contrast to the earlier vision, at Jaén Mary
gave no explication.

☆

Chronology

On Tuesday, June 13, 1430 the four seers "put their hands on the cross and swore in the hand of the judge by God, Saint Mary, the sign of the cross that they physically touched, and the holy gospels wherever they might be" to tell the entire truth. Juan Rodríguez de Villalpando first questioned informally the seer who had the most complete view of the procession, Pedro, son of Juan Sánchez. Then he took formal testimony from:

1) Pedro, son of Juan Sánchez
2) Juan, son of Usenda Gómez
3) María Sánchez, wife of the shepherd Pero Fernández
4) Juana Fernández, wife of the shepherd Aparicio Martínez

In the translation below I have put the testimony of Juan first and omitted Pedro's informal statement, as it coincides with his formal testimony.

TESTIMONY OF JUAN

Juan, son of Usenda Gómez, resident in Jaén of the parish of San Bartolomé, a witness received by the judge regarding the above matter, said under oath that last Saturday night, June 10 of the present year, at what seemed to him to be midnight, when he was sleeping in the district beyond the walls near San Ildefonso in some houses belonging to Alfonso García with three others in a bed, in the middle next to Juan, the miller's son, who was on the side by the door, this witness awoke and saw that there was a light in the house as if from a candle, and thought it was daylight. Then he heard dogs barking—there were seven hunting dogs outside the house—and many other small and big dogs who sounded far away. This witness thought it was already day since there was so much light, and he arose in his underclothes and opened the door a little, staying inside the house and looking out with his head between the door and the wall.

He saw five crosses come one after another as is the custom in processions. The crosses were like those of Jaén, all
white, and were carried by five clean-shaven youths. At
the end of the procession of the crosses went a lady dressed
and wrapped in white clothes and a kind of mantle, and it
appeared to him from her shape that she was in a bed, or
on a dais or a large chair that appeared to be of silver, and
that she was half a cubit taller than everyone else, but nobody carried the lady, who walked very slowly. From this
lady issued so much brightness that she shone as the sun
shines at its zenith on a clear day, so that the entire street
could be seen. This lady wore behind her a train as much
as three arm-lengths long and carried on her right arm a
small baby about a year old, which to him appeared very
beautiful, dressed all in white, and on her head she wore
something white.

No one was nearer to the lady than the length of her
train. After her it seemed that there came priests on both
sides, as in a procession; in the middle of the street there
was no one except for the priests on both sides as in a
procession. There were about ten priests—he knew they
were priests because they were tonsured and prayed as
they walked—but he did not understand a word of what
they were saying. After this procession of priests there followed a hundred persons, armed and dressed all in white.
Their weapons could be heard, and they seemed to carry
lances.

This witness did not wait until all had passed by, but
quickly got inside and pulled his head in and closed the
door behind him. But he did see the last of the people in
the street and that no more people were coming. He closed
the door well and tried to wake up Juan, who was in bed,
but he could not. And he thought about it and called
Pedro, son of Juan Sánchez, and said to him, "Pedro, see if
you can figure out what is going on, for there are some
people dressed in white and a lady going by in the street."
And Pedro got up and put on his nightshirt and went into
the yard. This witness put on his clothes and lay down on

a bench in the houses. At first he sat, thinking about what he had seen, and then he lay down. For a while he stayed awake, then he fell asleep, so when Pedro went back to bed he did not see him.

Asked if when he saw those people he took pleasure or fright, he said that when he saw the crosses he thought they were in a procession; and after he saw the people in white he saw that the brightness was not the brightness of day, but rather of another kind. He was thereby in doubt and had neither pleasure nor fear, except that when he first went outside the brightness seemed to warm him, although not as much as the sun.

Asked when he talked about it afterwards, he said that when he got up in the morning he told the woman of the house and the others there, and that Pedro was there and said he had seen the same thing.

TESTIMONY OF PEDRO

Pedro, son of Juan Sánchez, housekeeper of the wife of Ruy Díaz de Torres, resident of Jaén in the parish of San Ildefonso in the district beyond the walls of the very noble city of Jaén, a witness received by the judge regarding the matter described above, said under oath when asked the appropriate questions that last Saturday, June 10 of the present year, not long before the clock struck midnight, this witness was sleeping in a bed in the house of Alfonso García, which is in the same parish near the church of San Ildefonso, and that Juan, son of Usenda Gómez, citizen of this city, normally slept with him. This witness woke up and saw that the street door of the compound of houses was open and that Juan came in quickly and slammed and barred the door, threw himself down on a bench as if frightened, and in that position said to this witness, "Pedro, get up and look at all the people." And this witness said, "Where are they going?" And Juan told him, "They are going up there toward San Ildefonso."

This witness then got up in his nightshirt, went out into the yard, and by way of a low wall got out on a higher wall of the houses, from which he could see very well the entire street and the back of the chapel of the church of San Ildefonso. When he looked over the wall he saw going toward the church on the upper street seven crosses, one behind another, which were like the crosses of the city, carried by seven men dressed all in white from head to toe. On both sides of the crosses walked about twenty persons similarly dressed in white to their feet as in a procession, praying.

At the end of this procession went a lady taller than the other people and dressed in white garments with a train as long as 2½ or 3 arm-lengths. She walked alone behind the procession, and this witness did not see her face, but it seemed to him that so much brilliance went out from her face that it shone brighter than the sun. And everything was so bright that the houses of the neighborhood could be seen, the tiles of the roofs, the church, and everything as if it were noontime. It was so bright that it blinded this witness as if or worse than if he looked straight at the sun. This lady carried in her arms a small baby dressed in the same way in white, and he did not see anything else the baby was wearing, and she carried it in her hand with her right arm only.

Close behind the lady's train came about three hundred people, men and women, the women near her and the men behind, all dressed in white and grouped together, not lined up as in a procession. After these people came about a hundred armed men all in white. Their weapons could be heard one against another (that is how he knew they were armed), and it seemed to him they carried something like lances on their shoulders. All these people who went behind the lady walked silently and very slowly, so that when this witness got on top of the wall the procession had not yet reached the church. There would be a distance of the throw of a fist-sized stone from the house to the chapel of the church.

Against the back outer wall of the chapel he saw that a great altar as high as a lance had been erected, and it shone very brightly and was very dignified and elegant, with white and red hangings on the entire wall above it. He saw that about twenty persons dressed in white were singing, and their voices seemed weak, like those of the sick after they recover from sickness. This witness did not see the faces of any of these people, but at the altar he saw no one dressed like a priest. He did not even see anyone go to the altar, or anyone tall enough. When the people reached the top of the rise near the chapel, the lady and all the other people sat down, and it seemed to him that so many people were there that the hill was covered, and that it could accommodate more than* persons. When they arrived, this witness could no longer bear to look at such a bright light, and he lay down on the wall and did not look at the people, although the wall and its environs were well lit by the light emanating from the lady.

After a while when his eyes were rested and he recovered his sight he looked again at the lady and the other people. He saw she was seated, wearing clothes that shone as if she was a silver image, and the other people were seated. Those who were singing were standing on both sides of the altar. The lady was seated near the procession, and all the other people were close around behind her. This witness, after he had seen the people seated in that way and his eyes had recovered their sight, began to get down from the wall, and got down the way he had gotten up. He would have gotten down before, but he could not see very well, and so he was afraid to. He was on the wall for about a half-hour; when he climbed up, the clocks were striking twelve, as he said, and when they finished ringing, the church of Santa María and some of the other churches rang for matins. And when these people were coming he heard many dogs barking behind them.

When asked if he was frightened or pleased or what he felt when he saw these people, he said that, when he first

* in the original left blank; in a copy published in 1639 "eight hundred."

saw the people, he felt pleasure in his heart as he would in
seeing anyone, and that as soon as he saw the soldiers he
was frightened. He thinks his pleasure was because every
night in this district outside the walls people fear the
Moors, and as soon as he saw the procession, the people,
and the crosses, he was relieved, for if those people were
safe from the Moors, so was everybody else outside the
walls. But when he saw the soldiers he became afraid and
unsure. When he came down he went to sleep, said nothing to anyone, and slept almost until dawn. When daylight
came he went out to see whether the people had left any
footprints or traces, and he found none.

Asked when he told about it and where he first mentioned it, he said that on his return from looking in the
cemetery for footprints, before entering the house [he was
present as] Juan was speaking with Miguel Fernández de
Pegalajar about what had happened, saying how he had
seen five crosses go by and other people who went in a
procession. At that point this witness declared, "I saw it
all." Juan's face was very yellow when he got up in the
morning, and this witness said to him, "Why are you so
yellow?" And Juan said to him, "From the fright I got last
night." And they asked him on the following Sunday what
he had seen, and he told what he had seen.

He also said that the previous Wednesday, about midnight, he woke up and heard a voice tell him, "Do not
sleep and you will see good things." And that Thursday
after falling asleep he awoke and heard a similar voice; Friday he heard nothing; and Saturday he saw what he has
recounted.

TESTIMONY OF MARÍA SÁNCHEZ

María Sánchez, wife of Pero Fernández, shepherd, citizen
of Jaén in the parish of San Ildefonso, a witness received
by the judge regarding the above matter, said under oath
that last Saturday night, June 10 of the present year, she
was in the houses of her compound on the main street that
leads to San Ildefonso in the district beyond the walls of

this city. Between eleven and twelve, when she got up to
get water for her son who was sick, she saw a great light
inside her houses, which seemed to be shining like gold in
sunlight. The witness thought it was lightning and was
afraid and got down on her knees on the ground and
looked out into the street through a wide crack between
the doors of her compound and saw that a lady was passing
by in the street dressed in white clothes [decorated] with
bright white flowers that stood out in the cloth. It seemed
to her that the mantle the lady was wearing was lined with
silks the color of sunflowers. She was carrying a baby boy
on her right arm held by the left, and the child was
wrapped in a cloth of white silk. She was more than a
cubit taller than the other persons, and the baby appeared
to be about four months old and well fed.

On her right was a man who appeared to be like the image [or depiction] of Saint Ildefonsus in the altar of the
church of San Ildefonso. He was wearing a stole around his
neck and carried a book in his hand, and he wore the stole
as priests do to say mass and carried a maniple in his hand
with the book with a white cover open in both hands as if
he was holding it in front of [the lady] so she could see it.
On the other side of the lady walked a woman like a beata,
a little behind, and she did not know who she was.

All the brilliance issued forth from the lady's face; and
on seeing the lady and the brilliance she suddenly took
fright. Afterward she realized that it was the Virgin Saint
Mary and she saw a crown [or halo] on the lady's head, as
portrayed in the altar of the church. She recognized her
because of what she has said, and because she was very
similar to the image of Our Lady in the altar. Saint Ildefonsus also had a crown [or halo] on his head and a ton-
sure wide and open like a monk's, as portrayed in the
church. After the lady, came people all dressed in white.
She saw no crosses or candles, just the brilliance, and after
[the lady] had gone by, it was as bright in her houses and
the street as when [the lady] was going by.

Because she was alone, she did not dare open the door to

see more, but instead went back to her room, for there
was no man with her, just two children, one about eight
years old and another about four. The lady and the other
people went as if in a procession from the church of San
Ildefonso toward the city. When she was in her room she
was much comforted, and then she heard the clock strike
twelve, and when it finished the bells rang for matins. And
this witness said that at the time she heard singing, but it
did not appear to her to be singing of this world, and when
she heard it she was very relieved and comforted.

TESTIMONY OF JUANA FERNÁNDEZ

Juana Fernández, wife of Aparicio Martínez, shepherd
citizen in the parish of San Ildefonso, a witness received by
the judge regarding the matter described above, said under
oath that she was in her houses, which are in the parish of
San Ildefonso in front of the cemetery, last Saturday night,
June 10 of the present year, after the first sleep but before
the rooster called. She got up to go into the yard of her
houses because she had diarrhea (*pasyon en las tripas*) and
had gotten up three times already.

In these circumstances she saw a sudden great brilliance
near the back of the chapel of the church of San Ildefonso.
At first she thought it was a lightning bolt, but then decided it could not be because the light was so strong, resplendent, and continuous. As she pondered this, she saw
between the doors of her compound a lady coming with
many other people from the direction of the pottery works
up the street toward the chapel. It appeared that the lady
carried in her arms at her breast an object, but she could
not see what it was; and it seemed to her that the brilliance shone forth from her face and the object. They came
as in a procession over the *muladar** near the chapel, and
behind [the lady] came other people dressed in white. It
seemed that some of them carried staves upright in their
hands, but because the sill of the doors to her compound is

* dunghill, rubbish heap, or midden.

low, she could not see if they were crosses or scepters or what they were. This brilliance did not seem like that of the sun, the moon, or candles, but rather was a brilliance she had never seen.

When this witness saw it she fell down, paralyzed with fright, and began to tremble all over. And because she was blinded she turned toward the wall with her back to the light and stayed there a while. Then she got up and felt her way along the wall to her room. The brilliance continued. Before, when she was looking, it appeared that the lady stopped behind the chapel, and hence she lost sight of her, because she could not see that from her house, but the brilliance remained. And this witness out of fear went to bed with her husband, and a child was with him, and she moved it and lay down trembling beside her husband.

Asked if the people went in a procession or in a group, she said that, because she was afraid, she did not notice, except that many people came dressed in white. Closest to the lady came two persons, although she could not tell if they were men or women, one on one side, one on the other. And the lady appeared to be taller than the others. Soon afterwards she heard matins ringing. It appeared to her that the lady and the other people came very slowly in procession.

On the night of Saturday, June 10, around midnight, the four witnesses, two young men living in one house and two wives of shepherds in their own houses, all saw, in the vicinity of the church of San Ildefonso, a procession of people dressed in white, with a tall lady who gave off a blinding light carrying a baby or what could have been a baby. These are the only matters on which the viewers agreed.

Three of the viewers specified that the blinding light issued from the lady's face, but for all of them the light itself was what first attracted their attention. Two of them, Juan and Juana, said that the light was not one they had ever known and was unlike that of the sun or the moon. The women at first thought it could be lightning, but rejected the idea as the light was continuous. The light remained after the lady had passed, and Juan said he felt warmed by it.

In terms of the direction and time of the procession, three were in agreement. Pedro, Juan, and Juana all saw the procession go up the hill to pause at the open space behind San Ildefonso and heard the bells ring for midnight and matins. But María Sánchez, who lived on the street joining the city and San Ildefonso, saw the procession going by her house in the opposite direction—away from the church toward the city, before midnight struck.

In terms of the composition of the procession, Pedro and Juan, on the one hand, and María and Juana, on the other, appear to have partially coordinated their stories, but the overall picture is quite confused. Pedro and Juan both saw men dressed in white carrying crosses, a lady, priests who were praying, and armed men, and heard dogs barking. Pedro saw seven crosses, Juan five; for Pedro a total of twenty priests walked on both sides of the crosses in front of the lady, for Juan the crosses went in front of the lady, but the priests (only ten of them) followed her. Both of them saw that the lady wore a train about three arm-lengths long, but only Pedro saw that she was followed by a large group of people, women first, then men. Both saw about 100 armed men bringing up the rear, and both were frightened.

Pedro specifically said that no one was near the lady. Both María and Juana placed two figures near her. Juana could not see who they were, but María identified one as Saint Ildefonsus and the other as a beata, or nun.[30] María saw a group of people following Mary, and Juana saw men carrying pole-like objects, which could have been crosses or lances.

Discrepancies like these are not important if our task is not to see whether Mary actually visited Jaén that night, but rather to understand what this story meant to the witnesses and townspeople. Certainly the discrepancies did not stop the people from eventually taking the whole matter very seriously. Our Lady of the Capilla is now the patroness of the city, and from the sixteenth century on she has been turned to for help in major disasters.[31] To the witnesses, however, the meaning of their visions was not so clear. Three of them thought they were seeing some sort of religious activity, identifying priests at prayer. Pedro was the only one who saw an outdoor altar behind the church, but both he and María heard singing. Only María offered an explicit identification of the lady as Mary and pointed the way to the meaning that the people of Jaén subsequently assigned to the episode. Her interpretation, however, was consistent with the testimony of the other witnesses.

María saw the lady as Mary because she was like an image in the altar of the Church of San Ildefonso. The present image of Our Lady of the Capilla is almost always covered by a robe, but a 1950 monograph on the devotion includes a photograph of the image undressed.[32] The statue appears to be from the fourteenth century or early fifteenth century. Mary wears a gold robe with white daisies; she is standing and carrying a child. The back of the image is broken off, as if it had been part of a reredos and was removed. María Sánchez described white flowers on Mary's dress. Possibly, the present statue was once part of a reredos and was broken off, after the visions, to be venerated in a special chapel.

María Sánchez also claimed to recognize Saint Ildefonsus, the seventh-century bishop of Toledo noted for his Marian writings, walking next to Mary and showing her a book. She recognized him, too, from his image in the church. The combination of Mary and Ildefonsus inevitably leads to the early legend of Mary bestowing on Ildefonsus a chasuble. The story as told in the life of Ildefonsus by the monk Cixila in the ninth century is as follows:[33]

For the Feast of the Annunciation of the Blessed Virgin, Ildefonsus had composed a new *missa*, the seventh in number, and when he was going to the Church to celebrate the *missa*, preceded by the clergy with lighted torches, the portals of the church opened and a heavenly splendor shone round about them all. Whereupon the clergy dropped their lamps and fled; but Ildefonsus remained among the choirs of the Blessed. Then he saw the Heavenly Queen sitting on the ivory throne where he as bishop was accustomed to sit whenever he preached to the people. And she addressed

him with these words: "Hasten, loyal servant of God, to
receive from my hand a gift I have brought you from the
treasure of my Son; you may wear this vestment only on
my feast days, and because you have remained in this life
with the vesture of glory, in the life to come you shall en-
joy with other servants of my Son the realm of glory."

This story was known throughout Europe by the end of the
eleventh century. In the compendia of Marian miracles, it was
almost invariably the first or second miracle, not only in Western Europe but also in the Orient.[34] The Cathedral of Toledo
was a shrine largely because of this tradition, and the stone on
which Mary supposedly stood was venerated within it. Even
today many persons entering the cathedral touch the holy stone
and say a brief prayer[35] (see Figures 3 and 4).

Our witnesses, living as they did in the parish of San Ildefonso, appeared to know the story. Juan saw the lady traveling
on her feet but also, strangely, on some kind of a platform,
perhaps the throne in the legend. Pedro, who viewed the ceremony behind the church, saw an unearthly choir, an elaborate
altar, and Mary seated on a throne. That what was involved in
the matins ceremony was a heavenly, not an earthly choir was
made clear both by Pedro (who thought the voices were weak
like recently recovered sick people) and María (for whom "it
did not appear to be singing of this world"). Pedro did not see
Mary give the vestment to Saint Ildefonsus (would that be the
cape lined with silks the colors of sunflowers María saw?); in
fact he says the lady walked alone, hence without the saint
altogether.

All in all, the visions seem to be informed in part by the
legend, but they do not reproduce it. Instead, like the Santa
Gadea story, they are inventive, using elements from the legend,
together with elements from Jaén ceremonial, as the mind makes
creative combinations from known elements when dreaming.
Both Juan and Pedro remarked how the carrying of the crosses
and the crosses themselves were similar to standard Jaén processions in which every cross would stand for a parish.

Such a visit would logically resemble two kinds of ceremonies familiar to any resident of Jaén. Undoubtedly, like other Iberian cities of the time, Jaén held daytime petitionary processions to invoke divine assistance, whether for health, rain, or victory. Barcelona processions in 1425 and 1427, for instance, also included crosses of parishes, clergy dressed in white singing the litany, major relics or statues, and, bringing up the rear, the people. The second kind is the city's solemn reception of royalty. Such an entrance would have taken the form of a Corpus procession and would have included stops at specially decorated sites, like the improvised altar behind San Ildefonso.[36]

The presence of armed men is another innovation in keeping with local conditions. Pedro saw them as protection for the procession, and the very fact they might be needed frightened him. But his own evidence that all were dressed in white might indicate that all in the procession belonged to the realm of the dead, the realm of heaven, and the soldiers might also be seen as martyrs who died in the crusades against the Moors, and who perhaps were buried in that cemetery, as with the martyrs of Santa Gadea. In this, the entire vision evokes the processions of souls of the dead said to be seen until recent times in Galicia.

Later interpreters saw the soldiers' presence and the apparition as a whole as a sign that Mary would protect the city in the future. This message of special Marian attention and protection, building on the legend of the Descent to Toledo and the liturgical customs of the city, would have been very welcome to a jumpy frontier city. Just as Mary came to Toledo to single out Ildefonsus for attention, and in the process honored the city itself, so Mary came to Jaén, perhaps introduced by Ildefonsus, to defend the city from Moors.

The city of Tortosa, at the mouth of the Ebro River, also has a tradition of an apparition that appears to derive from the legend of Saint Ildefonsus. There in the cathedral is preserved a holy belt, "la Santa Cinta," supposedly given by the Virgin to a holy priest at a midnight matins ceremony in 1178 (see Figure 5). There is no document for the apparition, and the story may well have been made up centuries later. The holy belt was there as early as 1354 and was used at that time for women in childbirth, like numerous "girdles" or "*ceintures*" of Mary prized in towns in France, England, Italy, and Flanders. No mention of an apparition comes until a special prayer was approved for it in 1508. In the seventeenth and eighteenth centuries, the belt was taken to the queens of Spain as a holy aid in childbirth.[37] One wonders whether the belt might not originally have been a *"mide"*—a talisman-measurement of some place in the holy land of the kind ordinarily secured by Western pilgrims. The legend is more evidence for the popularity of the original miracle of Ildefonsus.

The apparitions of Santa Gadea and Jaén bear resemblances uncanny for places so far apart and matters of only local importance. Such resemblances, it turns out, are more the rule than the exception. If they appear uncanny, then perhaps our notions about rural ignorance or segmented cultural systems need revision. Both apparitions involve a procession that includes a lady clad in white who gives off a blinding light. The bedazzled seers have to cover their eyes or periodically look away. One seer has to feel her way with her hands along her wall to her room; another has to wait before he feels clearheaded enough to get down off a wall without falling. Seers in both places refer to the light as brighter than the sun.

Both processions are liturgical, take place at midnight, and end with a matins ceremony. In both, the saints and angels are doing things that priests or monks do, and both choirs sound unearthly. Both are outdoors in public, not private, space. Other heavenly matins processions were not uncommon in the Middle Ages. Thirty-three of the miracles mentioned by Caesarius of Heisterbach occur during matins, the office in which it is most difficult to stay awake, that which takes place at the hour of midnight. Although villages did observe matins during Holy Week, it was essentially a monastic ritual, and the motif of heavenly matins doubtless grows out of monastic tradition. This makes special sense for Santa Gadea, where the Virgin calls for a monastery.

The seers, too, are similar. Pedro and Juan are the names of seers in both, and in Jaén, as in Santa Gadea, Pedro is the main seer. In Jaén it is Pedro who reveals, virtually as an afterthought, that he received locutions warning him to stay awake to see good things the third and second nights before the vision. Again there is a reminiscence of Peter, who three times was unable to stay awake in the Garden of Gethsemane. At Jaén it is Pedro who, of all the seers, has the most complete view of the procession. He alone gets a glimpse of the ceremony behind the church. His importance as chief seer is shown by the fact that the judge took him aside and questioned him first informally. In both cases, Pedro is the chosen one whose testimony gives impetus to the shrine or devotion, as Peter founded the Church. It is Pedro's account of the Jaén procession that is considered definitive by later historians.[38]

In keeping with the epoch, both apparitions have in the background as the enemy or the "other," the Moors. In later visions this "other" becomes Christian heretics, "reds," and finally, liberal clergy. Almost always, however, implicitly or explicitly, there is some "other" with an alternative system of belief, against which the seers and the community can affirm their faith in their own gods.

What features distinguish these two stories from later visions? The lady so intensely brilliant does not return to the peninsula until the apparition of Fatima in 1917. In later years there are no more supernatural processions. And by and large the visions get simpler. These two apparitions conform to the efflorescence of symbolism that is associated with the waning of the Middle Ages. In that of Santa Gadea, the symbolism is deciphered, and the Virgin gives Pedro a detailed explication of what he saw. That of Jaén is left for the people to figure out; there is no direct communication, aside from Pedro's premonitions. Both are complex signs, sacred riddles.

The Mary that appears in these two visions is not the benevolent friend of later visions. She is indeed benevolent, but as a hieratic mother goddess rather than a person. The face that sends forth light that blinds is a terrifying image of power. The Marian image is halfway between the enthroned God-mother of the twelfth and thirteenth centuries and the graceful standing lady of later years. Three of the Jaén visionaries see her walking, but taller by a forearm than everyone else, and Juan sees her paradoxically both walking and seated at the same time. Pedro, who saw her walk, also saw her sit in a silver chair behind the church. At Santa Gadea, where she is (presumably seated) in the hawthorn tree, there are overtones of divinities of trees and pre-Christian cults, as with the fairies that Jeanne d'Arc knew about in a tree in her village.[39]

Perhaps the greatest shock to Catholics versed in the saccharine images of Mary of later centuries is the whipping of Pedro by monks in Santa Gadea, supervised by Mary herself. Punishment, in Catholic popular theology, was thought to be administered by God or Christ, but here is a very stern Mary indeed. It is true, she works through agents, and also that mothers of Santa Gadea may also have had their children punished; but the beating was bad enough to cause an uproar in the town, good evidence that it would not have been tolerated from any parent.

Nor was the beating without precedent in European religious legend. Bede says Saint Peter himself thrashed Bishop Laurence when he was going to abandon his see in England. In that case, as at Santa Gadea, the wounds served as proofs of divine intervention, for when Laurence showed his wounds to the king, the king was converted. Caesarius of Heisterbach, writing in the thirteenth century, told various stories—a nun was cured of her lust for a priest by a clip on the jaw from the Blessed Virgin, "a grievous disease requires harsh medicines"; a sexton was attacked by a cross in his bedroom; and a canon was kicked in the stomach by John the Baptist. The *Libro de los exenplos*, compiled 1400-1420, contains a story taken from Gregory the Great about the Lord appearing to a priest to give him a message for a saintly bishop. The priest did not dare approach the bishop, and finally during the third apparition the Lord severely whipped the priest, who thereupon went to the bishop, showed him his wounds, and delivered the message.[40]

These attacks are in keeping with a notion of divinity that inspired an awe akin to terror, with whom contact is more to be feared than desired. It is an early medieval notion, one that was changing even as the Spanish visions we describe took place. Divine assault and battery was rare in the late Middle Ages;

it occurs in none of the Spanish public visions I know of after Santa Gadea.

Subsequent apparitions of Mary have her seem and act like a human being. The seers do not know who she is until she tells them. She is kind, gentle, and very beautiful. In the Santa Gadea and Jaén testimony, beauty is not mentioned. Glory and power, high wattage, is more like it. The more human and humane apparitions follow shortly after. Is it a coincidence that these two more god-like visions occurred earlier? In any case, the change aptly represents the shift in the image of Mary so clear in the iconography of the late Gothic period.

MARY OF THE CROSS IN CASTILE

Cubas (Madrid), 1449

The village of Cubas is about forty km. southwest of Madrid, just off the road to Toledo. In 1978 it was still beyond the area of urban expansion, with neither chalets nor apartment houses. Visitors who ask there for the convent of Santa María de la Cruz will be met with blank stares. When they explain what they want they are directed to "Santa Juana," a small convent lying in a depression a few hundred meters east of the town by a dirt road. The gently rolling fields around the town are still, as in 1449, used for grain and vines.

More is known about the apparitions in Cubas to Inés Martínez in 1449 than virtually any Spanish apparitional episode until the twentieth century. This is not because it is an important shrine now—it is not a shrine at all—but rather because a copy of the investigations of the visions and the affidavits taken of the subsequent miracle cures is still available. Although the convent was destroyed in the Civil War, the nuns were able to preserve a full transcription of the documents.[41]

In March 1449, Inés Martínez, called Inesica by her friends, was 12½ years old. She was born August 3, 1436. She herself told the judges in the investigation that she normally said 150 Hail Marys and Our Fathers when keeping her pigs, and that

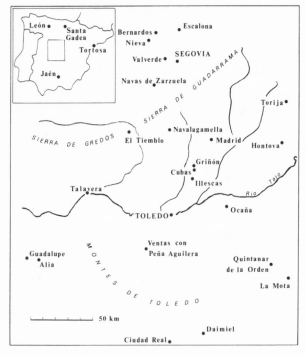

Map 1. Central Castile

she knew two other prayers. The other witnesses confirmed that she was exceptionally devout. She first confessed at age six, and she confessed more often than the other children her age. She first received communion at about age nine. From about that time she had abstained from wine and fasted for half the days of Lent and all the days of Mary. Devoted to Mary, she often prayed at Mary's altar in the morning. If she heard the church bells ringing she went to the church "to see God," even if she had to interrupt a meal. The judges seemed to measure debauchery by behavior at weddings; unlike others her age, Inés rarely attended weddings, and, when she did, she did not dance or sing.

In keeping with the poverty of her parents, Inés dressed modestly. For the year before the visions she worked watching pigs; at home she spun and prayed. Sometimes she ate at the home of her friend next door. Her good character was one reason why some of the townspeople believed in the apparitions. One villager said, "All who hear Inés believe what she says because they know she is a good daughter." Her neighbors considered her incapable of fabricating the story.

Inés's father's occupation was variously given as the town pigherder (*porquerizo*) or as a blacksmith (*ferrero*). He and his wife were described by their fellow villagers as poor and simple. Probably the majority of the peasants would have characterized themselves as poor to Church or government officials. If Inés's parents were among the poorest in the village, probably some other qualifiers would have been added. In any case they were neither rebellious (*revoltosos*) nor crafty ("*no entienden en mal*"). The judges wondered if Inés's parents could have coached her to invent the visions. Their neighbor thought that neither father nor mother was smart enough. One witness said they were the simplest in the village.

☆

Chronology

Inés's visions of Mary took place over seventeen days in March 1449. Mary appeared to her a total of six times, always in fields outside the village, as follows:

1) *Monday, March 3: Inés was to tell the people to confess for an epidemic was on the way.*
2) *Tuesday, March 4, and*
3) *Friday, March 7: Mary pressed Inés to deliver the message.*
4) *Sunday, March 9: Inés was instructed by village men to ask Mary for a sign, and Mary pressed Inés's fingers into the sign of the cross.*
5) *Sunday, March 9, later: the climactic vision occurred. The village waited nearby in procession as Mary took a cross from Inés and planted it in the ground to mark a church site.*

On Monday, March 10, Inés's testimony was taken before a notary public, and a copy was sent with her and some village men to Guadalupe, where the Virgin had instructed her to go.

6) *Wednesday, March 19: on her return, Inés had a final vision, in which the Virgin announced another sign.*

On Friday, March 21, she described this final vision in a deposition, which together with the earlier document was sent by the town to the archbishop of Toledo.

On April 23 there opened an official enquiry ordered by the archbishop. I have translated below Inés's testimony on March 10, March 19, and April 23.

PRELIMINARY INVESTIGATION BY TOWN AUTHORITIES, CUBAS, MARCH 10, 1449

In Cubas, town of the noble caballero Luis de la Cerda, March 10, 1449, in the church of San Andrés in the presence of us, notaries and public scriveners, and of the undersigned witnesses, there appeared Juan González, chaplain, assistant curate in the church; Rodrigo de Arévalo, commander and lieutenant for Señor Luis de la Cerda in his towns of Griñón and Cubas; Lope de Lorbes, commander of Piedrabuena; Juan González and Juan Ferrándes, alcaldes in the town; and a number of other citizens of Griñón and Cubas. They said that Inés (daughter of Alfonso Martínez, pigkeeper of the town, and Mari Sánchez his wife, citizens of Cubas), who was present, claimed that the Virgin Mary spoke to her, and that she witnessed certain things that the Lady Virgin Saint Mary had said to her and done. Because of this, today the clergy and councils of these towns and other neighboring towns made a general procession in honor and reverence of the Lady Virgin Saint Mary and had two masses said at her altar in accord with what Inés said she had ordered. Then the men named above told Inés to tell all she had seen and experienced in the past few days in the presence of us, the notaries and witnesses given below. What Inés said follows.

Testimony of Inés

Inés said that on Monday, March 3 of this year, when she was watching pigs in the area known as Fuente Cecilia, about noon, she saw a very beautiful lady, who seemed to be dressed in cloth of gold, who came to her and said, "What are you doing here, *carita?*" And that Inés said, "I am watching these pigs." And she says the lady then asked why she fasted for the days of Saint Mary on Fridays. And she replied, because her parents told her to. And then she says that the lady said that she did well, and that she had little to fast this year. And then the lady ordered her to fast on the days on which they fall, that whoever fasted on the days on which they fell earned pardons of eighty thousand years. And she ordered her to tell all the people to confess and put their souls right, for they should know that a great epidemic of pain in the side (*dolor de costado*) would come, and rose-colored stones covered with blood, from which many people would die. And Inés said she asked the lady if from this epidemic she, her father, or her mother would die. And she says the lady answered it would be as God willed. And when the lady finished saying this, Inés saw her no more.

Inés said she did not dare tell anyone. And that the following Tuesday when she was walking with the pigs in the area known as Arroyo de Torrejón at noon, the lady came to her in the same way she appeared the day before and said, "Daughter, why did you not say what I ordered you to say yesterday?" And Inés said, "Because I did not dare say it for fear I would not be believed." And the lady said, "Pay attention: I order you to say it, and if they do not believe I will give you a sign so they will believe you." And then Inés says she asked the lady to tell her who she was. And she says the lady replied, "I will not tell you that now." And then she saw the lady no more. Inés says she told her father, her mother, and other people in Cubas.

And after this Inés said that on Friday, March 7, when she was watching her pigs in the area called el Prado Nuevo, near the town, the lady came to her for the third

time at the same hour, dressed as before, and asked
whether she had said what she had ordered her to say.
And Inés said yes, that she had told her father, her
mother, and other people. And the lady told her to tell it
and make it known to the priest and to all the people without fear or dread.

And Inés said that after this on Sunday, March 9, she
went to herd the pigs in the area called La Ciroleda, and
she says that when she was in the valley on the side of
Ciroleda near the town, kneeling with her mouth on the
ground offering her prayers to her and asking that the lady
appear to her, the lady came to her in the form that she
had appeared the other times and said, "Get up, daughter."
And that she was frightened and got up at once. And the
lady said to her, "Do not fear." And Inés then asked her
who she was, and the lady replied, "I am the Virgin
Mary." And that she came up to her and took Inés's right
hand with the thumb and pressed it and left the hand with
all the fingers pressed together and the thumb on top,
making a cross, as she showed. All of us who were there
saw it. And when her fingers were pressed together, Inés
cried out, and the lady said to her, "Now go with this sign
so they will believe you, for you will suffer this for their
sake. Go to the church. You will arrive when they are
coming out of mass. Show it to everybody, so they will
believe what you say since you bring a sign."

Inés said she went to the town and the church and arrived when the priest was finishing mass, as the Lady Saint
Mary had foretold. When she entered she knelt in front of
the altar of the Virgin Mary and declared to the priest and
people everything given above. Then the priest, alcaldes,
regidores, and omes buenos, with great reverence to the
Lady Virgin Mary who had manifested this miracle in Inés,
all assembled in a barefoot procession, carrying with great
devotion the crosses, lighted candles, and large wax tapers,
together with Inés and all the children who could be found
in the town. A cross of sticks was brought to put in the
place where the lady had taken [Inés's] hand and made a
sign out of it. When the procession was moving, beginning

to leave the threshing floors and enter the vineyards, Inés, who was in front with the children, turned and told Lope de Lorbes and Andrés Ferrándes, the regidores, who were keeping the children in line, to stop, for she heard the Lady Virgin Saint Mary calling her, saying twice, "Come here." Inés said she wanted to go and see what the Lady Virgin Saint Mary wanted. At that point Andrés Ferrándes, who was carrying the cross of sticks, gave it to Inés, and Inés went off with it. She said when she left the procession the Lady Virgin Mary came and went with her on [Inés's] right to the place where she had given Inés the sign. The Lady Virgin Mary said nothing until they reached the spot, and when they got there she took the cross in her hands and knelt against it. Then she got up and placed it sticking into the ground upright. And she ordered Inés to kneel facing the procession, which would come, and told her to hold the cross there until the procession came, and that they should build a church there called Saint Mary. And she instructed her that they should return with the procession to the town, and that Inés should spend that day and the night until today in the church of Cubas before the altar of the Virgin Mary with some innocent young children (*criaturas inocentes*). And that they should say two masses to Saint Mary at her altar, and that they should put Inés beneath the gospels of the masses.

And after the two masses they should take Inés to the church of Lady Saint Mary of Guadalupe, where she should remain for two days, and with her they should take four *libras* of wax to the Lady of Guadalupe. When they return, they should bring Inés to the place where the lady had taken her hand and made the sign. And that as soon as Inés prayed there, the sign would be undone. When she finished speaking she disappeared.

The witnesses to this first declaration included five citizens of Griñón (the next village to the north); two men from Cubas, including an alcalde; and three from Humanes, the next village to the west. It was made before four notaries.

Inés's hand came unfixed at Guadalupe, not on her return,

and on March 21, two days after she came back, she was questioned once more before notaries public, this time by the titular priest of the parish, who was probably absent at the time of the first visions.

PRELIMINARY INVESTIGATION CONTINUED, MARCH 21, 1449

Subsequent to the above in the town of Cubas on March 21 of the same year, with Inés, a girl (*moza niña*) of twelve or thirteen years old, present with her hand loose and healthy as she demonstrated in the presence of us Juan González de Roa and Benito Ferrández, notaries, and the witnesses written below, Ferrnand Alonso, Racionero of the Church of Toledo and parish priest of the town of Cubas appeared before us. He asked the girl on her conscience, admonishing her greatly to speak the truth and not the contrary, if everything contained in the above document, which was repeated in its entirety, happened as it said. Inés said that as certain as God is true, everything had taken place the way she said, and she had understood it and said it as given above. Then Ferrnand Alonso asked how it was that she had said her hand was not to come unstuck from the sign until she returned from Guadalupe, and how or why did this not happen? Inés said she had certainly understood it that way, because when she was in Guadalupe, the Prior and friars and the alcalde, after they had examined and looked at her hand, had tried to open it, and they could not believe that she had not been born that way. They had put her in front of the main altar of the church of the monastery of Guadalupe and asked her if the lowest image on the altar of Guadalupe was, or was like, the [image or woman] that appeared to her. And Inés said it was not that one, or like that one. Then they showed her the image of Saint Mary that is higher up on the altar of Guadalupe, which is a small one. And Inés said it was that one for sure. And it was said to Inés that the small image is not covered with gold, nor has such a gleaming face as Inés had said. And Inés said that it certainly seemed very white to her, and covered with gold as she had ap-

peared to her here, and it was for certain the same. And
that afterwards the monks, who had put Inés in a room,
locked it from the outside, and the girl remained shut in
there. And that afterwards* the monks came back with the
mayor of the town and others. And when they entered
where the girl was they told her to hold out her hand.
When she raised her hand to show them, they found it
well. And Ferrnand Alonso asked her if the Virgin or anything else appeared to her, or if they did anything to un-
stick it. Inés said that she saw nothing, and they applied no
medicines, just that she found her hand loose without
seeing or knowing how, and so they returned.

And when they came close to here, Inés says she went
on ahead to pray in the place where the sign was given,
and when she got to the spot and was praying the Lady
Virgin appeared to her. And Inés said to her," Lady, your
worship told me that my hand would not open until I returned here. Why did it not happen that way?" And she
says that the Lady Virgin Mary told her, "You did not understand because of your haste to question me. That is
why I sent you to my House of Guadalupe, so that when
you went there it would come undone." Inés says she said,
"Lady, may it please you to give another sign so they will
believe me, for they do not wish to believe my message
from you." And the lady said, "This I can well believe.
But do not worry, daughter, for I will give them such a
sign, that even if they want to they will not be able to believe, for blessed are those who saw it and believed it*,"
and at once she disappeared.

And this took place on her return from Guadalupe,
which was last Wednesday, March 19, in the afternoon,
when the Lady told her all that has been recounted this
last time. Ferrnand Alonso asked her if the Lady Virgin

---

* after an hour

* variants reported by other witnesses Inés had spoken to: did
not see it, and believed; blessed will be those who see it and believe
it.

Saint Mary had said what sign she would give or when it would be. And Inés said she said nothing more, and that she, Inés, did not know what the Lady thought of doing.

Ferrnand Alonso asked that an account of all this be given as a signed affidavit as often as asked for from us, Juan González and Benito Ferrándes, notaries. . . .

The matter had certainly aroused attention between March 10 and this declaration on March 21. The titular priest had come in, presumably from Toledo, where he was a prebend. The witnesses to the March 21 declaration included not merely men from Cubas but also the parish priest of Fuenlabrada, two citizens of Toledo, and two pages of the duke of Medinaceli.

Both of the declarations were dispatched by the concejo of Cubas to Alfonso Carrillo, archbishop of Toledo. On April 7 he replied from Benavente giving the town permission to build the church and instructing the archpriests of Madrid and Illescas to document the matter more fully.

The new investigation was opened in Cubas on April 23, 1449, by the clerical investigators placing the archbishop's letter upon their heads and saying they would obey him. The Cubas priest presented the witnesses, Inés first of all. With her previous depositions in hand, they led her through her testimony about the four days of apparitions one by one and asked for additional details for each day. Translated below are their questions and her answers. The questions themselves reveal much about the meaning of apparitions in fifteenth-century culture.

DIOCESAN INVESTIGATION, CUBAS, APRIL 23, 1449, TESTIMONY OF INÉS.

Asked by the señores judges who was with Inés on Monday at the time she says the Lady Virgin Mary appeared.

Inés replied there was no one, but that she saw two shepherd boys who were watching sheep a crossbow shot away from her [ca. 450 yds.], Perico, son of Alfonso Ferrándes, and Pasqual, son of El Callejano.

Asked if she noticed whether the shepherd boys were looking toward the place Inés said the lady was talking,

she said that they were eating, but she did not notice if
they were watching.
Asked if she was afraid of what she saw when the Virgin
Mary went up to her,
    she said that she was afraid when [the Virgin Mary]
    went away and she stopped seeing her.
Asked if she brought with her beautiful odors,
    she said she did not smell anything.
Asked if the lady wore a crown on her head,
    she said she did not see it.
Asked what she wore on her head, and what clothes she
wore,
    she said that she saw her face was shining, and that she
    wore something like a skirt (*saya*), and an *abrochada* in
    front, and that it was white as snow, and a coif on her
    head.
Asked if the coif was white,
    she said that no, that everything seemed like gold, the
    coif and the skirt.
Asked if she wore a belt,
    she said she did not see it.
Asked if she wore jewels on her hands,
    she said she did not see them, but that her hands were
    white as snow.
Asked if she wore clogs,
    she said no, she wore golden slippers.
Asked if the slippers had points,
    she said she thinks they were without points.
Asked if when the Virgin Mary left her and, as she says,
she was afraid, she went over to the shepherd boys, or
what she did,
    she said she stayed there and lunched on bread and
    water.
Asked what she did for the rest of the day until evening,
    she said she watched her pigs and again said one
    hundred and fifty Ave Marias with their Pater Nosters,
    which she was accustomed to say, and other prayers.
She was asked if she knew the Ave Maria and the Pater

Noster. And then the judges had her say them in front of them, and she said them simply (*simplemente*). Asked what other prayers she knew,

> she said two others, which she repeated, and they were of good words and holy devotion, one to the Virgin Mary and the other almost the same as the Pater Noster.

And asked whether on that day she said anything to anyone of what she had seen,

> she said that on her way back to Cubas with her pigs, she walked with the shepherd boys, and on the path she asked them if they had seen anything, and they said no. And that she asked them, "Didn't you see at noon today that woman who came to me when you were eating?" And they said, "No, why do you ask?" And she said, "A very beautiful woman came to me and asked me if I fasted on the days of Saint Mary. And I told her I did." And they said, "We didn't see anything; maybe it was a traveling prostitute." And she told them, "I do not know who it was," and they did not pay much attention and went off with their animals.

Asked about the second article in the deposition, that which Inés said that she saw the following Tuesday, in different ways to see if she changed the story she gave before, Inés did not say anything differently, but repeated the very words contained in the deposition.

Asked by the judges what clothes the Virgin Mary wore on that Tuesday,

> she said she saw her the same that day as the day before.

Asked if the Virgin Mary wore an overskirt [or train— *falda*],

> she said no, that the skirt (*saya*) was rounded.

[The judges asked about the Friday apparitions and Inés repeated the substance of her earlier statements.]

Asked if she was afraid when she saw the lady,

> she said that at first when she saw her she was afraid,

but as soon as she spoke she had no fear. And when she came up to her, she was afraid again.
Asked how far away from her the Virgin Mary was,
    she said she was a little way off.
Asked if she was on foot or kneeling,
    she said that both were standing.
Asked what time it was when she came that day,
    she said it was about noon.
Asked if she had eaten that day,
    she said no, because she fasted that day.
[The judges asked about the Sunday apparitions and Inés repeated the substance of her earlier statements.]
Asked in addition by the judges if on that Sunday when she says the Virgin Mary called her and said, "Get up, daughter," if [Mary] came as she had seen her before,
    she said yes.
Asked if she came with stockings or bare-legged,
    she said she came bare-legged.
Asked if she then was more afraid of her than other times,
    she said yes.
Asked if she said any other words besides those contained in the deposition she made,
    Inés said that when she got up and said to the Virgin Mary, "Give me, Lady, a sign, because they do not believe me," the Lady replied, "I can well believe that."
Asked if when the Virgin Mary called her the first time, she saw her,
    she said no.
Asked if the second time she called her, she saw her,
    she said that then she saw her.
Asked if the Virgin Mary came in the path walking, or how did she see her,
    she said that she saw her standing in the path where the cross is now erected.
Asked how far away she saw her,
    she said the distance of the throw of a stone (*tejo*). And that the lady was standing still, and Inés went over to her.

Asked if she walked with her,
>   she said when she got to the lady, then the lady began
>   to walk, and Inés with her.

Asked if by her walking or in her demeanor or form she
appeared to be a woman,
>   she said yes.

Asked if she was afraid of her,
>   she said yes.

Asked if her voice was thick or fine,
>   she said it was very fine and beautiful.

Asked if she was dressed as other times,
>   she said yes.

Asked if when she went to the place where she planted the
cross, she went quickly or slowly,
>   she said she did not go quickly, but rather slowly, yet
>   they got there right away, and she does not know how
>   they got there so soon.

Asked if she saw the lady leave footprints where she went,
>   she said no.

Asked if she saw her leave footprints where they arrived,
>   she said that where they arrived and the Virgin Mary
>   planted the cross there was a stretch of sand, and that it
>   seemed to her that some small footprints remained
>   there.

Asked if when she went with the lady on the path, the
lady said anything to her, or she to the lady,
>   she said no.

Asked why she did not say anything,
>   she said that she was never able to say anything, that it
>   seemed that her feet were not touching the ground.

Asked if when the lady took the cross, where or by which
arm did she hold it,
>   she said she took it a little lower than midway in its
>   length.

The judges showed the cross to her, and she pointed out
the place she had mentioned. Asked with which hand the
Virgin Mary grasped it,
>   she said with the right hand.

Asked how she stuck it in the ground,
> she said that she did not, that she merely put it down,
> and that it went down into the ground a palm and a
> half, and that she left it this way for Inés and told her,
> "Hold it here until the procession arrives."

Asked in what direction the Virgin Mary went off, or what
path she took,
> she said that after she stayed with her a little, she
> moved away from her a little, and then she disappeared.

Asked with great diligence the other questions or articles in
the deposition to see if she changed what she said, Inés still
repeated the substance of what appears in her testimony.

Asked if when she looked at the Virgin she could look at
her easily,
> she said that she shined so much that she blinded her,
> and that day she did not see her as well as before.

Asked whom the image that the monks of Guadalupe
showed to her resembled,
> she said it resembled the Virgin Mary whom she had
> seen here, and so did the clothes.

Asked if it seemed to her that it was alive,
> she said yes.

Asked if the eyes were open,
> she said yes.

Asked if it said anything to her,
> she said no.

Asked if while Inés was seeing [the image], the Virgin
Mary was watching her,
> she said yes.

Asked how long she was looking at her,
> she said the entire day she was there.

Asked if when Our Lady closed her hand it hurt,
> she said, up to the elbow.

Asked if it hurt much,
> she said that it did not hurt much; rather her arm
> seemed paralyzed or numb.

Asked if after her hand was opened the pain went away,
> she said yes.

And by the oath she took this was the truth, and she did
not know anything more about this matter.

Twenty-one other witnesses were questioned by the judges:
Inés's brother and parents; the two shepherd boys who were
nearby at the first apparition; Inés's next-door neighbors, who
heard about the apparitions from their daughter on Tuesday,
March 4; their married son, whose own son was one of the first
cured; the acting priest; one of the commanders, who instructed
Inés on Sunday morning to ask for a sign; three small children
from the procession who heard the Virgin call Inés, one of
whom saw the Virgin from behind; two men who went with
Inés and her father to Guadalupe; three local men who were
protagonists of miracles recorded on April 15, and two others
from nearby towns who were at the shrine on April 23 to give
thanks for their cures. There are no blatant contradictions in
the stories, but enough minor variations to indicate that the
testimony had not been coordinated in advance.

The testimony provides alternative explanations for the visions. The shepherd boys gave their initial reactions to Inés's
story as, "if she was so beautiful she was a traveling prostitute
(*mondaria*)" and, "if she was an earthly woman we would have
seen her." Inés's parents could not shrug off the matter so
easily. They told her she lied ("*Calla loca que mientes*"), and
the neighbors reported that Inés's parents had said to her, "They
will say you are drunk (*beoda*)."[42]

The villagers describe the public events in more detail than
Inés. When Inés came to the church on Sunday, they said, she
was weeping; after she knelt at Mary's altar, the people gathered
around her and heard her story. They tried to pry open her
hand, and they kissed it. After the general procession reached
the cross, men were left to guard it all night, and the next day
another procession was held to retrieve it.

Even after the deposition and the procession, people were not
entirely convinced. One of the men who accompanied Inés to
Guadalupe, Martín Ruíz, measured the position of Inés's thumb
on her fingers against a stick and checked later to see if she had
moved it. He also examined her hand at night while she was

asleep and found it unchanged. Ruíz was struck with a fever
and *dolor de costado* while going up a pass on their return, and
was cured when Inés touched his side. He became a firm be-
liever.[43] When Inés talked to Mary for the last time, March 19,
she complained that people still did not believe her, but enough
believed to convert the apparition site into a shrine.

The pattern of the Cubas apparitions is similar to that of
Santa Gadea and a large number of legends. A single seer or
two seers have visions in the countryside that they prove to
their town after repeated attempts with a sign provided by the
divine figure. The proof is revealed in some dramatic way, and
the seer, often of humble status, undergoes a kind of local
sanctification. Many of these seers were buried at the shrines
they helped to found, at least according to legend. The essential
drama of the story is the rejection, then the vindication of the
less credible, marginal seer in the face of the skepticism not
only of the authorities but often of their own families. The
stories validate the local as opposed to the governmental or
bureaucratic, and the common person, even the weak, as opposed
to the nobility and the strong. Power structures are surprised
and converted; ultimately they assume control of the sacred
enterprises they first refused to accept.

The small but critical differences between the different cases
include the iconography or attributes of the divine figure; any
message the saint gives in addition to the standard one indicating
protection and requesting a shrine; and especially the particular
form of proof.

What were the distinctive features of the Cubas story? Which
Mary appeared to Inés? Mary of the Cross, as she became
known, shares some of the characteristics of the two earlier
visions described above. On the day she gave the sign, her face
was so bright that Inés had trouble looking at it. But the previous
days she appeared to be a human lady, betraying herself as
something more only by her sudden disappearances. In spite
of the brightness, this is a different Mary from the distant
goddess of Jaén.

From the very first, Mary takes a friendly, maternal role.
"Que haces aqui, carita?" is the kind of friendly, rhetorical

greeting which one villager addresses another even today. In fact "carita," literally little face—we might say "honey"—was such a colloquial form of address for the Virgin Mary to employ that when the village notary recopied Inés's first deposition for it to be sent off to the archbishop, he substituted the slightly more formal, but still affectionate, "hija"—daughter, or child, a term the Virgin used at other times to Inés. "Carita" was what Inés really said that the Virgin had said, because that is also what she told the shepherd boys. The Virgin maintained this informal tone throughout the dialogues, which seem to echo the interactions of a village child and an approachable noblewoman. The Virgin addressed Inés in the *tu* form, and Inés replied in the respectful *vos* form, once calling the Virgin "*vuestra merced*" (your grace).

So Inés was not afraid of the lady until the lady disappeared. Unlike the other two cases, where Mary was aloof, here she touched Inés. Even the painful fixing of Inés's hand is a more human, closer relation than the distant majesty of Santa Gadea and Jaén.

And this is a strangely diminutive Mary. Inés's mother testified that Inés told her that Mary was "a small woman, although not her size" (one is unsure whether she meant Mary was not as small or not as tall as Inés).[44] Witnesses who saw the footprints said they were tiny.[45] Inés said they were those of a person about eight years old. The small size matches Inés's identification of the Virgin with the image at Guadalupe, which appeared to Inés to be alive and watching her. Here there is another similarity to the Jaén story—María Sánchez saw the Virgin and Saint Ildefonsus as portrayed on the altar. There, however, the Virgin was larger than the people around her; it was as if the image had been blown up. Mary's size when she appeared to Inés was more like the size of the statue. A small Mary, which was common to many of the early modern apparitions, is a less fearsome, more approachable spirit, like the little people of Celtic countries.

This Mary, a standing image, is not a queen; she is a lady, has a refined voice, very white hands and face, and is beautiful. In the earlier visions the seers cannot even see Mary's face.

Perhaps the cross is the most distinguishing feature of this vision sequence. The high point comes when Mary kneels in front of the cross, then plants it in the ground, leaving her footprints. For a moment she was in the recognizable stance of Mary at the foot of the Cross. The ground immediately became sacred for the people of Cubas. The spot was guarded; the sand taken as a relic and used for cures. People walked two or three times around the apparition site as part of the cures, or went on their knees, as they would in a shrine, or around a saint's tomb.

The sign of Inés's hand also was a cross, one that served as a test. Some believed and some did not. On March 19, on Inés's return from Guadalupe, the Virgin said she knew that some did not believe. She implied that those who did not believe had lost their chance. She also said that those who saw it and believed it would be blessed. This message was garbled by the priest in his testimony; he was apparently confused by the mention of a new, unidentified sign. He understood the message as, "Blessed will be those who will see and believe," as if referring to a future sign.[46] A seventeenth-century historian reported the message as, "Blessed are those who did not see, but believed," giving it a Biblical twist.[47] He, too, seemed to interpret Mary's statement as referring to the future sign. But Inés's version is clear enough. Those who saw and believed the sign of her hand as a cross would be blessed. Those who did not believe it had lost their chance, because by March 19 the sign was gone, her hand was back to normal. The cross was the test.

The villagers wanted to know more about any further signs. When the Virgin announced an epidemic, Inés immediately wanted to know if her family would be affected. After Inés testified to her last vision on March 19, the priest Ferrnand Alonso asked her only one question: what would the sign be, or when? Inés said she knew nothing more.

A second sign at Cubas was the footprints of the Virgin in the sand. They are almost incidental signatures to a tableau already complete. The Archangel Michael also left tiny footprints in his church on Monte Gargano to show that it was he who helped the Sipontines in a naval battle against pagans in

663. This story was part of the martyrologies used in Mozarabic and Roman ritual in Toledo. The motif is not common, however, in Spanish legends or in modern apparitions.

By contrast, the contorted hand as a sign and proof of a vision is found in many shrine stories. There are many variations:[48]

a closed hand: Virgen del Risco,Villatoro (Av.), supposedly c. 1200

hand fixed to cheek: Na. Sa. de la Carrodilla, Estadilla (Huesca); Na. Sa. de las Sogas, Bellvís (Lleida); Na. Sa. de Carramia, Abella de la Conca (Lleida)

hand fixed to stone: Na. Sa. de la Soterraña, Nieva (Segovia)

hand fixed to ear: Na. Sa. del Prado, Vivel (Teruel) supp. bef. 1349

arms fixed in cross: Na. Sa. del Pueyo, Villamayor (Zara.) supp. bef. 1369

The cure of seers with previously paralyzed arms and hands is also common as a proof.

Three kinds of contexts may have given the Cubas visions their meaning for the villagers: the political struggles of the Castilian monarchy and their local repercussions; the Lenten season; and the imminence of death by disease.

Alfonso Carrillo, the archbishop of Toledo, authorized the building of the shrine and the taking of testimony on April 7, 1449, from Benavente (Zamora). He was part of a conspiracy of nobles, including the count of Benavente, against Alvaro de Luna, Juan II's condestable. In January 1449, open rebellion had broken out in Toledo, when Alvaro de Luna had tried to levy a special tax; and on May 3 the king's representative there, Pero Sarmiento, joined the rebellion, which included the pillage of converso merchants. Sarmiento sent a complaint to the king about converso influence and in June promulgated a decree denying conversos the right to hold office in the city.[49]

It is difficult to see a direct connection between the rebellion and the apparitions. It may be that, as a supernatural restatement of Christian power, the apparition was a reaction to converso influence. By implication, if the epidemic were conditional on confession, and the conversos did not confess, then they would be the ones at fault when the epidemic came (cf. the scapegoating of the Jews in 1391). But there is no internal evidence to support this proposition. A clear example of an anti-Jewish shrine is that of the Niño de la Guardia, not far away, a shrine to a child supposedly crucified by Jews c. 1485. Several conversos were tried and executed for the crime in 1490.

A second political context was the presence of marauding Navarrese in the area. The villagers reported to Philip II more than 125 years later that these incursions, apparently based on the castle of Torija, involved mass kidnappings, with the victims ransomed off at the castle of Zorita de los Canes. There would seem to be a parallel to the kind of security the Virgin offered against the Moors in Jaén twenty years before. Juan, son of Benito Sánchez of Paracuellos de la Rivera (now Paracuellos del Jarama) came to Cubas and told his story on March 3, 1450, the anniversary of the first vision. In December 1449 he was lying in bed with his wife and children when archers, footsoldiers, and about sixty mounted men pillaged his town and took off forty men and youths to Torija, about seventy km. northeast. There they were imprisoned "under seven locks" and fed only entrails and, each Sunday, a small loaf of bread. Juan was kept chained to a wooden ball weighing seven libras for seven weeks. One night with others he was taken out to work at a lime kiln. He remembered hearing of the miracles of the Virgin Saint Mary of the Cross near Cubas, he invoked her aid, leaped from a high wall, miraculously eluded his pursuers, and escaped. After struggling a league and a half with his ball and chain, he broke it with rocks. On his visit of thanks to the shrine he brought a ball of wax and donated thirty days of work on the construction.

Villages that mentioned the raids in Philip II's survey included Esquivias, about fifteen km. south of Cubas, which was virtually wiped out, and Fuencarral, about thirty km. to the north, as well as towns closer to Torija such as Berniches, Jadraque, and Tendilla. The raids were therefore a clear threat to Cubas and at the very least must have contributed to a generalized sense of insecurity, on which apparitions through the centuries have thrived.[50]

What of the formal religious context? The Virgin Mary revealed indulgences (nothing less than 80,000 years) for those who fasted on her days. In the diocese of Toledo at that time, six days of Mary were observed, and on none of them was fasting compulsory.[51] In some dioceses bishops granted indulgences (a maximum of forty days) for fasting or not working these days. The practice of fasting on the nearest Friday to the Marian day was not as rigorous as fasting on the day itself, since on Fridays meat could not be eaten anyway. Here Mary gave guidelines to the devout with scruples. From other sources it is known that villagers were very open to signs instructing them to observe the days of very popular saints, such as Saint Anne, whose days were not obligatory feasts. This kind of specification of duties in matters that the Church has left undefined characterizes vision messages throughout Europe to the present day.

The Cubas apparitions occurred in the first week of Lent, and another message of the Virgin is to set the soul straight by confession. Lent for most villagers would be the time for their one, annual, confession anyway, but the confession prescribed by Mary would not be a normal one, but rather a preparation for death. For in her deposition Inés reported the Virgin saying that an epidemic was definitely on the way. Others, the priest, Inés's mother, and a neighbor, when they told what Inés had told them, put the warning in a conditional form. That is, people should confess in order to avoid the epidemic and the bloody stones. Inés's direct words, however, are in keeping with the Virgin's ominous statement in the final vision that even if unbelievers want to, they will not be able to believe. The contrast in the testimony is revealing, for one sees how a visionary's statements that might be disproved by time are consciously or unconsciously adjusted by her audience, whether to enhance her credibility or to avoid facing death.

From Inés's statement, it is unclear whether the stones that would accompany the epidemic were a physical symptom, such as kidney stones, or whether, as the priest understood, they would fall from the sky. Rains of blood or rains of stones were considered dire portents and signs of divine displeasure by specialists in divination. In 1438 some very light stones, perhaps volcanic in origin, had fallen on the Segovian village of Maderuelo; an official sent by Juan II of Castile brought specimens back to the Court.[52] The priest's interpretation of the chastisement as stones falling from the sky with blood may also have been influenced by a version of the Heavenly Letter. A Catalan manuscript of the Letter dating from around 1400 warned of "sharp and hot stones from the sky. . . and the stones will be mixed with blood, and will kill you and your sons and daughters."[53]

Finally the Virgin asked that a procession be held, a shrine built on the site of the cross, and two masses said in her name, with Inés and two children standing in front of the congregation. Inés was sent on what must have been the dream trip of a devout youngster of New Castile—to the great shrine of Guadalupe. Pilgrims would have been passing through Cubas on their way to the shrine; and possibly the shrine's questors had visited Cubas, bearing small images and gathering alms and money from villagers' vows. Some citizens of Cubas may well have been there, four days away to the southwest.

Two contemporaneous Italian visions resemble those of Inés both in the devotional instructions and in the vision motifs. In 1426 and 1428 an elderly married woman, Vicenza Pasini, had visions of Mary instructing her to tell the people of the town of Vicenza that if they built Mary a church on the site of the vision they would be spared a plague; and if they went there the first Sunday of every month and the days dedicated to Mary, they would receive copious graces. The Virgin traced the plan of the church on the ground with a cross made from olive branches. In 1426 the seer was not believed. In 1428, after the second vision during a serious plague, she was believed, partly because as the Virgin foretold a spring issued forth at the barren mountain site. Mary left a mark on the seer's shoulder with her fingers. A notarized account of the events was made in 1430, and the original is still extant. The shrine is known as the Vergine sul Monte Berico.[54] The motifs in common with the Cubas visions, besides the almost universal connection with an epidemic, are the Virgin dressed in gold, giving devotional instructions, handling a cross, and touching the seer.

A vision four years later by another married woman at Caravaggio, in Lombardy 150 km. east of Vicenza, had another feature of the Cubas visions—the Virgin left her footprints. There Mary appeared in a field and said that her son was angry, that for him people should fast on Fridays and for her they should celebrate Saturdays after vespers. There, too, she left a spring. The Madonna di Caravaggio, or delle Fonte, is now an enormous shrine; in the sixteenth, seventeenth, and eighteenth centuries, it inspired a number of satellite shrines and some imitative visions.[55]

While a direct connection is possible between the Italian cases and that of Cubas, it is more likely that all three cases partake of a culture of visions. The authorities of Cubas, while they were skeptical of Inés's story at first, knew what to do when she came with her proof. They arranged a procession in which children were prominent, and had the foresight to rig up a cross with which to mark the spot. I suspect there were precedents for this kind of event. Before these cases, whose documents are among the earliest that have survived from Western Europe, there must have been many others.

Although I do not know the history of epidemics in the Cubas area immediately prior to the visions, the documents of the shrine show how much people needed a divine helper for medical reasons. The same copyist who in 1789 transcribed the investigations, copied out the notarized versions of sixty-eight miracles performed at the shrine, more than half of them for the years 1449-1451.

In every community at any time, people have a number of everyday minor ailments, and some people suffer chronic infirmities. The quick curing of local people typically provided the initial impetus for the formation of a regional curing center. One of the first cures was at the nearby village of Ugena. Inés was on her way to Guadalupe and stopped there for the night. When the villagers heard her story, a man with his head swollen from a toothache got her to touch his face, and he was cured.

On the return trip she cured the doubter Martín Ruíz of the dread *dolor de costado* mentioned in the Virgin's message. "He felt so sick that he no longer worried about his wife, his children, or his property; rather he thought about the danger to his soul and his need of penance for salvation. And he asked Inés to help him ask the Lady Virgin Saint Mary who appeared to her near Cubas to give him strength so he would not die before taking the Sacraments."[56]

Sudden death when not in a state of grace was the great fear of the Middle Ages, and this fear constituted part of the power behind Inés's message. Martín Ruíz's greatest fear was not of death itself, but of damnation.[57] Dolor de costado could bring damnation with a sudden death. Mary spoke to the villagers' real preoccupation with salvation both by warning them to confess because death was nigh, and also by providing indulgences that would ease their passage to another world.

Other cures in Cubas and surrounding villages in March and early April included a four-year-old girl who suddenly seemed to die on Wednesday of Holy Week, a three-year-old girl, dying, for whom a shroud had been prepared, a child who woke up with crippled legs, and a carpenter with badly swollen feet.

In April the radius of attraction for cures spread as far as Madrid (forty km.), and a woman came from Mondejar (seventy km. east) to hold a novena. Thereafter the zone of curing stayed about the same—about a 100-km. radius. Most pilgrims lived within twenty km. of a NE-SW axis from Talamanca through Madrid to Toledo. After 1455 few miracles were recorded—only the more spectacular ones, such as escapes from Moorish captivity in Granada and Murcia.

About four out of five of the fifty-five miracles recorded for the first six years of the Cubas shrine have to do with ailments. Few concern epidemic diseases, the only possible exceptions being four revivals from unspecified deaths and three cases of dolor de costado. The medical treatment for this latter problem was bleeding, and it was usually accompanied by a fever. Was it plague, appendicitis, nephritis, pneumonia, or something else?

Aside from a variety of ills that turned up only once—men with rabies, hernia, bad eyes, infected ear, toothache, weak

heart, and seizures; women with sciatica, a dangerous preg-
nancy, and blindness—the majority of miracles involved some
kind of disabling paralysis. These paralyses were often sudden,
and must have raised the specter of death without grace. They
occurred to a woman working on the threshing floor; a man
who fell over when sowing cucumbers; a son delousing his
mother on a street in Madrid; a girl sweeping; and a soldier
lying in bed in an inn in Vallecas. No less than three children
and one woman woke up paralyzed. Several of these paralyses
were total and lasted for a few hours until a vow was made.
Others were partial and lasted much longer. Partial paralyses
included muteness, crippled hands, and crippled legs.

Local practitioners knew that these paralyses were beyond
their ken. When the four-year-old son of a man in Rejas, a
village just west of Madrid, woke up crippled on November 1,
1454, his father took him to a healer (*maestra*) in a nearby
village. She referred him to the shrine. "The healer said that
his ailment was incurable and that she could not make him well,
but that he should make a promise to the Virgin Mary of the
Cross, and it would please God and the said Virgin Mary to
make him well and healthy." The following Sunday he took
his son to the shrine and offered him before the altar along with
some money for the construction. Three pilgrims from Yepes
witnessed the cure.[58]

The practitioners who were tried and rejected before praying
or coming to the shrine included *fisicos* (mentioned in five cases,
for dolor de costado, sciatica, muteness [2] and "sickness"). But
the fisicos were expensive; one passing through the village of
Fuenlabrada would have charged "muchos dineros" to cure a
twenty-two-year-old mute woman; instead the woman made
a promise to the shrine. Fisicos were above all located in Madrid
and Toledo, where villagers would normally have to go to con-
sult them.

Bleeding, however, could be done by local *barberos*. They too
knew their limits. When a woman in Serranillos had a heart
attack, the barber in the adjacent village advised her to turn to
the shrine, since it was a heart problem. A man with rabies
consulted a young man who was a *saludador*, someone with a

gift for healing hydrophobia;[59] but after a woman treated by the saludador died, the man gave up and went to the shrine. There were probably other healers as well. In 1569, about a century later, supplicants coming to see a miraculous cross in Griñón, the next village north of Cubas, had previously tried *medicos* (again, in cities, no longer called fisicos), *cirujanos* (no longer called barberos, they did cauterizations and bleeding), *algebristas* (orthopedists), *bizmadors* and *herbolarios* (who cured wounds and bruises with poultices), and *maestros* (in Toledo, who operated on hernias). A simple bizmador in Nominchal charged four ducats, an enormous sum for a peasant, and his cure did not work.[60]

With this kind of competition, the shrine at Cubas and others in early modern Spain flourished. At shrines the fee was reasonable, it could be paid in kind, it was payable only if the cure was successful, and it was generally set by the patient.

A fifth of the miracles concerned non-medical problems. In addition to the villager who escaped from Torija, others escaped with the Virgin's help from prisons in Madrid, Illescas (debtors prison), and from the Moors in Vera (Granada). Others were saved from accidents—falls out of windows or into wells, drowning and choking; and three horses and a cow were cured.

The apparition was integral to the shrine and enhanced its attraction as a source of healing grace. Some of the people calling out for help from Mary of the Cross invoked the fact that she appeared to Inés, someone like them from their region and their station. Three years after the visions when Juan González of San Martín de Valdeiglesias died, his wife prayed, "O Lady Saint Mary blessed and glorious, just as by your holy mercy you chose to appear to that girl near Cubas, so by your holy mercy see fit to give me my husband alive, and I promise you to take him to your shrine with all the alms we can muster." The fame of the shrine is indicated in another way by this story. Juan's wife was moved to make her vow, although her husband was dead and the church bells were ringing for him, because her two-and-a-half-year-old son said, "Saint Mary of Cubas cured a man." Even infants knew about the miracles of the shrine over fifty km. to the east.[61]

As in the above case, most cures occurred when a vow was made that included a quid pro quo. Of the cures made at the shrine, the rituals involved were probably copied from other curing sites. Sometime between April 1 and April 23, when the building was already under way, a man "sick in the eyes" with a bandage over them came from San Martín de la Vega, thirty km. east. Inés made the sign of the cross over him and cured his eyes with some sand that the Virgin had walked on. "And they told him to bring for the construction a measure of lime, and two libras of wax to burn before the Virgin Mary on the spot where she appeared. This was also to protect one of his mares, which was wounded."[62]

Inés intervened in few of the miracles, however. Most of the cures that took place at the shrine occurred at certain critical junctures—the moment a person left for the journey; when first coming in sight of the shrine, on entering the shrine, when praying there, or when walking around it.

The offerings of those cured included working for a certain number of days on the shrine construction, sending workers, lime, stone, or wood; or other traditional Mediterranean votive offerings such as money, figures in wax of eyes, tongues, hands, faces, or entire bodies; a wax model of a cured horse, or wax symbols of captivity, such as chains or manacles. People spared from death or raised from the dead sent or brought shrouds, the crosses of wax with which they were laid out, and other funeral paraphernalia. People offered their own physical penances—coming barefoot or on their knees from a cross erected where the village procession waited during Inés's vision. At the shrine they might spend the night praying or even stay for nine days of a novena.

As at modern apparitions, even before the shrine was built or an image was present, the place or the site of the apparition was venerated and candles were burned there. At Cubas there was no image miraculously found. Eventually one was made, but the true relic of the appearance, besides the holy ground itself, was the cross the Virgin had held. In the early miracles there is no mention of its use in cures. In the sixteenth century it became the focus of devotion at the shrine, which by that time was a cloistered Franciscan nunnery. In 1556 a mute girl sick with fever for two years indicated by signs to her parents that an image of Mary by her bed told her to go to Cubas and have the famous cross placed on her head. Her parents took her and secured permission from the abbess and the chaplain. When a nun took the cross down from the altar and gave it to the girl to kiss, then put it on her head, the girl fainted. When she woke up fifteen minutes later she was cured both of the fever and of her muteness.[63]

In the 1570s a procession was held regularly from the village to the nunnery on March 9, the anniversary of the general procession and the planting of the cross in 1449, and the nuns exposed the cross for all to see. People came from far away to see it on this day. Perhaps it is a measure of the growth in devotion to the Cross and the Crucifix over the intervening century that in 1580 the villagers knew more about the cross than we do from the original, voluminous testimony. The cross was made, they say, from boards from a loom.[64]

From the report of the apparition villagers sent to Philip II in 1580, we can see the ways in which the original story was modified, the extent to which it had become a legend. The 1580 version was essentially faithful, but there were some divergences from the original facts. The villagers said that nine visions took place March 1-9 (to correspond to a public novena held at the shrine those days?) instead of six visions March 3-19. They gave Inés's age as nine or ten (a more innocent age?) instead of twelve or thirteen. They did not mention messages about epidemics or injunctions to confess; instead the Virgin's only instruction was to build a church. The sign of the crossed fingers, the planting of the cross, and the trip to Guadalupe were faithfully remembered, but predictably the confusion over where the hand was to come unstuck was eliminated.

They also reported, briefly (as given above), an apparition of Saint Blaise, who instructed a plowman to stop working and have a chapel built. That tradition probably existed in the village before Inés's visions, for the first women in the new monastery while awaiting its construction lived in a house next to the Saint Blaise chapel. It may have been one of the most immediate sources for Inés's visions.

Seventeenth-century clerical historians, with documents in hand, could give a more complete story. But they printed only brief excerpts from the vision document, and they too simplified the tale. For instance, they had the Virgin explicitly ruling out a second sign, and they changed the announcement of an epidemic to a threat. Hence, over time, the complex events of the original vision became simplified, both in oral and written history, to the point that the vision resembled the stories that could more properly be called legends.

From the miracles, we know that by early 1450 the representative of the lord of the village who helped order the original procession was administrator of the shrine and a shrine hospice. In 1454 the shrine had at least one servant, and as late as 1471 the cleric in charge of the shrine was still the Toledo prebend who was titular curate of Cubas in 1449. According to seventeenth-century historians, a group of women, members of the Third Order of St. Francis, in 1464 moved into a nunnery on the site constructed in part with their own money. Among them was Inés.[65]

These beatas were not cloistered, but rather held a kind of intermediate status between religious and secular, probably subject only to simple vows of chastity, which, unlike solemn public vows, could be set aside should a beata decide to marry. In the first years, two chaplains probably served the beatas as well as the public.

The women supported themselves by weaving and by begging in neighboring villages. They watched over their own animals. Individual or collective, non-binding, retirement was common throughout New Castile until the end of the sixteenth century. It gave poorer women like Inés the possibility of a religious life without the need for a dowry. The seventeenth-century commentators ascribed the initial failure of the Cubas quasi-nunnery to the women's exposure to the world. For whatever reason, Inés as well as other women left and married. "Inés tired of the delicious manna and returned to the onions and garlic of Egypt, an example of human instability and our lack of perseverance in the good."[66]

The beateria was reformed by a holy woman named Juana de la Cruz. Under her leadership (1499-1510), the shrine once again became a pilgrimage center. Juana had revelations and worked miracles; indeed, her body worked miracles even after she died in 1534. Some of her writings are in manuscript in the Escorial; a play was written about her by Tirso de Molina; and biographies of her issued in 1610 and 1622 enjoyed phenomenal success. Juana served as a model for many Third Order Franciscan women of the seventeenth century. It was her memory, not that of Inés, that lasted the longest. That is why the convent is now known as "Santa Juana."

Cubas and Guadalupe

The Cubas apparition is an instance of a phenomenon common throughout Spain beyond a certain radius of very powerful shrines: the formation of a satellite. Satellite shrines meet the needs of people devoted to a shrine image who live too far away for frequent contact. For instance, in Spain today in Almería, Granada, Córdoba, and Ciudad Real, there is a circle of shrines to Our Lady of the Cabeza, about three days away on horseback from the famous shrine in the Sierra Morena.

Naturally the keepers of the major shrine tried to keep distant devotion under their control, whether by the establishment of brotherhoods or by setting up minor shrines by the same name under franchise. The satellite shrines of Montserrat were well organized by its Benedictines in cities throughout Spain where there were major concentrations of Catalans; their income in promises was fed back to the mother shrine. Similarly, in the early seventeenth century, the Minims of San Francisco de Paula tried to control the brotherhoods and images of the popular Our Lady of the Soledad in cities where they had convents, because they had commissioned the original image in Madrid.[67]

Hieronymite monasteries tried to keep a monopoly on publicly venerated images of Our Lady of Guadalupe in a given city, but it was difficult for even the most litigious order to maintain a monopoly over a devotion when they were simultaneously propagating it throughout the land with questors. By the eighteenth century, there were independent shrines of at least district attraction to Our Lady of Guadalupe in Rianxo (Galicia), Fuenterrabia (Basque country), and Ubeda (Andalusia), in addition to the controlled proxy images in Hieronymite monasteries in major cities. That of Ubeda may have originated like that of Cubas. Although there are no documents to prove it, it was supposedly founded after a farmer's vision in 1381.[68] The apparitions at Cubas of a lady eventually identified as Our Lady of Guadalupe in effect established a new satellite shrine.

Guadalupe, favored by privileges by the Castilian monarchy and used by them as a palace and a bank, was the richest and most popular shrine in fifteenth-century Castile. Indeed, it maintained its preeminence among Castilian shrines until the nineteenth century, drawing pilgrims from Portugal, the entire Castilian meseta, and Andalusia. The shrine would have been well known in all of the Castilian villages where apparitions took place.

As at most shrines, the legend of the origin of the holy statue was an integral part of the Guadalupe experience. Pilgrims in the fifteenth century not only kissed the slab of marble on which the image was discovered, some of them were cured by drinking scrapings of the rock with water. This custom was common at the tombs of saints.[69] Well into the twentieth century, dirt from the tombs of Santa Marina de Aguas Santas (Orense), San Wentila (Pungín, Orense), and Fray Pedro de Ulloa Santa María (Ois, La Coruña) was drunk with water to cure malaria and other sicknesses.[70]

It is not known when the Guadalupe legend was formed. The earliest version I have found is a manuscript dated 1440 in the National Historical Archive.[71] I have translated the relevant passages.

The Guadalupe story begins with the alleged gift of the image of Mary and other relics from Saint Gregory in Rome to Saint Leandro in Seville. When the Moors invaded Spain priests from Seville fled to the north,

> until they came to a river called Guadalupe and encoun-
> tered some very high mountains. In these mountains these

saintly priests dug a cave that was like a tomb, surrounded
the cave with large boulders, and placed inside it the image
of our lady Saint Mary, and with her a little bell and a
letter that said the image of Saint Mary had been sent
from Rome to Saint Leandro, archbishop of Seville, with
other relics by the Doctor Saint Gregory. And when they
had put it inside they covered the cave with large stones
and earth and departed. And in the area of Almaraz they
buried the cross in the same way and fled to the mountains
of Old Castile. . . .

After the Moors had taken over most of Spain,

the Lord God was pleased to strengthen the hearts of the
Christians so they would go back and recover the lands
they had lost. And thus they regained much land held by
the Moors. And to make the story short we will tell you of
the noble king Don Alfonso, who won from the Moors
much of Castile. He fought very great battles with them,
especially that of Las Navas de Tolosa, where the holy
cross of our lord Jesus Christ was upraised. There he
struck them such a blow that they never raised their head
again. On this occasion he captured Ubeda, Baeza, and
many other places north of the Guadalquivir and in the
Sierra Morena. He rested in peace and our lord God took
his soul to his holy glory. And his grandson, the king Don
Fernando, reigned in Spain and captured the very noble
city of Seville and many other towns; and he rested in
peace and our lord God took his soul to his holy kingdom.

And his son Don Alfonso reigned, who won Algeciras
and died at Gibraltar. And when this king Don Alfonso
reigned in Spain, our lady the virgin Saint Mary appeared
to a herdsman in the mountains of Guadalupe in the following manner. Some herdsmen were guarding their cows
at a place called Halia in a grazing ground known today as
the Dehesa de Guadalupe. And one of them found he was
missing one of his cows and went hunting for it for three
days. Not finding it, he went into the high mountains
upriver and into a tall oak grove, and there he saw his cow

lying dead near a small spring. When the herdsman saw his cow was dead, he examined it and was surprised that it was not bitten by wolves or wounded in any way. He took his knife from the sheath to butcher it, and when he was opening its breast in the form of a cross, as is customary when butchering, the cow stood up, and the herdsman drew back in great fear.

The cow remained still, and all of a sudden our lady the virgin Saint Mary appeared to the herdsman and said to him, "Have no fear, for I am the mother of God by whom the human race achieved redemption. Take your cow and go and put it with the others, for from this cow you will have many others in memory of this appearance here. After you put it with the other cows, go to your home and tell the clergy and the other people to come to this place where I appear to you and to dig here, and they will find a statue of me." And when our lady told him these things and others mentioned below in this chapter, she suddenly disappeared.

The herdsman took his cow and went with it and left it with the others and told his comrades everything that happened to him. His comrades made fun of him, and the herdsman replied saying, "Friends, do not dismiss these things; if you will not believe me, then believe the mark the cow bears on her breast." When they saw the mark in the shape of a cross the cow carried on her breast, they believed him.

He bade farewell to his comrades and went to his home. And know that wherever he went he told everyone he met about the miracle that had occurred to him. And know that this herdsman was from Cáceres and had a wife and children there, and when he reached his house he found his wife weeping, and he asked her, "Why do you weep?" She replied, "Your son is dead." And he said, "Do not sorrow or cry, for I promise him to Saint Mary of Guadalupe, who will give him back to me alive and well, and I promise him as a servant in her house." And at once the youth arose alive and well and said to his father, "Señor, father, get

ready and let us go to Saint Mary of Guadalupe." And all
who were there were amazed and believed everything he
said about the appearance of our lady Saint Mary.

And this herdsman went to the priests and said to them,
"Sirs, know that Saint Mary appeared to me in some
mountains near the Guadalupe River and ordered me to
tell you to go where she appeared to me and dig in the
very spot she appeared and that you would find there a
statue of her and that you should take it out and make a
house for it. She also ordered me to tell those in charge of
her house to give the poor people who came there food
once a day. And she also said to me that she would have
many people come to her house from many regions because of the many miracles she would work on sea as well
as land. She also told me that on that great mountain she
would make a large town."

When the clergy and the other people heard these
things, they acted at once and went to the place where our
lady Saint Mary appeared. As soon as they arrived, they
began to dig where the herdsman indicated that Saint
Mary appeared to him. Digging there they found a cave
like a tomb, and out of it they took an image of our lady
Saint Mary, a little bell that was with it, and the stone on
which it was resting. And you should know that they
broke up all the other stones that were around and took
them away as relics. And at once they put up a very small
building of stone and green poles and covered it with cork,
for you should know that there were many cork trees
nearby. And know that many persons sick with diverse ailments came with these people, and as soon as they reached
the image of Saint Mary they recovered from all their sicknesses. And they went back to their home lands praising
God and his blessed mother for the great miracles and
marvels he had worked. The herdsman remained as a
guardian with his wife and children and his descendants as
servants of Saint Mary.

And since these miracles were manifest in all of Spain,
many people came from all regions to visit this image in

reverence of Saint Mary for the many miracles and marvels she had worked for them.

Here we are dealing with a fable and not a real event. There
is no attempt at documentary proof, no date given for the event,
and a 120-km. expedition of priests and sick people to check out
a dubious discovery in deserted country seems highly improb-
able. The ultimate models for the story were probably the hag-
iographic descriptions of the discovery of saints' bodies. The
elements are all here—a divine revelation, a devout messenger,
even a tomb.[72] Yet this imitative, ex post facto story provided
the same kind of ideological contract for the shrine as the real
apparitions.

The Guadalupe story in turn seems to be the inspiration for
a number of scenarios of discoveries of buried images, especially
in the Segovia region. We saw how the image of Nuestra Señora
de la Soterraña, in Santa María la Real de Nieva, was supposedly
discovered underground in 1391 after a shepherd saw a sign in
the sky. The pattern was repeated and fully documented in
relatively modern times at Valverde del Majano (Seg.) (1623)
and Bernardos (Seg.) (1728).[73] In the 1455 story of San Antonio
del Cerro (discussed below) as at Guadalupe, the critical proof
is a very opportune resuscitation.

Guadalupe shares with the legend of Saint Michael of Monte
Gargano the ancient theme of a lost animal leading a herdsman
to a holy site, and with that of Rocamadour in France and Nuria
in the Pyrenees the discovery of an image underground with
a bell. The different legend items are like beads; the assembled
legends like necklaces. Familiar items are rearranged in apparitions into new patterns. The repetition of individual items
maintains a recognizable continuity in divine behavior. A different arrangement and occasionally a new motif distinguish
the story of one sacred place from another. All of the shrine
legends and actual apparitions feed on the same cultural repertoire, one that at the very least encompasses Iberia, France,
and Italy. The more important a shrine becomes, the more
weight it carries in the creation of new scenarios, whether in
the minds of creative clerics, in the unconscious of lay vision-

aries, or in the minds of those who hear what the seers say and by their understanding determine what is written as history.

Two Saints in the Sierra de Guadarrama

Documentary evidence for the apparitions of Santa Gadea, Jaén, and Cubas survived because it was the basis for devotions that have continued to the present day. There were doubtless other visions at the time for which testimony was taken but has not survived. Probably a kind of natural selection has favored Marian documents, as opposed to those of other saints. As devotion to saints other than Mary declined, their shrines were not maintained and their archives disbanded.

A second kind of selection occurs in the process of dissemination of vision stories. Marian devotion has been fairly constant since the thirteenth century, so devout people have always been interested in keeping the evidence and letting other people know about it. Documents attesting the apparitions of other saints probably exist, but because over the years few people have bothered to make collections of saints' legends, nobody knows they exist beyond the village where they took place, and I have not heard about them. Even in the village of Navas de San Antonio, studied here, the people and priest were unaware of documentary evidence of the apparition in the parish archive.

The visions of Santa Gadea, Jaén, and Cubas are mentioned in most collections of Spanish Marian legends by the end of the nineteenth century. The next two cases were more difficult to locate. The vision of Saint Anthony I located through a nationwide survey of some seven hundred shrines; that of Saint Michael was in the manuscript reports of parish priests to Cardinal Lorenzana of Toledo in the 1780s.

Apparition traditions in general were rare; those of saints other than the Mother of God were even rarer. Only four out of 464 villages in New Castile reported them in 1580, and three out of 534 in 1780. The ratio of saints:Mary apparition traditions declined from 1:2 in 1580 to 1:8 two hundred years later.[74] Traditions of apparitions of other saints were not given the same weight as the Marian traditions. Two of the towns reporting saints' apparitions in 1580 were surveyed in 1780. In both, the apparitions had been forgotten in the intervening years. Yet all those towns with Marian apparition legends in 1580 that were also surveyed in 1780 remembered them. Selective memory discriminated against the saints, since generally they were more specialized and less powerful helpers, and more subject to replacement.

Hence Jeanne d'Arc, who from 1424 until her execution in 1431 regularly saw Saint Catherine and Saint Margaret, and occasionally Michael the Archangel, may have been the exception and not the rule for late medieval seers. In Spain, visions of Mary among lay persons outnumbered those of all other saints combined. In this respect Jeanne's competitor, Catherine de la Rochelle, who in 1430 had regular visions of a lady dressed in white (as in Jaén and Santa Gadea) was more typical.

The two saints who may have "appeared" in Castile are fitting exceptions. Anthony of Padua's fame as a miracle worker and preacher was widespread even before his death in 1232. Today he is still the most frequently invoked saint in Spain, after Mary. Throughout Europe the Archangel Michael was considered one of the most powerful divine figures from the sixth century until the early modern period.

Anthony of Padua, Navas de Zarzuela (Segovia), 1455

Navas de Zarzuela is now known as Navas de San Antonio because of a shrine that supposedly originated in an apparition in 1455. The present shrine appears to have been built in the sixteenth century. It is reverently administered by a brotherhood of townspeople. The traditional procession of brothers on the feast days is a popular event in the region, attended by busloads of emigrants now living in Madrid, and was included in the film *Marcelino Pan y Vino* (see Figure 6).

In the fifteenth century, the village produced and processed wool. Now the villagers have large and prosperous herds of milk cows. Their continued prosperity perhaps explains in part the maintenance in a rather pristine form of the old devotion. Some of the most prosperous rural areas of Spain, such as Navarre and parts of Rioja, have best preserved old traditions and customs, even if the economic base of their prosperity is completely modern.

Under the choir loft in the nave of the shrine of Saint Anthony hang two large framed transcriptions, in very large print, of the original notarial affidavit of the apparition story. One is apparently from the sixteenth or seventeenth century, the other from the late nineteenth century. Because the oldest *tabla* is mutilated (washings appear to have removed much of the text, and it was used as a bulletin board), the best earliest copy of the document is one in the parish archive dated 1737. The 1455 original, on three sheets of parchment, was lost by the seventeenth century, when a transcription was made from the *tabla* for a legal dispute over control of the shrine between the priest of Zarzuela and the Navas brotherhood.[75]

TESTIMONY ABOUT THE APPARITION OF SAN ANTONIO

In Las Navas de Zarzuela, village of the city of Segovia, Friday, August 4, 1455,[76] in the presence of me, Martín Gómez, citizen of this town and scrivener and notary public of the king our lord in his court and all of his kingdoms and domains, and of the witnesses named below, in some houses where Juan González de Avila lives, a citizen of this town. Present were Luis González, clothmaker*, a citizen of this town, and Juan his son, along with certain clothmakers whom he invited to meet there at the behest of God and San Antonio. As soon as these artisans arrived, Luis González said they well know that he told and admonished the town to form and establish a brotherhood in honor of San Antonio and build a church where he could stay at the yglesuela on the road to Segovia where it crosses the Monte de Sancho. This is something his son

---

* I have translated *official peraile* as "clothmaker" rather than simply as "carder." In Barcelona a *peraire* was the owner of the cloth, who might do several operations, including carding, beating, drying, and dyeing. Similarly, for Castile it is a general term from which weavers and dyers began to distinguish themselves around 1430. The *perailes* of Las Navas might have been substantial citizens, relatively speaking.[77]

Juan had said to him three times as a message from the
blessed San Antonio, who appeared to him. "I never believed him until once more he asked me on behalf of God
and blessed San Antonio to get them to establish the
brotherhood and build the church, and that if they did they
would see some miracles happen to those who entrust
themselves to him."

Then Luis González told his son to tell those present and
testify to me the present scrivener in what manner or how
San Antonio had appeared to him. And Juan said, "One
day when I went to the village church to read I saw a man
in a friar's habit, and he called me and said, 'Come here,
child. Tell the people of this town to build a church at the
yglesuela on the road to Segovia where it crosses the
Monte de Sancho.' The friar disappeared and soon afterward my friend Antón Garzía, the sexton, came, and I told
him what the friar had told me. My friend told me to keep
quiet or else he would whip me. And I did not dare to say
anything to anyone but my mother and father, and they
told me I was lying."

"Later, on the sixteenth of the same month and year,"
said Juan, "when I went to ring the Ave Maria, I saw the
friar and he called me. I was scared, and he said, 'Tell me,
boy, did you do as I ordered?' I said, 'I do not know what
you ordered.' 'I told you to tell the people to found a
church and a brotherhood.' I answered, 'Are you the one
who ordered that?' 'Yes.' 'Well I told it to my friend and
my father, and he threatened to beat me, and they said I
should keep quiet.' As I left to go to my father's house,
because it was dark, he said to me, 'Tell the people of this
town to believe what you say.' And I saw him no more. I
went to my father's house and sat by the hearth, and my
father asked me what was wrong, why was I so quiet. I
told my father that the friar from the other day had come
back, and that I was supposed to tell the villagers to found
a church at the yglesuela and a brotherhood. My father
told me not to say anything or he would beat me, and that

I was lying. The next day I went to the church and told
my friend, and he said that I lied and that it was some
kind of phantom (*fantasma*) appearing to me, and that if I
told him or anyone else he would whip me. So I did not
dare tell anyone."

"Another day my father sent me to the Enzinar pasture
for a burro, and when I was looking for it I saw the friar
coming, and I was afraid and ran away. He called me and
said, 'Come here, boy, don't run away.' I could not run
any more, and he came to where I was and said, 'Tell me,
boy, why didn't you do what I ordered?' I said, 'I already
told my father and my friend, and they threatened me and
ordered me not to say anything to anyone, because it was
some kind of phantom.' Then he said, 'Pay attention. I order that you tell the people of this town to build me a
church and set up a brotherhood so that all will join to
build my church.' And as I was going off he spoke again,
'Tell the people of this town that I am San Antonio, and it
is my will that they build me a church where I have indicated and establish a brotherhood.' I went to my father and
told him what happened."

Then Luis González, who was present, said that everything his son had said was true, and that he had not believed him, and that he therefore besought the artisans to
order and organize the above with the townspeople; and if
the town did not want to do it that they themselves should
organize the brotherhood in the service of San Antonio.

Then the artisans said they would begin to organize the
brotherhood and approach the bishop to establish the
brotherhood and church, but that first they had to report
to the town about it. While they were discussing this the
church bells rang for a funeral, and the people called out in
the town to come and bury the wife of Antonio Fernández
de Mazarías. Luis González, because of what his son had
said, devoutly knelt on the ground in the presence of me
the scrivener and the witnesses and the town authorities
and said, "O San Antonio, I beseech you that you beseech

my Lord Christ that by his love the woman for whom the bells toll be brought back to life, and from here I promise in her name to carry her shroud to the church."

We left for the church to accompany the cross to bring back the dead woman, and the moment we entered with the cross where the dead woman was, she opened her eyes and raised her head and said, "O Saint, blessed be your holy name, for you have brought me back from death to life." Luis González then said, "O San Antonio, blessed be your name for working this miracle." And in a loud voice he proclaimed to everybody what his son had said.

When they heard it they gave thanks to God and San Antonio and promised to found the church and brotherhood in his service. And Luis González told me the scrivener to put down in a notarized affidavit what I had seen and what had happened and what his son Juan had said in order to give notice to the king and to other bishops in all places so that it would be believed.

On another day, the 28th of the same month and year, the town gathered together and formed a devout procession and went to the place the boy had indicated. When they had all gathered where the church was to be built, in the presence of me the scrivener and witnesses they made a vow to build the church and established a brotherhood in honor of San Antonio.

After this, on September 10 of this year in the house of Antón Garzía, nephew of Juan González, when his wife was sick from a tumor, thinking her dead her husband with great devotion promised her to San Antonio, and on the third day she was on her feet. Her husband asked to have it all taken down.

The witnesses to everything were Sancho González, Juan González de Avila, the nephew of Pedro Sanz, blacksmith, Bernabé Sanz, tax collector, Gómez Garzía, cloth shearer, Antón Garzía, sexton, and Diego Sanz Díez, weaver, citizens of this town. I Martín Gómez, scrivener and notary, was present at the above with the witnesses, and at the re-

quest of Luis González and Juan his son I had it put in
writing on three sheets of parchment and sealed below
with my seal and on top three strokes of ink with this one
that is my signature: in witness of the truth Martín
Gómez.

In Spain devotion to Anthony of Padua partially absorbed
that to Anthony the Abbot, protector of animals. At the shrine
of Los Santos Antonios de Urquiola (Vizcaya), the figure of
Anthony of Padua had to be added to that of Anthony the Abbot
because of confusion between the two.[78]

A third major shrine to Anthony also points up the connection. San Antonio del Tiemblo is located in the Avila town of
El Tiemblo, near the pass over the Guadarrama mountains between Toledo and Avila.[79] Like the other two Antonine shrines,
it is on a main road near a pass. It is also on a cañada, or
transhumant sheep route. Another cañada passes through Navas
precisely where the shrine is. In fact transhumant shepherds
used to sleep at the shrine guesthouse within living memory.
Both shrines were undoubtedly used to seek protection for sheep
(and now milk cows) and to find lost animals.

One of the ways Anthony of Padua used to be portrayed was
with a mule. The legend behind this depiction was that the
mule's owner, who did not believe in the real presence of Christ
in the holy sacrament, was converted when his mule knelt before
Anthony, who was carrying a consecrated host. Is there a hint
of this legend in the Segovia story, when the saint appears to
Juan when Juan is looking for a burro?

A cañada also ran through Guadalupe, and the Saint Anthony
apparition shares with the Guadalupe legend the most dramatic
part of the proof: the resurrection of a dead person in front of
the assembled funeral procession. In both cases, when the dead
person awakens, they confirm the intervention of the saint.

The Saint Anthony story has in common with the Cubas
visions the demeanor of the appearing saints and the language
they use. Both treat the young visionaries with familiarity.
Certain phrases are repeated (Cubas: fija por que non dijiste lo

que te mande ayer decir? Navas: di niño porque no a dho lo
que te mande?; Cubas: Catta que te mando digas a los del pueblo
. . . Navas: Cata que te mando que lo digas . . .).

Michael the Archangel, Navalagamella (Madrid), 1455

The parish priests of Fresnedillas and Navalagamella, a little
south of El Escorial in the foothills of the Sierra de Guadarrama,
reported in the 1780 survey the 1455 apparition of Saint Michael
to a shepherd.[80] Their descriptions were based on records in the
parish and town archives of Navalagamella and, very likely, on
a book entitled *Grandezas de San Miguel Archangel*, published
around 1760 in Madrid, which included a chapter on the apparition. The author of the book obtained a notarized copy of
the first investigation made in 1520, 65 years after the event,
from the Navalagamella town archive.[81]

I have been unable to find a copy of the investigation or of
another one made in 1617, so the story must be treated with
circumspection. In an ecclesiastical inquiry from 1610 to 1618
some of the townspeople claimed the story was a fabrication.
The story as it appears in the book is as follows:

Late one afternoon in 1455, Saint Michael appeared on an
encina, or holm-oak tree, and a *jara*, or rockrose plant, to a
shepherd, Miguel Sánchez. The site of the apparition is about
halfway between Navalagamella and Fresnedillas, near a hamlet
then known as Los Degollados (The Beheaded). Saint Michael
told the shepherd not to be afraid, that a chapel should be built
on the spot and a brotherhood founded, both in honor of the
angelic messengers. Sánchez said the people would not believe
him, but the angel told him to go and tell his employer. "I will
make them believe you so they build a shrine here to the holy
angels." Michael then left the print of his hand in the tree
trunk.

Sánchez, who lived in the hamlet of Los Degollados, did not
dare tell the story. After a few days he woke up crippled, his
legs folded back at the knees so that his calves stuck to his
thighs, and his heels touched his buttocks. His employer, Pedro
García de Ayuso, tried to cure him with herbs and oils, but to
no avail. When Sánchez finally told his story, García de Ayuso

called in the authorities. They carried Sánchez to the apparition site, where they found the tree with the hand-mark on it. They then marked off the site for a chapel and carried Sánchez in a devout procession to the parish church. There a mass was said for the shepherd's health, attended by people from the surrounding towns. At the words *ite missa est* Sánchez stood up, cured. He became the keeper of the shrine.

Some of the children in the procession—Pedro Sánchez, weaver; Alonso Martín, maker of roof-tiles; and Pedro González— were still alive and able to testify at the investigation made by the mayor and scrivener of the town on February 14, 1520.

Miguel Sánchez's vision of his namesake follows the standard pattern. Unless there are corroborative witnesses, the visionary must have some kind of proof to be believed. Miguel's contorted body is a proof similar to the crossed fingers of Inés at Cubas, and as at Cubas, when the villagers go with the seer to the shrine site, they find the mark of the saint.

The imprint of the saint's hand on the oak tree links the story with the tradition of Monte Gargano and takes us out of Spain as surely as the reference to the burning bush took us to Saint Catherine's shrine in the Sinai. The legend of the discovery of the shrine to Michael on Monte Gargano in Apulia by a shepherd hunting an ox is still repeated in the Roman martyrology. The shrine in a mountain cave became very popular throughout Western Europe in the seventh century, partly due to a Lombard victory in 663 over the Saracens that they ascribed to Saint Michael's intervention.[82] The French Mont Saint Michel is thought to derive from the Gargano cult in the eighth century. Legend had it that the Lombard victors found the imprint of Michael's foot near the south door of his temple when they went to render thanks to God for their victory.

Cumque domum reversi victores vota Domino gratiarum ad templum referebant archangeli, videntes mane iuxta ianuam septemtrionalem, quam predixi, instar posteruli pusilla quasi hominis vestigia marmori artius inpressa, agnoscuntque, beatum Michaelem hoc presentiae suae signum voluisse monstrare.[83]

Still in the twentieth century, pilgrims to the shrine, in memory of this footprint, outline their own hands or feet and add their initials on the steps of the shrine as they leave. The handprint on the tree in Navalagamella may be connected with the legendary footprint, the pilgrim handprints, or both. By 1782, when the priest reported to the archbishop, there was no vestige of the tree; he presumed the villagers had gradually removed it for use as relics. The shrine still exists, rather barren; and a romeria is held there every year which villagers of Navalagamella and Fresnedillas attend. The brotherhood still exists. In recent years the priests who have served the village have considered the devotion slightly superstitious and have not promoted it.

The cult of Saint Michael in Spain, to judge from church dedications and place names, peaked by the thirteenth century.[84] As in many parts of Europe, many of Michael's shrines were located near mountain tops, where they may have replaced pre-Christian devotions. Two shrines to Michael remain today with regional significance: San Miguel de Aralar, the most important shrine in the traditionalist, Basque-speaking sector of Navarre, consecrated in 1074 on the site of an earlier shrine;[85] and San Miguel de Liria, a shrine maintained by a religious community on a hilltop twenty-five km. northwest of Valencia. The Navalagamella story does not resemble the legends of either shrine.

Both the Navas and the Navalagamella visions were of a male saint calling for a brotherhood in 1455. In all likelihood one influenced the other. But both are hazy in regard to dates, and one does not know which came first. The towns were not far apart; both were in the jurisdiction of the city of Segovia, and the villagers of Navalagamella may have had to pass through Navas on their way to the city. They may even have shared grazing grounds in the mountains.

Even more than the Saint Anthony vision, that of Saint Michael resembles that of Mary in Cubas, fifty km. south, only six years before. In addition to the parallel proofs—contortions and prints—both seers served after the visions as keepers of the shrine. In the years following the visions, pilgrims from as far as one hundred km. away went to Cubas to be cured or to give thanks for cures. Although the miracles recorded do not mention Navalagamella, there were pilgrims from Cebreros, San Martín de Valdeiglesias (where the two-and-a-half-year-old knew about Cubas) and Valdemaqueda, all towns beyond Navalagamella to the northwest.

The skein of replication continued. An innovation in the Saint Michael vision was that the shepherd's body was released from its contortion at the end of the mass, at the words *ite missa est.* Similarly, about forty years later, a visionary from a village north of Segovia was freed from her contortion (her mouth would not open) at the end of a special mass, when she spit out two mouthfuls of water.

MARY OF THE CROSS, A REPRISE

Escalona (Segovia), c. 1490

Visions very much like those of Inés in Cubas occurred in the village of Escalona, about thirty km. north of Segovia, around 1490. The town clergy made a retrospective canonical investigation in 1617, with authority from the diocese, and questioned thirteen villagers about the original visions, the shrine, the relic cross, popular devotion, miracles, and votive offerings. The following testimony of María Herranz, aged about sixty, was taken on October 23, 1617. It is her answer to the question about the apparitions.[86]

☆

Chronology

seer: *Joana, servant of Sancho Herrero*

1) *Saturday, Joana, gathering thistles for mules, saw Mary, who instructed her to have a chapel built. Her master dismissed the story.*

2) *Two or three days later, Joana saw Mary again in the fields. A youth was with Joana but saw nothing. Mary embraced a cross and repeated her instructions.*

3) *Another day the same thing happened. This time the youth
saw small birds around the cross. Mary pressed Joana's
lips together as a sign. Joana was believed.*
4) *The next morning the town went in procession to the cross
and marked the site of the chapel. At the end of mass
in the church Joana's lips came unsealed.*

TESTIMONY OF MARÍA HERRANZ, AGE OVER 60, OCTOBER 23,
1617

[2r] Question 1
    First let them be asked if they know or have notice of,
or have heard their ancestors say how long ago the most
holy Virgin Mother of God known as of the Cross of this
town appeared, and in what form and to whom and how
she appeared and in what place. Let them say what they
learned from and heard their ancestors and elders say.

[18r-21v]
    To the first question in the questionnaire this witness
said she often heard her husband Joan Herrero's mother,
Madalena Gonçález, a woman of the greatest knowledge
and memory, say that Sancho Herrero, the father-in-law of
Madalena Gonçález and the grandfather of this witness's
husband, had a servant called Joana, who was very virtuous, humble, and fearful of God, and who lived with
much modesty. Never while Joana lived with Sancho Herrero did they see her swear or blaspheme either at people
or animals for any reason or provocation, although it was a
house with much traffic of people and animals.
    The wife of Sancho Herrero, Madalena Gonçález'
mother-in-law, sent this servant girl one Saturday to
gather a sack of thistles to feed her master's mules when
they came back from plowing. The servant girl went for
them to the fields called Carramaxuelos, in the territory of
this town of Escalona. When she had gathered a skirtful,
Our Lady the Mother of God appeared to her very resplendent and shining. When the girl saw her she felt
much fear, terror, and confusion. And the Mother of God

said to her, "What are you doing, daughter? (*que aces hixa*)."

The girl replied, "Lady, I gather these thistles."

The Mother of God said to her, "Run, daughter, and tell your masters to tell the priest and the council that where the cross of the meadow path is they should build a chapel in my name called Saint Mary of the Cross, which will be of much devotion, consolation, and help for all of Christianity and even more in the times to come."

The girl replied, "My lady, I will gather this sack of thistles, and then I will go and say it."

And the Virgin Our Lady told her, "Go along, the sack is already full," and at once the Virgin Mother of God disappeared from her.

The girl went to the sack and found it quite full of thistles, which confused her even more, and with Our Lady giving her strength, she took her sack and went to the house of her master, Sancho Herrero. Her mistress, when she saw her come so soon, was surprised and said to the servant girl, "How can you have finished with the thistles so quickly? I can't understand it."

The servant girl said, "Aunt, the Mother of God came to me, a lady very shining, beautiful, and resplendent, and filled up the sack, for I had only gathered a skirtful when she came to me. She told me it was already full, and that I should come and tell you and my uncle that where the meadow cross is a chapel should be built in her name called Saint Mary of the Cross, which will be of much devotion and consolation for all Christians and even more in the times to come."

The mistress marveled at what the girl said and told her, "Say nothing until your master comes, for he is not at home, and we will tell him together." And when her husband, the master of the girl, arrived, the mistress and the girl recounted the story as it transpired, and Sancho Herrero made fun of it, and scolded them for what they said and ordered them not to tell it or open their mouths about it.

After two or three days Sancho Herrero and his wife, parents-in-law of Madalena Gonçález, sent Joana their servant to gather thistles in a fallow field they had in La Graneruela, very near the cross where Our Lady ordered that a chapel be built to her. And they sent with the girl a servant of the house named Bartolomé. When Joana was gathering thistles she saw coming toward them through the upper meadow the Virgin Mother of God in the same form in which she had appeared the time before, and above her came a great multitude of very beautiful birds. And the Virgin Mother of God went up to the cross and knelt down and embraced it. And the girl said to the youth, "Bartolomé, Bartolomé, look at the lady who came to me the other day—she is coming there in the meadow very re-splendent, and above her is a great infinitude of birds. And she has gone up to the meadow cross and has knelt down and embraced it." The boy, although he looked as much as he could, saw nothing.

The Mother of God asked Joana why she had not told her master what she ordered. The girl replied that she had already told it, and they had not believed her. The Mother of God ordered her to tell them again to build the chapel where she had said for it is the will of both her son and her, and it will be of great consolation and assistance to the Christian world.

The girl went to the house of her masters and reported it, and Sancho Herrero refused to believe it and contradicted the girl, called her crazy and silly, and told her not to repeat it or open her mouth about it, for everyone would have a good laugh at her. And so the girl spoke no more of it.

And another day, the girl and the boy were sent by their masters to gather thistles in the same fallow field. And when Joana was gathering thistles she saw the Mother of God come very luminous, beautiful, and resplendent with a multitude of birds above her. And Joana said to the youth, "Ay, Bartolomé, the lady who came to me these past days is coming through the meadow, and she is kneeling and embracing the cross there—look at her, look at her!" The youth though he looked as hard as he could saw nothing except some small birds flying around above the cross.

The Mother of God went up to the girl and asked her why she had not done what she ordered. And the girl said, "My lady, I already said it, but they do not believe me."

And the Mother of God said, "Yes, I know, but now they will believe you." And then with her fingers the Mother of God touched Joana and pressed her lips together, and ordered her to go to the house of her masters the way she was, and she would be believed so they would build a chapel.

The girl went to the house of her masters and was mute and could not speak except by signs. Her master had the priests called and told them the story as the girl had told him. A council was held, and all the people of the village came to see the girl, and it was agreed that the next morning they would go in procession to the meadow cross.

The next day the clergy and the entire town went in procession to the cross, and they took along the girl with her lips stuck together, and with a pair of mules they marked the site where the chapel had to be built.

They returned in procession to the church and said the mass of the Holy Spirit. When the words *yte missa es* were pronounced Joana's mouth became unstuck, and she spit out two or three mouthfuls of water. Then she spoke and began to praise God and his Blessed Mother and recounted the whole affair from beginning to end. And the youth Bartolomé told everything the girl had told him when she saw Our Lady. The entire town was gathered there for this event and miracle and praised God and his Blessed Mother.

Soon the chapel was built, and an altar erected with an image of Our Lady the Mother of God. And on the altar was painted and depicted this miracle of the way the Queen of Heaven appeared to Joana, as today it can be seen on the same altar, with the same fallow field where they were gathering thistles.

From that day on the priests gave Joana the name Joana of the Cross because of the apparition. So that is what she was called, and they made her the hermitess in the chapel, and everyone touched her clothes out of devotion, and cut pieces from it to take as relics, because they held her to be a saint.

This is what she said she knows, and what she heard her mother-in-law Madalena Gonçález relate. She heard the same thing in the same way from many old people, men and women, who lived in this town. This has always been known and is public, notorious, well-known, and generally accepted. This is her response to the question.

Thirteen witnesses, the youngest 47, most of them over 70, told the same story, with very minor variations. Several said that a spring came forth from the ground where Mary pressed Joana's lips together, and water from the spring performed cures until it was profaned by a woman who dipped in it the diapers of a baby with leprosy, at which point the spring dried up.[87]

By and large the investigators and witnesses avoided the topic of what happened to Joana after her visions. One woman over 70 had had an aunt who remembered Joana. "Her aunt knew Joana and talked with her, and heard her recount several times with the greatest awe and reverence the appearances that the Mother of God made to her."[88] Perhaps they thought further references to the post-visions Joana would have hurt the chances of approval of the shrine from Segovia. In about 1618 a priest began a record of miracles at the shrine and an entertaining chronicle of the various hermits who lived there. In this book he put down everything the villagers had heard about Joana's later life.

The tradition is that in the apparitions the most holy Virgin ordered her not to marry, or else to remain a virgin—which is not clear, and that afterward she lived in voluntary retirement in the chapel. But some bad women began to go there and lead her astray. They started having many feasts in the chapel and dances and other things neither permitted nor decent for a hermitess, nor one retired from the world and in charge of a holy place. Because of this bad company Juana became distracted, and she married in the country around Cuellar—no one knows where for sure, but I heard it was in Los Yáñez. I have also heard from the old people that after marrying Juana came to visit the chapel many times a year. And that each time she came she caressed everyone who visited it and recounted everything that happened in the apparitions with much contentment and happiness and admonished them to be devoted to the chapel. And that until she died she came quite often every year to visit the holy chapel.[89]

In the process of the inquiry, on April 1, 1618, the investigators visited and described the shrine and its altar, including a painting that may have represented the apparition. "The Mother of God is painted with a golden skirt and a blue mantle, kneeling and embracing a gilded cross. From the nail of the cross issues an inscription that goes around above the crown and behind the Virgin, which reads in very old and large letters, *salbe crux preciosa que in corpore xpi, dedicata est et ex menbris eyus tan quam margaritis.* And then on the other side of the cross is a girl dressed in red in old style clothes with blond [or brown] hair let down without a coif. And she is kneeling adoring the cross and the Virgin, and at her knees is painted a fallow field that is very green with five stumps in it." The reredos was made in 1499, "in honor and reverence of Our Lady and reverence of the Cross," according to an inscription. So the visions of Joana occurred sometime before that.[90]

As at Cubas, the cross the Virgin embraced had become the center of devotion by the late sixteenth century. Its use in the ritual dispersal of a hailstorm in 1611 was in part responsible for the revival of interest in the shrine and was reported extensively in the 1617-1618 investigation. Pilgrims nipped off splinters with their teeth when they kissed it, and it had to be protected by a display case.

When I visited Escalona in 1977 and 1978, Mary, rather than the Cross, was once more the center of devotion. Devotion to Mary of the Cross is quite deep in Escalona, and the shrine is well maintained by a brotherhood. During the annual novena in September an ancient painting of Mary appearing to Joana, barely distinguishable, is placed at the center of the altar (see Figure 7).

The similarities between the episodes of Escalona and Cubas are striking. Mary knelt before the cross at Cubas, embraced it as at Escalona. The seers, both girls (although Joana is referred to exclusively as a *moza*, and thus may have been slightly older than Inés) see Mary in the countryside. Mary asks them what they are doing, then gives them her message. Both are eventually touched by the Virgin and given a deformity as proof. Both are taken to the site of the visions in a procession. The cross remains as a prized relic in both towns, and both seers first retire from the world, then escape to marry in distant parts. The confusion is compounded because Joana became Joana de la Cruz shortly before a holy woman of the same name, Inés's successor, as it were, was performing miracles and reorganizing the Cubas convent.

One also wonders about the influence of the apparition of Saint Michael of Navalagamella. Joana's sign was undone, like the shepherd Miguel's, at the words ite missa est. Is it coincidence that Saint Michael was the only other saint painted on the reredos of the Escalona chapel in 1499?[91] It is not entirely coincidental that retrospective investigations of both the Escalona and the Navalagamella visions were made in the same years, 1617-1618, in their respective dioceses. For throughout Spain in the first two decades of the seventeenth century, in a delayed reaction to the Council of Trent, extensive (but not exactly rigorous) investigations were carried out to justify the depiction of miracles and visions in churches.

Yet anyone who reads the transcripts of the Cubas and Escalona investigations will be convinced of the authenticity of the documents and the incidents. We are not dealing with literary imitation,* but a real life imitation, a scenario revised and replayed in a new setting.

---

* Such a duplication would theoretically have been possible, as at least two printed books had by 1617 described the Cubas apparitions—those of Pedro de Salazar (1607) and Antonio Daça (1610). But such a fraud would have entailed the collaboration of the entire town of Escalona and leaves unexplained the shrine, its paintings, and its relic cross.

TWO

Late Medieval Apparitions in Catalonia

THE CATALAN CONTEXT

The sacred ecology of Catalonia in the late medieval period was slightly different from that of New Castile. Reconquered earlier, it had a greater variety of divine helpers: more cults of local saints, more relics, more Mediterranean littoral devotions such as the Christ of Beyrouth. The fertile but mountainous terrain made for a more dispersed settlement pattern. This in turn increased the importance of district shrines, usually valley shrines, shared by a number of villages. In New Castile, only in the densely populated region of the Sagra and Maqueda do we see what for Catalonia was common everywhere, intricate networks of processions from different villages to common shrines. In New Castile district shrines brought together individuals from a wide area. In Catalonia they brought together whole communities from a smaller area.

In the mid-fifteenth century the major shrine, as now, was Montserrat. Located on a spectacular jagged outcrop in the center of the region, it was a very well-organized devotional establishment that attracted pilgrims from southern France, the Mediterranean islands, and even Italy. Montserrat and Guadalupe were the two poles of Iberian devotion.

Our Lady of Nuria, high in the Pyrenees, attracted devotees from the present-day provinces of Girona and Barcelona and what is now French Cerdegna as far north as Perpignan. The zone of devotion can be mapped from the many miracles in its miracle books. Many of those cured, or whose cures were considered worthy of note, were merchants, notaries, or officials of the cities of Barcelona, Girona, and Perpignan.[1]

Another shrine had only recently become popular, the Font de la Salut near Traiguera (Castelló de la Plana). There a statue of the Virgin Mary was supposedly found in a spring in 1438, and shortly thereafter it had acquired papal and royal privileges and was a thriving center for cures (see Figure 1).[2]

Historically older, but perhaps slightly eclipsed by 1450, were the relics of local saints in the region's cathedrals. Saint Felix and Saint Narciso in Girona, Saint Eulalia in Barcelona, and Saint Candia in Tortosa were martyrs whose bodies were once accorded the greatest veneration.

Pilgrims from Catalonia occasionally went to shrines elsewhere. Catalans went to Rome and Jerusalem, and to the French shrines of Rocamadour, Saint Quiteria, and Our Lady of Puy. Communities in serious straits sent paid romeros to represent them with their petitions to Saint James of Compostela.

In central Castile, with the exception of Our Lady of the Cabeza in northern Andalusia, shrines were not located in the mountains, whether those of Toledo or the Sierra de Guadarrama. In Catalonia the dense population even in mountainous regions led to the crowning of many promontories with chapels, especially in the dioceses of Vic and Girona. Much of Catalan devotion is that of people of the plains and valleys going up to the mountains. There is little reverse flow; the shrines of the plains and the coast do not attract the mountain people.

Historically, Catalan holy places were probably more likely to have been consecrated by hermits. Montserrat began as a series of hermitages, and the first miracles were worked there quite possibly before there was even an image of Mary. Recent studies have demonstrated that many Catalan shrines exist near or on the sites of early medieval hermitages, many of them caves. This would be an alternate historical explanation for the isolated location of images with finding legends.[3] Much of Castile was still unsettled or unconquered in the tenth and eleventh centuries when eremitism was at its height. One of the most popular Catalan shrines, now as well as in the fifteenth century, is that dedicated to a local hermit, Sant Magí de la Brufaganya, near Santa Coloma de Queralt in the mountains of Tarragona. The shrine of Santa Afra in Girona is also popular. It is dedicated to a prostitute converted by Saint Narciso who supposedly lived as a hermitess until martyred by the Romans. This legendary story, reminiscent of that of Saint Mary the Egyptian, reflects what for many Catalan shrines was a reality—an eremitic origin.

The population of Castile increased in the fifteenth century; that of Catalonia declined. If life in Castile was somewhat disordered, its economy was, on balance, healthy and its population thriving. Catalonia's decline has been partly explained by repeated waves of epidemics. As cities were decimated, villagers moved in, especially those heavily burdened by feudal duties, so that in rural areas emigration compounded the depopulation caused by the epidemics.[4] Pierre Vilar characterizes 1380-1420 as a time of economic difficulty; 1420-1440 as a time of relative stability; and 1440-1492, the period of the apparitions studied here, as a time of brutal crisis.[5]

On the one hand, whatever the differences between the two kingdoms, the possibility of epidemics was great enough in both to set a tone of constant anxiety, not only for the year-to-year survival of individuals and families but also for the survival of entire communities. No one would have forgotten that earlier plagues, especially that of 1348, wiped out thousands of villages across the peninsula.

On the other hand, the frequency and effect of the fifteenth-century epidemics seem to have been greater in Catalonia than in Castile. Certainly Catalonia was closer to the endemic sources in the Near East. In any case, although the Castilian visions involved the threat of epidemics, many of the Catalan visions took place while epidemics were in progress.

We know of one earlier supernatural response to the Black Death, high in the Pyrenees in the Valley of Arán. There in 1356 a crucifix in the church of Salardú, probably the same crucifix venerated there now, worked miracles.[6] Doubtless there were spates of miracles in other places, and probably other apparitions instructing people as to preventive or curative measures.

EL MIRACLE (LLEIDA), 1458

The first Catalan apparition for which there is documentary evidence is that of Our Lady of the Miracle, Santa María del

Miracle, near Riner (Lleida). It occurred in August 1458, in the midst of an epidemic of bubonic plague, to two young boys on the same day their father was helping to bury the child of neighbors. Within a week the chief seer, a boy about eight years old, had also died, but not before he told his story to a diocesan official. The apparition shares the iconographic motif of Mary with a cross with the visions of Inés at Cubas nine years earlier and Joana at Escalona thirty years later. As at Cubas, Mary appeared child-sized.

The setting for this apparition is a zone of dry piedmont in central Catalonia where large, semi-fortified farmhouses are dispersed over the countryside. The farmhouse of the seer, still called Cirosa, looks much the same now as it did five hundred years ago (see Figure 8). The hamlets of Riner and Sant Just d'Ardévol were also fortified, and are referred to in the documents as *castells*. It is a region in which banditry was prevalent, and in the nineteenth and twentieth centuries it was known for its conservative Carlism.

El Miracle is now an imposing shrine administered by Benedictines from Montserrat. It is about halfway between Cardona, a town wealthy from its salt mines, and Solsona, a market center that in 1592 became the seat of a diocese detached from Seu d'Urgell. El Miracle is one of the ten most popular shrines in Catalonia and has a large collection of votive paintings, some of which date from the sixteenth century (see Map 2).

☆

Chronology

seers: Jaume and Celedoni, aged about 8 and 9, respectively, sons of Joan Cirosa and Constança, his wife.
place: near Riner (Lleida)

Thursday, August 3, 1458. There was plague in the area.
  1) Joan, the father, went to help bury a neighbor's child, leaving his wife and sons to harvest wheat.

Map 2. Central and eastern Catalonia

> 2) *Late in the afternoon, Celedoni, the older son, was sent to get some mules. He saw a mysterious girl and ran away.*
>
> 3) *Constança, the mother, went to look, but was frightened and went back.*
>
> 4) *Jaume, the younger son, went to look, but saw nothing.*
>
> 5) *Later Jaume went back to fetch the sheep. He met a girl with a cross, who told him to warn the people to convert and then walked away.*

Monday, August 7, Jaume came down with the plague.

Tuesday, August 8.

> 1) *A doctor had a divine locution to go to the farm and talk to the boy.*

> 2) *Officials of Solsona and Riner asked the bishop's representative to investigate rumors of an apparition. They took Jaume's testimony.*
>
> *Thursday, August 10, Jaume died, and the rest of the family and the doctor made depositions.*

Order of Testimony
>   1) *August 8, Jaume.*
>   2) *August 10, Joan, the father [excerpted here].*
>   3) *Constança, the mother.*
>   4) *Celedoni, the older brother.*
>   5) *Pere dels Ots, doctor, of Sant Just d'Ardévol.*

On August 8, 1458, officials of the towns of Solsona and Riner asked Jaume Vilar, the representative in Solsona of the bishop of Urgell, to go with them to Riner to investigate "a great miracle." At the farm Cirosa Vilar questioned the child Jaume Cirosa under oath.[7]

JAUME CIROSA, AUGUST 8, 1458

And first the witness was asked if he had seen any vision in the last few days. And he said that yes, on Thursday.

Asked what it was he saw, he said that last Thursday, August 3, at the hour of vespers, for the shadow was already across the stream, he saw a being like a beautiful blond child, dressed, he thought, in a red cape. In addition he said he thought it carried a very beautiful cross on its shoulder.

The witness was asked if he could identify the cross. He said it seemed to him like one that is on the altar of Saint Sebastian of Riner.

He was asked what the vision like a child was doing, whether it was standing or kneeling. The witness said it was kneeling.

The witness was asked if he could tell if it was a boy or a girl. He said it seemed to be a girl.

He was asked why it seemed to be a girl. The witness said it was because she had very long hair, like a woman, and blond.

The witness was asked if he went close to her. He said
that yes, to two paces away.

The witness was asked if he saw her before he was close
to her. He said he had not seen her until he went to turn a
sheep back with the others, when he came upon the girl.

The witness was asked if he said anything to the girl before she said anything to him. He said no.

He was asked if when he saw the girl, the girl spoke to
him. He said yes.

He was asked what she said to him. He said she told
him, "Tell the people to make processions, and make them
devoutly, and to confess and convert and return to the side
of God, and that if they do, God will forgive them."

He was asked if the girl said to him that God would forgive you if they do those things. The witness said she did
not tell him.

He was asked if the girl said anything else. And the witness said that yes, she said, "Tell them that if they do not
believe you, my son will make them believe."

He was asked if the girl said anything else. The witness
said yes, that she said, "There is no child four or more
years old whom my son will not reap."

He was asked if the girl said anything else. The witness
said she said nothing more, but she arose and gave him the
cross in his left hand and kissed his right hand.

He was asked if the girl did anything else. The witness
said that no, she just walked away on the path to Torradenagó.

The witness was asked if he noticed, after the girl left
him, where she went and if she disappeared. He said he
does not know, except that she took the path.

The witness was asked where he saw the girl. He said in
a small meadow called the meadow of Bassa Dòria.

He was asked if he knows how old he is. The witness
said he does not know, but that his father and mother say
he is nine to ten years old.

The witness was asked if he could point out the place
where he saw the girl. And the witness said he could easily

show them if he could walk, but that his illness was so painful that it made him delirious, and he could not walk there; but that he had already shown his father and mother.'

The witness was asked what he was doing in the meadow when he saw the girl. He said he was watching his sheep. And that as he already said, it was when he tried to turn a sheep back with the flock that he saw the girl.

He was asked if anyone was there with him. He said no, just the animals.

The witness was asked if anyone asked him to say the things he had just said. And the witness said no, only the Virgin Mary, who told him to tell the people.

The witness was asked if he saw anyone with the girl. He said no, nobody.

The witness was asked if the girl had anything on her head. He said no, only her hair.

He was asked what clothes the girl wore. He said he only saw that she wore a red cape.

The witness was asked if he ever said anything to the girl. He said no, that he only listened to her.

He was asked if he had been suborned by anyone. He said no.

It was read to him and he confirmed it.

Two days later, August 10, 1458, Joan Cirosa, the father of Jaume, testified that he spent the day of the visions helping out neighbors who had one daughter sick and another to be buried. He repeated the story of his boys' visions as they had told him. As he remembered it, the Virgin's message to Jaume was, "Tell your father and mother to tell the people to confess and do penance and make processions devoutly, otherwise it is not worth anything to them, and that if they do this, God will forgive them. You tell them that my son will make them believe, and that there will be neither small or big, four years or older, whom my son will not reap." At the end of his testimony Joan was asked and answered the following questions by the priest.

Figure 1. The discovery of an image in a stream. Illustration, p. 326, Iayme Prades, *Historia de la adoracion y uso de las santas imagenes* (Valencia, Felipe Mey, 1597), courtesy Marian Library, University of Dayton.

Figure 2. The apparition procession in Jaén. Detail from the altar of the Descent of the Virgin by La Roldana, Church of San Ildefonso, courtesy Archivo Mas.

Figure 3. Mary bestows a chasuble on Saint Ildefonsus. On the left is Saint Helen, on the right Saints Lucy and Clare. Fifteenth-century mural in the cloister of the convent of Santa Clara, Toledo, courtesy Archivo Mas.

Figure 4. The sacred stone, behind two sets of bars, of the Descent of Mary in the cathedral of Toledo. The poem in ceramic reads, "When the Queen of Heaven put her feet on the ground, she placed them on this stone. Kiss it for your consolation. Touch the stone, saying with complete devotion, 'We venerate this place where the most holy Virgin put her feet.' " (Photo, Cristina García Rodero)

Figure 5. An early fifteenth-century painting of the Santa Cinta, part of a retablo by the Maestro of Guimerà in the museum of the diocese of Vic, photo courtesy Archivo Mas.

Figure 6. D. Cándido Pérez Campo, *santero* of the Brotherhood of San Antonio, Navas de San Antonio (Segovia), May 1977. (Photo by author)

Figure 7. Mary presses Joana's lips together. In the background, barely discernible, Joana shows the townspeople the site of her visions. This well-worn painting in the shrine of Nuestra Señora del Prado in Escalona (Segovia) is probably a copy of an older one. (Photo by author)

Figure 8. The Cirosa farmhouse in July 1980. (Photo by author)

Figure 9. The Font Santa of Jafre in 1911, courtesy Archivo Mas.

N. S. DE MISERICORDIA, CON SUS TRES MARTI.ˢ
VENERADOS ENSU ERMITA DE LA VILLA DE REUS.

Figure 10. The apparition of Mary to Isabel Besora at Reus.

JOAN CIROSA, AUGUST 10, 1458

The witness was asked if he knows if his son had ever been in any town. And the witness said that he had never been in a town or village, except Riner, where he went to hear mass some Sundays.

The witness was asked what kind of life his son led, and if he knew any prayers. And he said that his life was spent watching the animals, he only knew the Pater and the Ave Maria, which they made him say every day, and he never heard either of them blaspheme.

Asked if after the event he noticed that his younger son behaved better than before. He said that he always behaved well enough.

Asked if he knows if his son was given to lying. He said he cannot recall him ever saying a lie.

Asked if he knows if his younger son, who is dead, was healthy on the day he saw the vision. He said yes, healthy and happy.

Asked of what disease he died. He said the bubonic plague, which he had in the right underarm.

Asked when he died. He said today.

Asked when he became ill. He said last Monday.

Everything was read to him, and he confirmed it.

CONSTANÇA, WIFE OF JOAN CIROSA, AUGUST 10, 1458

And first the witness was asked if she heard her older son say that he saw any vision or found anything in the past few days. And the witness said that last Thursday her older son came to the field they were harvesting saying that he had found a beautiful thing, like a beautiful child, in the meadow near the Dòria pool, kneeling near the water's edge with a beautiful cross in its hands, a red cape that touched the ground, and beautiful blond hair; she did not ask him whether the hair was long or short. And this witness told him three times, "Watch that you tell the truth." And she told him, "If you are telling the truth I will go and look for it." And the boy, in reaffirmation, said, "It is as I have said." And the witness knew from his face that he was shaken and that it must be true. And she decided to go there, but she did not go all the way because she became afraid. Instead she looked at the place from a distance, but saw nothing. And a hare ran out from near her feet, and she then went back to the field being harvested, where she had left her son with another younger son, telling them she had not found anything. Then the younger son said, "Let me go there, and I will look for it." And so he went right off, but he found nothing then. And they turned back the animals.

The witness was asked if she heard her older son say anything else. She said yes, that the thing spoke very softly to him, but that he did not dare to listen to it; all he caught was that they should make processions. He said it told him other things, but he did not dare to listen, since he was so frightened.

She was asked if he said anything else. She said no.

She was asked if her younger son encountered the thing, or what he found. And the witness said that her younger son said that on that Thursday near dusk as the sun set into the trees, he had found the thing, resembling a beautiful child. It was near the Dòria pool, fairly close to where her older son said he found it. It was wearing a beautiful red cape; it had beautiful blond hair; and it was kneeling with a cross in its hands. It seemed like a very young child, and it came up to him and put the cross in his left hand, kissed his right hand, and then took the cross back. And it told him, "Tell your father and mother to tell the people to confess and return to God's side and make processions devoutly, otherwise they will not be worth anything to them. And if they do not believe you, say that my son will make them believe." And with that, with hands clasped, she went away from the boy on the path through the Dòria oak grove toward Torradenagó. And he also said that it told him that there was no one too small or too big, four years or older, that her son would not reap.

She was asked if she knew the ages of her older and younger sons. She said that they were about ten years old. She was asked if her son was given to lying. She said no.

Everything was read to her and she confirmed it.

CELIDONI CIROSA, THE OLDER SON, AUGUST 10, 1458

And first he was asked what vision he said he saw in the last few days. The witness said that on last Thursday after the hour of vespers, for the southern fields were in shadow, he went after the mules, which were near the Dòria pool. Near the pool in a small meadow above it, which he said he would point out, the witness suddenly came upon a thing like a beautiful child about three paces away from him. It was kneeling with its hands joined toward heaven, holding a beautiful cross with Our Lord who was crucified, similar, he thought, to one in Riner on the altar of Saint Sebastian. It wore a very fancy red cape, which touched the ground all around it as it was kneeling. As soon as the witness saw it, it came toward him, and he stepped back two or three paces along the right bank of the pool. Then it spoke to him, "O son, come here and tell the people . . ." and he could not listen to it any more for fear and fled while it was still talking. When the witness was a little way off he heard it say ". . . weeks . . . " and he heard nothing else. And he went back to reap all frightened and shaken. He told his mother what happened, and she went there right away but could not find anything.

Asked if it seemed very big to him. He said it seemed to be about the size of a child two to three years old.

Asked if he could tell if it was a man or a woman. He said he doesn't know if it wore anything on its head; since he was so afraid of it he did not notice.

The witness was asked how old he was. He said he was about eight years old.

Asked if he knew more, he said no.

Everything was read to him and he confirmed it.

PERE DELS OTS, THE DOCTOR, AUGUST 10, 1458

On the same day and year, Pere dels Ots, of the parish of Sant Just in the territory of the castle of Ardévol, a witness cited, sworn, and questioned to tell the truth.

And first he was asked what happened to him in the last few days near La Cirosa. The witness said that last Tuesday he was on his way back from Fornell de Riner, where he had gone to visit a boy stricken with the plague. And on his way home to Sant Just, when he was near a plowed field of Mas Vilaseca, by a large juniper tree near the main road from Estanys to Cardona, no matter how much he tried he could go no farther. And he crossed himself and wondered what this could be, as he felt nothing wrong with his body. And pondering this he sat down near a scrub oak. When he was seated, the witness heard a voice that said to him, "What are you doing here? Why do you not go to La Cirosa for a child who is sick there, who will repeat to you words the Virgin Mary spoke to him?"

When the witness heard this, he looked around to see who was speaking, his whole body trembling, and then he stood up, but he saw no one. And once more he tried to go toward Sant Just, but he could not move forward. And so, given what the voice said, he decided to walk to La Cirosa, thinking this must be some kind of mystery. When he arrived here at the house he found Old Estenya and the wife of Lordella. They told him that a child named Jaumet was sick, and they thought the sickness may have come to him because he had had a vision. The witness entered the room to see him and asked him about the vision and what he had seen, and the boy repeated everything, word for word, that is contained above. And after the witness questioned him at length, he asked him if the Virgin Mary had told him on what day to hold the processions. And he said the boy told him, "she did not tell me." That was all he could get him to reply.

Asked if the witness had planned to go to La Cirosa before he heard the voice. He said no, he never thought of it.

Asked if the witness heard anyone say anything about

the vision before he went to La Cirosa. He said no.

Asked if when he went back, there was any impediment in his way. He said no.

Everything was read to him and he confirmed it.

Five persons testified: Joan Cirosa; Constança, his wife; the chief visionary Jaume, Joan's younger son; Celedoni, the older son, both around ten years old; and Pere dels Ots, the doctor. Each boy's vision was recounted three times—by the boy, the father, and the mother. The different accounts coincided in substance, the parents remembering a few additional details from what their children told them previously.

The visions occurred at dusk on Thursday, August 3, 1458. Four days later, on Saturday, August 7, Jaume came down with the plague. The doctor received his locution to go to the child's bedside Sunday, August 8. Outside the house he met two neighbor women who thought the child's sickness was connected with his vision experience. Possibly it was the doctor who informed the officials of his hamlet and set the documentation process in motion. In any case, on the same day, August 8, the officials of the two nearest hamlets went to the priest, who came to take the sick child's declaration. On Tuesday the 10th, when they came back with witnesses from Solsona, they were too late. Jaume had died earlier in the day. They took declarations from the rest of the family and the doctor, and the older son, Celedoni, showed them the apparition site.

Finding the spirit when going after animals is in keeping with the discovery legends. Celedoni, who saw the child-Mary first, was going after mules; Jaume did not find it when he went to look; but when he went for sheep and was chasing a stray, he saw it.

The descriptions the witnesses gave of finding the child show they were aware of the significance of natural conjunctions of wildlife and landscape. They specify that the strange child was near the pool. Later they showed their parents the spot. When the mother, fearful, first went to look, she noted that a hare started up from near her feet. The Virgin went away through a live oak grove, beside some boulders. The doctor could not move past a juniper tree and had his locution by a *raboll*, a scrub oak. All of these features of the landscape were carefully noted and declared, for children, parents, and doctor all seemed to realize that, from what they said, what was sacred in the landscape would be distinguished from what was profane. And they were right. A stone cross marks the apparition site close to the imposing Baroque shrine, and a small chapel was built where the child-Virgin was last seen, called the Chapel of the Disappearance.

The child told the older son her message, but he ran away and did not hear it. The mother was frightened. Of the unknown? Or of stories she had heard about *velletas*—fairies who could take the form of little girls with golden hair. Two Catalan folk tales reported in the twentieth century are about "the damsel with the golden hair." The younger son was not afraid and listened. He died, his sickness a confirmation of the vision for the women who met the doctor on his arrival.

Jaume did not run away from this bright child with the cross. He recognized the crucifix. He had never been to any town or village other than Riner, but there he had occasionally been to church and had seen the crucifix, or one like it, on the altar of Saint Sebastian. Perhaps he had seen it recently, for Sebastian was the protector against the plague. The family and the parish might well have been paying special attention to that altar. In any case, the crucifix presumably remained on the altar after the vision disappeared, a concrete reminder, an image equivalent to the images "found" in the legends. Thus, too, the crosses venerated by Mary in the visions of Cubas and Escalona also remained.

Is it coincidence that Celedoni and Jaume saw a God-girl on the day their father went to bury a neighbor's girl dead of the plague, a girl they must have known? One is reminded that Jeanne d'Arc's most frequent divine visitor was Saint Catherine, and Jeanne had had a sister named Catherine who had died.

The Virgin never explicitly identified herself as she did in the Castilian visions; but she did implicitly, by referring to "her son." There is no sense of incongruity that a child two or three years old should refer to a son. For this is not exactly a child.

Throughout most of their testimony the boys refer to it as *"la cosa,"* the thing. In addition, it had long hair like a woman.

In fact there was a scriptural basis for the appearance of Mary as a child who acted like a woman. According to the Apocryphal Gospels, Mary was a very mature three year old when she was taken to the temple to be reared by her parents—"and when she was three years old, she walked with a step so mature, she spoke so perfectly, and spent her time so assiduously in the praises of God, that all were astonished at her, and wondered; and she was not reckoned a young infant, but as it were a grown-up person of thirty years old."[8]

The message of this child-woman was not unlike that of the great missionaries of Catalonia, especially Saint Vincent Ferrer, who had been active in the district thirty years before: confession, conversion, and devout processions would earn God's help. Disbelief would lead to certain, terrible punishment. All people four and older would be harvested, an apt image for a child coming from a wheat harvest. Most of the Castilian apparitions ask for direct worship and veneration and the establishment of a shrine, the kind of concrete contact with a given saint in a given place characteristic of much of rural religion. Several of the Catalan apparitions, like this one, ask for more—for conversion and penance, for a public confession of guilt and reparations. Here there is no request for a shrine. The emphasis is upon the crucifix, and the solution to the plague is in the redemptive procedures of penance.

The Catalan legend most similar to the vision of El Miracle is that of Our Lady of Carramia of the village of Abella de la Conca in the same diocese (Urgell) about eighty-five km. to the northwest. There, Camós reported, a herding girl also had a vision of a "noble and beautiful girl." Her message was simply to tell the village councillors to build a shrine on the site, and, as a proof, the girl's hand was fixed to her cheek. The councillors found an image on the site.[9] At El Miracle the message was more severe.

As in the Castilian apparitions, the gestures carry the most symbolic weight. At the start of the Cubas investigation, the investigators placed the archbishop's letter on their heads and promised to obey it. At Cubas the Virgin planted the cross with her hands, just as at Monte Berico in Italy she had used a cross to mark off the plan of the church. Here the Virgin-child handed Jaume the cross, kissed his hand, then took the cross back. Kissing his hand, as if he were a bishop or a saint, seems ominous in retrospect. Was it the kiss of grace, of death, or both? Giving him the cross would appear to symbolize pointing out the crucifix to the people as a special aid and an indication of the penance they would have to perform, imitating themselves the trials of Christ. In any case the chosen one died, like Pedro de Buenaventura of Santa Gadea and his friend Juan, both of whom were told they must die soon. Indeed, Jaume's death itself was the proof of the story; surely he had nothing to gain on his deathbed by lying.

In sum, the cross, the threat of epidemic, the appearance of Mary as child, and the premature death of the seer, if they did not come to Catalonia directly from Castile, shared with Castile and northern Italy a scenario common to fifteenth-century rural culture.

JAFRE (GIRONA), 1460

On September 15, 1456, the bishop of Barcelona received a dispatch from Pope Calixtus III telling of a great victory over Mohammed II, sultan of the Ottoman Empire. The Christian troops, the pope wrote, were led by Friar John of Capistrano, "at the counsel and instigation of a pilgrim," who gave him a shield with the sign of a crucifix on it. When the battle was over the mysterious pilgrim had disappeared. The bishop had a Te Deum sung in the Barcelona cathedral, and the news was put into the municipal record book.[10]

Four years later, two years after the visions at El Miracle, Catalonia had its own mysterious visitor, at whose instigation a cross was erected and a new shrine started. It still exists today, a small chapel on the outskirts of the village of Jafre on the road from Girona to the resort town of Estartit. The road follows the north bank of the Ter River through fertile farmland, and Jafre is about halfway to the coast. The chapel, which has in its courtyard a spring with a metal cup on a chain, gives little indication of its heyday as a healing center in the 1460s (see Figure 9).

COPY OF THE ACT FOUNDING THE CHAPEL OF OUR LADY OF THE HOLY SPRING (NOSTRA SENYORA DE LA FONT SANTA) AND DEPOSITIONS OF WITNESSES CONCERNING THE MIRACLES WORKED THERE.[11]

Testimony received about . . . spring shown to have power in the locality of Jafre, 1461

Ad perpetuam rei memoriam

On Tuesday, February 10, 1461, the following witness swore and testified in the city of Girona. Miquel Castelló of the parish of Jafre, a witness summoned and sworn, said that in truth last November he was plowing one of his fields called the field of the woods, in the parish of Jafre, and a man of medium height came up to him wearing a blue woolen tunic to mid-calf, blue woolen stockings, brown boots, and a blue hat, and carrying a pole about eight palms long. In the judgment of this witness the man was twenty to twenty-three years old, without a trace of a beard. When he was near he asked the witness his name, and the witness replied that he was Miquel Castelló. Then the man asked him how many crosses there were in the different crossroads of Jafre, and the witness said there was only one. The man then said to him that he should put one on his land if he could, or else at another crossroad.

Then he said to the witness these or similar words: I charge your soul that you tell the people of Jafre that the spring on the road to Colomés that makes a pond should be well enclosed and held in esteem, for its water once had great power. Because people washed their laundry there, they caused it to lose its power, but if they closed it off and respected it, the spring would regain its power.

The witness then said that if he repeated this to the people they would not believe it. The man told him that yes, they would, because a baby would die here soon, and he could give that as a sign, and then they would believe him. The witness asked whose baby it would be; and the man told him that he would know soon. The man then left him and went off toward Colomés along the River Ter. The witness lost sight of him and does not know who he was.

Subsequently the witness went to the town of Jafre, and as he came to his house he heard the bells tolling for a baby of Bernat Dolça, cloth-maker of Jafre, who had just died in that parish. The witness went to Mossen Joan Ballester, priest of Jafre, and told him everything related above, and Ballester repeated it the following Sunday from the pulpit of the Jafre church to the parishioners. This event took place on a Friday. Since then the witness has seen many people go there for certain ailments, and according to the witness they are cured.

It was read to him and he confirmed it.

This first testimony was recorded as part of a village request for permission to build a chapel on the apparition site. It was not made until three months after the apparition. By that time the seer could no longer remember the exact date, just that it was a Friday in the month of November 1460.

Mary is never mentioned in the vision. Within a year the priest and villagers knew they wanted the new chapel to be dedicated to Mary, but the important symbol here, as in El Miracle and the Castilian visions, is the cross. The mysterious man with a pole suggested the building of a cross at a crossroads.

The villagers subsequently decided that the man in blue must have been an angel, but he was not considered a major actor in the drama, simply a messenger. They did not dedicate their shrine to him. He is more like the mysterious traveling artists who left crucifixes painted on the walls of the farmhouses of New Castile two hundred years later; the crucifix, the cross, and the spring were the foci of attention. Similarly, the spot where the man appeared and even the exact date were not considered noteworthy. He walked away westward along the river and out of the story altogether.

Perhaps the vision was not granted much credit to begin with, even if the priest repeated it in church. For one thing the proof—the death of the child—was a little thin. Castelló told his story only after he heard of the child's death; hence that death could serve as a proof only to Castelló himself. But once the idea had been planted that the spring was miraculous, the proof to the villagers lay in the water. Indeed, that became the central question. Not whether a vision took place, but whether the water worked cures. Even the seer Castelló apparently faded into the background. He is not mentioned as caring for the spring or as one of the citizens appointed to manage the construction of the shrine or the quest for alms. Like the anonymous messenger from heaven, Castelló was simply an instrument. Other witnesses, in fact, made no reference to the apparition.

Two days after Castelló testified in Girona, a nobleman of the village told of being cured and of the cures of others. The illness in question, dolor de costat, may well be the plague, for the *costat* and the *coll* were places on the body where the lymph glands formed bubos. If the first baby, who died on the apparition day, died from the plague, then Castelló was probably taken very seriously indeed.

TESTIMONY OF BERNAT GUILLEN

Thursday the twelfth day of [February 1461], the following witness declared and swore: the honorable Bernat Guillen of Jafre, nobleman (*miles*), domiciled in the town of Jafre, admonished, sworn, and questioned to say and declare all the truth he knows about the matters below, was asked if he has heard it said that a spring was found in the parish of Jafre, and if it was good for any illnesses, and if the people are devoted to it, or if they go to it to carry any [water] off to cure illnesses.

He declared it was true that here in the parish of Jafre there is a spring on the road to Colomés that is very effective for many ailments. Three weeks ago on Friday the witness came down with a great illness and pain in the side (*dolor de costat*), and he was very frightened and was sure he would die and asked for water from the spring to drink. As soon as he was given the water he drank three or four

cups, and he felt his heart very clear (*clar*). Then he had
himself covered up and sweated profusely and by the grace
of God was perfectly cured. The witness believes that Our
Lord God by means of the water cured him, because he did
not think he would come out of it alive.

Similarly this witness says that before he was stricken
with his sickness he saw Miquel Trobat of Jafre with so
great an infirmity in the neck that he was given up for
dead, for his throat was already so swollen that he was
choking. They gave him water from the spring to drink,
and he quickly improved so that now by God's grace he is
all cured and well.

The witness also said that Gaspar Costa of Ullastret told
him that at Monells there were seven persons who had
drunk the spring water that the witness sent them. They
had the sickness of the side and the neck or shoulder (*mal
de costat, mal de coll*), and all were cured except for an old
lady, who died.

The witness heard that a slave of En Caramany was sick
and given up for dead, and they gave him the water and he
was cured, and that Caramany promised to leave them [sic]
for two months at Jafre to help build the chapel of the
spring if it is built.

And the witness sees in one day about a hundred people
come, and every day there are many people, because on
the spring they have put a box in which every day they
find six sous, and on one day as many as eight sous and
six diners. He sees that people carry off [the water] with
gourds and large and small wineskins, and they wash
themselves with it with great devotion. And the witness
has heard it said publicly that almost all who drink it are
cured of all ailments, and that it is very effective for eye
trouble.

It was read to him and he confirmed it.

From Bernat Guillen's testimony, then, by February 1461 the
holy spring was attracting the lame and the blind from many
of the neighboring towns—those he mentioned are about

twenty km. to the southwest. News that a spring somewhere could cure the plague must have spread quickly. Many of those interested in it would have been too sick to come, and the nobleman himself helped dispatch water to distant towns. By February the people of Jafre already had the idea of building a chapel. Alms were being collected, and a man had even offered to leave his slaves to help.

In June 1461, the vicar general of the diocese went to Jafre to see for himself what was happening and to question more witnesses. He was told of three people who had paralyzed hands cured: a woman, a *ungaro* (gypsy?), and a girl from near Vic (over 100 km. away, beyond a substantial mountain range). Later, with two priests, the nobleman, five church employees, and eight villagers, he drew up a document granting permission to build a chapel with separate curing pools for men and women, and set conditions for raising alms for the project throughout the diocese.

More miracles reported on July 12 demonstrate the wide area in which the spring had become known since February. Cured were people from Tarragona, Figueres, Santa Pau, and France. The Frenchman and the Tarragonés may have been beggars or travelers passing through, but the effective radius of the shrine, given the cured from Vic, Figueres, and Santa Pau, was at least 100 km.

One aspect of the original apparition message was supported by these latter miracles. The man in blue warned that the spring had once worked well, but that it became polluted when used for the mundane purpose of laundry. This need for the separation of sacred and profane is like the cases of Escalona and Monte Berico. At Jafre people noticed that the water stopped coming out when some people started to use it, and resumed its flow when they left. There was a striking case on July 12. Before noon the water stopped "because a man from Colomés named Besart wanted to draw a basin of water to drink. The witness said that Besart is a great sinner, which explains what happened. He committed many sins recently, especially all this year he carried Moors and horses in his boat to Granada, and with these horses the Moors had ravaged the people of Castile."

Calixtus III had excommunicated all persons helping to supply the Moors of Granada in 1456.[12]

The spring was thus not just a place for cures. It was a sacred test for purity and pollution. In faraway rural Girona, the Moors were still the "other," as at Santa Gadea, Jaén, and even somewhat Cubas and Guadalupe, where escapees from Moorish captivity came to give thanks. Curing is not a simple matter. At these holy places, health cannot be preserved or achieved mechanically; it must be earned through a state of grace and genuine devotion. Similarly, the Virgin at El Miracle told Jaume that the people, when they make processions, must make them devoutly, "or else they are worth nothing."

Jafre is quite close to Palacals (fifteen km. north), the only place in the diocese of Girona that Camós mentioned as having an apparition-finding legend. There an image of Mary supposedly spoke to a mute shepherd girl from an elm tree, telling her that the ox she was hunting was safe in the stable. When she told this in words to her amazed parents or employers, they went with her to find the image. Holy springs were not uncommon throughout Catalonia or indeed, throughout Western Europe, and the idea would not have been outlandish to those who heard Miquel Castelló tell his story in church. Apparitions are strange events, but they are usually not without precedent.

EL TORN (GIRONA), 1483

Between 1450 and 1530 there were many outbreaks of the plague in Catalonia. According to statistics from the city of Barcelona, the worst years were 1457 (with which the epidemic of 1458 connected to the El Miracle visions was associated), 1489-1490, 1501, 1507-1508, 1515, and 1530. A slightly lesser outbreak in the years 1482-1483 probably provoked the next apparition we can document.[13]

When the plague threatened Barcelona in late 1482, the city corporation, following a practice used in other parts of Spain, had a candle made the thickness of a finger and the length of the walls of the city—more than four miles long. Royal, Church, and municipal authorities accompanied the (presumably coiled) candle in a procession, crying out, "Lord, true God, have mercy on us." At the chapel of La Pietat in the Augustinian monastery, the enormous candle was cut into five-foot lengths and burned night and day before the image there of Mary.[14]

The next year the plague took about 1400 lives in Barcelona between March 15 and the end of September, and the villagers in the hills of Girona would have been wondering when or if it would come to them. These same villages had been hard hit in 1475, and perhaps also in 1460, for the abandoned chapel where Miquel Noguer spoke to a weeping Mary was only fifty km. northwest of Jafre.[15]

TESTIMONY OF MIQUEL NOGUER OF EL TORN TO DIOCESAN
AUTHORITIES IN GIRONA[16]

Thursday, November 30, 1483, Miquel Noguer, parishioner of Sant Andrés de Torn, diocese of Girona, said and declared what is given below. First he said and declared that last Saturday, October 25, eight days after the feast of Saint Luke, he was coming back from hunting near dusk, the time of the Ave Maria bell. Passing by the chapel of the Virgin Mary of Collell he went up to it with devotion to pray at the door of the church, which was locked, and to ring the prayer of the pardon. Praying on his knees he went to the door of the chapel, and after he prayed as God ordained and started to arise he heard within the chapel the lamentations of a little girl. The witness was very disturbed and surprised by the cries and sobs, and when he started to arise and ring the pardon the doors of the chapel, which, as he said, were locked, opened miraculously.

From his kneeling position the witness saw through the open doors, three or four paces within the chapel before him, a very beautiful girl between seven and eight years old, all dressed in clothes as white as the snow. She was continuously wringing her hands and with them joined she cried and asked for pity from Jesus Christ, beseeching him that it be his mercy and pity to take mercy and pity on his people. She was crying out loudly in a very sweet voice, and when the witness saw and heard her from his kneeling position, he made an effort to pull himself together, although he was very frightened, and questioned the girl with these or similar words: "O sweet child, will you tell me what is troubling you so?"

The girl replied as follows: "O my son, I charge you by your soul to charge the souls of the men of the parishes of El Torn, Milleras, El Salent, and Sant Miquel de Campmaior to charge the souls of the priests to ask the people to pay up the tithes and all the duties of the church and restore other things that they hold covertly or openly which are not theirs to their rightful owners within thirty days, for it will be necessary, and observe well the holy Sunday.

And second that they should cease and desist from blaspheming and they should pay the usual *charitats* mandated by their dead ancestors."

Also she charged me by the souls of the men now or in the future that when they see one of the above sins they should punish it.

When the girl had said these words and given these orders to the witness to transmit, she began to weep again, and weeping said to the witness, who was still on his knees, the following: that she charged the soul of the witness to charge the souls of the men mentioned above that within thirty days they remove and raise the interdict on the chapel. And once the interdict is removed, she orders the four parishes and all others who so desire to hold processions every Friday with all the people together and fasting. And they should come to this my chapel and do that good thing which God will ordain.

And further the girl told and ordered him to report all this to the Very Reverend Lord Bishop of Girona or to his Vicar in order to have the interdict on her chapel lifted. And that on his soul he should have this removed within thirty days.

After the girl said all these words and things to the witness, she disappeared, and he saw nothing more except that the doors of the chapel closed and locked themselves as miraculously as they had opened, with the witness still on his knees in the doorway. Then the witness stood up and went home. And everything said and described above he now declares to you, the monsignors and vicars of the Very Reverend Lord Bishop, in discharge of his soul and the charge he had.

The witness who reported these things was asked if he asked the girl he says he saw who she was. The witness said he asked the girl to tell him please who she was, and the girl replied that she was the Virgin Mary.

The witness was asked if when the girl disappeared he was disconsolate or sad, and the witness said that he felt very good (*aconsolat*) when the girl disappeared.

Asked if he asked her and she revealed to him if Our Lord God was going to punish the people, he said that yes, the girl told him that if the people did not convert she would send great mortal epidemics of bubonic plague over the land.

The witness was asked if he remembers anything else the girl told him, and the witness said [she said] nothing else, just that described, spoken, and contained above.

It was read to him and he confirmed it.

Luis Constans carefully researched the background for this vision, and his work confirms the historicity of the events. Miquel Noguer was married and had at least one child at the time of his vision. Two of his children later married, and one son became a priest. Noguer was still living in 1509. He appears to have been a prosperous peasant, and it is a measure of his respectability that his story was believed (at least enough to reopen the shrine) without any proof, sign, or corroboration.

Constans found two of Noguer's wills. Together they confirm not only the apparition but also Noguer's own belief in it. The first will was made in 1482. In 1487 he changed it to mandate his burial at the door of the chapel where the apparition took place and the burning of a lamp before the image every Saturday (the day the vision took place). Noguer's bones were recently uncovered under the doorway in the presence of diocesan officials.

The apparition document, reproduced in Constans's book, appears from the script to be the shrine's copy of testimony taken by diocesan officials in Girona. The vision was followed by an immediate revival of the shrine, which became one of the most popular in the diocese. Now it is also used as a summer seminary and a diocesan retreat.

As with all the Catalan visions of the time, this is a plague vision. One of the four questions officials in Girona asked Noguer was if God was going to punish the people. Similarly at Cubas, the one question the priest had for Inés was when the epidemic would come. The Virgin's essential message is an alternative: plague or moral reform.

A second, more proximate context was the abandoned chapel. Because of some profanation, whether its misuse as a stable, an intervillage brawl, or perhaps a failure to pay ecclesiastical duties, the chapel had been locked up, and the bishop had forbidden its use. As at Santa Gadea, the abandoned chapel must have been a matter of concern for the people living around it. A devout person such as Noguer, who went to ring the angelus on his way home from hunting, must have been sad not to be close to a representation of Mary of his devotion.

In the earlier visions, Mary had pointed to the Cross as the way to health and salvation. She was not reenacting a scene from the Passion, however, and neither was the Mary seen by Miquel Noguer. At El Torn, Mary (again, a child) wept alone, clasping her hands as at El Miracle, asking for mercy from a vengeful son. Her tears, perhaps due in part to the infidelity of the surrounding villages, could also be ascribed to her knowledge of the punishment the people would receive if they did not repent. Unlike either a pietà or a Mary at the foot of the Cross, Mary at El Torn was not weeping for her son, but rather *to* her son for her symbolic children, the human race. Her weeping was part of her intercession.

Of all the vision messages studied here, that of El Torn is the most clerical. The morality Mary called for was that defined by canon law. But it was not restricted to payment of tithes and removal of the interdict by the bishop or his vicar. It was a general call to order to a society seriously out of order after years of plague and depopulation. Miquel Noguer was an appropriate carrier for this message; a prosperous farmer would naturally be concerned about reorganizing a disordered society; children, on the other hand, would be less susceptible to such a theme. Through Noguer, Mary called on people who had misappropriated property to restore it to its rightful owners. The dead must also be paid their dues, and their salvationary bequests fulfilled. In addition to observing Sundays and abstaining from swearing—perhaps the two most ignored religious injunctions in rural Iberia—the neighboring villages were to make weekly processions on Fridays to the shrine. As at Cubas and Monte Berico, there were instructions for fasting, and they were to punish future violations of all these injunctions.

It may be that these late fifteenth-century Catalan apparitions were part of a religious revival, not simply because of the threat of the plague, but rather because, with the worst of the plague over, the people were in a position to restore some of the fabric of religious and moral life. The critical moments of these supernatural messages came in minor outbreaks of the plague, logical times to remind people what could happen to them if they did not reform.

The vision of El Torn had much in common with El Miracle and that of Pinós, which followed. As at El Miracle, Mary was a child who warned of plague and asked for conversion. Her message resembled that of a charismatic missionary. Her appearance came on Saturday, Mary's day, at dusk, Mary's time, when the angelus was rung.

PINÓS (LLEIDA), 1507

1507 was another plague year. Throughout the southeastern half of the Iberian peninsula, the population had been physically weakened by two years of bad harvests. The area around the shrine of El Miracle was again affected, not only by the bubonic plague but also by some other epidemic, possibly malaria. Mary appeared again with instructions, this time at an isolated wayside chapel about 20 km. south of El Miracle and 170 km. southwest of El Torn. The visionary, Bernat Casas of Matamargó, made

his declaration in the parish church of Cardona the day after
the vision.[17]

Today, Thursday, September 5*, 1507, in the following
form, the following deposition was taken from Bernat
Casas of the parish of Matamargó in the parish church by
Mossen Balle of Cardona and the venerable Mossen Joan
Pinyet, representing the Reverend Lord Bishop of Urgell,
together with the honorable Jofre Martí, consul of Cardona
for this year. And first Bernat Casas was asked how or
what was the vision or apparition that is said occurred to
him, and that he tell the truth, for this was not a laughing
matter.

Bernat Casas in response said in so many words that
Wednesday, September 1, Saint Giles's day, at seven
o'clock, or between seven and eight in the morning, he left
his house to go to Biosca to see his aunt. Because the road
he took led past the Virgin Mary of Pinós, he tried to say
a prayer to her, but he could not enter because he found
the doors locked. So he took the road behind the chapel
past the water cistern to go on his way. When he was next
to the church on the north side in front of the cistern, suddenly there appeared to him with a noise like dull thunder
a woman all dressed in red, and he was very afraid.

She said to him, "Fear not, good man, where are you
going?"

He said he was on his way to Biosca to see his aunt.

She asked him where he was from.

He said from the parish of Matamargó.

She said to him, "Tell me, how are things in Cardona?"

He replied, "Señora, as for the plague, all right; no one
has died for days. But there are some fevers from which
many are dying."

She said to him, "And in the towns nearby?"

He said, "Señora, now they are beginning."

She said to him, "Good man, I order you to go to Car-

---

* error; should be September 2.

dona and tell the jurats that there was a time when they remembered this chapel, and now they have forgotten it. They should tell all the castles, that is, Ardévol, Riner, Castelltallat, and other parishes around the chapel, that among them all they should arrange for a good priest. And that they should perform the obligations due to the chapel and to the service of God as in the past, and that he will have mercy on them."

He replied, "Señora, they will not believe me."

She said, "Go, and if they do not believe you, let them be." When she had said this she disappeared suddenly, and he saw nothing more, and no one else.

Asked what lady it was and what her face looked like, he said he could not understand, and his eyes did not dare look at her face.

Asked why he called her Señora, or who he thought she was, he said that in his opinion she was the Virgin Mary.

Asked the Articles of the Catholic Faith, he repeated them as a Catholic and a Christian. He was exhorted and sworn by the reverend official in virtue of said articles that he claimed to believe to say that what he said took place in the vision was true or else his soul be condemned.

He replied that everything should be in condemnation of his soul if it was not as he declared above.

Casas assumed that the woman who appeared to him suddenly with the sound of dull thunder was the Virgin Mary. She does not appear to have been child-sized. The plague was just beginning in Matamargó, as it spread out from Cardona.

Casas's visions may well have been influenced by those of El Miracle and El Torn. Ardévol and Riner, two of the castles or hamlets mentioned, were involved in the visions of El Miracle fifty years before. Mary appeared in red, as at El Miracle.

Questors from El Torn circulated throughout Catalonia and could have carried the story of that vision to eastern Lleida. As at El Torn, there was a context of epidemics and an abandoned devotion. As at El Torn, the vision came to a man who intended to say a prayer to Mary, and Mary told him that if the shrine were revived and maintained, God would have mercy on his people. Finally, as at El Torn, no proof was given, perhaps for the same reason—the credibility of the seer combined with the imminence of epidemic.

The day of the vision, San Gil, September 1, was to some extent a Marian day, celebrated at the famous shrine of Nuria. Giles, according to legend, supposedly lived at Nuria and left the shrine image there, to be discovered miraculously by an ox and a ram centuries later. One of the major holy days there was consequently September 1; it became a major feast day at Pinós, as well, known as Apparition Day.

Two Early Modern Visions:
Reus (Tarragona), 1592, and Sant Aniol (Girona), 1618

In Catalonia, as in Castile, there were very few visions leading to the establishment of shrines from 1500 to 1900. Two early modern visions in the present-day provinces of Tarragona and Girona, however, repeated the medieval patterns.

In 1587 a woman in Bagnères in the French Pyrenees had visions of a "belle demoiselle" asking for a general procession to her shrine and warning of a plague. The seer, a widow who lived alone with her daughter, was ignored, and in 1588, five-sixths of the population supposedly died of the plague. When the townspeople finally made a vow to Mary and held a procession with the woman and her daughter in the front dressed in white, the plague ended. The town fathers paid for the dowries of both mother and daughter, and they entered the Cistercian convent of Vallbona in Catalonia, for the wars of religion had disrupted conventual life in France.[18]

Vallbona is sixty km. north of Reus, where another apparition occurred on September 25, 1592, also during a plague. Most of the town councillors had abandoned the city a month before, just as the councillors and archbishop had left Tarragona. The seer, Isabel Besora, was sixteen years old, the daughter of a weaver. She saw the Virgin while she was tending sheep (see Figure 10).

There is no authentic text for this vision. Only an oral tradition of the Virgin's message remains—that Isabel tell the town councillors that Mary was the co-redeemer of the town, and that they should light the plague candle in the church if they wanted to be free of the epidemic. The councillors did not believe Isabel, who returned to the apparition site, where Mary touched her on the cheek (like Vicenza of Monte Berico, Inés of Cubas, and Joana of Escalona), leaving a mark of a red rose.

Isabel was then believed. The town held a procession to a chapel where there was an image that looked like the vision, and lighted the plague candle, perhaps a candle the length of the town walls. The following day there was a solemn mass, during which Isabel remained on her knees with a lighted candle. At the end of the mass (as at Escalona and Navalagamella) the mark on her cheek disappeared. This is the story recorded from traditional sources at the beginning of the nineteenth century.[19] In 1657 Camós gave a shorter version in which Isabel's proof was a traditional one for apparition-findings in Catalonia, the hand stuck to the cheek.[20]

The immediately relevant pages are missing from the town council register. The first documentary evidence for the apparition is the entry in the register for December 13, 1592, when the councillors unanimously agreed to purchase the land and build a chapel "where Our Lady appeared to the girl." The chapel was completed in 1601. Today it is the main shrine for the town. The image, a standing figure of Mary with child dating from the mid-fifteenth century, had been in a private chapel before the visions.

It is impossible to know how much of the tradition is historical, and how much an amalgam of other stories. What is known for sure is that a girl had a vision in the context of a plague, and that the statue subsequently venerated was already in the city. Whether or not the story told by the new nuns at Vallbona had reached Reus, it appears that the earlier pattern still had a hold.[21]

The final vision also referred to a preexistent image and devotion, Nostra Senyora dels Arcs, Our Lady of the Arches, in the jurisdiction of the town of Santa Pau (Girona), quite close to El Torn. The declaration I translate below is that which the seer, María Torrent, gave on December 8, 1618, at the shrine and confirmed eleven years later. Narciso Camós copied it down around 1651, and since then the originals have been lost.[22] The vision occurred on All Saints Day, and draws attention to the people's anxieties about their obligations to the dead. Note that María Torrent had a promise pending to the image of Collell, the Marian image that appeared to Miquel Noguer at El Torn, 150 years before.

VISION OF MARÍA TORRENT, SANT ANIOL, NOVEMBER 1, 1618

On All Saints Day, 1618, María Torrent, wife of Juan Torrent, laborer of the parish of Sant Aniol, barony of Santa Pau, of this diocese of Girona, left her house and went to the parish of San Miguel de Lacot, in which she was born and where her parents were buried, to have responses said for their souls and for those for whom she had obligations. For this she carried six diners. When she reached the parish church she found the priest busy and did not dare to say anything to him. Hence she returned very sad. When she reached the plain of Camias, as it was already dark she commended herself very sincerely to the Virgin of the Arches, beseeching her that she see fit to protect and favor her in that which was best for the good of her soul.

In this frame of mind she proceeded, reciting the rosary, and shortly thereafter a beautiful, elegant woman dressed in white appeared to her and said, "Good woman come here; have no fear; you come from the parish church of Lacot, where you were born, and you carry six diners to have responses sung for those to whom you are obligated, and you have not been able to have them recited, and so now you will have psalms said instead."

Then the lady told her that she should not wear colored clothing, only white, for a year; that she should not swear at the children God entrusted to her care; that every day for a year she should say the rosary to Our Lady before doing anything else if it was possible and she was able to; and that she should fulfill the promises she had made to Our Lady of Collell and Our Lady of the Arches with as much diligence and as soon as she could.

And she should tell the people of Sant Aniol that they should not blaspheme or swear against God, for he was very offended; that they should take great care not to bear false witness against each other; that they should punish each other severely for their vices, and if they did not that Our Lord God would punish them most severely; and that they should cease their rivalries and malice. She should tell the people of Sant Aniol that the Mother of God of the Arches had obtained mercy and forgiveness for them from her most precious Son, and they should go in procession to her Holy Chapel, and all those who could should go barefoot, except the parish priest. At her Holy Chapel they should say three Our Fathers and three Hail Marys for the most needy soul in purgatory, and they should continue this devotion for one year, and together with it they should recite five Our Fathers and five Hail Marys for the souls in purgatory in general, and ten Our Fathers and Hail Marys in reverence of the precious blood that Our Lord Jesus Christ shed for sinners. And every morning before doing anything else they should recite the rosary, and they should do the same every evening.

After she said this she took her leave with the following words, "Good woman go, for it is very late to get home." María left, and the lady passed her, and afterwards a brilliance followed her for the entire stretch of the path that was the roughest. María Torrent saw this lady once more on a lower path, seated on a stone near the spring of Mas Faja of Sant Aniol, and said that around her was a great brilliance. Torrent later arrived trembling at the house of En Font, farmer of the parish of Sant Aniol. When she was asked what was wrong and why she trembled, she told how the Mother of God of the Arches had met her at a certain place and everything that had happened to her. The wife of Font and many other people of the house were present. Let all be for the glory of God and Most Holy Mary of the Arches.

María Torrent was upset because she could not fulfill her obligations to her dead parents. Furthermore it was dark, she was on a mountain path and afraid. As at El Torn, Mary came after being invoked, dressed in white. First Mary reassured her, telling her not to fear, then she went back with the seer over the events of the day. Psalms, Mary told her, could be substituted for the unsaid responses.

After this solution to María's immediate problem, the Virgin gave her the kind of precise instructions that very devout people who did not know how to express their devotion would be glad to have. She was to wear white for a year, like the penitential habits still worn today, usually after a promise, by village men and women in Spain. She was not to swear at the children she cared for; she should say the rosary the first thing every morning, again for a year—a kind of sacred quarantine after seeing the Virgin. And she should fulfill the promises she had outstanding to the shrines of Els Arcs and Collell.

The people of Sant Aniol were given instructions like those given the people of El Torn. They were not to blaspheme or bear false witness, and they were to cease rivalries and malice and to punish each other's vices.

The theology of the vision was much the same as at El Torn. Mary was an advocate who obtained, not God's help, but his mercy. God had two options: punishment or the withholding of punishment. Mary could stay his hand. In return the people as a corporate body had to make penitential processions to her shrine, everyone (except the priest!) barefoot, reciting Our Fathers and Hail Marys for the souls in purgatory and Christ's precious blood. The reference to purgatory is something of an innovation, one in keeping with the increased attention to purgatory in southern Europe in the seventeenth century.[23]

CATALAN AND CASTILIAN MESSAGES

With its different levels of instructions for personal problems, personal piety, community moral reform, and community piety, something like a personal and communal examination of conscience, María Torrent's vision resumed much of the content of the late medieval Catalan apparitions. All in one way or another combined piety and moral reform.

For in fifteenth-century Catalonia, with the Moors distant and heresies yet to come or long gone, the "other" was within. The "other" was the blasphemer, the false witness; the "other" was the villager who carried horses for the Moors, not the Moors themselves. The "other" was the individual villager or the entire community lax in religious duties. In some of the visions the dereliction was made specific: shrines abandoned (not surprising, given the population decline), a spring polluted, and a ceremony of propitiation neglected. The vision message was not one of aid against an external enemy, but rather a warning against the enemy within and a call for conversion. Such a warning was especially useful for communities under the perennial menace of epidemics; it served at once as an explanation for their cause and a prescription for their avoidance.

Jews were not mentioned in these visions, but the cleansing of the body religious by self-reform and conversion was like an extension to the conversion of the Jews preached by Vincent Ferrer and others as a means of purging communities of impurity. Jews were persecuted as the cause of the Black Death of 1348 in Barcelona, Cervera (near El Miracle and Pinós), Tárrega, Girona, Solsona, Tarragona, and Lleida. For Jews were another internal "other," part of the fabric of Catalan society, rather than an external enemy. Arguments for purging or conversion of Jews could be applied also to lax Christians. Indeed, Vincent Ferrer used an exemplum in which Saint Macarius spoke with a skull whose soul was in hell. That particular soul had been a pagan, and reported to Macarius that there were different levels of hell. Jews were worse off than the pagans, and Christian sinners were worst off of all, even worse than the Jews.[24]

The distinction between Castilian and Catalan visions should not be pushed too far, given the limited number of cases and the essential similarity of both to French and Italian visions. The more dire tone and the more penitential message of Catalan apparitions are consistent with differences in the relative well-being of the two regions in the fifteenth century, and in keeping with the kind of theology preached in Catalonia by Ferrer and his disciples.

Vincent Ferrer had been dead for about forty years at the time of the visions of El Miracle, but his memory was very much alive. He had preached at nearby Cervera;[25] his disciples, mainly Dominicans, were still active; and it was precisely in 1458, the year of the visions, that the bull of canonization was proclaimed. His particular appeal came from the appropriateness of the solutions he offered to a society in very grave, long-term economic and demographic straits.

In the Catalan sermons of Vincent Ferrer, there is very little emphasis on the intercession of saints or Mary. In a sermon on Saint James, for instance, he mentioned in passing James's visit to Spain, but not the shrines of Pilar or Compostela. For Vincent the saints were examples to follow rather than intermediaries with God. His sermons emphasized good behavior and penance. Christ was often compared with a king, and Ferrer's exempla proposed how one would act when dealing with the king directly, as when one received an invitation to the wedding of the king's son or when one married his daughter. There are no powerful intermediaries in these exempla. Similarly the Catalan visions, unlike those of Castile, rarely involved the simple establishment of a relation of patronage between saint and town. Instead, the beings that appeared brought instructions for moral reform and penance.

The purpose and scope of the visions were comminatory, as Vincent described in one of his sermons: "When our lord God wants to destroy a town, city, or kingdom, first he is accustomed to send a messenger to warn the people." Ferrer gave as examples Noah, Lot, Amos, Saint John the Baptist, and the Apocalypse of John.[26] The saints that appeared to Catalan seers were above all messengers of God with warnings of disaster and the means for avoiding it. Even if the messengers themselves subsequently became cult figures at shrines (as Vincent himself did), this should not distract us from their immediate function in the fifteenth century.

A convention ultimately derived from twelfth-century reinterpretations of the Book of Revelation, a progressive, linear, view of history, its logic and its future revealed in visions, became a theological and literary convention in the late Middle Ages.[27] How much the apocalyptic revelations of John served as the underlying myth or template for the Catalan and Castilian lay visions is an open question. Certainly in the earliest ones in Castile, the reference to brightness greater than the sun recalls Revelation 12. Perhaps the very notion of a divine messenger foretelling disaster was reinforced by theological attention to Revelation. Scenes from the book were commonly portrayed on Catalan church walls. In addition, Vincent Ferrer had preached the coming of the apocalypse, though not as frequently as is generally supposed, and in rather vague terms.

The messages of these by and large humble visionaries were not really apocalyptic. There had been too many plagues, too many recoveries from the plague, perhaps too much apocalyptic preaching, for any particular epidemic to be seen as a sign of the end of time. Rather than the Judgment, the plagues were simply judgments; final enough for those condemned, but not part of the final act of the grand design.

The emphasis on the observance of Catholic precepts in the Catalan visions echoed the "Heavenly Letter," which was particularly well circulated in fifteenth-century Catalonia, to judge from the surviving manuscripts in Catalan verse and prose. The Letter was supposedly written by Christ and found on an altar in Jerusalem. Its central instruction was to observe Sundays, but different versions contained allusions to usury, mutual forgiveness, and a general conversion. Much of the text described the punishments that would befall those who did not heed the Letter (or priests who do not read it from their pulpits). In the Catalan versions, there was particular emphasis on the saving intercession of Mary.[28]

The Letter apparently began in the sixth century. The earliest extant version in Spain is one from Urgell in the tenth century. A variant version was circulated by the flagellants of the thirteenth century in Germany that promised remission of sins for those who joined them. The Catalan versions do not contain this clause, but it has been speculated that the circulation of the

Letter in Catalonia nevertheless coincided with the missions of Ferrer. Certainly the missions and the Letters would be mutually reinforcing. Comminatory visions and the Heavenly Letter were, similarly, alternative ways of explaining and managing recurrent plague and famine. Unlike the Letter, however, the visions had a special immediacy in that they were keyed to a specific time and place, and the seers were members of the community being warned.

Comminatory prophecies were also included in the revelations of Saint Bridget of Sweden (d. 1373). A Spaniard, Alfonsus of Jaén, edited her writings, and another, Cardinal Juan de Torquemada, gave them a certification, which was printed as a preface in the early editions. Christ told Bridget, "I shall send my friends to such as I choose, and they shall make ready a way to God."[29] Images of chastisement in her writings included a beast that led sinners down into hell, the Lord as a terrifying giant, and the Lord plowing the earth, sparing neither old nor young, poor nor rich.[30]

Though such warnings were a minor aspect of Bridget's writings, they seemed to have a special appeal in the last quarter of the fifteenth century. In north and central Italy a number of self-proclaimed prophets distributed broadsides with warnings described as the prophecies of Saint Bridget. Dressed in the sackcloth of apocalyptic messengers, they went from town to town warning of doom and calling for repentance, and until the novelty wore off they were received as saints by the common people.[31]

I do not know if there were similar amateur prophets in Spain at the time—rough lay versions of Vincent Ferrer. But the extent to which the Church at Constance and Basel accepted the prophecies of Bridget gave the spontaneous prophets of Italy, and Savonarola as well, a certain legitimacy. This temporary climate of toleration may have had a similar effect in Spain, where the notion of God "sending his friends to such as he chose" may have eased the acceptance of the local visions.

In spite of the more prescriptive nature of the Catalan visions, and in spite of differences in vision motifs (body contortion as proof was uniquely Castilian), the visions in both Catalonia and

Castile shared the basic pattern of the shrine legends. All but one were rural and implicitly regulated the relations between society and nature. On the one hand, there was the Virgin or saint's statements; but there was also a meaning of time, place, and gesture. Whether in zones of nucleated or dispersed settlement, the visions called for people to leave their homes and their parish churches and go out to sacred spots in the countryside. In some cases new shrines were to be built, in others, old shrines were to be revived. As with the legends gathered by Narciso Camós, natural objects were specified that would aid in cures—sacred trees, springs, and stones. Animal intermediaries had mostly, but not entirely, disappeared—bees showed the sacred spot at Santa Gadea, mules and sheep at El Miracle. The visionaries were still, predominantly, males. With the single exception of Jaén, these were not visions that sorted out urban space, but rather part of a continuing process of sacralization of the countryside—effectively, the establishment of societal outposts in non-urban space.

Three generations after the visions of Cubas, the original comminatory message had been forgotten. The subtext had become the text, the location of a sacred place in the countryside the message. This may also have been true at Escalona and Navalagamella, for which we have only hearsay testimony long after the visions took place. In those places, too, there may have been a more immediate, time-bound message, which was later forgotten as irrelevant.

So there were both historical and ahistorical messages in these visions. The second, the regulation of relations with nature, transcended the times and joined the preexisting corpus of legends and subsequent miracles as a general expression of divine protection for and divine availability at a particular place.

THREE

Repression of Apparitions: The Inquisition in La Mancha

The last "successful" (officially accepted) Castilian apparition before the nineteenth century occurred to a shepherd on the outskirts of León, some time in the years 1505-1513. Only the bare facts are known. In 1513 the cathedral chapter appointed supervisors for the alms of "nuestra señora del camino, que Agora Aparescio" (who recently appeared). In 1517 a papal bull referred to ". . . a certain shepherd to whom, whether in dreams or divinely, it was revealed that on a certain public road out of the city of León, a shrine or hermitage or oratory should be built in honor of the Blessed Virgin Mary." The image was a preexisting one, which allegedly as early as the twelfth century was in the Templo del Mercado. The seer, Alvar Simón, was employed after the visions as an alms-collector.[1] The shrine is thriving today and draws pilgrims from the entire province of León and much of Asturias.

After the vision at León, we hear of no more of this kind of public lay apparition. There are only rare cases, like those of Reus (1592) and Sant Aniol (1618) in Catalonia, until the twentieth century.

There were similar visions in Italy, where between the years 1440 and 1500 apparitions started at least seven of the present-day Marian shrines with the permission of bishops or popes. But in Italy, unlike Spain, visions that founded shrines continued, with at least four or five per decade until about 1590. I do not know whether the flurry of visions in Castile and Catalonia from 1449 to 1512 occurred in other countries as well.

There was another kind of vision in Italy at the turn of the century that indirectly may have affected the Spanish situation. For a papacy threatened by schism and seeking to consolidate a temporal and territorial base for its authority, Girolamo Savonarola provided an apt demonstration of the dangers of independent revelation. Savonarola was burned at the stake. But his temporary success, and that of other, wandering prophets, showed the need for a clear statement of apostolic authority over apparitions and revelations. Hence the Fifth Lateran Council in 1516, in a session dedicated to preaching, decreed as follows:[2]

> We wish that, according to normal law, supposed apparitions before they are made public or preached to the people, should be considered from now on reserved for the examination of the Apostolic seat. If this causes undue delay, or if some urgent need counsels other action, then the matter should be brought to the local bishop. . . . He, taking with him three or four learned and serious men, will examine this kind of matter with them diligently; when it appears convenient to them, on which we charge their conscience, they may grant permission.

Whether or not they were directly influenced by the council, Spanish bishops and the Spanish Inquisition appear to have taken a more rigorous stance toward apparitions than did the Italians. In Spain, in addition to the Savonarolan tendencies in religious ecstatics such as Sor María de Santo Domingo, the Beata de Piedrahita, even simple lay visions were punished.[3] The Spanish Inquisition extended its attention from Jewish and Moslem practices to Catholic heresies and independent revelation.[4]

Two investigations of village visionaries, not religious or semi-professional beatas, but relatively normal folk like those studied above, are preserved in the archive of the Inquisition of Cuenca.[5] The visionaries lived in neighboring towns in La Mancha, Quintanar de la Orden, and La Mota del Cuervo, where the borders of the present-day provinces of Toledo, Cuenca, and Ciudad Real meet (see Map 3). The suppression of lay apparitions that their stories show did not let up until the Inquisition itself was suppressed.

Map 3. The vicinity of La Mota del Cuervo (Cuenca)

VISIONS OF JUAN DE RABE, LA MOTA DEL CUERVO (CUENCA) c. 1514, 1516

INVESTIGATION OF THE INQUISITION OF CUENCA, 1517-1518[6]

Denunciation

March 28, 1517

Madalena, wife of Diego de Pozo, inhabitant of Santa María de los Llanos, a sworn witness, said in addition to what she has already said against others that she heard Juan de Rabe,* inhabitant of the said town and sometimes of La Mota, say that many times he goes into trances and sees God and Saint Mary in paradise and the saints, angels, and archangels. And that if someone says something bad about him he knows about it later and repeats it in front of the whole town, both in La Mota and Santa María de los Llanos. And this witness recalls that Juan de Rabe said in La Mota that he had seen Our Lady riding on a little ass. And when they heard about it they held a procession from the church and carried a cross, which the priest of Santa María de los Llanos carried on his back, to the place where the shepherd said he had seen Our Lady; and that this

---

* [marginal note] this shepherd lives with Martín Sánchez and Pedro de la Calle, inhabitants of La Mota

happened more than two years ago. And that this witness went with the town in the procession.

The sister of this witness, Ysabel López, and Alonso López, neighbors of this witness, and Juan Castillo, inhabitant of the town, said the same thing under oath, and their testimony is in the [papers] of Villamayor on the second of the loose pages.

Testimony of Juan de Rabe, probably in Belmonte
February 18, 1518

Juan de Rabe, citizen of La Mota, was ordered called in by their Reverences to the hearing room, being a prisoner in the jail of this Holy Office by their order. And when he was sworn in by the Inquisitor Juan Yañes he was asked by his Reverence what his name was. He said he was Juan de Rabe, and his parents were Juan de Rabe and Ynes Rodríguez, both deceased, inhabitants and natives of Villaverde and full-blooded Old Christians. His only sister lives in La Mota. She is named María de Rabe and is married to Pedro García, *labrador*, inhabitant of La Mota.

Asked if he is married or has ever been, he said no, and that he is about fifty years old. Asked why he did not marry, he said it was because he could not find a good match. Asked what property he owned, he said he owned nothing, that he maintained himself by working, digging, plowing, and sometimes herding sheep, as he did last year. Asked where he has lived in the past few years, he said in La Mota and in Santa María de los Llanos. Asked if he knows what year it is, he said that he does not know, but that he does know it is the month of February.

He was asked by his Reverence if he knew the Credo and the Salve Regina; he said he did not. And if he knew the Pater Noster and the Ave Maria; he said he did. He was ordered to say them. He said the entire Ave Maria, and the Pater Noster he said in its entirety but he did not know it well. He was asked by his Reverence if he confessed every year as the Holy Mother Church mandates. He said that he has confessed every year at Lent with the old priest in the town of La Mota, and that every time he confessed he received the most holy sacrament.

Asked if he knows the Ten Commandments and the Articles of Faith and the seven deadly sins and the five senses, he said he did not know any of these in whole or in part.[7] Asked by his Reverence what it was he confessed, if he did not know the deadly sins or the Ten Commandments or the five senses, he said he confessed what he did know about. He was asked if pride or envy or lust or the killing of a man or insulting someone with offensive words was a sin, and to each of these he replied he did not know. He was asked if theft was a sin, and he said that, God preserve us, theft was a very great sin.

First vision, near Santa María de los Llanos, c. 1514

He was asked what things he did confess, since he did not confess any sins at all. He said that about four years ago he was on his way alone to turn over the soil in a vineyard at Santa María de los Llanos that belonged to his cousin, Francisco Martínez. He was carrying a hoe, a wineskin, and bread for his lunch. On the road he heard a loud bolt of thunder in the sky and said to himself, "God in heaven help me! The sky is clear, why does it thunder?" He said he looked toward town and heard another thunderclap, and since the sky was clear he said, "God help me! What is this about?" Then he looked down, and he said he saw next to his feet Our Lady the Virgin Mary. She seemed to him like a tiny girl, and that she was riding on a tiny burro and dressed in white.

Asked what color the burro was, he said it was very pretty but he does not know what color it was.

Asked who came with her, he said that no one else came with her.

Asked how he knew or who told him that the girl he referred to was Our Lady, he said that she herself told him so. And that she said to him, "O how many bad people there are in this town of yours who do nothing but blaspheme and foreswear my son," and that it was not enough

that men should do this, but the women did it too. And
that he should tell the whole town and the priest to take
the cross and go in procession to the holy calvary in El
Pedernoso or on the way to El Pedernoso, and that they
erect a cross where she came and appeared to this witness.

And so later he went to tell everybody about it, and
they came afterwards with a cross and put it where this
witness told them Our Lady had appeared to him. And
from there they went to the holy calvary, which may be
more than four crossbow shots from there. And afterwards
they went back in procession to the town. And that before
he went to tell the people all this she disappeared, and he
never saw her again. And that this took place on a Saturday morning, and she told him not to report it until the
afternoon, which is what he did. And the priest would not
absolve him until he said it out loud in front of everyone
in church.

Asked if Our Lady, she who he says he saw, carried a
baby in her arms, he said all he saw was that she was
seated on the little burro.

Asked if he knows if it was a little burro or a little mule,
he said he does not know, just that it seemed like a little
burro to him, and very pretty. And that on no other occasion did she appear to him. . .

Second vision, near El Toboso, c. 1516
but that another time two years later Saint Sebastian appeared to him in Los Llanos de la Casa Sola wearing a
brown garment and his arrows with blood and a crown of
gold like a star. He was about half as tall as this witness,
and he came alone. This took place in the morning before
this witness had breakfasted, when he was tending the animals of Christobal Sánchez of La Mota. And He told him
He was Saint Sebastian, and that he should go to El Toboso because at that time many people were dying of the
plague and tell them to build two chapels. One was to be
in the Cerro Espartoso, which Our Lady had ordered them
to build and which they had not seen fit to build until the

epidemic returned as they had had it before when she ordered it. The other was to be below Saint Peter, which has been started. And that he does not know to what saint except that He ordered them that the one on the Cerro Espartoso should be dedicated to Saint Roch.

Sentence

When their Reverences had seen the confession of Juan Rabe and everything else there was to see and examine, they ordered him given one hundred lashes for the wrongs that appear in his confession. They ordered that these lashes be given in public in the accustomed streets of this city, accompanied by a herald, and that afterward he return to the jail for instruction in what is necessary for the health of his soul. And when this is done that he go with God wherever he wants to. And they instructed him that henceforth he should not go around proclaiming the vanities confessed by him since they are indeed vain things and detrimental to our Holy Catholic Faith and to the souls of the simple and Catholic folk who hear them.

This sentence was given on February 17, 1518, before the witnesses Lope Suárez, alcalde, and Francisco de Oyos, doorman of the Holy Office; I Francisco Ximénez notary was present.

Juan de Rabe lived with two other shepherds and shared the fate of probably half the workers in La Mota del Cuervo, who were landless laborers moving through the year from crop to crop, working off and on as shepherds. His formal religion was like that of the earlier seers: he knew the Lord's Prayer, the Ave Maria, and little more. He had learned one important lesson for the poor—theft is a "muy grande pecato."

On the face of it he was a *pauvre type*. He had no property. No one would marry him. He did not even know what year it was. But he did have some social resources. His married sister lived nearby, and a cousin owned land planted with vines. In 1514 when he told the people of La Mota or Santa María de los Llanos (it is unclear which) in church about his vision, Juan de

Rabe was believed, believed even though he said the Virgin Mary sat on a tiny burro.

We do not know how many of the approximately 2000 people of La Mota heard him, or how many went in the procession. The priest carried a cross on his back, so he must have believed. They erected the cross on the apparition site, then visited the Holy Calvary, probably, like most of those in New Castile, set up by a brotherhood.

Devotion to the Passion of Christ had existed in these towns before Juan de Rabe's vision. Again, as in the fifteenth-century visions, devotion to the Cross was ratified by instructions from Mary. Once more Mary appeared in diminutive form, very small indeed (*chiquitina*). As in all the visions from 1449 on, she was without the Christ-child. Her association was not with the baby Jesus, as in Romanesque and Gothic images, but with the crucified Jesus.

Again, as with the other Castilian visions, the doctrinal content was minimal, well in keeping with Rabe's professed ignorance about sin. Blasphemy by women as well as men was the only vice Mary mentioned. The apparition took place, as at El Torn, on a Saturday, and was accompanied, as at Pinós, by a thunderclap.

Rabe was believed without any sign, and there is no indication that there was even an epidemic at the time to lower the town's threshold of skepticism. His success, if one can call it that, did not appear to change his material circumstances. Two years later he was still a hired shepherd. It may, however, have gone to his head. For he denounced in public those who criticized him, and that kind of behavior was unwise when his neighbors could denounce him to the Inquisition.

Rabe did not say how the town of El Toboso, another large Manchego agro-town (800 households in 1575), reacted two years later to his vision of Saint Sebastian. But the vision of Juan de Rabe provides credible evidence that visions were expected and even looked for in epidemics. According to him, before his own vision, the Virgin in another vision had already ordered the people of El Toboso to build a chapel during a previous epidemic (the great plague of 1507?). The new plague of 1516 was a punishment for their failure to fulfill her orders.

Such an explanation would not have sounded outlandish to the people of El Toboso. New Castilians in times of trouble were especially on the look-out for divine helpers; and it was normal for them to set up chapels with devotion on their side in exchange for protection on the saint's side. Unlike Catalonia there was little intromission of "higher" theology, in the nature of moral reform. Both regions, nevertheless, shared a basic explanation: the plague came because people did not fulfill their obligations to the divine, whether maintaining chapels, burning candles, or, in this case, building a promised chapel.

Again, as two years before, the saint was a miniature one, perhaps the size of the statue in a chapel to Saint Sebastian that existed in La Mota. Sebastian, of course, was the plague saint. It is interesting that Rabe's Sebastian himself introduced the relatively new devotion to Saint Roch, who would gradually come to replace Sebastian as the chief plague saint over the next two hundred years.

Were the rules changed on Rabe? Was something suddenly out of bounds that had previously been permitted? He must have been bewildered to find himself whipped through the streets for something that his home town and especially his home priest had sanctioned.

Just because they followed Mary's orders, however, does not mean that town or priest believed him. In circumstances in which going against a saint's orders could bring down the plague, it might have been safer to obey in any case. After the threat of plague had passed, some people examined his visions more critically.

Indeed, the woman who denounced Rabe had gone in the apparition procession; but later she seems to have felt he was an ominous fellow to live with. Rabe was a poor man who found himself with a strange power over his neighbors. He may have gone too far, but it may also be that the Inquisitors were more aware of visions as a problem in 1518 than they had been before the Lateran Council. Six years later in the next town to the northwest, the case of Francisca la Brava confirmed the hard line the Inquisition was taking against visionaries.

VISIONS OF FRANCISCA LA BRAVA, QUINTANAR DE LA ORDEN, 1523

Francisca la Brava was born in Corral de Caracuel (20 km. southwest of Ciudad Real, 120 km. southwest of Quintanar) about 1498. Her father, Alonso, was a shepherd; she never knew her mother. Her father brought her to Quintanar as a child (she was there at age eleven, in 1509, if not before) and eventually moved on. In Quintanar she stayed, probably as a servant, in two households, and subsequently with her uncle until she finally married. By 1523, at age twenty-five, she had had several children, at least one of which, a son, had died.

In the eyes of the town mayors, she was one of the poor. Her husband was a wool-carder who left the house before sunrise to work and returned at night. Their house had at least two rooms—a bedroom and a kitchen. The kitchen had a door giving on the outside. There was no corral (yard).

Francisca was said to be bold, frivolous, and mocking. According to the priest, however, for the seven years he had known her she had faithfully attended mass and received communion every year. She knew the basic prayers: the Ave Maria, Pater Noster, the Credo (with a few words wrong), and the Salve Regina, and at night she prayed to God, Mary, the Santa Magestad (crucifixion), and Saint Bernard to deliver her from sins. Perhaps her prayer to Bernard was due to the influence of the Cistercian Order of Calatrava in the region where she was born. She fasted about half of the days of Lent and the eves of feasts, and a few of the fast days at the beginning of each season (*temporas*). The priest considered her a "good Christian" and did not know of any history of insanity or demonic possession. She was not considered especially devout by the other village women.

Quintanar may have had 300 households, or 1300 inhabitants at this time. The chapels of the town, in addition to the parish church of Santiago, probably included Saint Sebastian, Saint Christopher, Saint Anne, and Saint Bartholomew. There were probably a number of brotherhoods, as in neighboring El Toboso.

☆

Chronology

seer: *Francisca la Brava, wife of Pedro García de la Romera*
place: *Quintanar de la Orden (Toledo)*

1) *Tuesday night, October 20, 1523, Francisca had trouble getting to sleep.*
2) *Wednesday night, October 21, Francisca had a vision of Mary, who gave her devotional instructions.*
3) *Thursday, October 22, Francisca confessed to the priest and told her neighbors.*
4) *Friday, October 23, Francisca had another vision, at daybreak, of a penitential Mary with angels. Francisca brought objects given to her by Mary to the priest; women came to visit the vision site; and the alcaldes took testimony from two town women and Francisca.*
5) *Sunday, October 25, Francisca had some kind of trance, fit, or vision outside her door.*
6) *November 21, 26, and 28, Francisca and other townspeople were questioned by the Inquisition of Cuenca in Belmonte.*
7) *November 28, Francisca was sentenced and whipped.*

Order of Testimony[8]

1. *Investigation by town officials, October 23, 1523*
   Witnesses: María Fernándes
   Juana Martínez
   Francisca la Brava
2. *Investigation by the Inquisitor Mariana in Belmonte, November 21-28, 1523*
   Witnesses: Francisca la Brava, Nov. 21
   Pedro García de la Romera, Nov. 21

Alonso Fernándes Gajardo, parish priest,
Nov. 26
Alvaro de Cepeda, alcalde ordinario,
Nov. 26
Hernand Muñoz de Horcajada, Nov. 26
Francisca la Brava, Nov. 28
Sentence, Nov. 28

INVESTIGATION BY TOWN OFFICIALS, OCTOBER 23, 1523

In the town of El Quintanar, October 23, 1523, the
señores Alvaro de Cepeda and Hernand Muñoz de Horcajada, alcaldes ordinarios in the town, because they heard
that Francisca la Brava, wife of Pedro García de la Romera,
inhabitant of this town, said and was saying that Our Lady
the Virgin Mary appeared to her, heard in their official capacity the following testimony.

María Fernándes

On this day the señores alcaldes received a legal oath
from María Fernándes, wife of Juan Muños. When asked
what she knows or heard from Francisca la Brava, wife of
Pedro García de la Romera, the witness said that yesterday,
Thursday, at the sweet water well, she ran into the wife of
Pedro Garrydo, who said they should go into Juana
Martínez's house to see Francisca la Brava and ask her to
tell them how she had seen Our Lady. And this witness
said, "[?] Our Lady!" and was surprised. And not really
believing it or planning to ask her anything, she went into
Juana Martínez's house to see if she could use her oven for
baking. There she saw Francisca la Brava.

When Juana Martínez saw this witness, she said, "Come
on in, wife of Juan Muños, and coax Francisca la Brava to
tell you how she saw Our Lady." And when the witness
heard this she was so happy that tears fell from her eyes.
And then she thought about it and was surprised, saying to
herself, "May Our Lady bless me, how is it that in this
town there are so many devout people who do nothing but

pray, especially the wife of Pedro Ortyz and the wife of Villoslada, and She does not appear to them, yet She appears to this woman?" And with this in mind she said to Francisca la Brava, "Blessed are you if that is what you saw."

And then Francisca la Brava said to her, "It is true that I saw Her, and it happened in this way;" she got out of bed to urinate, and as it was at night and dark she could not find the door, and so she said, "Help me Our Lady" and "Why can't I find this door?" And that Our Lady replied saying, "She is helping you," and "I am Our Lady who sustains you on the face of the earth." And that She put Her arm on Francisca la Brava's neck, and as she was naked, Our Lady put the skirt of Her dress over Francisca la Brava's belly and said, "Do not fear, daughter."

And Francisca la Brava said to her, "Protect me, Our Lady, if it is a devil who has come to deceive me," and She repeated, "Do not fear, for I am Our Lady." And Francisca also told her that She had returned last night, toward morning, and that Francisca said to Her, "Mother of God, they will not believe that it is you, even though I say I have seen you." And Our Lady told her, "Then take this candle and a piece of silk and a magnet." And Francisca la Brava said she had seen all this, and all this had happened. And it is true by the oath this witness took that she heard Francisca la Brava say all this.

[signed] Alvaro de Cepeda, alcalde

Juana Martínez

On the same day, the señores alcaldes received a legal oath from Juana Martínez, wife of Francisco Sánchez Palomares, who was asked under oath what she knew about the present matter. She said that yesterday morning Francisca came to the witness's house, said she was on her way to mass, and asked for a stub of candle. The witness asked her why, and she said she wanted to confess. Francisca went to mass and on her way back she came to this witness's house. As soon as this witness saw her she said, "What's wrong, Francisca, what do you have to confess?"

Francisca told her, "I did not tell you this morning, but I will tell you now," and said that when she was in bed with her husband on Wednesday night she awoke wanting to urinate and got up and tried to open the door to see what kind of a night it was. But because the house was very dark she could not find the door and said, "Help me Our Lady," and that a voice responded, "She is helping you." As soon as Francisca heard these words she thought of calling her husband, but She who had said to her, "She is helping you," said, "Hush, do not wake him up. Do not fear for I am Our Lady who has come to visit you. Remember the day you punished your child and told him, 'Help me Our Lady,' and 'What is this, can't you be still?' " Francisca was very frightened when she heard this and said, "Blessed am I if it is true that Our Lady has come to see me." And She spoke again, saying, "Then do not fear, for I am Our Lady." Francisca said, "What if it is a devil who has come to deceive me?" And She replied that She really was Our Lady, and told her to have three masses said for her dead, to collect alms three Sundays for Our Lady of the Piedad and another three for Our Lady of Guadalupe, and to have seven masses said to the Exile of Our Lady. And She also said that She would return Thursday night. And Francisca told her today, Friday, that She had come last night when it was already daylight and gave her a wax candle and a magnet to show so they would believe her. On her oath this witness heard Francisca la Brava say everything above.

[signed] Alvaro de Cepeda, alcalde

Francisca la Brava

Confession

On this same day the señores alcaldes went to the house of Pedro García de la Romera, where they found Francisca la Brava his wife, and received her oath according to law. Under this oath the señores alcaldes ordered and asked her if it is true that she said and made known that she had seen Our Lady last Wednesday and Thursday nights.

She said on her oath that it is true she saw Our Lady,
and she told and made it known to many inhabitants of
this town. And that it was certainly Our Lady she saw, because if it were something else it would not have come as
it did. And that what she saw happened in the following
way. Last Tuesday night, the twentieth of October, when
they were by the hearth, her husband Pedro García wanted
to go to bed. She did not want to retire so soon, but her
husband said, "Let's go to bed because I have to get up
early to work carding wool," and he went to bed first. She
too went to bed, but could not sleep the whole night
because a sorrow came to her heart, although in her face
and body she did not feel bad, but rather healthy.
Sleepless from the sorrow in her heart, she prayed to Our
Lady the Virgin Mary to guide her in what was best for
the salvation of her soul to a completely sound mind, and
shortly after this she fell asleep.

The next night, Wednesday, she went to bed without
thinking about what had happened, and the same sorrow
and pain came to her as the night before. She asked Our
Lady, since she was so sad without knowing why, to guide
her and tell her what was the cause of the great sorrow she
felt in her heart, and when she was praying she fell asleep.

She said she awoke around midnight next to her husband and got up without knowing if she was in control of
her senses to urinate, completely naked except for a coif on
her head. And it was like she was in a trance, and she did
not know or think that she was in this world, but rather
the other. She tried to reach the door of her kitchen to
open it, but she was so befuddled she could not find it.
When she got to the door she was finally in her right
mind, and as she was opening it she said, "Help me Our
Lady, either I am not in control of my mind, or I am
batty." When she had said these words Our Lady replied,
"She is helping you." And she said once more, "Help me
Our Lady." And Our Lady said once more, "She is helping
you." And this witness when she heard this she said,
"Help me Our Lady, get back Satan, you are a devil come

to deceive me." And that She said, "I am she who will
protect you on the face of the earth, you and every Christian."

At this point the witness went to call her husband and
said, "Pe . . ." to call him, but could not finish saying it.
And Our Lady told her, "Daughter do not worry; do not
frighten your husband." And She came to the witness and
put Her cape over her belly because she was naked, then
told her to go and confess and receive communion before
telling anyone else. And she was to have three masses said,
one for her mother, another for her father-in-law, and another for her mother-in-law. And She said they should
hold a procession to a cross chosen by the Captain of the
Sinners and the town authorities, and they should an-
nounce in town that everyone had to go, and those who
did not go should be arrested so they would take seriously
the procession in progress. After the procession they
should go to Our Lady of the Piedad and say mass there,
and everyone commend himself to Her. Everything said
above was what Francisca experienced Wednesday night.

She also said that today, Friday, a little before dawn
when she was in bed alone, she felt the same sorrow as
before. And she prayed to Our Lady to reveal the source of
the sorrow and guide her to her senses, and she got up and
signed and crossed herself and opened the kitchen door.
When she opened it she saw Our Lady by the door with a
great company of angels. And she was so joyful and
pleased to see so many angels with so many lighted candles
that she fell to the ground in awe. And Our Lady told her
that for more than thirty days She had wandered outside
of Her blessed house praying to Her precious son to send
us health for our bodies and salvation for our souls. And
then Francisca said, "O mother my mother, they will not
believe me." Then She gave Francisca a candle wrapped in
a cloth and a magnet, all of which she gave to the priest of
the town. Then She disappeared.

This witness went at once to one of her neighbors, the
wife of Fernando Ximeno, and called, "Friend, come out

here." She replied, "Come on in." And she repeated, "Come out here at once, I do not want to come in." And the neighbor came out to her. This witness saw Our Lady again and pointed to Her, saying, "Look at Her there!" "I can't see her." Her neighbor could not see Her, but her neighbor's small son did. And Our Lady disappeared and went away. She said that all this is what truly happened and what she saw and is true by the oath she took.

[signed] Alvaro de Cepeda, alcalde

INVESTIGATION BY THE INQUISITION OF CUENCA IN BELMONTE

Francisca la Brava, First Interrogation

In the city of Belmonte, November 21, 1523, before the Reverend señor Licenciado Mariana, Inquisitor, and in presence of me, Pedro de Uranga, notary, appeared Francisca la Brava, wife of Pedro García de la Romera, inhabitant of El Quintanar, who was cited and called by order of his Reverence. When his Reverence appeared he received from her an oath in the prescribed legal manner on the sign of the cross and the holy gospels, under which she promised to tell the truth. His Reverence had me read the confession she made before the alcaldes of El Quintanar in which she said that Our Lady had appeared to her. And when the confession as given above was read to her word for word, Francisca said it was true as she had declared it and as it was read, and that she confirmed and ratified it, and that nothing else happened, by the oath that she took.

When asked, she said her father was named Alonso Bravo, but she does not know whether he is alive or dead, she does not know her mother's name because she never knew her, her father when he lived in El Quintanar was a shepherd, and she is a pure-blooded Old Christian. She said she was born in El Corral de Caracuel, and has lived since she was very young in El Quintanar, where she still lives. She lived with Alonso López de Horcajada and then with Antón de la Mota for a year, and afterwards was with Pedro Bravo her uncle, until she was betrothed and wedded to her husband. She is twenty-five years old.

She was asked if this Lent she confessed and received communion, and with whom. She said yes, that the parish priest of El Quintanar, Gallardo [sic], received her confession and gave her communion.

She was asked if she regularly hears mass on Sundays and Holy days. She said yes, except for some times when she does not go because of her children or bad weather.

She was asked about Christian doctrine. She said the Ave Maria and the Pater Noster and the Credo, in which she got a few words wrong, and the Salve Regina, and she signed and crossed herself. She did not know the Anima Christo or any other prayers, except that when she goes to bed she says the following prayer: "I pray to God the Father and to Saint Mary Mother and to the Holy Majesty (*Santa Magestad*) and to the flower [?] that is in it and to Saint Bernard, who is buried in Rome, to free and protect me from all sins made in compact and yet to be compacted, that I not be accused in life or deceived in death. I commend myself to that most sacred Virgin and blessed Mother of God." She knows no other devotions, and fasts half of Lent and the eves of feasts and some of the *temporas*.

She was asked at what time of day or night Our Lady appeared to her, and in what form, on the first occasion. She said that She appeared to her for the first time four weeks ago on a Wednesday about midnight after the roosters had crowed. And She appeared to her as a woman covered with a white mantle and white coifs, and she did not see the skirts She was wearing.

She was asked what size and what color She was, and if when She spoke She was standing or seated, and who accompanied Her. She said Our Lady was small and had a dark complexion, and when She spoke to her She was standing, and that the first time She was unaccompanied, and that as soon as She spoke there was a great brightness and splendour.

She was asked what She who she calls Our Lady said, and what she replied, and if she was frightened, and that she declare everything that happened. She said Our Lady said what she reported in her confession to the alcaldes. And that at first she was afraid.

She was asked if when she went back to bed she woke up her husband and told him what happened, or whom she told first. She said she did not wake up her husband or tell him, and the first person she told was the priest when she confessed.

She was asked when she told the priest. She said she told him Thursday, the next day, when she confessed and received communion and told him that the previous night she had seen Our Lady.

She was asked if at the time she says Our Lady appeared to her there was any noise or it was dark or light, and if she was asleep or half-asleep. She said that she heard no noise, that it was bright as day, that she was awake not asleep, and that her house has no yard.

She was asked if previously she used to get up in the night to urinate or do anything else. She said not unless she is pregnant.

She was asked if when she got up in the night when she was pregnant she left her bedroom to urinate. She said no, because in the room she has a pot to urinate in, and that night after she urinated she went out and opened the door and stood in the doorway to see what the weather was like.

She was asked if she went out in the street and if She who she says was Our Lady entered her house and room and embraced her or kissed her or knocked her to the floor or whatever. She said she did not go out in the street, just to the threshold, and Our Lady came up to her at the threshold but did not go inside. And She put her arm on her neck, and knocked off her coif, but that She did not knock her to the floor. And She told her to confess and receive communion and have three masses said. And that they should hold the procession she has told about already and say the mass after the procession, as she declared in her confession.

She was asked how long they were together. She said they were together for a very short time, less than an hour, she cannot say exactly except that it was a short time, and this witness did not speak.

She was asked what She who she calls Our Lady said or did as She left. She said that after all she declared in her confession took place, She disappeared. She told her husband nothing of this because Our Lady did not let her tell anyone, but rather sent her to confess and receive communion.

She was asked what was the size and stature of She whom she calls Our Lady, and if She came barelegged or what stockings and clothes She wore. She said Our Lady appeared in the size of a four year old, and that She wore a cape white as paper and white coifs. She did not see what clothes Our Lady wore or if She wore stockings or came barelegged, nor did she see a crown, just Her white coifs. She did not have time to notice.

She was asked if She smelled good or what scent She bore with Her, and if the brightness she mentioned could have come from the moon. She said that she did not have occasion to smell Her scents, and the brightness was not the moon, but rather She brought it with Her. She does not know what the coifs were made of, just that they were white.

She was asked if when these alleged events took place she was asleep, or in a trance, or half-asleep, or awake and in control of herself and her judgment. She said she was awake and as in control of herself and her judgment as she is now, not asleep, dozing, or in a trance; she well recalls everything she has talked about. The second time Our Lady appeared to her, as mentioned in her confession, was near dawn on Friday and She was surrounded by angels.

Asked how Our Lady appeared to her then, and what clothes and other things she wore, she said that she has already answered this in her confession, and that she says the same now. And She asked her if she had ordered the things done that She had said. This confessant replied that she had, but that they did not believe her. And when Our Lady was leaving, this confessant said, "Ay, my mother, they will not believe me," and then Our Lady gave her a candle and a magnet wrapped in an embroidered cloth, and told her, "This is so they will believe you." And then She disappeared and never appeared again. And later this confessant gave the candle and magnet to the priest, and the priest took it and put it in his breast.

She was asked what the angels were like that she says came with Our Lady—if they were big or small, what clothes they wore, if they carried musical instruments, candles, or torches, and if they wore wings. And if they were on the ground and walked or in the air, if they were singing, what clothes they wore, and if they spoke at all. She said she did not notice what they were like, except that they accompanied Our Lady when she went up into heaven. They were small, and she did not see if they wore clothes or stockings, but they did not wear wings or carry instruments or candles, nor did they sing. She only saw them when Our Lady went up into heaven, and she cannot declare anything else about them. This second time her husband was not in the house, for he had already gone to work.

At which I the aforementioned notary was present.

Inquisition. Pedro García de la Romera

In Belmonte November 21, 1523, before the Reverend señor Licenciado Mariana, Inquisitor.

Pedro García de la Romera, carder in the town of El Quintanar, was sworn in and questioned. He said it is true that he is the husband of Francisca la Brava, and that he is married and veiled with her according to law and benediction.

He was asked if he knows that his wife said that Our Lady appeared to her and how and in what way and how many times and where, and that he declare everything about this he has seen and heard said.

He said that little more than a month ago, on a Thursday or Friday before dawn, when he was dressing to go to work at his trade and Francisca his wife was in bed, she began speaking, "You have had much good in your house, Pedro García." And he asked her why. She told him she had gotten up that night and gone to the door to urinate, and as she opened the door she said, "Help me Our Lady." And Our Lady had responded, "This one is helping you." And she told him she was naked and Our Lady had covered her with Her mantle, and that she did not know whether or not she was in control of her senses. And this witness told her not to tell anything about these things, and went off to work. This was the first time that his wife said Our Lady appeared to her.

On a later day in the evening, his wife told the witness that Our Lady had appeared to her once more. When Our Lady was leaving his wife had complained that she would not be believed, and Our Lady had given her a candle and a stone. She had seen Our Lady come as white as a dove, Her knees running with blood, and that She had not entered Her house for many days, praying to Our Lord for sinners. Our Lady had ordered her to say three masses and that processions should be held. And with Our Lady came many angels, all dressed in white. His wife also said that as she was going out the door, Our Lady had put Her arm on her neck, and that she had kissed Our Lady's hand. And this witness told her not to say anything about it.

He also said that in that period Andrés Fernándes, *labrador*, inhabitant of El Quintanar, came to this witness and told him to punish his wife, because [he or she] could get into trouble, as she was going around saying that Our Lady had appeared to her with drums and trumpets. Juan Pintado, inhabitant of El Quintanar, said the same thing to him.

He also said his wife Francisca told him Our Lady when She appeared had said she should ask for offerings with the basin in church seven Sundays for Our Lady of Guadalupe. And that on the first night his wife told him about, he did not hear her get out of bed or get back in.

Inquisition. Alonso Fernándes Gajardo, priest

Belmonte, November 26

Alonso Fernándes Gajardo, parish priest of the town of
El Quintanar, a sworn witness, was asked if he knows
Francisca la Brava, wife of Pedro García de la Romera, inhabitant of El Quintanar, and that he declare what he
knows about what Francisca said about Our Lady appearing
to her.

He said that he has known Francisca la Brava for six or
seven years by sight, speech, and conversation. What he
knows about this matter is that about a month ago, more
or less, Francisca came to his house when he was praying
and told him that she was lucky or blessed that Our Lady
should appear to a sinful woman like her. And this witness
said to her, "Didn't I tell you yesterday that you should
shut your mouth and not repeat these things, for it is
probably the devil trying to deceive you?" And then Francisca said to this witness, "Well, Señor, Our Lady really
did appear to me; look at what she gave me." And she
showed and gave him a little candle and a piece of black
stone wrapped in a small cloth which had been embroidered a little. [The priest] then gave these things to his
Reverence. When the witness took them from Francisca he
again reprimanded her and told her to repeat nothing of
this, for it was probably the devil deceiving her. And so
she went away.

And three or four days later on a Sunday morning,
Pedro García, husband of Francisca, came to this witness's
house and said to him, "Señor, for the love of God go to
my house, for my wife has gone out and is seated in the
doorway with her hands locked together and will not
speak, and we cannot get her to go back inside."

So this witness got out of bed and went there and had
Francisca put back in the house and unlocked her hands;
and all this time she did not speak. And he gave her many
examples from the holy scripture telling her what appeared
to her must have been the devil, and when he was leaving

he told her to commend herself to Our Lady and She
would help her. And Francisca replied, "She does help me,
and to Her I commend myself." And so this witness left.
There were several women present. Since then he has not
spoken to her. He has heard many things that they say
Francisca has said, but this witness knows nothing else.

He was asked if Francisca is a full-blooded Old Christian.
He said that as far as he knows and has heard, she is.

He was asked if Francisca goes to mass every Sunday
and the obligatory feasts and other days, confesses and re-
ceives communion when the Church ordains, does the
other things a good Christian should, and has a good repu-
tation for them. He said that he regularly sees her go
many Sundays and other days to mass, and he has confessed her every year for the past seven years without fail,
and she is regarded as a good Christian and has a good rep-
utation for it.

He was asked if he knows that Francisca is sane, and if
she has ever been possessed by the devil or under suspicion
of it. He said that as far as he knows Francisca is sane and
has not been possessed by the devil.

He was asked if he believed that Our Lady appeared to
Francisca. He said no, on the contrary, that he reproved
her for what she said because he thought of it as frivolousness (*liviandad*).

He was asked if he knows or has heard why Francisca
made it known that Our Lady appeared to her. He said he
does not know, but he has wondered if she dreamed it, or
whether the devil deceived her.

He was asked why if, as he says, he considered it frivolousness, did he not come and denounce it to his Reverence, since the examination of this pertains to the jurisdiction of this Holy Office, for as parish priest he had a
special obligation. He said that he well sees that he was
obliged to denounce it, but since he was and is sick he put
off coming to say it.

He was asked if before all this occurred he heard the
Letter of Edict read in the church of El Quintanar, or knew

it was read. He said that he heard the letter read with all of its censures from beginning to end.

He was told that since he knew that this matter pertained to the jurisdiction of this Holy Office and he heard the Letter of Edict, why did he not denounce it or send notice of it by one means or another, especially since he was the parish priest and pastor of the town. He said he wrote his Reverence telling him about this matter and gave the letter to the parish priest of El Toboso to deliver.

He was asked if it was well-known in the town of El Quintanar and the surrounding area that Francisca had said and made public that Our Lady appeared to her. He said yes, for it was known in the entire town and the surrounding area.

Inquisition. Alvaro de Cepeda, alcalde

In Belmonte, November 26, 1523, before the señor Licenciado Mariana, Inquisitor, appeared Alvaro de Cepeda, alcalde and inhabitant of El Quintanar, who was called by a summons, from whom his Reverence received an oath in the proper form. He asked him under oath if he knew Francisca la Brava, inhabitant of El Quintanar, and for how long. He said he has known her by sight and conversation for the past twelve years.

He was asked to declare what he knows and has heard about what Francisca has said or made public about Our Lady appearing to her. He said that as alcalde of the town of El Quintanar he received testimony about it and Francisca's confession, all of which was ordered brought before his Reverence. This witness refers to it because he does not know anything else. And he said he heard that many women kissed and embraced Francisca la Brava and carried off pebbles and dirt from her house from where she said Our Lady sat down. This witness saw some women go to her house and heard that many others from the town of El Quintanar and other towns including El Toboso had gone and were still going to hear Francisca tell how Our Lady appeared to her and the rest of her story. He said this is well known in the town and the district.

He was asked if he knows or has heard what moved
Francisca to recount and spread the above story. He said he
does not know what moved her, and this witness considers
it frivolousness and falseness and a lie that Our Lady appeared to her. He believes that if anything appeared to her
it was the devil.

He was asked if he knows whether Francisca is an Old
Christian, and if she is known as a good Christian in her
conduct. He said he knows on her father's side that she is
an Old Christian, and on her mother's side he does not
know, nor does he know about the confessant. He has
heard it said that she well knows how to use obscenities [or
artful insults—*bien sabe echar pullas*].

He was asked why, since he held what Francisca made
public to be falseness and a lie, and he sees that it was to
the detriment of our holy Catholic faith and the diminu-
tion of its authority, and the examination of it pertained to
the jurisdiction of this Holy Office, did he not, as alcalde,
denounce it and remit it to his Reverence. He said that it is
true that this witness and his colleague, as alcaldes of El
Quintanar, seeing that the aforesaid was public knowledge,
received testimony about it, as he mentioned. And they
sent it to Licenciado Lillo of Ocaña for his opinion. The licenciado replied that they should not follow up on the
matter, but simply intimidate Francisca into not saying
anything about it. He did not give this opinion in writing,
but rather verbally by way of the *procurador* of this confessant, Pedro de Billanueva, with whom they had sent the
testimony. If he had sent them word that it was something
that pertained to this Holy Office, this witness would have
denounced it and forwarded it to this Holy Office. If by
inadvertence or neglect he has fallen into any excommuni-
cation or penalty he asks for mercy and absolution.

Inquisition. Hernand Muñoz de Horcajada

In the same city on the same day Hernand Muñoz de
Horcajada, alcalde of El Quintanar, appeared before the
señor Inquisitor. When he had sworn in in the prescribed
manner and was asked about the above matter, he said that

he does not know anything more about Francisca la Brava
than what is contained in the testimony that this witness
and Cepeda, as alcaldes of El Quintanar, received about it.
Except that he has heard many women went to the house
of Francisca to hear her tell how Our Lady appeared to her,
and that they kissed her mouth, eyes, and ears, and that
they carried from her house stones and dirt from the place
where they said Our Lady had appeared. This witness
thought badly of what they said Francisca said, because he
thought it was a trick (*burla*) and not certain or true.

This witness has known Francisca by sight, speech, and
conversation for the last fourteen years, and he considers
her an Old Christian and a woman sane, not crazy, although a little loose-mannered, frivolous, mocking, and ir-
reverent. He does not know what moved her to say the
above. And she is poor.

He was asked why, since he considered the above matter
a falsehood, did he not send it on to his Reverence, since
he saw that the knowledge of it pertains to this Holy Office. He said that they sent the testimony to a lawyer, who
sent them word not to worry about it, but just to tell the
woman not to say anything more about it. And had he
told them to remit it to the Holy Office they would have.
If by neglect he incurred any penalty or sentence of ex-
communication he asks for penance and absolution.

Inquisition. Francisca la Brava, Second Interrogation

In the town of Belmonte, November 28, 1523, the Reverend señor Licenciado Mariana, Inquisitor, in the presence
of me, the notary, ordered Francisca la Brava to appear before him. When she appeared, his Reverence asked her under oath if after she made it known that Our Lady appeared to her many people gathered at her house and
kissed her eyes and mouth and other parts of her body,
saying, "Blessed be the eyes that have seen Our Lady."
And if they carried off stones and dirt from the place this
witness said Our Lady had appeared.

She said many women came to her house one day,

which was Friday, five weeks from yesterday, and that Miguel Tgrado [?] also came. And the wife of Juan de Billanueba put her face up to this confessant's face and said, "Blessed be the face that has seen such a thing." No one else kissed her. It is true that the women carried off pieces of the stone on which this confessant said Our Lady appeared to her, which was next to the doorway of her house. They also brought a child of Alonso de Yepes who had an intermittent fever (*çiçiones*) and had him kiss the rock, and later he was cured. This confessant said she saw a son of hers who had died, now an angel, among the angels that came with Our Lady.

She was asked if when she first gave notice of this to Alonso Fernándes Gajardo, parish priest of El Quintanar, he ordered her to keep quiet and tell no one anything about it, because it was a matter of frivolousness and trickery. She said it is true that the priest told her to keep quiet and say nothing; that if it was Our Lady that he would pray that She return to her. This was the first time. After this she told several people about it, but before she confessed with the priest she told no one.

The candle and the stone and the slightly embroidered cloth that she says Our Lady gave to her were shown to her to identify. She said it is true that Our Lady gave her the candle, stone, and cloth, and she identified them as the same that were shown to her.

She was asked why, since her assertion that Our Lady appeared to her is a notorious falsehood, has she said, made public, and affirmed this and the other things in her confession. She said that what she has said is true, and she will always hold in her heart that She who appeared was Our Lady.

She was read word for word the entire deposition that her husband, Pedro García made on the twenty-first of this month before his Reverence, and she was asked if what he said was true. She said everything her husband said was true; that she told him, and that she told it to him as he says.

She was asked why, since she said she did not know whether or not Our Lady was wearing stockings, her husband said She had blood running from Her knees, and why she wanted to perjure herself. She said the first time she saw Our Lady she does not know if She came with or without stockings. And that the second time she did see blood running from Her knees and Her face, and it was then She told her that for over thirty days She had not entered Her house, praying to Our Lord for the health of our bodies and the salvation of our souls.

All of her confessions were read to her again, word for word, and the variations and contradictions were pointed out to her, how in many things she contradicts and perjures herself. Therefore his Reverence said that he admonished her in the name of God Our Lord and his blessed Mother Our Lady the Virgin Mary that she tell the truth and not perjure herself or condemn her soul, and that she declare what moved her to make known that Our Lady appeared to her, since it was patently a lie. Were she to do this and tell the truth, he would have mercy on her. And if she did not, he would order that justice be done to her, and she would be punished according to the law. She said that she says what she said before.

And then his Reverence ordered Pedro García de la Romera to appear before him together with his wife, and he asked them whether she wishes to conclude her confessions so that this matter can be settled, or whether they want to continue with his justice; that it is up to them. Then Francisca la Brava with the counsel and opinion of her husband said that she was done with her confessions and does not want to say anything more, for they do not want a trial.

At which I was present, Pedro Uranga, notary.

Inquisition. Sentence

We the Inquisitors of the Diocese of Cuenca have officially examined the present investigation and the confessions of Francisca la Brava and the testimony of witnesses against her. It is evident from everything that Francisca is much at fault for having seriously offended against our holy Catholic faith by publicly affirming that Our Lady appeared to her twice, in the manner and form that she states in her confessions, when it is all trickery and falsehood as is obvious from what she said in her confessions and the earlier investigation. In addition she has clearly perjured herself in many of these matters. By rights we could have treated her more rigorously, for the above matter was very public and scandalous for the Christian faithful, since she attracted them and induced them to believe in what she said and made known, when it was all vanity and frivolity. But in deference to certain just reasons that move us to mitigate the rigor of the sentence we decree as a punishment to Francisca la Brava and an example to others not to attempt similar things that we condemn her to be put on an ass and given one hundred lashes in public through the accustomed streets of Belmonte naked from the waist up, and the same number in the town of El Quintanar in the same manner. And that from now on she not say or affirm in public or secretly by word or insinuation the things she said in her confessions or else she will be prosecuted as an impenitent and one who does not believe in or agree with what is in our holy Catholic faith. And thus we pronounce and order it by our sentence and our signatures.

I, Licenciado [illegible]

Execution

On the same day I the notary at once notified Francisca la Brava of the sentence in person, and it was executed on her as to the first set of lashes. The witnesses were those above and I the aforementioned notary.

When Juan de Rabe was denounced, it was almost incidentally among other denunciations more than two years after his vision took place. The woman who denounced him had denounced others. Was she one of the persons whom Juan de Rabe exposed as talking badly about him? And in that accusation—that he knew what people were saying behind his back—was there a hint of occult powers that might come from the devil?

The denunciation of Francisca, six years later, was not based on a grudge. Rather it came in spite of an unsuccessful series of efforts on the part of her husband, the priest, the village authorities, her husband's friends, and outside consultants to *avoid* denunciation to the Inquisition. For by 1523, with the clear precedent of Juan de Rabe from the next town, the men were well aware of the danger Francisca faced. They all knew one thing; it did not matter what she saw as long as she did not make it public. She should simply be quiet.

What were her options? Francisca had a sorrow in her heart that did not allow her to sleep. One is reminded of the nocturnal premonitions of the seer of Jaén in 1430. Could her unease have anything to do with a dead son, the one who appeared with the angels? In the first vision Francisca was worried Mary might really be the devil. Mary's proof was that she remembered something that might have been bothering Francisca—her punishment of her son, and her invocation of Mary. For the incident to be significant to Francisca, it must have been serious, not just one of the many times she must have been angry at him. Perhaps it was when he was sick or injured, crying for a serious reason, perhaps before he died.

From what her husband said, she was not sure when she awoke whether it had all been a dream or not. She must have convinced herself it was true, however, for she went to confess. She did not fully convince the priest it had not been the devil. His attitude was standard, common today among priests. He warned her to keep quiet, but he left open the possibility the vision was true. He needed proof. So there was a prototypical return vision, one in which proof was delivered. Unfortunately the proof, objects not particularly difficult to obtain, convinced no one.

Francisca could not or would not keep the secret. Women friends and neighbors, not knowing whether to believe her or not, gathered in a neighbor's house. Some would testify in the investigation.

In his testimony to the Inquisition, the priest reported a final trance on Sunday, two days after the mayors drew up their report. Francisca would not speak or enter her house, and her hands were locked together. Was this a hysterical reaction to the authorities' disbelief? Or was it rather a last attempt, a resort to the traditional proofs of body contortions—hands together (like Inés's joined fingers at Cubas) and mouth closed (as with Joana at Escalona). If these were attempted proofs they too failed, for the priest was able to open her hands and get her to talk. The traditional patterns are as clear, perhaps more clear, in these failed visions, than in "successful" visions.

Only one of the village men mentioned in the testimony believed Francisca. Can we trust the mayors when they describe their disbelief to the Inquisitors? Is it not possible that theirs was the kind of investigation that might end up as a founding document for a shrine or devotion, depending on what the experts would say? Apparently not. For on the original document the word "confession" was written in the margin by Francisca's name. Furthermore, the kind of misgivings expressed by the first witness, María Fernándes—the internal reservations she described as she cautiously congratulated Francisca, seem to be those of someone who knows she speaks to skeptics.

Women, on the whole, did seem to believe. Many gathered at Francisca's house, making it a kind of pilgrimage site. Some came from El Toboso, the town where Juan de Rabe went seven years before when he had a vision of Saint Sebastian.[9] Why did the women believe when the men did not? It was not simply that women were more likely to believe another woman. Also important was doubtless the woman's informal role as the devotional representative of the household. Day to day religion was (and in Spain still is) woman's business—seeking out sources of divine power, getting that dirt and those chips of stone, taking the boy to kiss the rock, just in case. Total belief was not necessary. Probably the women would have gone even if there was only a slight chance that it was true. For it would be a slight chance of a very important event, the visit of the Mother of God to El Quintanar with precise devotional instructions not only for Francisca, but also for the whole town.

These instructions came from a Mary whose face and knees

were streaming with blood, who was exhausted from over thirty days of praying outdoors, like a weary pilgrim passing through the town on the way to Our Lady of Guadalupe, doing penance on her knees. Surely she must have looked to Francisca like the image of Our Lady of Piedad that is today and was probably then the most respected image in Quintanar. Our Lady of Piedad was one of the shrines Francisca was to beg for, and the final destination of the penitential procession.

Our Lady said she was praying for the health of bodies and the salvation of souls. That kind of intercession was what was keeping places such as Quintanar from the epidemics not only of plague but also of other diseases that periodically ravaged the area. In 1544 the next village to the west, La Puebla de Almoradiel, would be ravaged by a disease that would strike about half of its population and kill 200 children and 50 adults. It had also been hit by the great plague of 1507, as in all probability had all of these towns. Another epidemic occurred in 1516. Even the small possibility of help, therefore, could not be ignored.

In the second vision, Francisca found out about her dead son. He was an angel. She could not say the same for her mother, whom she never knew, or the parents of her husband. They were all evidently in purgatory, for she was told to have a mass said for each. As the family representative to the divine, she was responsible for her husband's, as well as her own, dead.

Seeing Mary, Francisca was also seeing her mother. "Madre mía madre," she cried out when she finally believed. It must have meant more than just a symbolic motherhood for this young woman who had never known her own mother to have Mary call her "daughter."

Was Francisca's evident preoccupation with her dead son connected with the apparition of the Mother saint as a child of four? She had Mary appear as a child, but she also had Mary put her arm on her neck. Mary was both tall and short, mother and child, the kind of paradox dreams are filled with. Ease in imagining children as angels or saints may facilitate a reverse transformation, the imagination of saints as children.

Not surprisingly, Francisca saw things others had also seen. One of the models for her story was probably the Descent of the Virgin to Saint Ildefonsus in Toledo. The piece of cloth Francisca received could be a vestigial equivalent of the chasuble given to Ildefonsus. As at Toledo, a stone was consecrated by the Virgin's presence. Mary as a child, or at least child-sized, praying for humanity was reminiscent of the vision of El Torn. At both places the Virgin mentioned obligations to the dead, a theme taken up again a century later at Sant Aniol. This vision contained, like that of Cubas, a reference to Guadalupe, destined to remain the dominant shrine of the region until the nineteenth century. As in almost all of these visions of Mary there was a reference to the Cross—here as a destination for the procession. Francisca may not have been believed, but her vision was the same kind of recombination of legendary elements and innovations as the previous visions and the shrine myths.

"Our Lady" (as she called herself) did not enter Francisca's kitchen. This was a point to which both Francisca and the Inquisitor paid particular attention. The visions studied above all took place in the public sphere; Mary never crossed the door sill. She belonged to everybody, not one person, and the places she went belonged to everyone. Another significant feature of this unbelieved vision may be that it happened in a town. Most of the other episodes of visions occurred in the countryside. Nevertheless, like all good visions, this one had a link with a tangible natural object like a spring or a tree. Here it was a rock on which Mary sat, from which the village women took chips.

Whether the seer was Francisca or her husband, or even her daughter, or whether it took place inside, outside, in town, or in the countryside, it was probably doomed. Visions themselves were no longer respectable; and with the Inquisition periodically soliciting denunciations, it may have been seen as suspicious even to believe in a new one, much less have one.

The criteria used to examine the truth of this apparition were applied far more rigorously than before. Inés Martínez at Cubas contradicted herself on details just as many times as Francisca la Brava. On the whole Francisca stuck to her story well, and one rather thinks that she herself believed it. Like Juan de Rabe down the road, she was reenacting an age-old scenario, fulfilling a role for her town by serving as its connection to the saints. Juan de Rabe was accepted, then retroactively rejected. Francisca was a little late, a participant in a divine drama from which a most essential character, the chorus, had largely been alienated.

That it was not enlightenment, rationalism, or high religion that produced this alienation is clear from the degree to which other, non-apparitional but miraculous signs continued to be seen and believed in this very district. In 1575 in nearby So-cuéllamos, a sexton was believed when he concocted a story of a transient having stolen and whipped a crucifix and the crucifix bleeding. In 1644 the entire town of Osa de la Vega saw a painting of the Veronica sweat during Holy Week.[10]

While some of the alienation of the visionary audience may have been due to a fear of the Inquisition, the immediate and negative investigation by the town mayors of Francisca la Brava indicates that this was only part of the story. In the early sixteenth century, the cultural form of public, lay visions itself may have worn out. This particular way of connecting with God was no longer believable enough. The itinerant prophets, dressed in sackcloth, who circulated in central Italy with pre-dictions of woe and calls to repentance were welcomed as holy men in the 1470s and 1480s yet laughed out of town by the 1530s.[11] By the same token, had there been too many visions in Spain? The less exceptional visions became, the more sus-picions they would arouse. Perhaps by 1523 the Inquisition was ratifying and enforcing a point of view that was more general in the society.

As the century progressed, the need to regulate lay initiatives in religious matters became more and more evident. In 1525 the Illuminist heresy was defined, and the first nuclei identified and destroyed. Although the Illuminists by their opposition to external devotion had little in common with our seers of saints and founders of shrines, they too believed in direct contact with the sacred unmediated by the church. Protestant doctrines raised some of the same issues. Throughout the century, bishops as-serted and parish priests exercised more and more control over religious institutions. The legislation of Trent confirmed prior Spanish reforms in matters of brotherhoods, hermits, miracles, and vigils. In the first years of the century, apparitions and independent revelations were some of the first of these matters to be affected. Village visions, orthodox and innocuous as most of them were, were almost incidental victims of a general climate of closure.

Although this form of knowing the divine will in time of trouble went into eclipse, others survived, including a species of visionary or prophetic monastic. At Quintanar de la Orden many women did believe Francisca; it was the men running the town who did not. A constituency for visionaries remained, but not among the people who decided what was officially acceptable. That may be why subsequent kinds of seers who were tolerated were those (particularly women) whose visions and revelations spoke largely to women as individuals, without encroaching on matters relating to town government or the town as a parish.

Amateur or professional religious women, beatas or nuns, from time to time over the next 300 years were consulted by individuals, especially other women, sometimes even by bishops and kings, on such varied matters as one's personal state of grace, whether one will have children, the appropriateness of a prospective spouse, and the destination of particular souls after death. Some, like Magdalena de la Cruz of Córdoba (1487-1560), María de la Visitación of Lisbon (fl. 1588), Luisa of Carrión (fl. 1635), and María of Agreda (1602-1665) became quite well known and influential. Others attained a more discreet and local fame. Most of these women had visions in trances, and the Inquisition investigated all of the best known, and many of the lesser known to see whether they were under the influence of the devil or fraudulent. But even though some were repressed, the cultural type survived throughout the early modern period. As persons subject to religious discipline of some kind, they seemed to have had an initial advantage over lay seers when it came to the Inquisition. [12]

Although the prophet-beatas served the same generic function of communicating the divine will, their specific tasks and the ways they performed them were quite different from those of the lay seers of apparitions. Generally the prophet-beatas were not consulted and did not provide information for communities about specific prospective disasters or plagues. Their activity was more habitual than that of the occasional seers studied here, and they tended to shy away from predictions that could be disproved. More than our seers, they served as living demonstrations of grace, whose communication was manifest by their trances and ecstasies. By contrast, the seers studied above had few spiritual pretensions. They were by and large average people, who merely conveyed simple information about where, through what image, on what days, and after what rituals grace could be obtained.

Only in the late visions of La Mancha were there references to trances, even there equivocal. Juan de Rabe apparently boasted that he often went into trances (*que se traspone muchas bezes*), but in his confession there is no indication that he was in a trance when he saw the saints he described. In her first confession Francisca la Brava described what might have been a trance (*que estava trasportada que no tenia notiçia ni pensamiento que estava en este mundo sino en el otro*) prior to her first vision, but that during the vision and those that followed she was "awake and in her free control and judgment." On the other hand, her parish priest described a final trance-like episode when she remained outside her house with her hands locked together.

There is no hint of a trance-like state in any of the other visions described in this book. Seers were fully awake, usually standing up, and had fully sensory experiences. In this fundamental way, their experiences differed from the mystical experiences of many medieval monastics, of Teresa of Avila, and of the habitual ecstatics of later times, including most of the seers of apparitions in the nineteenth and twentieth centuries.

There is another way in which the experiences differed, one not unrelated to trances. Even though these visions had a public vocation, virtually all of them took place without an audience, when the visionaries were alone with Mary, a saint, or an angel. Of all the cases studied, there were only three instances of non-visionary witnesses of seers—at Cubas when Inés saw Mary while in the procession (but then Mary led her off out of sight over the hill to deliver her message); at Escalona, where the boy Bartolomé saw Joana while she was seeing Mary; and at Quintanar, when Francisca called out her neighbor to see Mary. In all of these instances the accounts and questions focused on whether these witnesses saw Mary, not whether they saw the seers do anything unusual (like fall into a trance). Apparently it was not expected that the visionary would be in an altered state of consciousness.

Ecstatic visionary nuns and beatas, because many of their visions were public, served as mediums and conveyed personal messages back and forth between individual members of their audience and their divine contacts. The seers we have studied did not serve this function. They received messages for themselves and for their towns, but were not, properly speaking, diviners.

The attention to signs as proofs in the Castilian apparitions points to a role that trances subsequently played for the more habitual diviners; trances became a means for validating the presence of spirits, a kind of proof that supplanted the signs of the fifteenth century. Trances did not per se mean that good spirits were involved, and ecclesiastical experts were aware of some natural ailments that could appear to be trances, but for lay persons they seemed to have served as a kind of preliminary guarantee against pure fakery. Hence the trances and the visions had to be visible and public, as opposed to the more discreet and private colloquies we have studied. Indeed, most of the nineteenth- and twentieth-century lay visions are a hybrid form, conserving the basic pattern and purpose of the medieval visions, with the difference that they include trances, they are in public, and they contain messages for individual pilgrims as well as collectivities. In the twentieth-century visions, the altered state of the visionary is a form of immediate validation for fellow-citizens and visitors that is entirely lacking in the cases gathered here. The visionaries in modern times are central figures in a public sacred drama. In the fifteenth century, the drama took place offstage—in a field at night; on a dark street; by a pond in late afternoon; in an isolated chapel.

FOUR

General Themes in the Visions

Francisca la Brava's testimony was scrutinized and rechecked, and she was variously accused of lying, dreaming, or seeing the devil in disguise. Her case is a good introduction to the criteria used by villagers, parish priests, diocesan officials, and inquisitors to establish the truth or falsity of visions. The criteria were ancient.

Except in the cases of Cubas, El Miracle, La Mota, and Quintanar, the investigations of Spanish visions that have reached us were vestigial. In only three other inquiries were any of the investigators' questions recorded. There are, however, extensive records of the trial and rehabilitation of Jeanne d'Arc. These records provide in explicit form many of the theological and popular criteria implicit in the testimony of the Spanish visionaries.

Jeanne d'Arc had her first visions at age thirteen in her father's garden. First Saint Michael and later Saint Catherine and Saint Margaret appeared to her. These saints served her as advisers and helpers almost daily from 1424 until her execution in 1431.

Jeanne's interrogators in Rouen wanted to know why she believed the spirits she saw were saints, whether she had a sign, and whether she in turn could show others a sign. A consultant to the investigation, Zanon, bishop of Lisieux, said that only after signs, miracles, or special references in the scriptures should prophets be believed, because it is so difficult to tell true from false spirits. He cited as his authority a decree of Innocent III, *Cum ex Injuncto*.[1]

For Jeanne's interrogators, a sign would appear to be something that could be seen, smelled, or touched by others besides the seer, some manifestation of divine presence or impingement upon the natural world that could be independently verified.

They asked her, for instance, "what sign she had that the revelation comes to her from God and that Saint Catherine and Margaret are the ones who talk to her."[2] Jeanne avoided that question, but in a later interrogation she raised the issue herself.[3]

> She also said that whatever she did that was important [the saints] always helped her, and this is a sign that they were good spirits.
>
> Asked if she had any other sign that they were good spirits.
>
> She said that Saint Michael confirmed it, before the voices came to me.
>
> Asked how she knew it was Saint Michael.
>
> She said by his angelic speech and language. . . .
>
> Asked how, if the enemy [the devil] transformed himself in the form or visage of an angel, would she know if it was a good or bad angel.
>
> She said she would know well enough if it was Saint Michael or something disguised as him. She also said that the first time she was very unsure if it was Saint Michael. And the first time she was very afraid; and she saw him many times before she knew it was Saint Michael.

In short, Jeanne had no sign. She believed what she saw was what it claimed to be, and by the good doctrine Saint Michael taught her.

But Jeanne still had to convince the future Charles VII of her mission. It was not easy. For three weeks of March 1429, she had to plead her case before a commission of priests at Poitiers. According to Jeanne, Charles was finally persuaded not by the judgment of the clergy, many of whom were unconvinced, but by a sign.[4]

Michael had come to her, Jeanne said, in her boardinghouse in Chinon and accompanied her hand in hand to the king's room. There Saint Michael had bowed to Charles and presented him with a marvelous crown, telling him that with Jeanne's help he would chase the English from France. When Jeanne entered the room with Saint Michael, she said to the future king, "*Sire, vela vostre signe, preney lay* (There is your sign, take it)."[5] This incident was glossed over at Jeanne's posthumous rehabilitation. She may well have imagined or fabricated it. But it shows how well aware she herself had become of the importance of signs.

The story did not convince the interrogators at Rouen. They did not rule out the possibility that the devil had appeared in the guise of Michael to Charles as well as Jeanne, and so they asked her what sign *Charles* had that it was Saint Michael. The interrogators could not disprove Jeanne's visions any more than she could prove them, but they could impugn her signs. Since they appeared to have testimony from persons who had been present at Charles's court two years before (and who presumably saw nothing), they pressed Jeanne about the resplendence that she said accompanied her visions and voices—whether it could also be seen in the future king's chambers. They also asked whether anyone else saw the crown, and whether it smelled good or shone.[6]

From the start, Jeanne's interrogators were convinced that her voices were evil spirits. They persistently attempted to link Jeanne's voices and saints with the Lady Fees, or fairies that some people in her village had seen in a certain tree, and for whom the children made garlands.[7] Such fairies as pagan spirits were by definition demons, and if Jeanne had received their help and counsel, then she had been doing the devil's work. *Discretio spirituum*, or the discernment of good from evil spirits in disguise, was thus central to Jeanne d'Arc's trial and sentence.

The willingness of Jeanne's judges to see her visions as diabolical cannot be entirely ascribed to malevolence. For Jeanne's spirits were just as real to the interrogators as to her. Time and again when she would not answer a question, they asked her to obtain an answer from her voices. Articles 48 and 49 of the formal indictment charged that "she firmly believes that those she sees are saints, although she has no sign and she has consulted no bishop, priest, or prelate about whether to believe them," and that in fact they were evil spirits in disguise with which she had made an idolatrous pact.[8]

The interrogators saw as evidence for such a pact Jeanne's easy access to the spirits. It was suspicious, they thought, that the supposed saints visited, kissed, and embraced her frequently for no good reason, "something that saints are in no way accustomed to do in apparitions."[9] They therefore endeavored to find other incriminating evidence about the saints' behavior, asking if they ever contradicted themselves, or why Jeanne could not send them with their messages directly to the so-called king.[10] They noted that Michael bowed before Charles, "when there is no indication that such a bow or greeting had ever been made by angels or archangels to any holy man and not even to the Blessed Virgin, Mother of God."[11]

The spirits were evil, perhaps most obviously, because they were opposed to the English. One of the articles of the indictment charged that Jeanne said the spirits had "a mortal hatred for a Catholic kingdom and a people that practices the veneration of all the saints according to the prescriptions of the Church."[12] But the judges objected to other doctrines of the spirits as well. A very major objection was to the spirits' instruction that Jeanne wear men's clothes, a violation of scriptural and canon law. Another was to their instruction to Jeanne to ignore many of the judges' questions. Legitimate saints, they were sure, would on the contrary encourage her to cooperate with the Church.

These last objections point to a second criterion used to distinguish whether or not someone is truly possessed of the Holy Spirit—the character and comportment of the seer. Philibert, bishop of Coutances, when he assessed the articles of conviction, wrote, "Indeed, in her the two signs that, according to the blessed Gregory, are manifest in a person filled with the Holy Spirit, virtue and humility, are entirely absent."[13] His reference was to the *Dialogues* of Gregory the Great (Book I, Ch. 2). Jeanne's wearing of men's clothing reflected poorly on her virtue, as did her leaving home without permission of her parents and her leap from a tower in which she was imprisoned, which appeared to the judges to be suicidal. Jeanne's refusal to submit to the militant, earthly Church, as opposed to the victorious, heavenly Church of saints reflected poorly on her humility. So did her firm belief that she must be in a state of grace and virtually her entire career as a prophet and a divinely inspired military leader.

Character and comportment were emphasized by Jean Gerson also. Gerson was a recognized authority on the evaluation of spirits. Around 1400 he had written a treatise, *De Distinctione Verarum Visionum a Falsis*, in which, following Hugh of Saint-Victor, he asserted that a true seer would have five virtues displayed by Mary at the time of the Annunciation: humility, willingness to accept counsel, patience, accuracy, and charity.[14]

At the Council of Constance, in 1415, he was called on to help decide whether or not Bridget of Sweden's visions were authentic. He felt they were not and wrote another treatise, *De Probatione Spirituum*, which set out principles and procedures for distinguishing good spirits from evil ones in visions.

According to Gerson, the ideal evaluator would have personal mystical experience as well as knowledge of theology and canon law. He advised a careful preliminary investigation of the visionary, a detailed examination of the vision to see if it conformed to faith and morality, great prudence and caution in reacting to visions, consideration of possible motives for, and gains resulting from visions, scrutiny of the kind of life the visionary led, and then a judgment as to the nature of the spirits involved. These may be the Spirit of God, the good angel, the evil spirit, and the spirit of man. If it is a purely human matter, the visionary might be fabricating the vision consciously or unconsciously.

Gerson was not cited by Jeanne's judges in Rouen, for he was in the other camp. His opinion was apparently solicited by the earlier commissions of Charles VII at Poitiers and Chinon in 1429, and his response from Lyons was a favorable one. In it he pointed out that it was not necessary as a matter of faith to believe Jeanne entirely; all that theologians had to decide was whether there was anything questionable in her story or comportment. He found what he knew about her admirable.[15]

In all of his essays on visions, Gerson was very pragmatic.

He took the substance of a vision as a given and did not request additional signs. He did refer to miracles as favorable evidence, and also to clear references in the scriptures, but not to signs. The judges at Rouen by centering on signs, proofs that could be tested by the senses of others, used a much tougher criterion, but one that was easier to apply.

Almost twenty years after Jeanne's execution, Charles VII asked an adviser, Guillaume Bouille, to initiate Jeanne's rehabilitation. Bouille's preliminary evaluation of Jeanne's visions, written in 1449, once more used the criterion of comportment. He found that Jeanne possessed all five virtues recommended by Gerson and Hugh of Saint-Victor. Not surprisingly, Bouille evaluated her conduct differently from the judges of 1431. For instance he emphasized her willingness to accept the counsel of the saints, instead of her unwillingness to accept the counsel of the clergy. He praised virtues not mentioned in Rouen—her chastity, her abhorrence of violence, and her exemplary death. The accuracy of her prophecies was more evident in 1449 than in 1431, and accuracy was another of the five virtues.

Almost as an afterthought, Bouille mentioned yet another criterion, one not explicitly cited in Rouen, although clearly in the minds of Jeanne's interrogators there; nor is it mentioned by Gerson in his writings. Bouille cited Thomas Aquinas, who in turn cited the Life of Saint Anthony to the effect that ''the distinguishing of good from evil spirits is not difficult: If fear is followed by joy, we know that the help of God has come to us. The security of the soul is a mark of the presence of divine majesty. If, on the contrary, the fear remains, then the enemy is present.''[16] This criterion was probably influenced by neoplatonic ascetic doctrines. Iamblichus in the third century showed how higher or lower spirits could be distinguished by one's subjective reaction.[17]

Jeanne herself seemed to use this criterion. She similarly used her emotions to verify her state of grace. ''She also says that she has a great joy when she sees [Saint Michael]: and she thinks that when she sees him, she is not in a state of mortal sin.''[18] This same rule of thumb, a happy, untroubled spirit, is still seen by some people today as an indication of a state of grace.[19]

Both Jeanne and her interrogators seemed to realize the importance of her subjective reactions. At times Jeanne volunteered to tell them her feelings during or after the visions; other times they directly asked her about them. She emphasized how happy the visions made her feel. "I will not talk to you about the voice of Saint Michael, but I speak of *grant confort.*"[20] In her time *confort* could mean contentment and happiness. Twice Jeanne told how her revelations "conforte" her daily.[21] Her interrogator asked her once, "if, when the angel left, she was left happy (*joyeuse*) or scared and in great fear." She replied, "He did not leave me frightened or fearful at all, but I was sad that he went."[22] In her final condemnation, her internal feelings of *confortationem* were faithfully reported. For Bouille, Jeanne's feeling first of fear, then joy, confirmed the presence of good, rather than evil spirits.[23]

The main criteria used to evaluate Jeanne's visions, then, fall into three categories:

1. Independently verifiable signs, including miracles.

2. Her character and comportment, whether it was compatible with one filled with the Holy Spirit or guided by good spirits.

3. Her emotional responses to the presence of the spirits.

The prior question of whether she had visions at all was not treated seriously, probably because of her obvious sincerity and the magnitude of her accomplishments.

These criteria were also used in the verification of the Spanish visions. The Spanish seers, their villages, and the clergy felt, like Jeanne's judges, that signs were central. Except in instances of simultaneous plague, or corroborative witnesses, everything hung on some evidence that was visible. "But they will not believe me," the seers complained. "If they do not believe you I will give you a sign," Mary replied. "Ask her for a sign," the men of Cubas told Inés. A sign was sometimes even needed (as at Jafre) to convince the seer; it was virtually essential to convince the towns.

The devoutness, truthfulness, and virtue of seers was also

carefully checked in all of the significant Spanish vision investigations. When Inés of Cubas inaccurately predicted where her hand would come unstuck, a special session was held, and Inés testified that she had had another vision that clarified her previous mistake. But character evaluation in the Spanish cases was not directed, as with Jeanne d'Arc, at identifying what kind of spirit appeared, but rather at determining if the visionary was lying.

Indeed, the Spanish investigations are characterized by relatively little attention to Satan. In the Spain of these visions, no less than in the France of Jeanne d'Arc, it was common knowledge that the devil could provoke false visions. Yet only in the cases of Juan de Rabe and Francisca la Brava was there any mention of possible demonic participation.

Spanish writers knew of at least three ways the devil could counterfeit apparitions. One was by possessing the seer, who fell involuntarily under the devil's power. According to the Hieronymite Pedro Ciruelo, author of *Reprobacion de las supersticiones y hechizerias* (1530), at certain hours or on certain days the devil entered certain persons and moved their tongues to say many and varied things.[24] In view of this possibility the inquisitor asked the priest of Quintanar if Francisca la Brava had a history of being *"endemoniada."*

The devil could also get a seer to do his work by trickery. "Satan himself masquerades as an angel of light," warned Saint Paul in 2 Corinthians 11. The *Libro de los exenplos* told how the devil appeared in disguise to encourage the worship of false relics and a tree, surely a cautionary tale for our rural seers.[25] In two chapters of his sober *Treatise on the Spiritual Life*, Vincent Ferrer warned monks and nuns against visions and revelations as illusions and temptations of the devil. So, indeed, did almost every fifteenth- and sixteenth-century handbook for the spiritually minded.[26] The science of discernment was largely directed at this level of demonic activity, in which the seers themselves were deceived.

Francisca la Brava herself feared this deception, or at least said that she did, when she first saw Mary—"Get back Satan, you are a devil come to deceive me!" Already before her visions she was alert to the devil; her bedtime prayer referred to sins "in compact" and deception in death. A trick by the devil was what her priest warned her of and explained with examples from the Bible.

A seer who was deceived could not be blamed for being tricked, but was culpable if she or he communicated the false vision to others. Francisca would not have been punished if, even believing her visions, she had told no one but the priest. Her crime was in the publicity she gave the vision and the cult she encouraged by trusting her own discernment when it was at variance with that of the Church.

The most culpable level of dealings with the devil was the knowing, willing pact. It was due to such pacts that witches and necromancers gained their powers. Perhaps taking his information from *Malleus Maleficarum*, Pedro Ciruelo admitted that some witches actually flew around at night, while others merely fell into trances, the devil, "depriving them of all senses, and they fall to the ground as if cold and dead . . . and they feel nothing, though they be whipped, wounded, burned, or whatever injuries can be done to the body." Some of them, he said, speak many secrets while in these trances, and are taken for prophets because of a "strange wisdom unusual even for the holy doctors of the Catholic Church," much like some of those possessed by the devil.[27] It would seem that the woman who denounced Juan de Rabe thought he might have made such a pact, for she mentioned that he boasted of his frequent trances and he knew secret things.

Yet the investigators and inquisitors in Spain, in these particular cases at least, do not appear to have taken seriously the possibility of demonic involvement. Even with Francisca la Brava, whom the parish priest, one of the alcaldes, and even Francisca herself suspected of being tricked by the devil in disguise, the inquisitors did not think the devil was directly involved, but rather that Francisca concocted the story herself. They thought her motives were mere foolishness (*liviandad*) and vanity, the kind of attention she and Juan de Rabe received from their fellows when believed. Other non-diabolical explanations for visions, suggested by parents, townspeople, or investigators, included dreams (Quintanar, León), insanity (Cubas, Navas de Zarzuela, Quintanar), and drink (Cubas). Citing Saint Paul, Gerson warned that special attention should be paid to the character and comportment of female visionaries. "All the more it is true if these women, itching with curiosity, are the kind whom the Apostle describes: 'Silly women who are sin-laden and led astray by various lusts: ever learning yet never attaining the knowledge of the truth' (2 Tim 3:7). For where truth is absent, it follows that vanity and deception are present."[28] Elsewhere he wrote, "All doctrine of women, especially words or writings on religion, is considered suspect unless carefully examined previously by the other sex, and much more than the doctrine of men."[29]

Female visionaries were mistrusted long before and long after Gerson. A seventeenth-century commentator on the Cubas apparitions approved the town's slowness in believing Inés with this general caution: "Women easily believe in any spirit, and sometimes tell as revelations that occurred in the daytime the foolish things they dreamed at night; and so it is necessary to hear them with a prudent, mature, and cautious mind."[30] Women seers should be particularly mistrusted, according to Juan de Horozco in his *Tratado de la verdadera y falsa prophecia* (1588) because, once fooled, it was so easy for them, like Eve, to fool men.[31]

Several writers thought (as the inquisitors felt in regard to Francisca) that women were tempted to have visions as a way of gaining the attention and power they lacked in society. A "discreet lady" explained around 1700 to the Franciscan Antonio Arbiol, after watching a poor woman's public penance by the Inquisition, that "everyone naturally desires wealth and esteem. Men have many ways of achieving them, whether by arms, learning, or sainthood, . . . but women who are poor and of common birth, when they see that everyone praises them and gives them everything they need when they are considered virtuous and holy, are easily fooled in this way by the devil."[32]

Martín de Castañega in 1529 similarly used women's lack of power as one explanation for why women were more likely to be witches than men.[33]

These strictures applied in particular to sexually active ("sin-laden") women. Caesarius of Heisterbach wrote the following dialogue:

> Novice: I wonder if Our Lady visits good women as she visits men.
> Monk: There is neither male nor female in her eyes. She was born woman and she herself gave birth to the chief of all men, even Christ. Both sexes she visits and consoles, to both she reveals her secrets.[34]

The operant word here is "good." For Caesarius went on to give examples of women who saw Mary, and all were virgins. A panel of matrons examined Jeanne d'Arc at Poitiers to make sure she was a virgin as part of a theological investigation of her visions. Because her virginity was considered certain, the prosecutors at Rouen never impugned her visions on the grounds of gender.

So one is not surprised to find a double standard applied to the Spanish visionaries. In the cases studied, only one married woman, María Torrent, was the prime visionary and believed by the authorities (as opposed to six adult men, four boys or youths, and three girls). Probably the visions of adult women in the fifteenth and sixteenth centuries did not make it past an initial round of elimination. Many of them must have been rejected like Francisca la Brava by village authorities and priests before the matter went any further.

Prime Visionaries believed by Authorities

	Boys	
Pedro	Santa Gadea	1399
Pedro	Jaén	1430
Juan	Navas/Zarzuela	1455
Jaume	El Miracle	1458

Girls

Inés	Cubas	1499
Joana	Escalona	c.1490
Isabel	Reus	1592

Men

Miguel	Navalagamella	1455
Miquel	Jafre	1460
Miquel	El Torn	1483
Bernat	Pinós	1507
Alvar	León	c.1512
Juan	La Mota	c.1514

Women

María	Sant Aniol	1618

In addition to gender, Gerson directed attention to the social and economic standing of the seers, "also whether the visionary is rich or poor, for in the one we may suspect pride or secret sensuality, in the other deception."[35] All the Spanish visionaries, with the possible exceptions of Juan of Navas de Zarzuela and Miquel Noguer of El Torn, would have been considered poor by the authorities. As noted in regard to Inés, however, within their villages our visionaries, peasants and rural craftsmen, were not the true poor. None was a beggar, and only one was an adult day laborer (who was eventually whipped). It is true that for most of the visionaries a job as a shrine tender would mean an easier and more interesting life and would bring them respect from all levels of society, but it is hard to make a strong case, in these instances, for visions for economic gain.

The third criterion used in the Jeanne d'Arc case, that of the emotional responses of the seer, was on the minds of at least some of the Spanish investigators. That this doctrine was known in Spain can be seen from a Catalan sermon of Vincent Ferrer, probably delivered between 1412 and 1418. Ferrer was describing the appearance of the Archangel Gabriel to Zacharias, father of John the Baptist, an example of a Biblical vision used also by Gerson.[36]

And notice that one day Zacharias went to the temple to pray, and when he was praying the Angel Gabriel appeared to him on the altar, and Zacharias was terrified. "Fear not, Zacharias." You see that the doctrine is correct that when the good angel or a soul appears to a person, at first they make him terrified, because the flesh cannot bear so much; but then they console him (*aconsole*); hence, "Fear not."

Vincent's sermon shows not only that the doctrine was known to the clergy, which is not surprising, but also that it was considered important to communicate to the people. Vision evaluation was useful for laypeople in 1400.

In 1430 the vicar general of Jaén had only one or two of his many questions to each seer recorded. One of those, put both to Pedro and Juan, was whether they felt pleasure (*plazer*) or fear (*espanto, pavor*) when they saw the vision. He apparently asked the other two women also, for although no questions to them were recorded, they both reported their emotions. María Sánchez's response, like the rest of her vision (she was the only person to identify Mary and Ildefonsus), was letter perfect; she felt fear (*pavor*) then happiness and pleasure (*gasajado y consolacion*)—Saint Anthony's test for a vision of a good spirit.

The diocesan officials who questioned Miquel Noguer of El Torn in 1483 put down only three of their queries. One was how Miquel felt when Mary disappeared—was he *desaconsolat* or *desconfortat*? Miquel's answer was "correct"—*molt aconsolat*, very pleased. At Cubas, too, the diocesan officials were insistent on this point. In regard to four separate visions they asked Inés whether she had been frightened (*si ovo miedo*), the same question asked of Francisca la Brava (*si ovo temor*). Note that at Jaén, El Torn, Cubas, and Quintanar, the interrogators were high diocesan officials or Inquisitors, who could be expected to know the right questions to ask. The questions were not asked at El Miracle and Pinós, perhaps because the investigations, made on short notice, were by local priests. In the latter cases it is possible that the questions were asked but not recorded, for in any case the seers volunteered their emotions.

Even apart from the critical importance for discernment of

terror or joy, the Spanish visionaries, like Jeanne d'Arc, seem to have constantly monitored their emotions, and to have been remarkably open, compared to their modern counterparts, in telling about them. For modern Westerners, emotions are the signified, the net result of experience and physiology, clear data that can be acted on. For these people five hundred years ago, certain emotions seem to have been moral indicators, or signifiers. Just what they meant was not always clear. Some emotions were unidentified, which I do not think is true in modern times. Francisca la Brava felt a pain in her heart, not her body, and anguished and prayed to know what it meant. As with that pain, some emotions were not truths in themselves, but rather a form of obscure communication from God. Like dreams, they were messages to be deciphered. Unusual emotions seem to have been discussed and commented upon among neighbors like symptoms in a moral etiology.

The Spanish authorities also made sure that complete descriptions of the saints were put in writing. In Francisca la Brava's case, repeated, detailed, inquiries about the Virgin and her clothes were designed to catch her in inconsistencies. There may have been another kind of test in these questions. Greek and Roman dreamers and visionaries were warned to observe their visions closely for deceptive features. Artemidorus of Daldis advised in regard to the appearances of heroes and demons that "each of them must be wearing his own proper attire and that he must not change it or cast it off. He must not appear in simple clothes or be without his usual weapons, since, then, whether the god signifies something good or bad, he is lying and deceiving."[37] Martin of Tours realized a vision of Christ was really the devil when he noted Christ wore the purple robes of a king rather than the dress and stigmata of the crucifixion.[38] Similarly, Jeanne d'Arc's interrogators may have had this criterion in mind when they asked for details about her saints. Did Saint Michael carry scales, they wanted to know.

However, the Spanish questions, except those put by the Inquisitors, seem to have had a different purpose. They were intended, I think, to make an accurate picture for posterity, especially to make a statue or painting of the saint. Visions of

Mary would lead to a new type or advocation, with its own clothes and stance, and here the information would be especially important.

In a canonical investigation, questions put to witnesses are often not recorded. I have summarized the recorded questions relating to Mary's appearance below:

Information wanted about Mary in the five cases in which questions about her were recorded (Cubas 1449, Miracle 1458, Pinós 1507, La Mota 1518, Quintanar 1523). The answers are summarized in parentheses.

her size (*tamaño*)—C,Q (small, see below)
her age—M (about 4)

her face—P,Q
her complexion—Q (*morena*)
hair length—Q,M (dk, long)
timbre of voice—C (delicate)

clothes, color—C,M,Q (see below)
belt—C (no)
falda—C (no)
headwear—C,M,Q (coif, none, coif)
crown—C (no)
color of coif—C,Q (gold, white)
calza or *descalza*—C,Q (varied)

carrying child—LM (no)
alone—LM,Q (yes)
walking—Q,C (yes)
woman's gait—C (yes)

odor—C,Q (no)
aura—C,Q (yes)
departure—Q,M

Whether or not it was requested, this kind of information, particularly the color of the saints' clothes, was given by nearly all the seers. Mary wore white in six visions; she wore red (*vermell*) at El Miracle and Pinós; and she wore gold at Cubas. Colors were not given in the hearsay reports of Reus and Escalona. At least six visions were of small saints; they are discussed below.

SPANISH VISIONS AND THE RENEWAL OF THE LOCAL DEVOTIONAL SYSTEM

Jeanne d'Arc was told in 1431 that her visions were a threat to the Church and the Faith. "The great danger was shown to her that comes of someone so presumptuous as to believe they have such apparitions and revelations, and therefore lie about matters concerning God, giving out false prophecies and divinations not known from God, but invented. From which could follow the seduction of peoples, the inception of new sects, and many other impieties that subvert the Church and Catholics."[39]

The Spanish visions documented above were less momentous. The relatively local, stereotyped visions, offering pious solutions to immediate crises and identifying long-term protectors, were doctrinally harmless. Only in the sixteenth century were such visions perceived as threatening. Then they were suppressed with similar reasoning. "They are indeed vain things and prejudicial to Our Holy Catholic Faith and the souls of the simple and Catholic folk who hear them" (from the sentence of Juan de Rabe).

But even in the trials of Juan de Rabe and Francisca la Brava the language and the punishments were relatively mild for the Inquisition at that time. People did not need much persuasion to learn that times had changed. Other ways would have to be found to know for sure who were their holy helpers.

In point of fact, Jeanne d'Arc did not really threaten the Church and the Faith, although she could have if she had continued her revelations for life and taken an unorthodox turn. Certainly the theologians who rehabilitated her in 1455 and the pope who canonized her in 1920 did not consider her a threat. Jeanne was, however, a substantial threat politically for the Anglo-Burgundian cause. Lay visions in Spanish villages in the fifteenth century posed no such threat to local or royal power. On the contrary, miracles and shrines meant more business for a town's merchants, construction work for its laborers, masses for its priests, and documents for its notaries. Validation was itself in the hands of the town government and the clergy. It was the priest of Santa Gadea who followed up on the vision to set up a Benedictine monastery. The Jaén visions eventually led to a new addition to the parish church. One of the seigniorial officials of the duke of Medinaceli became the majordomo of the Cubas shrine; he was the person who made sure that miracles were recorded. New grace threatens no one. The only persons possibly affected adversely would be those devoted to or profiting from preexisting grace at other shrines. But major apparitions rarely occur in towns that already have active sources of grace. The competing sources of grace belong to other towns or villages, not the political unit that decides on validation.

Hence the inquiries that have come down to us of early Spanish visions were not primarily investigations, but rather ratifications. A more thorough questioning of witnesses could give a nascent devotion more weight, but was certainly not intended to challenge it. The archbishop of Toledo gave the mayors of Cubas permission to build the new shrine in the same letter in which he ordered a thorough documentation of the visions. Patently unbelievable lay visions probably never reached the stage of a public document; and there would have been no particular reason to preserve such a document should it have been drawn up. That is why, in these rather pro forma investigations, one has only glimpses of the theological criteria applied to more serious matters. Castilians did use such criteria in earnest. Juan de Torquemada, uncle of the head of the Castilian Inquisition, had been called upon at the Council of Basel, like Gerson at Constance before him, to evaluate the revelations of Bridget of Sweden. But the Castilian Inquisition in its first years concentrated on ill-converted Jews, and only after the turn of the century did it expand its attention to other matters.

The influence of late medieval Castilian and Catalan visions rarely extended beyond a radius of 100 miles. Even that radius would be a temporary one, during the first wave of miracles. None of those studied here was reported in the official chronicles of Castile or Aragon. They were not considered earthshaking

events. For unlike the visions of Jeanne d'Arc, Bridget of Sweden, or Savonarola, their objective was limited and local—the
establishment of a regular link of clientage and patronage between a social group and a sacred protector. As mentioned in
the introduction, they were far from the only way to set up this
link. Alternatives included the trial and error system of conditional community vows; the selection of protectors by lottery;
and the decipherment of striking anomalies or coincidences (like
the collapse of a church portal during mass on a given saint's
day). Apparitions were clear, easy to read, explicit solutions.
The messages given by the saints, however, rarely went beyond
what the villagers could deduce from their more normal systems
of selection. The theology explicit and implicit in these visions
was orthodox. A general theological statement like that of Mary
to Francisca, "I am She who sustains you on the face of the
earth, you and every Christian," was hardly adventurous.

Nor were these visions exceptional because of the miracles
they provoked. Spates of miracles were set off by the discovery
of saints' bodies, fraudulently or not; the finding of statues;
and most commonly of all, a striking cure at a preexisting shrine
that sparked an explosion of new wonders. Such an "activation"
of a statue was relatively easy to counterfeit, and such frauds
were decried in diocesan decrees.[40] Inés and her visions were
virtually forgotten at Cubas by the end of the fifteenth century
because Santa Juana was there working miracles herself.

Of all the visions studied above, only those of León (c. 1512)
and El Miracle (1458) resulted in shrines that maintain a significant radius of attraction today. When in 1530 the Italian
humanist Lucio Marineo Siculo listed the twelve major shrines
in Spain, not one of those studied above was included. He cited
the Marian shrines of Guadalupe, Pilar, Montserrat, Valvanera,
and Peña de Francia; shrines to Santiago, Santa Casilda, and
Santo Domingo de la Calzada; the Camara Santa of Oviedo, the
Corporales of Daroca, and the Christ of Burgos. He mentioned
the Veronica of Jaén, but not Our Lady of the Capilla.[41]

These visions were local, devotional, and protective. In the
sixteenth to eighteenth centuries when the Castilian nation-
state turned its weapons on its Catalan and French neighbors,

and Spanish soldiers were fighting heretics in Germany and the Low Countries, the visible signs that succeeded true apparitions took on, or were given, political meanings. In the late medieval apparitions, these wider significances were by and large missing.

That the visions had a relatively local significance is a virtue for historians, who know least about local, personal religion. The visions of Jeanne d'Arc, Bridget, Savonarola, Teresa de Avila, and John of the Cross are well known and documented precisely because they were exceptional in their political and religious significance. Paradoxically, because the visions studied here were far more common, less is known about them; only at the most local level did they have meaning and impact. Whether viewed as true epiphanies or as exercises in religious imagination, they provide clues to the whys and hows of local religion for the Spanish towns and regions in which they occurred; and they offer terms for questions about local religion throughout Western Europe.

Like the Catalan legends collected by Camós, visions served to strengthen relations between communities and the forces of nature. The overall pattern of the human drama of the visions was similar. The saint appeared to one or more seers, generally in the countryside, almost always in the public sphere. If the saint was not already established as a protector, the seer had to persuade the town of the truth of the vision. The people were persuaded by signs such as contorted bodies, a beating, the death of a seer or a villager, the resurrection of a dead person, or the testimony of adult witnesses. Other additional signs, such as the imprints of a saint's hand or foot, or the testimony of small children, were essentially corroborative. When the town believed, the people went out to the site of the vision in procession. They then set up regular devotions and established a shrine for the saint, in return for the saint's protection. A new link was thereby made between the society and its environment, a new sacred spot defined where people could seek help.

Very few of these visions created both a new image and a new sacred place. For these towns already had many of both. The sacred geography was constantly in flux, with some places and some images gaining and others losing power and popularity. So that, other things being equal, one would not be surprised if a "retired" image or place reasserted its sacred power in the visions. In fact all but two of the visions studied here explicitly or implicitly redirected the people's attention to a preexistent image or place.

Preexistent Images

Jaén	altar images in church of San Ildefonso
Cubas	Our Lady of Guadalupe in Extremadura
Miracle	Cross on altar of San Sebastian
Escalona	Cross in the field
León	Our Lady of El Camino
Quintanar	Our Lady of Piedad
Reus	Image in private chapel
Sant Aniol	Our Lady of Els Arcs

Preexistent Shrine/Site

Santa Gadea	abandoned parish church
Navas/Zarzuela	"la yglesuela"
Jafre	profaned spring
El Torn	interdicted shrine
Pinós	untended shrine
El Toboso	previously designated shrine sites

New Image at New Site

Navalagamella	Saint Michael in countryside
Sta María/Llanos	Cross on road outside town

What happened, then, was a rearrangement of priorities within a previously existing pantheon. The old system was shaken up. Some old saints were tacitly demoted, and the village redistributed its devotion to new saints in old sacred places, or old saints in new places. Continuity was built into this process; each new devotion had a comfortable, known aspect.

SOURCES AND DIFFUSION OF THE VISION STORIES

The combination of continuity and innovation in the sacred geography and pantheon of the community is similar to the combination of creativity and tradition manifest in the stories of the visions themselves. Reading the visions in roughly chronological order, one sees the extent to which each was a recombination of known elements, with a moderate touch of novelty. The vision scenarios built on techniques used for the discoveries of saints' bodies; the legends of the discoveries of statues both in nearby villages and at the major Iberian shrines; the legends and iconography of the international Mediterranean shrines; Spanish and European legends and *exempla* of miracle visions; the apocryphal lives of Mary, and the Bible itself. But most of all, they built on each other, borrowing a motif from two or more visions in the preceding years, and combining them in new ways.

The relation between apparitions and legends was symbiotic. Apparitions borrowed from legends, and over time they became legends. The investigations and subsequent restatements of the visions correct them, simplify them, and remove contradictions. One sees this best in the bias toward certain stereotypical motifs. For instance, visionaries were supposed to be shepherds. This process was facilitated in Castilian because the same word, *pastor*, refers to any kind of herding. Thus images or paintings of apparitions often have the seer with sheep, even if the seer was watching pigs or chasing a donkey. Scholars have termed this kind of vision, and those involved in the finding of statues, the cycle of the shepherds.[42]

Only four of the visions occurred to people tending sheep, however. Jeanne d'Arc was nicknamed the "shepherdess of Domremy," but her testimony was quite clear—she was not a shepherdess. She came from a well-off peasant family, spent much of her time sewing, and only occasionally took the animals back and forth from pasture. None of her visions occurred while watching sheep, because that was not one of her jobs.[43]

Occupations of Seers, 1399-1618

Tending Sheep	*Tending Pigs*
2 Santa Gadea	1 Cubas
1 Navalagamella	*Servants*
1 El Toboso	2 Jaén
1 Reus	1 Escalona

Plowman	*Young Children*
1 Jafre	2 of peasants Miracle
Day Laborer	1 of clothmaker Navas
1 La Mota	(1 of blacksmith Cubas)
Wives	(1 of weaver Reus)
2 of shepherds Jaén	*dk = prob. Peasants*
1 of carder Quintanar	1 El Torn
1 of laborer Sant Aniol	1 Pinós

Stephen Sharbrough has written about the reasons for the legends of shepherds—analogies with shepherds who first heard about the birth of Christ; and the association of the Mother Goddess with animals and as symbolic shepherdess of mankind.[44] These legends may have had more effect as symbolic statements of human-divine relations and charters for shrines than what really happened in the visions.

The iconography and the stereotype may also have been influenced by the Christmas plays put on in cathedrals—the Officium Pastorum. At Rouen, for instance, the shepherds approached a manger, and at a dramatic moment the mid-wives opened a curtain to reveal a statue of Mary with the baby Jesus, brilliantly lit up. Some such play is known to have been given in fifteenth-century Girona.[45] It is possible that the "discovery" of a venerated statue by shepherds in these plays could be transformed over time into a replaying of a supposedly historical "*inventio*" of the image itself by shepherds. The dramaturgy and the stereotype may in turn have influenced some real shepherds to have "real" visions. But the fact remains that only a few of the late medieval visionaries were shepherds.

How did these motifs reach the people of Castile and Catalonia before the time of print and radio? How did they hear about visions? A prime source must have been preachers. Some of the early legends, like that of the apparition of Saint Michael, would have been read and commented on in church. Clerics might know stories about Saint Catherine's in the Sinai from pilgrim accounts. There was a certain amount of circulation of members of any given order through its monasteries throughout Europe.[46]

Another source would be simple travelers or pilgrims, who criss-crossed Catalonia and Castile on their way to Santiago de Compostela, Guadalupe, and Montserrat to fulfill promises. Yet another would be iconography. One of the Jaén seers identified what she saw with an altarpiece. In Quintanar there was a pietà that may have resembled the tired and bleeding Mary seen by Francisca la Brava. One wonders if there were paintings of Mary embracing the Cross in or around Cubas and Escalona. A partial explanation for the appearance of Mary and Saint Sebastian as child-size adults would be that they appeared the size of their statues in the churches. Similar visions in twelfth-century England have been interpreted this way.[47]

People would know the legends of the nearby shrines. They would also know those of the district, regional, and national shrines, for questors gathering income from vows and carrying tokens from these shrines circulated through all of Spain's villages, as they still do in some regions today. When the shrine of Jafre was under construction, its keepers were allowed to beg for alms throughout the diocese. Questors from El Torn received permission to circulate through all of Aragon in 1493. For a shrine starting from a vision, a questor would naturally tell about the vision to gain acceptance and alms. The questors I have known in present-day Galicia circulate on foot or horseback, gathering grain or money, visiting the most remote places as well as devotees in cities. They are very thorough, and would have been so in the fifteenth century as well. A vision story in rural districts would have been big news, especially if it could mean cures for the chronically ill. In 1514, only two years after the dream or the vision of the shepherd in León, the church administrators of Our Lady of El Camino were complaining about fake questors "proclaiming bulls of our lady Saint Mary of el Camino." The shrines of Santa Gadea and Santa María de Nieva obtained papal indulgences for contributions to their construction, and these too must have been widely publicized. In some cases the visionaries themselves were sent around to gather alms and tell their story, like Alvar Simón of León.[48]

Once the word was out, its circulation had its own logic. For if a shrine proved miraculous, the people who were cured served as living advertisements to its power. With the story of its cure, they would doubtless tell how the shrine started with a dramatic vision. Hence the incantations that led to the curing of villagers some distance away from Cubas referred to the fact that Mary appeared to Inés.

That visions and miracles were news, and that information was avidly sought by the populace as it was distributed by the shrine tenders, can be seen from its commercialization. Shortly after a crucifix was discovered in 1514 by a dog in a field near Albalate de Zorita (Guadalajara), the story of the discovery was put into verse and printed up *"en letras de molde"* on broadsheets sung and sold by blind men.[49] This is one of the earliest references to the blind selling broadsheets in Castile. Subsequently they organized themselves into a guild.[50]

In Catalonia and Aragon, pilgrims at a shrine would hear and sing hymns that told the story of the image's origin. Just how early these song-legends, known as *goigs* or *gozos* (from *Septem Gaudia*, the seven joys of Mary) were printed up is not clear, but certainly the hymns date from long before their publication.

Any souvenirs the pilgrims brought away from an apparition site would remind them of the vision. Indeed, according to the *Siete Partidas* as cited above, pilgrims went to holy places precisely "in order to take something away," presumably for home cures and protection against disease and enemies. Pilgrims similarly descended on the vision sites, carrying off sand from Cubas, splinters of the cross from Escalona, water from Jafre, and stones and dirt from El Quintanar. The same occurs with the twentieth-century visions where entire trees have been removed piecemeal; and the legend of Guadalupe stated as a matter of course that all of the stones around the image's hiding place were broken up and carried off by the first delegation of pilgrims from Cáceres "as relics." The photograph of the stone of the Descent of Mary in the Toledo Cathedral shows the extent to which the reminders of holy visitations have had to be protected from pious vandals. The distribution of these relics of a holy presence ensured the repetition of the vision story.

Surely this kind of relic quest provides poignant evidence for the hunger for contact with the sacred that was met by apparitions. Modern people too easily dismiss this as "superstition." For those who believe in divine apparitions, the sand on which Mary left her footprints, the leaves of a hawthorn or live oak on which she appeared, and the stone on which she sat bore her signature and were meant by her to be kept and used in memory of her visit. Perhaps this tangible immanence was the ultimate attraction of an apparition. Certainly of all the effects of a vision, it lasted the longest.

The Logic of Divine Behavior

The sacralization of a place or the revitalization of a sacred place was one critical purpose of an apparition. But from Mary's messages and the peoples' questions to the seers we know that the visions had more immediate and specific meanings for the villages where they occurred. These meanings can be summarized as a series of questions.

1. Who is interceding for them?
   Answers: Mary (12), Saint Anthony of Padua (1), Saint Michael (1), Saint Roch (1), not given, assumed Mary (1)

   This question underlies all of the visions. By the same token, people want to know where the saints can be approached and when during the year is the best time (usually, by implication, the apparition site and time).

2. What will the future bring? Will the plague come or go?
   plague will come (2), plague will depend on response (4)

3. How can they affect that future?
   A. What should they cease doing that they have done wrong?
   theft (1), blasphemy (3), village rivalries (1)

   B. What should they do that they have not done?
   masses (5), fasts (1), prayers (1), processions (10), pay tithes and other duties (1), build shrine (10), erect cross (2), set up brotherhood (2), punish lapses (2), general conversion (3)

4. What is the situation of the dead? How can it be remedied?
   fulfill last wishes (2), have masses said (1), honor dead martyrs (1), have psalms sung (1)

5. What are the emblems, signatures of God to use for curing?
   sand, water, stones, dirt, leaves
6. What is the logic of divine behavior?

This final question is more ours than theirs. The visions reveal the character of the gods only implicitly, for this is something the seers and their communities already know. At most, the visions serve to reconfirm procedures of punishment and intercession. For the communities, the visions are living exempla, like skits sometimes acted out during sermons. They already know the sermon. The visions made known doctrine alive and immediate as something to be acted on. They also localized doctrine, gave it physical referents in time and space. That is, the visions integrated a theological system of punishment and grace into a local pantheon of saints.

At the apex of the system was a distant and severe God, named in the visions as Our Lord God, Jesus Christ, and My Precious Son. God did the punishing. "There is no one four or more years old whom my son will not reap," warned the child-Mary at El Miracle.

This God did not appear as an actor in the visions; he was always a power brooding offstage. Even as the passive child-Jesus in Mary's arms, he appeared only once, at Jaén. Although Mary at Cubas was supposed to be Our Lady of Guadalupe (an image seated with a child), Inés made no mention of a Christ-child when describing her vision in detail. Similarly, although by 1617 Our Lady of the Cross at Escalona was represented as a mother with a child in the shrine statue, Joana apparently mentioned no child, and the original painting did not show one as Mary embraced the cross. God was present only symbolically in two of the other visions, on the crucifixes and crosses the Marian figures embraced or presented.

When God was offended, he had to be persuaded, sometimes by tremendous effort, not to punish. At El Torn a child-Mary wept and prayed to "Jesus Christ, asking him to take mercy and pity on his people." She told Miquel Noguer that if the people did not convert, God would send great mortal epidemics of the plague. Vincent Ferrer had preached just this kind of preventive

penance and organized penitential processions not far from
Pinós and El Miracle in 1415, so neither the theology nor the
response was new to Catalonia. Towns and cities regularly held
penitential processions when faced with major disasters. Mary
fulfilled the same role at Quintanar de la Orden, telling Francisca
la Brava she had been out of her house for more than thirty
days praying to her precious son to send health for bodies and
salvation for souls.

To a certain extent, people could do their own penance and
their own persuading of God. But these penances and persua-
sions were best channeled through intermediaries. By appearing
in visions, saints spontaneously offered their services, or rather
revealed the role they had already assumed. Mary appeared to
María Torrent of Sant Aniol in 1618 to tell her that God was
angry and that She, "The Mother of God of Los Arcos, had
obtained mercy and forgiveness for them from her precious
son."

The saints seemed to take two kinds of stances in these visions. One was that of a cool, benevolent messenger who informed the community of its alternatives, stating the terms, as
it were, for the avoidance of disaster or the maintenance of
friendly relations. Such saints appeared more or less as God's
agents. It was at God's initiative that Mary came to Santa
Gadea—"They should know that her coming was willed by her
precious son, redeemer of the human race." This stance predominated among the Marian visions and applied to all of the
other saints. Michael, Anthony of Padua, and Sebastian simply
delivered messages or warnings, like the unnamed divine messenger who turned up in Jafre dressed in blue.

The second stance was seen in the tearful, pleading, or penitential Marys of El Torn (1483) and Quintanar (1523). The
role of the saint in this second stance was one of active, self-
motivated intercession. Mary's role as the supreme advocate of
sinners was not new in this period. According to contemporary
miracle books and chronicles, a shepherd boy of eleven in
twelfth-century Soissons, a boy of thirteen in 1126, and a Benedictine novice in 1161 in Germany all had visions of Mary
interceding with God.[51] Around 1230 the abbots of the Cister-

cian order were told at a general chapter about the vision of William of Clairvaux. He saw the beginning of the last judgment, but after the first trump had been sounded, "the Mother of Mercy, the Virgin Mary, knowing the world would be ended if [the trump] sounded again, whilst the rest of the saints remained silent, rose and threw herself at the feet of her Son and urgently entreated him to defer His sentence and spare the world."[52] In the late fifteenth-century Spanish visions, Mary's intercession was more emotional, desperate, and vulnerable, less stately, queenlike and dignified. It represented the ultimate humanization of her figure, the final step from the removed goddesses of Santa Gadea and Jaén and the subsequent approachable ladies of Cubas and Escalona.

In the messenger role, the saints helped people by conveying clear signals between God and the people. Devotion subsequently made to them by the people was presumably forwarded to God. In the intercessor role, Mary helped the people in two ways—first by obtaining God's mercy, and second by showing how to pray. For with her weeping, or praying on bloody knees, embracing the cross, or walking in a procession, Mary was endorsing certain procedures of penitential piety. Similarly, in some twentieth-century visions, Mary instructs the seers in how to say the rosary correctly and dictates new kinds of prayers and devotions.

In neither of these two roles is there any question about the source of ultimate, or even approximate, power. Punishments and rewards come from God. The saints, even Mary, help only indirectly. When the villagers of New Castile replied about their religion to a questionnaire of Philip II in 1575, they occasionally attributed some effective action, beneficent or vindictive, directly to a saint. There are no such slip-ups in the vision testimony.

CHILDREN, SAINTS, AND THE PLAGUE

Scholars working from "high culture" sources would have us believe that there was no notion of childhood and that children were treated cavalierly in late medieval communities; that high infant mortality led to a low emotional investment of parents in children. Le Roy Ladurie, in his detailed ethnography of the Pyreneen village of Montaillou, has challenged that view.[53] The documents of visions in Spain support his position and indeed elaborate it in certain critical ways. Children were symbols of purity used by communities for intercession with God.

The visions at Cubas are telling. When the priest and the village men first listened to Inés's story on Sunday morning, they heard her out and did not call her crazy or say she was tipsy as her father had predicted. Instead they asked her to obtain a sign. Her treatment after the sign was received showed the town's attitude toward children as sacred objects in general.

What was a child? The children nine and ten years old with Inés in the penitential procession were referred to as *niños*. Inés, who was twelve and a half was referred to as a *moza*, *mozuela*, or *moza niña*. *Moza* seems to have referred to a girl past puberty. The term was especially used when inquiring about Inés's moral comportment. Witnesses were asked whether she was a "moza de buena fama" and whether she danced at weddings "like the other mozas." When asked how long he had known Inés, her neighbor said, "since she was a niña"; apparently she was a niña no longer. So the cut-off point for niña/moza would seem to have been about age eleven or twelve.

Inés was enough of a moza so that she was not considered automatically innocent; hence the investigation of her behavior. Mozas were potentially sinful; their purity had to be preserved by rigorously avoiding occasions for sin, such as dances. The judges' persistence on this question came from a long tradition. *El Libro de los exenplos* (1400-1420) contains the following story:[54]

> Saint Gregory in the *Dialogues* tells of a girl (*moza*) to whom the Virgin Mary appeared, showed some other girls of her age, and asked if she wanted to be with them. She replied that she would. And the Virgin Mary said to her, "Then from now on do nothing that the other girls do" and also told her to keep away from foolishness (*risos*) and games, and that in thirty days she would come to be with the virgins

she had seen. The girl did this, and when she was dying after thirty days she saw the Virgin with the girls she had come with the first time, and the Virgin called her. She replied twice, "Lady I come, Lady I come." And saying this she gave up her soul to God, and thus she died in the company of the holy virgins. From which it clearly appears that it is forbidden to holy virgins to be at dances.

Unlike mozas, niñas (and niños) had some intrinsic innocence. Little children were put with Inés at the head of the Cubas procession. The villagers' idea seems to have been to put the village's best foot forward. They decided this without any explicit instructions from the Virgin, and two of the town officials went with the children to keep them in line. The strategy bore fruit, for a boy nine years old and a girl ten years old did hear the Virgin call to Inés, and another girl nine years old saw the Virgin, although the town official who was at the front of the procession with them saw and heard nothing. Children were privileged communicators with the divine, or at least privileged receptors.

The town fathers of Cubas did not invent the idea of a children's procession. The history of the children's crusades bears witness to the mobilization of the sacred child. In the fifteenth and sixteenth centuries, Barcelona children were prominently situated in penitential processions. In 1427 boys and girls (*fadrins et fadrines*) flagellated themselves in a penitential procession because of an earthquake. The procession may have been inspired in part by a Sicilian Franciscan, Mateo di Agrigento.[55] In the years 1455-1459 children 8-12 years old set out from Switzerland, Germany, and Belgium on group pilgrimages to Mont-Saint-Michel to beseech divine aid against the Turks.[56] In Girona, in April 1483, seven months before Miquel Noguer saw Mary as a small girl in nearby El Torn, children were paid to cry out, "Lord true God have mercy," when the host was raised in the Cathedral of Girona during a votive mass against the plague.[57] In Barcelona in a 1529 procession, boys and girls (*minyons y fadrines*) walked behind a crucifix crying "Señor Ver Deu Misericordia." On June 23, 1533, a set of boys (*min-*

yons) barefoot and wearing shirts, and a set of girls (*donzellas*) barefoot with their hair let down walked at the front of a general procession in Barcelona for the sick queen of Charles V. The next night the Augustinian friars organized a procession in which "small boys (*minyons petits*) barefoot in shirts walked whipping themselves between men who carried lighted candles."[58]

Those who ordered the Cubas procession (the priest, the mayors, the "*omes buenos*") certainly had a sense not only of childhood but also of the sacred importance of childhood. The Virgin shared their notions, for during the climactic apparition when she planted the cross, she also instructed Inés, now in a special consecrated state, to spend the night in the church "with some innocent young children (*algunas criaturas inocentes*)."

When was innocence lost? Inés, who was twelve had not lost hers, and this appeared to have weighed heavily in her favor. She was a moza who out of exceptional religiosity had maintained the purity of a niña. We might get a hint of the age of the loss of innocence from the age at which children began to confess or receive communion. Inés confessed for the first time at age six, and received communion for the first time at age nine; the first appears to have been typical, the second, precocious, doubtless because of her unusual piety. Vincent Ferrer instructed people to send their children to confess at age six, and to receive communion at age eleven or twelve.[59] It would seem, then, that there was a period between ages six and twelve in which there was still a degree of innocence.

The arrangement of children in a separate, advanced place in processions points to their separate sacred estate, like the separate legal estates of women, men, nobility, and clergy. In this sense it is certainly mistaken to assert that in medieval society the idea of childhood did not exist. In religious terms it was far more demarcated and accentuated in fifteenth-century Europe than in the industrial West of today. Rather one might say that *our* idea of childhood did not exist.

Children's sacred condition persists in devout areas of rural Spain, although it is no longer mobilized in processions.[60] Certainly children are carefully controlled, but they are also respected, observed, and privileged until they reach the age of sin and the world of work. When, after long intervals, I revisit a village where I have lived, I am disoriented by the passage of whole sets of children from a pampered and appreciated category to the profane, taken-for-granted status of fallen angels.

There is every indication that, in the late Middle Ages, high infant mortality, rather than hardening parents to the death of children, had the opposite effect—that of heightening their anxiety for, and love of, children. Two of the visionaries were reproved by Mary for getting angry or swearing at their children (Francisca la Brava in 1523 and María Torrent in 1618), indicating a high degree of sensitivity to child treatment. The miracles reported at Spanish shrines often involved cures of crippled children of poor parents who had escorted them from shrine to shrine over long distances.

The cases of Francisca la Brava and El Miracle drew us to the connection between Mary as a child and the dead child as an angel. The purity of young children ensured their passage to heaven. Hence Francisca la Brava was doubtless not surprised that her dead son appeared as one of the angels accompanying Mary back to heaven. It is perhaps a measure of the anxiety and attention devoted to children in these times of epidemic that Mary appeared as a child. The village next to Francisca's reported a child mortality rate four times as high as that of adults in a 1544 epidemic.[61] At El Miracle Mary appeared as a girl the same day a girl dead from the plague was buried on a nearby farm. Jeanne d'Arc's guardian saint, Catherine, bore the name of Jeanne's deceased sister.[62]

Philippe Ariès suggested that the motif of Mary as a child in late medieval art may have come as a result of the spread of the apocryphal gospels.[63] The explanation might just as well run the other way. The great plagues, with their disproportionate mortality of children, might have directed the attention of society more toward children as fragile and precious beings, and this attention in turn had repercussions in iconography, emphasizing the childhood of the two great religious figures, Christ and Mary, and by the same token the motherliness of Mary and Saint Anne. The popularity of the apocryphal gospels would then be a response to a need to know about and identify with the Gods as children. For these visions of Mary-as-child and child-sized Marys occurred in conjunction with or announcing epidemics, epidemics that would almost certainly strike children the hardest, like the baby in Jafre whose death, perhaps the first from that wave of the plague, confirmed Miquel Castelló's vision.

The role of children as intercessors is graphically illustrated by an account of another procession in Barcelona, one in which child mortality was explicitly mentioned. On April 12, 1507, in the midst of the great plague, the city held an elaborate procession to found a chapel to the plague saint, Sebastian. In the procession walked a man dressed as Saint Sebastian, his clothes pierced by arrows, "and after him a group of children in shirts and barefooted, flagellating themselves. Saint Sebastian would turn to the children and ask them what they wanted; and they would fall to their knees and reply, 'We all ask our lord God that we do not die so quickly from such a severe plague, and we say Lord God have mercy.' And those who said this wept with tears and lamentations so piercing that it almost broke the hearts of those who cried and those who heard them."[64] Such a drama reenacts, in a way, the apparitions studied above. For in at least eleven of the sixteen visions, children served as intermediaries between society and God, whether as seers, saints, or both.

The plagues and other insecurities of late medieval society may also account for the particular form of piety encouraged in these visions: a penitential devotion to the crucified Christ. The priest of Santa María de Llanos, when he heard Juan de Rabe's confession, decided to carry on his own back the cross they would set up. Mary presenting the Cross—planting it in Cubas, embracing it in Escalona, giving it to a child in El Miracle—would seem to mark a transition from a pre-plague rural devotion centered on a powerful Mary to a post-plague devotion centered on penance. (Similarly, Saint Sebastian appeared near El Toboso to present Saint Roch.) The Mary most appropriate to accompany the Cross was the pietà, foreshadowed in the weeping child of El Torn and the Mary with bloody knees of El Quintanar.

Although the major shrines of Castile and Catalonia remained Marian, overwhelmingly dedicated to Romanesque and Gothic images of Mary with the child Jesus, the miraculous signs of the sixteenth and seventeenth centuries were almost exclusively dedicated to crucifixes and images of the Passion. The only exceptions, in addition to the two late Catalan visions of Mary already mentioned, were images of Mary that wept.[65]

It was not uncommon for lay people in fifteenth-century Europe to imitate Christ's passion by public self-flagellation. Some of the processions held at Mary's request at El Miracle, El Torn, Sant Aniol, La Mota, and El Quintanar, and spontaneously at Cubas, Navas de San Antonio, Navalagamella, Escalona, and Reus, may have included flagellants. As a lay, as opposed to monastic, ascetic discipline, flagellation spread from Perugia in 1260 to much of central Europe. In Italy it was soon incorporated as a regular practice in religious brotherhoods.[66] It is not known when public flagellation was first practiced in Spain, but in the fourteenth and fifteenth centuries it was used there only on special occasions, such as after a mission or during a plague, or by a special group, such as the band of flagellants that circulated with Vincent Ferrer. Before 1500 public flagellation may have been more common in Catalonia than in Castile. Juan II of Aragon permitted it in 1394, and there were flagellant processions in Barcelona in 1425 and 1427.[67] One suspects that Mary's requests for processions in 1458 and 1483 were considered requests for flagellation.

The first penitential brotherhoods in Castile and Catalonia to practice flagellation regularly were dedicated to the True Cross and the Blood of Jesus, respectively.[68] They overlapped, if at all, only with the last of the visions described. ("The Captain of the Sinners" referred to in the visions of Quintanar may have been an official in a penitent "company.") Both the visions and the brotherhoods would seem to be independent manifestations of a devotional style new to Spain, but common in Germany and Italy.[69]

The association of the Franciscan order with the care of the shrines in the Holy Land, and Saint Francis's identification (to the point of stigmata) with Christ's passion, make the Franciscans those most likely to have propagated devotion to the Cross and the Passion.[70] They were by far the most numerous order in rural Spain. The first outside preacher to give a sermon at the site of the Cubas vision of Mary of the Cross, in 1449, was a Franciscan, possibly from the nearby convent at Recas. But it would be misleading to identify with a single order what was undoubtedly a broad movement of lay piety. The Augustinians, for instance, were in charge of the most popular Castilian shrine to the Crucified Christ—the Christ of Burgos—and devotion to Christ's passion was, of course, common to all orders.

Although the visions studied here were mostly of Mary, it was the nature of the times that they and others like them in Italy should emphasize Christ and the Cross, a warning of judgment and a model of penance. Both the Cross and the child were ultimately references to the plague. The children in Barcelona processions walked directly behind a crucifix; and it was to children that Mary presented crucifixes at Cubas, Escalona, and El Miracle. Children, like Christ, would be innocent victims for the sins of the community. They were the ideal messengers, human or divine, for warnings of judgment or imitations of Christ.

Notes

ABBREVIATIONS

ADC Archivo Diocesano de Cuenca
ADG Archivo Diocesano de Girona
ADT Archivo Diocesano de Toledo
AHN Archivo Histórico Nacional, Madrid
Dietari Barcelona, Consell de Cents Jurats, *Manual de Novells Ardits* (Barcelona, Henrich, I 1892, II 1893, III 1894, etc.).
Relaciones G I-VI Juan Catalina García, Manuel Pérez Villamil, *Relaciones topográficas de España (Memorial histórico español* XLI 1903, XLII 1903, XLIII 1905, XLV 1912, XLVI 1914, XLVII 1915)
Relaciones Cu I-II Eusebio Julián Zarco Bacas y Cuevas, *Relaciones de Pueblos del Obispado de Cuenca hechas por orden de Felipe II*, 2 vols. (Cuenca, Biblioteca diocesana conquense, 1927).
Relaciones M Carmelo Viñas y Mey, Ramón Paz, *Relaciones histórico-geográfico-estadísticas de los pueblos de España hechas por iniciativa de Felipe II; Provincia de Madrid* (Madrid, C.S.I.C., 1949).
Relaciones To I-III *Idem; Reino de Toledo*, Part I 1951, Part II (2 vols.), 1963.
Relaciones CR *Idem; Provincia de Ciudad Real*, 1971.
T Pierre Tisset, *Procès et Condemnation de Jeanne d'Arc*, 3 vols. (Paris, Klincksieck, 1960-1971).

INTRODUCTION: WHEN PEOPLE MEET GOD

1. Thomas Kselman, "Miracles and Prophecies: Popular Religion and the Church in Nineteenth-Century France." Unpublished Ph.D. thesis, Dept. of History, University of Michigan, 1978.

2. Bernard Billet et al., *Vraies et fausses apparitions dans l'Église* (Paris, Letheilleux, 1976).

3. The best study to date of the phenomenon of apparitions, in Spain or elsewhere, is Carlos María Staehlin, *Apariciones* (Madrid, Razón y Fe, 1954).

4. Caesarius of Heisterbach, *Dialogue on Miracles* (2 vols. London, Routledge, 1929).

5. P. Prigent, *Apocalypse 12; Histoire de l'Exégèse* (Tübingen, 1959).

6. Clemente Sánchez de Vercial, *El Libro de los exenplos por a. b. c.*, ed. John Esten Keller (Madrid, C.S.I.C., 1961). See also John Esten Keller, *Motif-Index of Mediaeval Spanish Exempla* (Knoxville, University of Tennessee Press, 1949); Frederic C. Tubach, *Index Exemplorum: A Handbook of Medieval Religious Tales* (Helsinki, Suomalainen Tiedeakatenia, 1969); and J. Th. Welter, *L'Exemplum dans la litterature religieuse et didactique du Moyen Age* (Paris and Toulouse, Occitania, 1927).

7. I treat the signs of the early modern period in Chapter Six of *Local Religion in Sixteenth-Century Spain* (Princeton, Princeton University Press, 1981).

8. Agne Beijer, "Visions célestes et infernales dans le théâtre du moyen-âge et de la Renaissance," 413 in Journées Internationales d'Études, *Les Fêtes de la Renaissance*, Vol. 1 (Paris, CNRS, 1956) 405-417.

CHAPTER 1. LATE MEDIEVAL APPARITIONS IN CASTILE

Introduction: Rural Life and Religion

1. Annie Molinié-Bertrand, "Le Clergé dans le royaume de Castille à la fin du XVIe siècle," *Revue d'histoire économique et sociale* 51 (1973) 5-53.

2. Mischa Titiev, "A Fresh Approach to the Problem of Magic and Religion," *Southwestern Journal of Anthropology* 16:3 (1960) 292-298.

3. Narciso Camós, *Iardin de Maria plantado en el principiado de Cataluña* (Barcelona, Iayme Plantada, 1657). The latest edition was published by Editorial Orbis, Barcelona, 1949. I cite (as *Jardín*) the 1657 edition.

4. Stephen Sharbrough, "The Cult of the Mother in Europe: The Transformation of the Symbolism of Woman." Unpublished Ph.D. thesis, Dept. of History, University of California, Los Angeles, 1977.

5. Eric R. Wolf, "Society and Symbols in Latin Europe and in the Islamic Near East: Some Comparisons," *Anthropological Quarterly* 42:3 (1969) 287-301.

6. Peter Brown, *The Cult of the Saints* (Chicago, University of Chicago Press, 1981).

7. Patrick Geary, *Furta Sacra* (Princeton, Princeton University Press, 1978).

8. Alfonso el Sabio, *Setenario*, ed. Kenneth H. Vanderford (Buenos Aires, Instituto de Filología, 1945) 73-76.

9. Eduard Junyent, personal communication.

10. For more on the Castilian legends and the *Relaciones topográficas* of Philip II see Christian, *Local Religion*, 75-91.

11. Legends from the *Relaciones*: San Pablo To II 392-3; Iniesta Cu I 32; Almonacid de Toledo To I 64-5; Fuenlabrada M 269; Cubas M 212; Hontova G IV 143; Ventas con Peña Aguilera To II 218-9; Daimiel Crosses CR 238-243; Daimiel Peace CR 237.

12. Jean Delumeau, *La Mort des pays de Cocagne* (Paris, Université de Paris, 1976) 65-6. Lucien Febvre, *Le Problème de l'incroyance au XVIe siècle* (Paris, A. Michel, 1962).

Santa Gadea

13. My source is a transcript of the original document in fifteenth-century script made in or after 1471 on a large parchment (AHN Clero, Carpeta 373, No. 15). The parchment does not have a notary's signature, and appears to have been destined for display in the shrine, for the apparition text is followed by a transcript of indulgences. In the Spanish version in the appendix below, I have put in brackets additional words or significant variants in a seventeenth-century transcript in the parish archive, as printed by Luciano Huidobro Serna in "Nuestra Señora del Espino en Santa Gadea del Cid (Burgos)" (Lérida, Imprenta Mariana, 1922). The text of the 1410 proceso is in AHN Clero Carpeta 373 No. 3, 1-7. There are licences for questors and mentions of miracles in AHN Clero Legajo 1366[2].

14. In 1399 "Santa Maria de Marzo" (presumably March 25, the Annunciation) was Tuesday of Holy Week. This was the day Pedro and Juan discovered the beehive. It was therefore the

following day, "miercoles de tiniebras," that they went to get the honey and had their vision. Assuming that "el jueves seguiente" means "the following Thursday," Pedro would have had the second, explanatory vision the next day. By the same token his beating took place either Easter eve or Easter night, and the public declaration was Easter morning or Easter Monday. But it is strange that Sunday in the document is not referred to as Easter. The document was drawn up Sunday, April 20, three weeks after Easter. It would appear to constitute a second, formal, notarized retelling by Pedro of what happened to him.

15. AHN Clero Leg. 1366 No. 1.

16. AHN Clero Carp. 373 No. 3, f. 6.

17. Mahfouz Labib, *Pèlerins et voyageurs au Mont Sinai* (Le Caire, Institut Français d'archéologie orientale, 1961) 50-51.

18. Kurt Weitzmann, *The Monastery of Saint Catherine at Sinai: The Icons (6th-10th century)* (Princeton, Princeton University Press, 1976) Plate XXVIII, 70-71; also his "Icon Painting in the Crusader Kingdom," *Dunbarton Oaks Papers* 20 (1966) 67, fig. 35, for a version from the thirteenth century.

19. Jean de Mandeville's account was perhaps the most widely read around 1400. Heinz Skrobucha, *Sinai* (London, Oxford University Press, 1966) 36-40.

20. E. Misset, *Une Église de Victorins en Champagne; Notre Dame de l'Épine près Châlons-sur-Marne; la legende, l'histoire, le monument et le pèlerinage* (Paris, Honoré Champion, 1902) 96, 28-41.

21. Legend was first published in P. Poiré, *Le Triple Couronne*. It can be read in Hamon, *Notre Dame de France* (7 vols., Paris, Plon, 1862-1866) V (1865) 402; and J. B. Drochon, *Histoire illustrée des pèlerinages de la Très Sainte Vierge* (Paris, Plon, 1892) 1214. Puiseux, *Notre Dame de l'Épine; son histoire, son pèlerinage* (Châlons-sur-Marne, Martin Frères, 1910) 24, has the engraving, cf. Misset, *Une Église*, 48-51.

22. *Acta Sanctorum*, Vol. 1 (1643), January 11, 708-712.

23. Labib, *Pèlerins*, 38.

24. Alfonso el Sabio, *Las Siete Partidas*, trans. Samuel Parsons Scott (Chicago, Commerce Clearing House, 1931) Part 1, Title X, Law X (p. 160).

25. Alfonso el Sabio, *Setenario*, 47: Ca antoiança el nonbre muestra que non es ssinon commo cosa que sse parase ante los oios e sse tolliese luego, ssegunt lo que vee o lo que oye arrebatadamiente, e por ende non es firmeza ninguna.

26. See note 48 below.

27. Alonso de Venero [O.P.], *Enchiridio delos tiempos*, 4th ed. (Burgos, Juan de Junta, 1551) cxxi r: . . . a intercession de la ymagen de la virgen Maria que fue hallada en el mesmo lugar: cerca de los años del Señor de Mcccc.

Jaén

28. The original document, a parchment 40.5 cm. x 61 cm. in script appropriate for the time, is in the parish church of San Ildefonso. It appears to be genuine. I greatly revised the version published by Vicente Montuno Morente, *Nuestra Señora de la Capilla: Madre, Patrona, y Reina de Jaén (Ensayo histórico)* (Madrid, Blass Tipografía, 1950) 305-313, Información testifical del descenso de Nuestra Señora.

29. Montuno Morente, *Nuestra Señora de la Capilla*, 35-39.

30. María Sánchez could not identify the beata. Subsequent portrayals of the event in Jaén depict her as Saint Catherine, who supposedly aided in the capture of the city by Fernando el Santo, and to whom the castle on a bluff outside the town is dedicated (Montuno Morente, 49, note). Another possibility is Saint Leocadia. The legend of her appearance to Saint Ildefonsus and her praise for his Marian devotion was widely diffused.

31. Montuno Morente, *Nuestra Señora de la Capilla*, 139-164.

32. *Ibid.*, Plate XVI, 100-106.

33. Sister Athanasius Braegelmann, *The Life and Writings of Saint Ildefonsus of Toledo*, Studies in Medieval History, New Series, Vol. 4 (Catholic University of America, Washington, D.C., 1942). Braegelmann's translation is from p. 24; life by Cixila in *Patrologia Latina*, XCVI c. 46.

34. Braegelmann, *Life*, 28; A. Mussafia, "Studien zu den mittelalterlichen Marienlegenden," I, II, III, *Sitzungsberichte der Wiener Akademie*, phil.-hist. Klasse, CXIII (1886) 917-994;

CXV (1888) 5-93; CXIX (1889) 1-66; and L. Villecourt, "Les collections arabes des miracles de la sainte vierge," *Analecta Bollandiana* XLII (1924) 21-68.

35. *Relaciones* To III 496, 528, 540, 545.

36. Barcelona, *Dietari* I 238 (II-8-1425) and 251 (VI-6-1427). Procession of king in 1390, I 3.

37. J. Vives in *DHEE* IV 2245 gives references. Also E. Bayerri Bertomeu, *Los códices medievales de la Catedral de Tortosa* (Tortosa, Gráficos Algueró, 1962) 447-449. A. Durand, *L'Écrin de la Sainte Vierge* (Lille, Desclée, 1885) 107-242.

38. Montuno Morente, *Nuestra Señora de la Capilla*, 379-390.

39. Pierre Tisset ed., *Le Procès et condemnation de Jeanne d'Arc* (Paris, Klincksieck, 1970) Vol. 2, 65-67.

40. Bede, *Ecclesiastical History*, II 6; Caesarius, *Dialogue*, II 501-502, 26, 52-3; Sánchez, *Libro exenplos*, 70-71.

Cubas

41. Gaspar Calvo Moralejo, "Santa María de la Cruz," *Antonianum* 50 (1975) 561-575, and "Santa María de la Cruz; Apariciones marianas en el siglo xv y nueva advocación de la Virgen," Cuadernos de historia de la Teología, 5 (Santiago, El Eco Franciscano, 1979).

The Cubas text given here is a transcription made by Joaquín Díaz from the original and from another transcription in 1789. It is a leather-bound *cuaderno* kept in the Cubas convent. The existence of the original is mentioned in the *relación* of Cubas to Philip II (M 212-213). A history by Antonio Daça (1610) cites directly from the original or an earlier transcription. The contents of the 1789 cuaderno are as follows:

folios

1-8, declaration of Inés, March 10, 1449, Cubas.

8r-11v, declaration of Inés, March 21, 1449, Cubas.

12r-23r, presentation of the official commission from Archbishop Alonso Carrillo for an investigation, including versions of the foregoing declarations forwarded to the archbishop.

25r-72v, interrogation of 21 witnesses, beginning with Inés on April 23, 1449.

75v-138, 68 miracles from 1449 to 1600, recorded by village notaries.

There are two versions of the first depositions of Inés—that taken down directly (1r-11v), and an edited version sent to the archbishop (12r-23r). I have translated the first, putting the few variants in substance from the second in brackets. I am indebted to Fr. Gaspar Calvo Moralejo and the Franciscan Sisters of Santa María de la Cruz for their assistance.

42. Cubas cuaderno, 48r, 63v, 60r, 62v.

43. *Ibid.*, 64v-68r.

44. *Ibid.*, 57rv.

45. *Ibid.*, 39r, 46r, 62r, also Inés: "muy chiquita," 47r.

46. *Ibid.*, 38r, 57v, 63r.

47. Pedro Navarro, *Favores de el Rey de el Cielo hechos a su esposa la santa Juana de la Cruz* . . . (Madrid, Thomas Iunti, 1622) 21.

48. Soterraña: the basic legend is given in Esteban de Garibay, *Compendio historial de las chronicas* . . . (Anvers, Christophoro Plantino, 1571) II 1049, but not the proof of a hand stuck to a stone, which is in Diego de Colmenares, *Historia de Segovia* [1637] (Segovia, 1969) I 230-232.

Risco: Juan de Villafañe, *Compendio histórico en que se da noticia de las milagrosas, y devotas imágenes* . . . , 2nd ed. (Salamanca, 1740) 500 ff.

Carrodilla: Camós, *Jardín*, 178-184.

Sogas: Camós, *Jardín*, 244-250.

Carramia: Camós, *Jardín*, 230-231.

Prado: Roque Alberto Faci, *Aragón, Reyno de Christo y dote de María SSma* (Zaragoza, Joseph Fort, 1739) Part 2, 163.

Pueyo: Faci, *Aragón*, Part 2, 79.

49. Eloy Benito Ruano, *Toledo en el siglo XV; vida política* (Madrid, C.S.I.C., 1961).

50. For razzias of the Navarrese see the *Relaciones* of Fuencarral (M 258), Esquivias (To I 401), Berniches (G I 30), Jadraque (G I 266-267), and Tendilla (G III 71), and Fidel Fita, "Fuen-

carral. Su destrucción a mediados del siglo xv. Datos inéditos,'' *Boletín de la Real Academia de la Historia* 35 (1899) 359-364. Paracuellos abductions Cubas cuaderno, 98r-99v.

51. The Marian days observed in the diocese of Toledo in 1449 were the Purification, the Annunciation, Saint Mary of the Snows, the Assumption, the Nativity of Mary, and the Expectation (José Sánchez Herrero, *Concilios provinciales y sínodos toledanos de los siglos XIV y XV*, Universidad de La Laguna, Estudios de Historia, 2, 1976; see texts of synods of 1356 and 1379).

52. Jean Céard, *La Nature et les prodiges; l'insolite au XVIe siècle* (Geneva, Droz, 1977) 76, 259. Fernán Pérez de Guzmán, *Crónica del Señor Rey Don Juan Segundo* (Valencia, Benito Monfort, 1779) 383-384.

53. "La Pístola de Sant Miquel," text in Daniel de Molins de Rei, "Notes sobre la 'Lletra caiguda del Cel,' Les versions catalanes en prosa," *Estudis Franciscans* 43 (1931) 79: pedres tallants he calents del cell . . . he les pedres seran mesclades ab sanch, de que mataran ha vosaltres he ha vostres fylls e filles.

54. Sebastiano Rumor, *Storia documentata del Santuario di Monte Berico* (Vicenza, Officina grafica pontificia S. Giuseppe, 1911) Processo 397-428. For a similar story, including the planting of a cross by a Mary-girl in 1420, see Antonio M. Vicentini, *Storia documentata del santuario di S. Maria della Crocetta in Godego* (Vicenza, Giovanni Galla, n.d., ca. 1920). This vision is not well documented.

55. The earliest source I know of for the Caravaggio story is the Latin inscription on a painting at the shrine around 1638, transcribed by Donato Calvi (b. 1613) in *Delle grandezze della Madonna Santissima del Sacro Fonte di Caravaggio* (Milano, G. Batista Messaggi, 1832) 38-40. The shrine was important at least as early as 1470 (135-136).

56. Cubas cuaderno, 79v.

57. Thomas N. Tentler, "The Problem of Anxiety and Preparation for Death in Luther, Calvin, and Erasmus." Unpublished Ph.D. thesis, Dept. of History, Harvard University, 1961.

58. Cubas cuaderno, 119v-120r.

59. On saludadores: Pedro de Ciruelo, *Reprobacion de las*

supersticiones y hechizerias rev. ed. (Salamanca, Pedro de Castro, 1541) Part III, Ch. 7; Antonio Torquemada, *Iardin de flores curiosas* (Salamanca, Iuan Baptista de Terranoua, 1570) 161.

60. In Griñón an *Informazion* was made June 21, 1569 by order of the señor of the village (and of Cubas) Alonso de Mendoza y Toledo. An eighteenth-century transcription in the parish archive of Griñón has 43 numbered pliegos (182 pages). Sixteen miracles were recorded from July 3, 1569, to April 3, 1570.

61. Cubas cuaderno, 110r.

62. *Ibid.*, 41v.

63. *Ibid.*, 136r-138r.

64. *Relaciones* M 212-213.

65. Antonio Daça, *Historia, vida, y milagros, extasis, y revelaciones de la bienaventurada virgen santa Iuana de la Cruz* (Madrid, Luis Sánchez, 1610); Navarro, *Favores*, 1622; additional bibliography in the essays of G. Calvo Moralejo, note 41 above.

66. Navarro, *Favores*, 43.

Guadalupe

67. Anselm Albareda, *Historia de Montserrat*, 5th ed. rev. (Montserrat, 1974); Germán Rubio, *Historia de Nuestra Señora de Guadalupe* (Barcelona, Industrias Gráficas Thomás, 1926). Guadalupe in Madrid in 1604: Jeronimo de Quintana, *Historia de la antiguedad, nobleza, y grandeza de la Villa de Madrid*, Imprenta del Reyno, 1629 (Madrid, Artes Gráficas Municipales, 1954) 895-896. Minims and La Soledad: Antonio Ares, *Discurso del Ilustre Origen* (1640) 234v-235v.

68. Rubio, *Historia de Guadalupe*, 51.

69. Diego de Ecija, *Libro de la invención de esta santa imagen de Guadalupe* (Cáceres, Biblioteca extremeña, 1953) 49, also AHN Clero, Cod. 101, 5v-6 (ca. 1500).

70. Galician shrines: personal communications, shrine keepers and villagers, 1978. See William A. Christian Jr., "La Religiosidad Popular, Hoy," in J. A. Durán ed., *Galicia, Realidad económica y conflicto social* (La Coruña, Imprenta La Voz de Galicia, 1978) 551-569.

71. AHN Clero Cod. 48 B 5v-8v. This history of the foundation of the monastery appears to have been written, possibly by Fr. Alonso de la Rambla, for use in sermons or in guiding pilgrims (viz. the frequent use of *sabed que* . . .) sometime between 1400 and 1440. A different writer made additions and corrections on the original, but I have omitted them. A later codice (AHN Clero Codice 101) that dates from around 1500 appears to be a more literary version of this one.

72. On the pattern of discoveries of relics, Patrick Geary, *Furta Sacra*, 12, 46, 154-157.

73. The image of Nuestra Señora del Sepulcro was found in a grave in Valverde del Majano (Segovia) on November 27, 1623. The original *expediente* with the testimony of four witnesses, drawn up by Pedro Arias Davila on May 11, 1624, is in the parish archive. For Bernardos (Segovia), Ildefonso Llorente Fernández, *Historia de la aparición de la Virgen del Castillo* . . . (Valladolid, Julián Pastor e hijos, 1867), and Rufino Nuñez, *Bernardos y su Virgen del Castillo* (Segovia, 1928).

74. Legends of apparitions in the towns of New Castile (excluding the Province of Cuenca) as reported by town elders 1575-1580 to Philip II and town priests 1782-1786 to Cardinal Lorenzana:

	1575-1580 (464 towns)	1782-1786 (534 towns)
Mary	7	25
Saints	4	3
Crosses	0	2

Navas de Zarzuela

75. The transcript was made by the notary Juan Negrillo of Segovia. It is in the parish archive in a book labeled Legajo 4, numero 3, Testimonio dela Aparicion de S. Ant°. y Papeles tocantes asu Capillan, y Capp^{nia}. The pages are unnumbered.

76. The date of the document is not correct, and its chronology uncertain. In 1455, August 4 was a Monday, not a Friday. The first apparition is not dated; the second was on the sixteenth of an unspecified month; and the third apparition is also undated. The cure of the woman appears to have happened the day before the procession, which was on the 28th of some

month, and the document, dated August 4, appears to have been drawn up later, with the final miracle of September 10 appended.

77. Throughout the fifteenth century, textile craftsmen formed guilds in Castile, first of pe	railes (as in Cuenca by 1428), then of specialists. In rural Catalonia pe	railes at this time had the most goods of all artisans. One in 1461 had many books, including a rhymed New Testament, story books, and works of grammar, logic, and philosophy. J. Serra Vilaró, *Baronies de Pinós i Mataplana* (Barcelona, Ed. Balmes, 1947) Vol. 2 378; Pierre Bonnassie, *La Organización del trabajo en Barcelona a fines del siglo XV* (Barcelona, C.S.I.C., 1975), Anuario de Estudios Medievales, Anejo 8, 16; Paulino Iradiel Murugarren, *Evolución de la industria textil castellana, XIII-XVI [Acta Salamanticensis* 84 (1974)] 12, 78; Soterraña Martín Postigo, "Expediente para reformar las ordenanzas del obraje de los paños hechas en 1500," *Estudios Segovianos* 15 (1953) 363-412.

78. Urquiola: Benito de Vizcarra y Arana, *Reseña histórica del multisecular santuario de los Santos Antonios de Urquiola* (Vitoria, Imp. del Montepío Diocesano, 1932).

79. El Tiemblo: The brotherhood of San Antonio in El Tiemblo has been in existence at least since 1542, the date of the oldest ledger kept there now. There is no legend; only that the saint was chosen by lottery. The zone of attraction of the shrine is largely the southern slope of the Guadarrama, especially the adjacent area of the province of Toledo. In this it complements the Navas shrine, which draws devotion almost exclusively from the northern slopes. Interview with D. Julio González, parish priest of El Tiemblo, VI-3-1977.

Navalagamella

80. Relaciones del Cardenal Lorenzana, ADT Navalagamella (Madrid), X-18-1782, and Fresnedillas (Madrid) III-17-1783.

81. The only copy of *Grandezas de San Miguel Archangel* I have seen is in the parish archive; it is damaged, and the title page is missing. The chapter on Navalagamella is pp. 104-121. I gratefully acknowledge the assistance of the parish priest, D. Enrique Herrero García.

82. Armando Petrucci, "Origine e diffusione del culto di San Michele nell' Italia medievale," in Michel Baudot ed., *Culte de*

Saint Michel et Pèlerinages au Mont (Paris, Lethielleux, 1971), Vol. 3. of _Millénaire Monastique du Mont Saint-Michel._

83. _Monumenta Germaniae Historica_, Scriptores Rerum Langobardicarum et Italicarum, saec. vi-ix (Hannover, 1878) [1964] 542.

84. E. Moreu-Rey, "La Dévotion à Saint Michel dans les pays catalans," in Baudot, _Culte de Saint Michel_, 369-388.

85. José M. Jimeno Jurio, _San Miguel de Aralar_ (Pamplona, Dip. Foral de Navarra, n.d.) 10-12.

Escalona

86. "Informacion judicial de testigos" (X-17-1617 to IV-1-1618) made by the parish priest Juan Mancio Davila before the notary Juan de Adrados with permission of the provisor general of the Diocese, Salazar. The información was approved April 7, 1618, by Pedro Suárez de la Concha. I used a first copy of 95 folios in the parish archive, and a Miracle Register that had in it a history of hermits at the shrine, dated 1618. Some of the material was published in a booklet by Francisco Sanz de Frutos, _Historia de Nuestra Señora de la Cruz_ (Vitoria, Hijos de Pujol, 1887). I am indebted to D. Mariano Tejedor, parish priest of Escalona, for his help.

87. Similar explanations for holy springs drying up due to profanation are found at one of the Italian Marys of the Cross, Monte Berico, where the apparition spring dried up in 1509, supposedly because a man watered his sick horse there, and at the Font Santa of Jafre, below.

88. Escalona "Informacion" 32r.

89. Escalona miracle register, 37-8.

90. Escalona "Informacion" 91v-92r.

91. _Ibid._, 91v.

Chapter 2. Late Medieval Apparitions in Catalonia

The Catalan Context

1. Fortià Solà, _Història de Nuria_ (Barcelona, Editorial Estel, 1952).

2. Iayme Prades, _Historia de la adoracion y uso de las santas_

imagenes, y de la imagen de la fuente de la salud (Valencia, Felipe Mey, 1597).

3. VI Semana de Estudios Monásticos, *España Eremítica*, Analecta Legerensia, Abadía de San Salvador de Leyre, Navarra, (Pamplona, Editorial Aranzadi, 1970).

4. J.-P. Cuviller, "La Population catalane au XVe siècle. Comportements sociaux et niveaux de vie d'après les actes privés," *Mélanges de la Casa de Velázquez* 5 (1969) 159-187.

5. Pierre Vilar, *La Catalogne dans l'Espagne Moderne* (3 vols., Paris SEVPEN, 1962) I 481-2.

6. Archivo de la Corona de Aragón, Reg. 1154 14v, in Amada López de Meneses, "Documentos acerca de la peste negra en los dominios de la Corona de Aragón," *Estudios de Edad Media de la Corona de Aragón* 6 (1956) 423.

El Miracle

7. The text I have translated was drawn by P. Cebrià Baraut (*Santa María del Miracle*, Montserrat, 1962, 163-170) from two sources: A, "Llibre calendari de totas les terras y proprietats de esta casa del Miracle" (17th century) fols. 9-15, in the archive of El Miracle; and B, a book of notes from the parish archive of La Curriu, probably kept by the parish priest, Juan Blanch, from 1580 to 1596. This latter version was first published by J. Viladrich, *Memoria histórico-descriptiva de la imagen y santuario de Nuestra Señora del Milagro de Riner* (Lérida, Imprenta Mariana, 1898) 144-153. The translation is of Baraut's preferred text, and I include the variants in the original in the appendix. I gratefully acknowledge Cebrià Baraut's permission to reprint the text.

8. Apocryphal Gospel of Matthew, Ch. 6. See also Gospel of the Nativity of Mary, Ch. 6. *Apocryphal Gospels, Acts, and Revelations*, Vol. XVI, The Ante-Nicene Christian Library, (Edinburgh, T. and T. Clark, 1870).

9. Camós, *Jardín*, 230-231.

Jafre

10. Barcelona, *Dietari*, II 242-243.

11. Jafre texts are from Libro de la Confraria del Roser 1622,

f. 6 ff., compiled with what remains legible of the original in the ADG Section C, No. 16, lligall 71 by Maruja Arnau i Guerola in *Jafre i el santuari de la Font Santa* (Girona, Gráficos Taberner, 1974) 145-152, and they are reprinted here by her kind permission. In the diocesan archive is the permission for almsquestors within the diocese dated July 10, 1461. It refers in particular to cures of the plague (ADG T/26, Regesto de Questoriorum 72v-73r).

12. José Rius Serra, *Regesto Ibérico de Calixto III* (2 vols., Barcelona, C.S.I.C., 1948) Bull of August 6, 1456 (II, 214).

El Torn

13. Barcelona, *Dietari*, II and III *passim*.

14. Camós, *Jardín*, 39-40.

15. Luis G. Constans, *Historia de Santa María de Collell* (Santuario del Collell, 1954).

16. *Ibid.*, 87-90, corrected as per photograph of original document. In a similar Italian vision, Mary appeared as a girl dressed in white to an elderly man praying in Motta di Livenza (Treviso). Mary instructed him on March 9, 1510, to fast for three consecutive Saturdays, for nine days to preach to the people of the town and the surrounding region that whoever fasted with repentence would be forgiven, and to ask for a church. His testimony is preserved in the Biblioteca Comunale di Treviso. See Prosdocimo Prodomi, *La Madonna dei Miracoli in Motta di Livenza* (Motta di Livenza, Santuario, 1954).

Pinós

17. Camós, *Jardín*, 384-385. He cites a document in the archive of the collegiate church of San Vicente de Cardona by Juan Nogués, notary public, September 5, 1507. I have not been able to find this document in Cardona. In Camós's time there was a copy in the chapel of Pinós notarized by Jerónimo Alsina and Juan Torrebruna, who were notaries in Cardona from 1620-1640. Their notebooks are in the Archivo de la Corona de Aragón in Barcelona and possibly would include a transcript.

Reus

18. Alexis Théas, *Notre-Dame de Médoux; aujourd'hui Notre-Dame d'Aste*, 2nd ed. (Tarbes, Clément Larrieu, 1896). Evidence is the town council records of sending the seer to Spain and an official retrospective investigation in 1648 with 18 witnesses, excerpted in this edition and printed in full in the first edition, 207-266.

19. Juan Bertrán Borras, *Nuestra Señora de la Misericordia y su santuario de Reus* (Reus, Santuario, 1966) 8-10, cites manuscript history destroyed in 1835.

20. Camós, *Jardín*, 4-5.

21. Hamon, *Notre Dame de France*, III 105, gives an almost identical vision occurring in Perpignan at the end of the seventeenth century—a vision of Our Lady "de la Miséricorde" to a shepherdess during a plague; "Tell the consuls to make a solemn procession with candle in hand." Could this be a satellite shrine from Reus?

Sant Aniol

22. Camós, *Jardín*, 101-102, has text and names of witnesses to declarations of December 8, 1618, and July 28, 1629. Local historians have been unable to locate the original documents. Miguel Juanola Benet, *Historia y tradición del Santuario de Na. Sa. dels Arcs* (Santa Pau, 1950).

23. Michel Vovelle and Gaby Vovelle, *Vision de la mort et l'au-delà en Provence du XVe au XXe siècle*, Cahier des Annales (Paris, A. Colin, 1970).

Catalan and Castilian Messages

24. *Quaresma de Sant Vicent Ferrer*, ed. Josep Sanchis Sivera (Barcelona, Institut Patxot, 1927) 283; also in *Sermons* II (Barcelona, Ed. Barcino, 1971).

25. Henry Dominique Fages, *Historia de S. Vicente Ferrer* (2 vols., Valencia, A. García, 1903) II 76-77.

26. Vincent Ferrer, *Sermons*, II 38.

27. Barbara Nolan, *The Gothic Visionary Perspective* (Princeton, Princeton University Press, 1978).

28. Hippolyte Delehaye, "Note sur la légende de la lettre tombée du ciel," Académie Royale de Belgique, *Bulletins de la Classe de Lettres*, Bruxelles, 1899, 171-213; R. Aramon i Serra, "Dos textos versificats en català de la carta tramesa del cel," *Estudis Universitaris Catalans* XIV 2 (1929) 279-298; D. Molins de Rei, "Notes sobre la 'Lletra caiguda del Cel'; les versions catalanes en prosa," *Estudis Franciscans* 43 (1931) 53-94; Norman Cohn, *The Pursuit of the Millennium*, rev. ed. (New York, Oxford University Press, 1970) 129-132, 134, 347.

29. *The Revelations of Saint Birgitta* (London, English Early Text Society, 1929) Book IV, Ch. 41.

30. *Ibid.*, Book I, Ch. 41, Ch. 57; Book IV, Ch. 41.

31. Ottavia Niccoli, "Profezie in piazza. Note sul profetismo popolare nell'Italia del primo Cinquecento," *Quaderni Storici* 41 (May-August, 1979) 500-539.

Chapter 3. Repression of Apparitions

León

1. Arturo Alvarez, *La Virgen del Camino, en León* (Vitoria, Imp. Fournier, 1968) 56-58.

2. *Conciliorum oecumenicorum decreta* (Bologna, Herder, 1962) 613. Apparitions may also have been discredited by certain well-known frauds; Dominicans at Bern in 1507 impersonated Mary, having her say that she was not conceived immaculately. This case was known in the Spanish Court. See Pietro Martire d'Anghiera, *Opus Epistolarum* (1530), letter of May 14, 1507, from Hornillos. Louis Lavater in *De Spectris* (Zurich, 1570) Part 1, Chapters vii-ix, recounts this and other similar cases.

3. Luis Salus Ballust, "Espiritualidad española en la primera mitad del siglo XVI," *Cuadernos de Historia* 1 (1967) (Madrid) 169-188; Marcel Bataillon, "Sur la diffusion des oeuvres de Savonarole en Espagne et en Portugal, 1500-1560," *Mélanges de philologie . . . offerts à M. Joseph Vianey* (Paris, 1934); V. Beltrán de Heredia, "Las Corrientes de Espiritualidad entre los Domínicos de Castilla durante la primera mitad del siglo XVI," *Miscelánea Beltrán de Heredia* (Salamanca, Ed. OPE, 1972-1973) III 519-671.

4. Bartolomé Bennassar, *L'Inquisition Espagnole* (Paris, Hachette, 1979) 25.

5. For Cuenca, Sebastián Cirac Estopiñán, *Registros de los documentos del Santo Oficio de Cuenca* Vol. 1 (Cuenca and Barcelona, 1965).

La Mota

6. ADC Inquisición, Legajo 70: 1039.

7. These are standard categories used by confessors at the time; cf. Thomas Tentler, *Sin and Confession on the Eve of the Reformation* (Princeton, Princeton University Press, 1977) 110-113.

Quintanar de la Orden

8. ADC Inquisición, Legajo 83: 1190.

9. The women of Quintanar doubtless told those of El Toboso at the market held on Thursdays in El Toboso. *Relaciones*, To III 584.

10. Christian, *Local Religion*, 196-197.

11. Niccoli, "Profezie in piazza," 514-515.

12. Henry Charles Lea, *A History of the Inquisition of Spain* (New York, Macmillan, 1907) IV 36-41, 81-93; Bennassar, *L'Inquisition espagnole*, 197-240; Julio Caro Baroja, *Las formas complejas de la vida religiosa; Religión, sociedad y caracter en la España de los siglos XVI y XVII* (Madrid, Akal, 1978) 86-90; Antonio Arbiol, *Desengaños mysticos* (Barcelona, Thomas Piferrer, 1772) 75-81, 410-416; T. D. Kendrick, *Mary of Agreda: The Life and Legend of a Spanish Nun* (London, Routledge and K. Paul, 1967). On non-ecstatic diviners and magicians, Julio Caro Baroja, *Vidas mágicas e inquisición* (Madrid, Taurus, 1967) Vol. 2 9-94.

CHAPTER 4. GENERAL THEMES IN THE VISIONS

Jeanne d'Arc

1. T I 320-321; T II 277-278.

2. T I 73; T II 74-75.

3. T I 161-162.

4. T I 115-118; I 133-137; T II 107-109; T II 120-124.

5. T I 136.

6. T II 56, 74, 123.

7. T II 85-86, 163.

8. T II 192, 208-210.

9. T II 210-211.

10. T I 340; T II 145, 295.

11. T II 214.

12. T I 244.

13. T I 318.

14. Jean Gerson, *Opera Omnia*, ed. Ellies du Pin (5 vols., Antwerp, 1706) I 43-59. Paschal Boland, *The Concept of Discretio Spirituum in John Gerson's "De Probatione Spirituum," and "De Distinctione Verarum Visionum a Falsis,"* Studies in Sacred Theology, Second Series, 112 (Catholic Univ. of America, Washington, D.C., 1959).

15. Dorothy G. Wayman, "The Chancellor and Jeanne d'Arc," *Franciscan Studies* 17 (1957) 273-303. Wayman's text is more in keeping with Gerson's earlier treatises than the questionable essay, possibly a forgery, used at the 1455 trial and reprinted in almost all editions of Gerson's works.

16. P. Doncoeur and Y. Lahors, *Documents et Recherches relatifs à Jeanne la Pucelle* (Paris, Librairies d'Argences, 1956) Vol. 3 70 ff.; Saint Athanasius, *The Life of St. Anthony*, trans. Robert T. Meyer (Westminister Md., The Newman Press, 1950).

17. Iamblichus, *De Mysteriis*, ed. Ed. des Places (Paris, Les Belles Lettres, 1966) II 3.

18. T I 87.

19. William A. Christian Jr., *Person and God in a Spanish Valley* (New York, Academic Press, 1972) 139.

20. T I 73.

21. T I 86, 122.

22. T I 138.

23. Doncoeur and Lahors, *Documents* II 80-83.

24. Pedro Ciruelo, *Reprobacion delas supersticiones y hechizerias* [first ed. 1530 (?)] Rev. ed. (Salamanca, Pedro de Castro,

1541) Book III, Ch. 8. An edition was printed in the Colección Joyas Bibliográficas, Madrid, 1952.

25. Sánchez, *Libro exenplos* 329-330.

26. J. M. de Garganta and V. Forcada, *Biografía y escritos de San Vicente Ferrer* (Madrid, B.A.C., 1956) 465-541 and V. Beltrán de Heredia, "Los alumbrados de la diócesis de Jaén," in *Miscelánea* III 324-334.

27. Ciruelo, *Reprobacion*, Book II, Ch. 1.

28. Gerson, "De Probatione Spirituum" in Boland, *The Concept*, 37.

29. Gerson, *Omnia Opera* I 15 cited in J. L. Connolly, *John Gerson, Reformer and Mystic* (Louvain, Librairie Univ., 1928).

30. Pedro Navarro, *Favores de el Rey de el cielo . . .* (Madrid, Thomas Iunti, 1622) 7.

31. Juan Horozco y Covarrubias, *Tratado de la verdadera y falsa prophecia* (Segovia, Iuan de la Cuesta, 1588) 57rv.

32. Antonio Arbiol, *Desengaños mysticos a las almas detenidas, o engañadas en el camino de la perfeccion* Impresion Nona (Barcelona, Thomas Piferrer, 1772) 78.

33. Martín de Castañega, *Tratado de las supersticiones y hechicerias* [1529] (Madrid, Sociedad de Bibliófilos Españoles, 1946) Ch. 5.

34. Caesarius, *Dialogue* I 481.

35. Gerson, "De Probatione Spirituum" in Boland, *The Concept* 30-31.

36. Vincent Ferrer, *Sermons* (3 vols., Barcelona, Ed. Barcino) II (1971) 15: E veus que hun dia Zacaries anà al temple per fer oració, e, axí com fahia oració, l'àngel Gabriel li apparech al cap del altar, e Zacaries hac-ne terror. 'Ne timeas, Zacaria.' E sapiats que doctrina és certa que quan appar l'àngel bo o la ànima a qualque persona, tantost le dóna terror, car la carn no u pot sostenir; mas, tantost aconsole la persona; e per ço: 'No temats.' This was a common illustration. See also C.S.M. Kniazzeh and E. J. Neugaard eds. *Vides de Sants Rosselloneses* (3 vols., Barcelona, Fundació S. Vives Casajuana, 1977) III 318.

37. Artemidoris of Daldis, *On the Interpretation of Dreams*, trans. Robert J. White (Park Ridge, N.J., Noyes Press, 1975) II 40.

38. Sulpicius Severus, *Life of St. Martin of Tours*, trans. F. R. Hoare, in *The Western Fathers* (New York, 1954) 89.

Spanish Visions

39. T I 340-341.

40. Christian, *Local Religion*, 103-105, 247.

41. Lucio Marineo Siculo, *De las cosas memorables de España* (Alcala, Miguel de Eguia, 1530) 91r-93r, "De las casas que ay en España de deuocion y Romeria."

Sources and Diffusion of the Vision Stories

42. Vicente de la Fuente, *Vida de la Virgen María con la historia de su culto en España* (2 vols., Barcelona, 1879) II 41; Staehlin, *Apariciones*, 148-149; Sharbrough, "The Cult of the Mother," 90 ff.

43. T II 45, text and note.

44. Sharbrough, "The Cult of the Mother," 93-100.

45. Richard B. Donovan, *The Liturgical Drama in Medieval Spain* (Toronto, Pontifical Institute of Medieval Studies, 1958) 110-118. On the *pastorets*, Catalan nativity plays acted out by children, see Francesc Curet, *Història del teatre Català* (Barcelona, Aedos, 1967) 41-43.

46. Ronald C. Finucane, *Miracles and Pilgrims; Popular Beliefs in Medieval England* (London, Dent, 1977) 160, for circulation of information on miracles among preachers by letter.

47. *Ibid.*, 34.

48. Alvarez, *La Virgen del Camino*, 86, 56.

49. Investigation in Albalate de Zorita (Guad.) was made in 1555; transcript in parish archive is from end of the eighteenth century.

The Logic of Divine Behavior

50. Jean-François Botrel, "Les aveugles colporteurs d'imprimés en Espagne," *Mélanges de la Casa de Velázquez* 9 (1973) 417-482, 10 (1974) 233-272.

51. Mario Martins, "Narrativas da Apariçoes de Nossa Senhora (ate ao sec. XII)," *Acta Salamanticensis* (1958) 703-722.

52. Caesarius, *Dialogue* II 344.

Children, Saints, and the Plague

53. Emmanuel Le Roy Ladurie, *Montaillou, village occitain de 1294 à 1324* (Paris, Gallimard, 1975) 306-309.

54. Sánchez, *Libro exenplos*, 84.

55. Barcelona, *Dietari*, I 251, 238; Jordi Rubio, "El b. fra Mateu d'Agrigento a Catalunya i Valencia" *Gesammelte Ausatze zur Kulturgeschicte Spaniens* (Munster) 11 (1955) 115.

56. Lionel Rothkrug, "Popular Religion and Holy Shrines," in James Obelkevich ed., *Religion and the People, 800-1700* (Chapel Hill, University of North Carolina Press, 1979) 20-86, 61-62; E. R. Labande, "Les pèlerinages au Monte-Saint-Michel pendant le moyen-âge," in Baudot, *Culte de Saint Michel*, 247-248; bibliography in Ulrich Gabler, "Die Kinderwallfahrten aus Deutschland und der Schweiz zum Mont-Saint-Michel 1456-1459," *Zeitschrift für Schweizerische Kirchengeschicte* 63 (1969) 221-231. See also Richard Trexler, "Adolescence and Salvation in Florence," in Trinkhaus and Obermann, *The Pursuit of Holiness in Late Medieval and Renaissance Religion* (Leiden, Brill, 1974) 200-264, and Chapter 11 of his *Public Life in Renaissance Florence* (New York, Academic Press, 1980).

57. Gabriel Llompart, "Penitencias y penitentes en la pintura y la piedad catalana bajomedievales," *Revista de Dialectología y Tradiciones Populares* 28 (1972) 229-249, gives other instances.

58. Barcelona, *Dietari* III 405, 468-470.

59. Vincent Ferrer, *Sermons* III (1975) 185, 285. See also Jacques Toussaert, *Le Sentiment Religieux en Flandres à la fin du moyen-âge* (Paris, Plon, 1963) 107-108. According to Antonio de Cordova, *Tratado de casos de consciencia*, rev. ed. (Toledo, Diego de Ayala, 1578) 164-169, the normal age of discernment, beyond which children could mortally sin, and therefore beyond which they had to confess such sins, was seven. The age for obligatory annual confession was 11-12. Communion was obligatory after age 12-13 for women and 14-15 for men.

60. Christian, *Person and God* 155-157.

61. *Relaciones* To II 252 (Puebla de Almoradiel).

62. For a Florentine dream vision of Saint Catherine in 1407

intimately connected to the death of the visionary's 10-year-old son from disease, see Richard Trexler, "In Search of Father: The Experience of Abandonment in the Recollections of Giovanni di Pagolo Morelli," *History of Childhood Quarterly* III 2 (Fall 1975) 247-251.

63. Philippe Ariès, *Centuries of Childhood* (New York, Vintage Press, 1962).

64. Barcelona, *Dietari* III 201.

65. Christian, *Local Religion*, 195-199.

66. *Il movimento dei Disciplinati nel settimo centenario dal suo inizio* (Perugia, Deputazione di storia patria per l'Umbria, Appendici al *Bollettino* 9, 1962); P. Bailly, "Flagellants" *Dictionnaire de Spiritualité* V 392-408.

67. Gabriel Llompart, "Desfile iconográfico de penitentes españoles," *Revista de Dialectología y Tradiciones Populares* 25 (1969) 31-53.

68. Christian, *Local Religion,* 185-190.

69. For votive prints of the Crucifixion, the intercession of Mary, and even the child Jesus bearing a scourge, which were used to ward off the plague in Germany 1450-1520, Peter Streider, "Folk Art Sources of Cranach's Woodcut of the Sacred Heart," *Print Review* (Spring 1976) 160-166.

70. It was the explicit policy of the order in the last half of the fifteenth century especially to promote devotion to Christ's Passion. Raphael Huber, *A Documented History of the Franciscan Order* (Milwaukee and Washington, 1944) 909-910.

Documentary Appendix of Spanish Texts

NOTE ON TRANSCRIPTIONS

I have respected the spelling and punctuation of the originals, even in cases of patent errors. I have, however, made the following adaptations to make the texts more readable:

1. I have written out abbreviations, italicizing only those letters added for which there could be any doubt, and then only the first time the abbreviation occurred in a text.
2. I have separated or joined words according to modern usage.
3. In the longer texts I have made paragraphs and indentations, which correspond to those in the translations above.

For fuller information on the original documents I refer to the respective notes, above. The numbers in brackets are the pages of the translations in the text.

1. Santa Gadea (Burgos), 1399. Parchment c. 1471, AHN Clero Carpeta 373 (see above Ch. 1, note 13).

Este es traslado de vn testimonio que fue tomado en la villa de sancta gadea segunt que por el paresçia escripto en pargamino de cuero & signado de escriuano publico. El thenor del qual es este que se sigue.

En sancta gadea domingo veynte [veinticinco] dias andados del mes de abril año del nasçimiento del nuestro saluador *iesu christo* de mill & trezientos & nouenta & nuebe años. Este dia en la iglesia de sant pedro de la dicha villa de sancta gadea estando y presentes ruy m*artines* & juan perez de rio clerigos curas de la dicha iglesia & asy mismo los otros clerigos & cabildo della y el alcalde diego garcia de arbolancha con el procurador & regidores & conçejo de la dicha villa juntos a repique de campana & seyendo y presente yo juan martines de sancta gadea escriuano & notario publico por nuestro señor el rey & de los testigos que en fin deste testimonio son escriptos paresçio y

presente ante los dichos curas & clerigos & alcalde & procurador
& regidores & conçejo vn moço de la dicha villa el qual avia por
nonbre pedro fijo de yñigo garcia de arbe vezino otrosy de la
dicha villa
   & dixo que el andando guardando las ouejas de su padre en
vno con juan fijo de juan de enzinas dia de sancta maria de
março deste presente año en termino de la dicha villa çerca de
vna iglesia que se llama sant millan & asy andando cerca de vn
robre que esta en el cimiterio de la dicha iglesia que fallaran en
el dicho robre vna ensanbre de avejas & por la avertura del dicho
robre parescia mucha miel & cera en el robre donde las dichas
auejas estauan & que concertaron como por el miercoles de las
tiniebras metido su ganado en la dicha villa de sancta gadea que
quando sus padres fuesen ydos a las dichas tiniebras viniesen
ellos a tomar la dicha miel & cera del dicho robre
   lo qual veniendo el dicho dia pusieronlo en obra. E ellos
venidos al dicho robre començando a sacar la dicha miel & cera
que vieran como se junto mucha gente con vestiduras blancas
enderedor de vn espino muy grande & que tenian tres lunbres
que alunbrauan muy claramente a toda aquella gente & que
vieran estar vna dueña ençima del dicho espino que relunbraua
mas que el sol en manera que les quitaua la vista que buenamente
non la podian mirar. E que estando asy que oyeran vna voz de
aquellos que ally estauan que dezia altamente venit a las tiniebras & a estas vozes que asomaran de partes de sancta maria
de guinicio por ençima del su viso muy grant gente a manera
de proçession en vestiduras blancas & la mayor parte dellas que
trayan vestiduras coloradas & ençima bandas blancas & otras
muchas colores & que trayan en las manos vnos ramos como
palmitos & que trayan dos lunbres que alunbrauan toda la
proçession como si fuera dia claro. E que se vino a juntar esta
proçession con la dicha gente que estaua alderredor de aquella
dueña & que el resplandor della yba fasta el çielo & que alderredor della estauan tres lunbres a manera de hachas que eran
en tanto grado que alunbrauan todo aquel termino & que paresçia que subian fasta el çielo & que oyan el cantar que paresçia
que dezian horas como clerigos & que de las sus vozes fueron
espantados E que dexaron su miel & çera de tomar & que dieran

a fuyr para la dicha villa. En quando llegaron a la llana que es
a medio camino que se voluieran a mirar & que vieran como
todas las lunbres se ayuntaron en vno & que su canto pujaba
al çielo & con tanto que non se atreuieron caminar alla.

E luego el juebes seguiente andando el dicho pedro guardando
las dichas ouejas del dicho yñigo garcia de arbe su padre en el
termino açerca del dicho lugar que le paresçiera supitamente vna
dueña muy resplandesçiente en tanto grado que buenamente
non la podia mirar synon en partes. E que le dixiera que la
vision que auia visto la dixiese y publicase a los curas & clerigos
& conçejo de la villa de sancta gadea. E por todas partes sopiesen
como ella era la virgen maria en persona glorificada la qual era
aquella que el avia visto sobre el espino & aquellas gentes que
el avia visto en çerco della que eran los angeles del çielo aquella
compaña muy linpia & que supiessen que su venida era por la
voluntad del su precioso fijo redemptor del humanal linaje. E
por quanto al tienpo de la estruyçion de españa era ally vn lugar
que se llamaua montañana la hyerma & avia ally vna iglesia
titulada en mi nonbre en la qual con grant inportunidat de los
grandes & muchos infieles se ovieron de acojer en ella & en su
çimiterio los huyentes del dicho lugar de montaña la yerma. E
en la dicha iglesia & çimiterio fueron çercados & tomados por
fuerça de armas & non queriendo venir en conosçimiento de su
seta fueron todos por martirio degollados en tanto grado que
toda la iglesia & çimiterio & todo su çircuito fue vañado en
sangre de los gloriosos martires.

E por quanto la memoria deste misterio yba peresçiendo con
mucha continua & assidua instançia asy de los martires & virgines que ende avian padesçido por muchos tienpos continuado
[sic] & en su supplicaçion ovo el glorioso fijo mio redemptor
del humanal linaje de se inclinar a sus preces & fue su voluntad
que yo viniese en persona glorificada con los angeles a celebrar
el oficio de las tiniebras & que ende serian aquellas animas
gloriosas comigo presentes a visitar los cuerpos que en tal dia
como este ende avian dexado

que assy como vino dios padre en la sarça a moysen la qual
non se quemo por bien de su pueblo assy fuy yo inviada en el
espino por bien de las animas & personas fieles del humanal

linaje el qual non fallaras quemado ni en alguna parte dañado
el qual sera medeçina para las enfermedades que del parte abran.
E la voz que oyste del que llamaua andat a las tiniebras era la
voz del angel sant miguel que asy como fue presente en aquel
lugar a resçeuir las animas de los gloriosos martires para las
leuar a la gloria al tienpo del su martirio asy fue voz de llamar
que viniesen a ser en celebrar aquel sollemne officio las quales
plogo a nuestro señor que respondiessen prestamente en manera
de procession muy gloriosa segunt viste. E las dos entorchas
que trayan la vna significaba la corona del sancto martirio. E
la otra significaba la virginidat de muchas donzellas virgines que
ende avian padesçido. E las otras tres antorchas que viste estar
en mi cerco significaban las tres personas del padre & del fijo
& del spiritu sancto. E las vozes que oyste eran las vozes del
dulçor de los angeles que trataban el offiçio. Et quando el offiçio
acabado fueron las entorchas consumidas en vno significando
la vnidat con la qual subimos a la gloria todos juntamente cada
vno a su silla & lugar establesçido. E mandote que digas como
este lugar es sagrado & ocupado de muchas reliquias de los
cuerpos que aqui padesçieron por martirio.

E mandote que digas como la voluntad del mi fijo glorioso
es que sea ende hedificado vn monesterio & iglesia de la orden
de sant benito con la qual memoria sea resurgido este secreto.
Et como digas que todas las gentes que vinieren o inviaren sus
ayudas & limosnas para hedificar la iglesia & monesterio & para
sustentaçion de los religiosos que ende seran abran remission
de sus peccados & sus animas seran en compañia de los dichos
martires & sus personas & cosas seran anparadas & guardadas
en cada hora que con grant deuoçion en mi se encomendaren
& en mi remembrança de la mi apariçion en este spino traxiere
mi señal asy como aparezco sobre sy sera librado de poderio del
diablo & el diablo non le podra enpeçer vista la mi señal & sy
la traxiere con grant deuoçion sera librado de pestilençias y toda
enfermedat otrosy te mando que digas a los curas clerigos &
alcalde & procurador & regidores de la villa de santa gadea en
concejo junto sy quieren que su pueblo sea aumentado & las
personas en prosperidat & las animas en estado de graçia que
luego se dispongan a desmatar las malezas & quitar que estan

en aquella iglesia & sito donde tuviste aquella apariçion & que
sepan que asy como por la parte de la aspereza & lugar fraguoso
han resçebido enojo robos [& muertes] assy abran refrigerio en
los cuerpos & salud para las animas. E sy quieren ser aumentados
en sus buenos deseos que sean en principiar la dicha iglesia &
monesterio & durante que lo faran & ternan su deuocion que
sienpre les yra de bien en mejor & por semejante a todos los
pueblos & personas donde quiera que sean.

Esto te mando que non ceses luego de lo denunçiar publicamente a los curas & clerigos & alcaldes & regidores del concejo
de la villa de santa gadea & a todas las comarcas & tierras
mientra turares ese poco tienpo que has de veuir & tu ave por
tu nonbre propio pedro de buena ventura que digno eres de te
lo llamar. E diras a juan tu compañero que luego se arme de
las armas de la caualleria de la bienaventurada uirgen sancta
cathelina luego prestamente pues en ellas ha de morir. E su fin
ha de ser partiendo de ieruzalin allegando al sepulcro de sancta
catelina dentro de nuebe dias. Como yo te lo mando luego
prestamente lo denuncia & non lo dexes por ocupaçion de la
verguença synon sabe que en mi presençia tu seras atormentado
en aquel grado que tu veras & con tanto que se desaparesçiera.

E que el dicho pedro que con grant verguença del temor que
non seria creydo que callara la dicha aparicion. E que dende al
domingo seguiente en la noche a ora de los segundos gallos
estando el dicho pedro en su cama cerca del dicho su padre que
veniera a el la virgen maria en la forma que el juebes ante la
avia visto & que tenia consigo [dos antorchas &] dos omes en
figura de religiosos & que el vno dellos le diera mano por el
braço & que le sacara de la cama & que el otro tomara su çinta
& que le diera con ella muchos golpes & feridas & que a las
grandes vozes que el daua que lo oyan por el varrio & que se
leuantaran de sus camas en espeçial diego garçia de arbolancha
alcalde que era a la sazon con los de su casa. E por semejante
los del dicho varrio & que venieran a las puertas del dicho yñigo
garçia & llamauan a grandes vozes & ninguno non les respondia
& con el grant quexo que el dicho pedro tenia & por le acorrer
que dieron con las puertas del dicho yñigo garçia en el suelo
& que ellos subiendo por las escaleras ariba que vieron estar la

casa tan clara como a medio dia la qual claridat çesara ellos subidos & con las candelas que las mugeres leuaban que fueran adelante & fallaran al dicho pedro metido en vna sala en suelo con muchas feridas de açotes & muy fatigado.

E a esto que despertara el dicho yñigo garçia & su muger & la gente de su casa. E que se leuantara ayrado diziendo que a tal ora en tal manera que que buscauan en su casa & que le respondiera el dicho diego garçia de arbolancha que eran venidos a anparar aquel moço de la grant crueldat que en el facia. El padre que se marabillara diziendo que non avia tal cosa nin tal sentimiento en su casa non avia seydo. E a esto que fabrara el dicho pedro & que dixiera en como su padre nin otro alguno de casa non le tenia culpa por ende que les rogaua en espeçial al dicho diego garçia de arbolancha asy como alcalde que mandase ayuntar a curas & clerigos & regidores & conçejo en su iglesia & a el fiziese lebar alla para les denunciar el fecho en como avia passado lo qual el dicho alcalde en amanesçiendo puso en obra & asy todo el pueblo junto traydo el dicho pedro & visto por todos sus açotes & fatiga dixo por su boca propia todo lo ante relatado.

E yo el dicho escriuano do fe en como vi las dichas señales & feridas que el dicho pedro tenia & oy de su propia voca todo lo en este testimonio relatado. Testigos que fueron presentes ruy martines & juan peres de rio curas & juan martines de fontecha & *martin* ruyz clerigos de la dicha villa & diego garçia de arbolancha alcalde & lope martines de miiala & lope *sanches* de velandia & juan peres de lodio & juan martines del varrio & ferran martines escriuano vezinos de la dicha villa de santa gadea & otros.

2. Jaén, 1430. Original document in church of San Ildefonso, Jaén. Words entirely in italics are missing from the original because of holes in the parchment and have been supplied from later copies. (See above Ch. 1, note 28.)

En la muy noble çibdad de jah*en* martes treze dias del mes de junio año del naçimiento del nuestro saluador iesu xpto de

mill r quatroçientos r treynta años: este dia el honrrado r dis-
creto varon iohan rodriguez de villalpando bachiller en decretos
prouisor ofiçial r vicario general en lo espiritual r tenporal en
todo el obispado por el muy reuerendo in xpo padre r señor don
gonçalo de astuñiga por la gracia de dios r de la santa eglesia
de roma obispo de jahen e en presençia de nos los notarios
publicos r testigos yuso escriptos el dicho prouisor dixo que por
quanto en esta çibdad se dezia r era fama publica que el sabado
que a postre avia pasado que se contaron diez dias del dicho mes
r año que algunas presonas avian visto çerca de la eglesia de
santo ylifonso que es en el arraual çerca desta dicha çibdad çiertas
visiones marauillosas de çiertas presonas que avian apareçido
en çierta forma r con muncho resplandor de claridad r por quanto
el queria saber que presonas eran aquellas que avian visto la
dicha vision r reçebir enformaçion de aquello que avia pareçido
r avian visto porque la verdad dello manifiestamente pudiese
pareçer r no oviese mezclamento de falsedad con ella r por ende
que nos requeria r rogaua que diesemos fe de lo que ante no-
sotros pasase r para la dicha enformaçion tomo çiertos testigos
que delante del fueron traydos r presentados de su ofiçio los
quales fueron pedro fijo de iohan sanchez casero de la muger
de ruy diaz de torres que dios perdone morador en jahen en la
dicha collaçion de santo ylifonso r juan fijo de vsenda gomez
morador en jahen en la collaçion de santo bartolome e juana
ferrnandez muger de apariçio martinez pastor vezina de la dicha
collaçion de santo ylifonso los quales pusieron la mano en la
cruz r juraron en la mano del dicho prouisor por dios r por santa
maria r por la señal de la cruz que con sus manos tanieron
corporalmente r a los santos euangelios do quiera que estan que
bien fiel r verdaderamente diran la verdad de todo lo que sopiesen
en aquel caso sobre *que* alli eran traydos r presentados r que
non lo dexarian de dezir por amor nin desamor nin temor nin
por otra cosa nin por aprouechar a uno nin dapnar a otro mas
que como fieles xptianos diran la verdad de todo lo que avian
visto syn mezclamento de falsedad r juraron segund r por la
forma que el dicho señor prouisor les mando r tomo el dicho
juramento respondiendo ellos r cada vno de ellos si juro e despues Amen segund la costunbre.

[*Pedro*]

e luego el dicho señor prouisor apartada r secretamente pregunto al dicho pedro si [?] el sy avia visto aquel dia sabado suso contenido alguna vision que fuese marauillosa çerca de la dicha eglesia e dixo que le mandaua r mando r requirio so el cargo del dicho juramento de lo que avie visto r a que ora r por que manera.

e luego el dicho pedro dixo que el dicho dia sabado que el estando echado en vna cama en casa de alfonso garçia que es en la dicha collaçion r çerca de la dicha eglesia de santo ylifonso de noche a ora de media noche r como quando el relox da doze oras que desperto r vido la puerta de las dichas casas que sale a la calle abierta r que luego vido entrar a juan fijo de vsenda gomez vezino eso mismo de la dicha çibdad que pareçe que la avie abierto para salir por quanto dormia eso mesmo aquella noche en la dicha cama r en la dicha casa con el dicho pedro r con juan fijo del molinero e que vido como el dicho iohan entro rezio r que çerro la puerta r echo rezio vn palo que estaua por tranca de la dicha puerta e que se echo luego en vn poyo frontera de la dicha puerta que salia a la calle r echose como a manera que venia espantado e que assi echado dixo a este testigo pedro leuantate r veras quanta gente va por la calle.

e que este testigo que dixo por donde van. r que el dicho juan dixo ay ariba van de cara a santo ylifonso. e que luego se leuanto este testigo en camison r se entro a vn corral que es dentro de las dichas casas fazia la dicha eglesia r que subio por vna pared baxa a otra mas alta que son amas de las dichas casas r que de aquella pared pareçia bien la eglesia r de toda esa plaça que esta en las espaldas della con el muladar r la calle por do dezia el dicho iohan que yua la gente r estando este firma echado de pechos sobre la dicha pared vido yr la calle ariba de cara la dicha eglesia syete presonas que pareçian omes que lleuauan syete cruzes vno en pos de otro como suelen yr en proçesion en esta dicha çibdad r que las dichas cruzes pareçian a las cruzes de la dicha çibdad r los omes que las lleuauan yuan vestidos de blanco r las vestiduras conplidas fasta los pies r que vido fasta otras veynte presonas vestidas eso mismo de blanco fasta los pies que yuan de vna parte r de otra a manera de proçesion reglada r que

yuan juntos con las cruzes r eso mesmo vestidos de blanco r
pareçia que yuan rezando r que en fin de la dicha proçesion que
yua vna dueña mas alta que las otras presonas vestida de ropas
blancas e lleuaua vna falda tan grande como dos braçadas r media
o tres.

e ella yua por si en la proçesion atras r que non yua çerca de
ella otra presona r que este firma non le vido la cara pero que
le pareçio que salia de su cara tanta resplandor que alunbraua
tanto r mas que el sol que con el resplandor pareçian todas las
casas de arededor r avn las tejas de los tejados se determinauan
asi como si fuera medio dia r el sol bien resplandeçiente e a
tanto era el resplandor que le quitaua la vista de los ojos asi
como si mirara de hito en el sol. e que esta dueña lleuaua en
los braços vna criatura pequeña vestida eso mesmo de blanco
r que lleuaua la dicha criatura en el braço derecho. e que vido
que atras de la dicha dueña que venian fasta tresçientas presonas,
omes r mugeres las mugeres çerca de la falda de la dicha dueña
e los omes mas atras e que estas mugeres r omes no fazian
proçesion mas yuan todos juntos las mugeres delante r los omes
detras como dicho es r todos vestidos de blanco e que a postre
de estos omes r mugeres venian fasta çiento omes armados todos
en blanco r que sonauan las armas.

[Pedro]

pedro fijo de iohan sanchez casero de la de ruy diaz de torres
morador en jahen en la collaçion de santo ylifonso del araual
de la muy noble çibdad de jahen testigo reçibido por el señor
prouisor en el negoçio yuso escripto so cargo del juramento que
fizo r syendole fecho las preguntas al caso perteneçentes, dixo
que el sabado que agora a postre paso que se contaron diez dias
deste mes de junio r año presente en que estamos asi como a
ora de en quirendo dar las doze oras del relox a la media noche
estando este firma en vna cama durmiendo en casa de alfonso
garçia que es en la dicha collaçion que es çerca la eglesia de santo
ylifonso e otrosi estando con el en la cama iohan fijo de vsenda
gomez vezino en la dicha çibdad que dormia con el que este
testigo que desperto a la dicha ora r que vido la puerta de la
calle de las dichas casas abierta r que vido entrar al dicho juan

r que como entro rezio que çerro la puerta r echo la tranca rezio
r que se echo en vn poyo a *manera que venia* espantado e que
asi echado que dixo a este testigo pedro *leuantate r veras quanta
gente r que este* testigo dixo por donde van. r que el dicho juan
le dixo *ay ariba van de cara de santo ylifonso.*

e que luego que este testigo que se leuanto en camison r se
*entro a vn corral que esta en las dichas casas r que por vna
pared* baxa que salio a otra pared *mas alta que esta en las dichas
casas de la qual dicha pared podia* muy bien mirar toda la calle
r las espaldas de la capilla de la dicha eglesia de santo ylifonso.
r que en asomandose por en somo de la dicha pared que vido
yr por la calle de ariba de cara la dicha eglesia syete cruzes que
lleuauan syete omes vna en pos de otra que les pareçian a las
cruzes de la dicha çibdad r los omes vestidos todos de ropa blanca
fasta los pies. e que vido que luego junto con las cruzes que
yuan fasta veynte presonas vestidas eso mesmo de blanco fasta
en pies de amas partes a manera de proçesyon r rezando

r en fin desta proçesyon que yua vna dueña que era mas alta
que las otras presonas e vestidas de ropas blancas r leuaua vna
falda a tan grande como dos braçadas r media o tres r ella yua
sola en la proçesion atras que le non vido la cara este firma pero
que le pareçio que salia tanto resplandor de su cara della que
alunbraua mas que el sol r que todos estauan en tanta claridad
que se pareçian las casas de la comarca r tejas de los tejados r
la dicha eglesia r todas las cosas asi como si fuera medio dia r
tanto resplandor era que le quito la vista de los ojos a este firma
a tanto e mas que si mirara al sol de hito r que leuaua esta
dueña en los braços vna criatura pequeña vestida eso mesmo de
blanco r que le non vido otra cosa que leuaua la dicha criatura
r que lo lleuaua en la mano con el braço derecho solo

e que luego detras de la falda de la dicha dueña que venian
fasta trezientas presonas, omes r mugeres las mugeres çerca
della r los omes atras r todos vestidos de blanco r que yuan
todos juntos r non en proçesion r que despues desta gente atras
que venian fasta çiento omes armados todos en blanco r que
sonauan las armas vnas con otras. r que en esto conoçio que
eran armados r que le pareçio que trayan de figura de lanças en
los onbros r que toda esta gente que yua detras de la dueña

yuan callando r de su espaçio muncho paso a paso e por manera
que quando este testigo fue subido en somo de la pared que la
proçesion non era avn llegada a la dicha eglesia e que avria desde
la dicha casa fasta la capilla de la dicha eglesia echadura de vna
piedra puñal

r que en las espaldas de parte de fuera de la dicha capilla que
viera aparejado vn grande altar tan alto como vna lança r que
relunbraua muncho y muncho honrrado r conpuesto el dicho
altar r con paramentos toda la pared en somo [?] dellos blancos
r dellos colorados r que vido que cantauan a alta boz fasta veynte
presonas vestidas eso mismo de blanco r que las bozes pareçian
flacas como suelen tener los enfermos desque se leuantan de la
dolençia r que este testigo non vido la cara de ninguna de aquellas
presonas pero que en el altar non vido presona alguna de manera
de clerigo vestido nin avn otro que llegase al altar nin fuese tan
alto e que llegando la dicha gente al altoçano çerca de la dicha
capilla que se asento la dicha dueña r toda la otra dicha gente
que le pareçio que era tanta que todo el dicho altoçano estaua
lleno el qual podia caber mas de . . . . presonas r que quando
fueron llegados que su vysta deste firma non podia sofrir la
claridad tan grande que se echo de pechos sobre la pared r non
miraua la gente avnque estaua bien claro la pared alderredor de
la luz que resultia de aquella dueña

e que despues estando asi vn poco como que le descansaron
los ojos r le recobraron la vista que torno a mirar a la dueña r
a la otra gente r que vido a la dicha dueña asentada como en
ropa que resplandeçia como figura de plata r que estaua asentada
toda la otra gente r que los que cantauan estauan en pie r que
estauan de amas partes del altar, e la dueña asentada açerca de
la proçesion r toda la otra gente junta alderredor detras della.

e que este firma desque vido la gente assi asentada r sus ojos
ovieron cobrado su vista que se enpeço a deçender de la pared
ayuso r se deçendio bien como subio r que se deçendiera antes
synon porque tenia torbada la vista r ovo miedo de deçender r
que estovo asi en somo de la pared contia de espaçio de media
ora poco mas o menos r que quando subio que daua el relox las
doze como dicho ha e en acabandolas de dar que tañeron a
maytines en la eglesia de santa maria r en algunas de las otras

eglesias r que quando venia *esta* gente que oyo que venian munchos perros ladrando en pos dellos.

preguntado si *quando vido esta* gente sy ovo espanto o sy ovo plazer o que syntio dixo que quando vido la gente *primera que sintio* como plazer en su coraçon como sy viera otra gente e que desque vido la gente armada ovo *espanto r que aquel* plazer que ovo que le pareçio que era por quanto en el dicho arraual han miedo de moros cada noche r que desque vido la proçesion r *la gente r las* cruzes que ovo plazer como que aquella gente segura estaua de moros, e que asi que todos los que estauan en el dicho arraual *estarian seguros* e que quando vido la gente armada que ovo espanto r dubdo r que quando se deçendio que se echo a dormir r non dixo *nada a otra* presona e durmio fasta çerca del dia. e que quando fue de dia claro que vino a ver sy aquella gente si avia fecho fuelliga o rastro alguno e que non fallo fuelliga ninguna

preguntado que como lo dixo r en que logar lo dixo primero dixo que torrnando el del çemeterio de ver si avia fuelliga a las dichas casas r antes que entrase en casa que el dicho juan que fablaua con miguell ferrnandez de pegalhajar torrnandole lo que avia visto diçiendole como avia visto pasar çinco cruzes r otra gente que yuan en proçesion. e que entonçes que este testigo que dixo yo lo vi todo. e que el dicho iohan que tenia la cara muncho amarilla quando se leuanto r que este testigo que le dixo como estas asi a tan amarillo r que el dicho iohan que le dixo del miedo de anoche. e que despues este domingo syguiente que le preguntaron lo que avya visto r que lo dixo segund lo avia visto

r otrosi dixo que el miercoles de antes asi como a media noche desque desperto de dormir que oyo vna boz que le dixo non duermas y veras muncho bien. e que el jueues como al primer sueño que desperto r oyo semejante boz. e que el vierrnes non oyo cosa r que el dicho dia sabado que vido lo que dicho ha.

[Juan]

iohan fijo de vsenda gomez morador en jahen en la collaçion de santo bartolome testigo reçebido por el dicho señor prouisor en el dicho negoçio r so cargo del juramento que fizo, dixo que

el sabado en la noche que a postre paso que se contaron diez
dias deste mes de junio año presente que le pareçio que seria
a ora de media noche estando durmiendo en el araual açerca de
santo ylifonso en vnas casas de alfonso garçia con otros tres en
vna cama que estaua este firma en medio çerca de juan fijo del
molinero que estaua çerca de la puerta de la calle de la dicha
casa en la cama r que este testigo que recordo aquella sazon r
que vido que en la dicha casa que daua claridad como de candela
r que penso que era de dia r que oyo luego como ladridos de
perros que eran syete perros caçadores que estauan fuera de la
dicha casa r otros munchos perros chicos r grandes que sonauan
como lexos de aquella casa r que este firma que pensaua que era
ya de dia a tanto vido la claridad r que se leuanto desnudo r
abrio la puerta vn poco r que estouo mirando de dentro de casa
r la cabeça fuera para mirar por entre la puerta r la pared

 e que vido çinco cruzes venir vna tras otra como suelen venir
en proçesion r que las trayan çinco omes mançebos como bar-
uirrapados r que las cruzes eran asi como estas de jahen todas
blancas r que en fin de la proçesion de las cruzes que yua vna
dueña vestida r cobijada con ropas blancas r a manera de man-
tillo. e que le pareçio segund el bulto que leuaua como que
estaua en cama o en estrado o *como* en vna sylla grande que
pareçia de plata r que ella yua mas alta que los otros quanto
medio cobdo pero que non la leuaua nadie a la dueña que ella
se yua por sus pies r que yuan muy paso r que salia desta dueña
tanta claridad que resplandeçia asi como el dia resplandeçe
quando haze sol claro r esta en su virtud. e asi que se veya toda
la calle r que leuaua esta dueña vna falda rrastrando que avria
en ella fasta tres braçadas r que leuaua en el braço derecho vna
criatura pequeña de fasta vn año r que le pareçio bien fermoso
r vestido todo de blanco r que leuaua en la cabeça una cosa como
blanca

 e que a la dueña non llegaua presona en quanto estaua su
falda r en pos della que le pareçio que venian clerigos como en
proçesyon de vna parte r de otra en medio de la calle non yua
nadie saluo los clerigos que yuan de vna parte r de otra como
a manera de proçesion que serian fasta diez clerigos porque
conoçio que eran clerigos que trayan coronas abiertas e yuan

rezando r que non entendio palabra de lo que dezian r despues
desta proçesyon destos clerigos que venian contia de çiento presonas armados r vestidos todos en blanco r que sonauan las
armas r que leuauan como lanças

r que este firma non espero que pasasen todos que luego se
entro r metio la cabeça r çerro la puerta tras sy pero que vido
el cabo de la gente por la calle que non venia mas gente. e que
çerro bien su puerta r quiso llamar al dicho juan que estaua en
la cama r que non pudo r que se delibero r llamo a pedro fijo
de iohan sanchez y que le dixo veras pedro que cosa es esta que
gente va por la calle en blanco r vna señora r que el dicho pedro
que se leuanto r se vistio su camison r se fue al corral. e que
este firma se vistio su ropa r se acosto en somo de vn poyo
dentro en las dichas casas r que primero estouo posado en el
dicho poyo maginando de lo que avya visto e que despues se
acosto r estouo vn rato que non durmio e que luego se durmio
por manera que quando el dicho pedro se bolvio a acostar que
lo non vydo.

preguntado que quando vydo aquella gente sy tomo plazer
o sy ovo pauor. dixo que quando luego vido las cruzes que penso
que andauan en proçesion. e despues que vido que aquella gente
en blanco r vido que la claridad non era tal claridad como de dia
saluo claridad de otra figura que estouo asi dubdoso que non
ovo pauor nin plazer saluo que quando luego salio al comienço
que aquella claridad como que lo escalento avnque non tanto
como el sol.

preguntado que como lo dixo despues. dixo que de mañana
quando se leuanto que lo dixo a la muger de alli de casa r a los
otros que estauan en casa r que el dicho pedro que estaua alli
r que dixo eso mismo lo avia vissto.

[María Sánchez]

mari sanchez muger de pero fernandez pastor vezino en jahen
en la collaçion de santo ylifonso testigo reçebido por el dicho
señor prouisor en el dicho negoçio e so cargo del juramento que
fizo, dixo que el sabado en la noche que a postre paso que se
contaron diez dias deste mes de junio año presente estando esta
firma en las casas de su morada que son en la calle maestra que

va a santo ylifonso que son en el araual de la dicha çibdad asi
como a ora de entre las honze r las doze que se leuantaua esta
firma a dar agua a vn niño su fijo que tenia doliente que vido
grand claridad dentro en las dichas sus casas que pareçia asi
como resplandor de oro reluziente quando le da el sol e que esta
firma que penso que era relanpago r que ovo temor r se puso
de rrodillas en el suelo r que miro fazia la calle por vn resquebrajo
grande que esta entre las puertas de las dichas sus casas r que
vido que pasaua por la dicha calle vna dueña con paños blancos
r con flores blancas mas claras que los dichos paños r que se
conoçian en el paño r que le pareçia que el manto que leuaua
la dicha dueña que yua aforrado en çendales como colores de
torrnasol r que leuaua vn niño en los braços r en el braço derecho
r abraçado con el yzquierdo r que el dicho niño yua enbuelto
en vn paño de seda blanco e que ella era alta mas que otras
presonas quanto vn cobdo r que el niño pareçia como de quatro
meses r bien criadillo

r que yua a la su mano derecha vn ome que le pareçia semejante a la figura de santo ylifonso segund esta figurado en
el altar de la eglesia de santo ylifonso r que leuaua vna estola
al cuello r vn libro en la mano r que leuaua la dicha estola
segund la ponen los clerigos para dezir missa r vn manipulo en
la mano, e el dicho libro abierto en sus manos como que lo
lleuaua delante della para que lo ella viese con vna cobertura
blanca. e que de la otra parte de la dicha dueña que yua vna
muger a manera de beata vn poco atras que no ovo conoçimiento
quien era.

e que del rostro de la dicha dueña salia todo el resplandor r
que en veyendo la dicha dueña r el dicho resplandor que ovo
pauor subitamente. e que luego ovo en ella reconoçimiento que
era la virgen santa maria. e que le vido a la dicha dueña vna
diadema puesta en la cabeça segund esta figurada en el altar de
la dicha eglesia r que este conoçimiento ovo por lo que *dicho
ha r que* porque era muncho semejable a la ymajen de nuestra
señora que esta figurada en el dicho altar. e que el dicho santo
ylifonso que tenia otra diadema en la cabeça r su corona abierta
grande como de frayle segund que esta figurado en la dicha
eglesia r que despues de la dicha dueña yua gente vestida toda

blancas vestiduras. r que non vido cruzes nin candelas *saluo el dicho* resplandor. e que despues de ella pasada que tanta claridad daua en las dichas sus casas como de antes *quando ella* pasaua r por semejante pareçia en la calle

que porque ella estaua sola non oso mas llegar a la puerta para ver mas saluo que se entro a su palaçio que non estaua con ella ome saluo dos criaturas vna de fasta ocho años e la otra de fasta cuatro años r que la dicha dueña r la otra gente que yua a manera de proçesyon de facia la eglesia de santo ylifonso fazia la çibdad r que entrada en su palaçio que ovo gran consolaçion e que oyo luego que el relox dio las doze oras r acabado que tañeron luego a maytines r dixo este firma que a la sazon que oyo como canto pero que non le pareçia el canto segund deste mundo e que en lo oyr ovo muncho gasajado r consolaçion.

[Juana Fernández]

juana ferrnandez muger de apariçio martinez pastor vezina en la collaçion de santo ylifonso testigo reçebido en enformaçion por el dicho señor prouisor en el negoçio de yuso escripto r so cargo del juramento que fizo dixo que estando esta firma en sus casas que son a la dicha collaçion de santo ylifonso que son de cara el çementerio el sabado en la noche que paso que se contaron diez dias del mes de junio del año presente asi como despues del primer sueño antes que cantase el gallo que se leuanto este firma al corral de sus casas por quanto tenia pasyon en las tripas r se avia leuantado antes otras tres vezes

r que estando asi que vido subito vn resplandor grande açerca de las espaldas de la capilla de la eglesia de santo ylifonso r que magino en si luego subito que era relanpago r que delibero que non seria relanpago por quanto era grande r muy resplandeçiente la claridad r que era continua aquella claridad r que estando asi parando mientes entre las puertas de las dichas sus casas e que vido venir vna dueña que venia con otra mucha gente de fazia las cantarerias la calle ariba [?] fazia la dicha capilla r que le pareçia que traya la dicha dueña en los braços ante sus pechos vn bulto que non pudo determinar que cosa seria r que le pareçio que de su faz della r de aquel bulto salia aquel resplandor r que venia por en somo de vn muladar que estaua çerca de la dicha capilla como a manera de proçision r que detras della venia otra gente vestida ropas blancas r que le pareçia que algunos dellos trayan palos en las manos enfiestos e que por quanto el vnbral de las puertas de las dichas sus casas es baxo non pudo ver sy eran cruzes o çetros nin que cosa era. e que esta claridad non le pareçia de sol nin de luna nin de candelas antes le pareçia como de vn resplandor que ella tal nunca vido.

e quando vido esta firma esto que se cayo amorteçida con temor r que começo a tremeçer toda e porque se le quitaua la vista que se echo torruada fazia la pared r las espaldas fazia la claridad que avya visto e que estouo asi vn poco e se leuanto r las manos por la pared se fue a su palaçio r que la claridad que se quedo alli e que antes quando ella miraua que le paresçio que esta dueña se paro tras la dicha capilla e asi que la perdio de vista porque de su casa non la podia ver pero que quedaua la claridad e esta firma con temor fuese a la cama con su marido r que estaua vna criatura con su marido que la quito r se acosto tremiendo cabo su marido.

preguntada sy la gente venia en proçesyon o junta dixo que con el temor non paro mientes saluo que venia muncha gente vestidas en blanco. e que mas çercanos de la dicha dueña venian dos presonas non sabe sy eran omes o mugeres vna de vna parte r otra de la otra r que esta dueña que le pareçio que era mas alta que los otros e que luego dende a poquito que oyo tañer a maytines r que le pareçio que la dicha dueña e la otra gente que venian muncho paso a paso en proçesion.

A lo qual todo fueron presentes por testigos r vieron fazer el dicho juramento a los testigos suso dichos r a cada vno dellos pedro de plazençia r alfonso fijo de lope perez escriuanos r aluaro de soberado vezinos r moradores en esta dicha çibdad e asi mismo grauiel diaz clerigo conpañero en *la eglesia* de jahen que tomo el dicho señor prouisor para ver fazer la dicha enformaçion. va escrito sobre raido // o diz en somo // r entre lineado // o diz segund esta figurado en el altar de la eglesia de santo ylifonso //.

E yo juan rodriguez de baena escriuano de nuestro señor el Rey r su notario publico en la su corte r en todos los sus reynos en vno con el dicho señor prouisor r por ante aluaro de villal-

pando r fernando diaz de jahen notarios publicos e por ante los
dichos testigos a todo lo suso dicho presente fuy r soy ende
testigo e lo fize escreuir e por ende ffize aqui este mi signo en
testimonio de verdad. Juan Rodriguez.

3. Cubas (Madrid), 1449. Transcript in *cuaderno* in Convent
of Santa María de la Cruz, Cubas, made in 1789 (see above Ch.
1, note 41).

Testimonio de los santos Aparecimientos de nuestra Señora
Santa Maria de la Cruz, hechos a la Pastorcita Ines, vecina, y
natural de la Villa de Cuvas, sacado de su Original antiguo de
un libro en quarto, y de otro traslado del menos antiguo, pero
muy devorados, y carcomidos con la injuria de los tiempos, y
antiguedad. Trasladados por mi fray Joachin Diaz Bernardo
Religioso Menor de la Observancia de N. P. S. Francisco y
Vicario en este Convento de Santa Maria de la Cruz (vulgo
Santa Juana) Año de 1789.

(1r-8r)
En Cuvas, Logar del noble Cavallero Luis de la Cerda diez
dias del mes de Marzo año del nascimiento de nuestro Salvador
Jesu Christo de mil quatrocientos, quarenta, y, nueve años dentro en la Iglesia de San Andres del dicho Logar Cuvas, en presencia de nos los Notarios, e Escrivanos publicos, e de los testigos
yuso escriptos, parecieron presentes Juan Gonzalez Capellan
teniente logar de Cura en la dicha Yglesia, e Rodrigo de Arevalo
Alcayde, e logarteniente por el dicho Señor Luis de la Cerda en
los sus Logares Griñon, e Cuvas, e Lope de Lorbes Alcayde de
Piedrabuena, e Juan Gonzalez, e Juan Ferrandes Alcaldes en el
dicho Logar, e otros asaz Vecinos de los dichos Logares Griñon,
e Cuvas. E dijeron, que por quanto Ynes fija de Alfonso Martinez, porquerizo del dicho Logar, e de Mari Sąnchez su muger
vecinos del dicho Logar Cuvas, que estaba presente, afirmaba
haverla hablado la Virgen Maria, y haverla visto, ciertas cosas,
que la dicha Señora Virgen Santa Maria le havia dicho, e fablado,
e fecho. Sobre lo qual oy dicho dia los Clerigos, e Concejos de

los dichos Logares, e otros Logares circunvecinos havian hecho
vna Procesion general a honor, e reverencia de la Señora Virgen
Santa Maria Madre, y le havia dicho dos Misas en el Altar de
la Virgen Santa Maria, segun que la dicha Ynes dijo que le avia
mandado decir. E los susodichos preguntaron, y dijeron a la
dicha Ynes que dijese todo lo que avia visto, y le avia acontecido
en los dias pasados hasta oy dicho dia en presencia de nos los
dichos Notarios, y testigos yuso escriptos, la qual dicha Ynes
dijo esto que se sigue.

E luego la dicha Ynes dijo que el Lunes, que se contaron tres
dias del dicho mes de Marzo del dicho año, que ella andando
en el campo guardando los dichos puercos al pago que se llama
de la fuente Cecilia, dis que podia ser al medio dia poco mas,
o menos vio que veno a ella vna muger muy fermosa, y que
le parescio que venia vestida de paños de oro, e que le dijera:
Que faces aqui carita [hija]? E que dijo la dicha Ynes: Guardo
estos puercos. E luego la dicha Señora dis que le dijo: Que por
que ayunava los dias de Santa Maria en Viernes? E ella que
respondio: Que por que gelo mandavan sus Padres. E luego la
dicha Señora dis que le dijo: Que bien facia, que poco tenia de
ayunar por este año. E que despues dijo la dicha Señora: Que
le mandava que los ayunase en el dia que cayesen. Que quien
los ayunase en el dia que cayesen, que ganava de perdones
ochenta mil años. E que le mandava que dijiese a todas las
gentes, que se confesasen, e que aderezasen sus animas, que
sopiesen, que avia de venir gran pestilencia del dolor del costado,
e de piedras rosias embueltas en sangre, de lo qual moriria
mucha gente. E que luego la dicha Ynes dijo: Que preguntara
a la dicha Señora: Que si de esta pestilencia, que si moriria ella,
y su Padre, y su Madre? E dis que le respondio la dicha Señora:
Que eso seria como Dios quisiese. E que acavado esto de decir,
que no vido mas a la dicha Señora.

E luego la dicha Ynes dijo: que esto, que no lo oso decir ni
lo dijo a ninguna persona. E que luego el Martes·siguiente dijo:
Que ella andando con los dichos puercos al pago que dicen del
Arroyo de Torrejon a la dicha hora del medio dia dijo: Que
viniera a ella la dicha Señora en la manera que el dia de antes
le avia aparescido, e que le dijera: fija por que non dijiste lo que

te mandè ayer decir? E dis que dijo la dicha Ynes: Por que no
lo avia osado decir por rezelo que no seria creyda. E la dicha
Señora dis que le dijo: Cata que te mando que lo digas, e si no
te creyeren, yo te darè señal por que te crean. E luego la dicha
Ynes dis que dijo a la dicha Señora: Que le dijiese quien era?
E la dicha Señora dis que la respondio: esso no te dire agora.
E que luego no vido a la dicha Señora. E que luego la dicha Ynes
dijo, que lo avia publicado, e dicho a su Padre, e a su Madre,
e a otras personas del dicho Logar Cuvas.

E que despues de esto Viernes siete dias del dicho mes, dijo
la dicha Ynes, que ella andando guardando los dichos puercos al
pago que se llama el prado nuevo cerca del dicho Logar Cuvas,
que viniera a ella la dicha Señora la tercera vez a la dicha hora
vestida como dicho es, e que le dijo: Que si avia dicho lo que
le havia mandado decir? E luego dis que dijo la dicha Ynes: Si,
y que lo avia dicho a su Padre, e a su Madre, e a otras personas.
E que luego la dicha Señora, que le dijo: Que lo dijiese, y
publicase al Clerigo, e a todas la gentes sin ningun miedo ni
temor.

E que despues de esto dijo la dicha Ynes, que el Domingo que
se contaron nueve dias del dicho mes, e año susodicho, que la
dicha Ynes que fue a guardar los dichos puercos al pago que
dicen de la Ciroleda. E dijo: Que ella estando en el Valle, que
es en el dicho pago de la dicha Ciroleda acerca del dicho Logar
fincadas las rodillas, e puesta la voca con el suelo ofreciendole
sus Oraciones, e rogandole que le aparesciese la dicha Señora:
Que viniera a ella la dicha Señora en la forma que las otras
veces le havia aparescido. E dis que le dijo: Levantate fija. E que
entonces la dicha [Ynes] que ovo miedo, e que se levanto luego.
E dis que le dijo la dicha Señora: No ayas miedo. E que entonces
la dicha Ynes que le preguntara: Que quien era? E que le dijo
la dicha Señora: Yo so la Virgen Maria. E que se llego a ella,
e que la dicha Señora tomò la mano derecha de la dicha Ynes
con el pulgar, e gela apretò, e le dejo la dicha mano con todos
los dedos juntos, e apretados, e el pulgar encima fecho Cruz
segun que los mostrò, e vimos todos los que ay estavamos. E
que quando la junto los dichos dedos, que se quejo la dicha Ynes,
e que luego le dijo la dicha Señora: Anda vete con esta señal

por que te crean, que aqueso pasaràs tu por ellos, e vete a la
Yglesia, e llegaràs en saliendo de Misa, e enseñalo a todas las
gentes, por que te crean lo que dijieres, pues que llevas señal.
E que luego la dicha Ynes dijo: Que se fue al Logar, e luego a
la dicha Yglesia, e llego al dicho tiempo que la dicha Señora
Santa Maria le dijiera en acavando la Misa el Clerigo. E como
entro que finco los hinojos ante el Altar de la Virgen Maria, e
que dijo publicamente al Clerigo, e a todo el Pueblo todo lo
susodicho. E que luego el Clerigo e Alcaldes, e Regidores, e
omes buenos del dicho Logar aviendo mucha devocion en la
dicha Señora Virgen Maria, que tal miraglo avia mostrado en
la dicha Ynes, movieronse todos con gran devocion con las
Cruces, e con candelas, e hachas de zera encendidas en las manos
todos en Procesion, e descalzos con todos los niños, que se
podieron aver del dicho Logar, e con la dicha Ynes. E que levava
vna Cruz de palo para la poner en el logar do la dicha Señora
le avia tomado la mano, e en ella fecha la dicha señal. E assi
yendo las dichas gentes en la dicha Procesion, que queriendo
salir de las Heras del dicho Logar, e entrando entre las viñas
venia la dicha Ynes delante de los Niños, e bolvio la caveza, e
dijo a Lope de Lorbes, e Andres Ferrandes Regidores, que ivan
ordenando la Procession de los dichos niños, que estoviesen
quedos, que avia oydo que la llamava la dicha Señora Virgen
Santa Maria, e que le dijiera dos veces: Anda aca. E que la dicha
Ynes dijo: Que queria ir a ver lo que le mandava la dicha Señora
Virgen Santa Maria. E que luego el dicho Andres Ferrandes,
que llevava la dicha Cruz de palo, que la dio a la dicha Ynes,
e que assi fue la dicha Ynes con la dicha Cruz. E dijo, que luego
quando se aparto de la dicha Procesion, que veno la dicha Señora
Virgen Maria, e fue con ella fasta el logar donde le avia dado
la dicha señal, e que venia al lado derecho de la dicha Ynes. E
que nunca le avia dicho palabra ninguna fasta que llegaron al
dicho Logar. E que como llegaron al logar donde le avia dado
la dicha señal, que la dicha Señora Virgen Maria, que le tomara
la dicha Cruz en sus manos, e que finco los hinojos contra la
Cruz, e despues que se levantò, e que la puso fincada en el suelo
enfiesta. E que le mando a la dicha Ynes que fincase las rodillas
de cara do venia la Procesion, que venia, e le mando que toviese

alli la dicha Cruz fasta que llegase la dicha Procesion, e que fiziesen alli una Yglesia, que llamasen Santa Maria, e le mando que se volviesen con la dicha Procession al Logar, e que estoviese la dicha Ynes en la Yglesia de Cuvas ante el altar de la Virgen Maria con algunas criaturas inocentes aquel dia con la noche fasta oy dicho dia, e que le dijesen dos Misas de Santa Maria ante su Altar. E que pusiesen a la dicha Ynes devajo de los Evangelios de las dichas Misas. E que dichas las dos dichas Misas, que llevasen a la dicha Ynes a la Yglesia de Señora Santa Maria de Guadalupe, e que estoviese alla dos dias, e que llevasen con ella quatro libras de zera a la dicha Señora de Guadalupe. E que a la venida, que la truyesen a la dicha Ynes por el dicho Logar donde la dicha Señora le avia tomado la dicha mano, e fecha la dicha señal. E que como luego que la dicha Ynes fiziese alli Oracion, seria desfecha la dicha señal, e acavado esto que desaparescio. E de esto en como paso los susodichos, e cada vno de ellos dijeron, que pidian, e pidieron, e rogaron a nos los dichos Notarios, e Escrivanos, que gelo diesemos por testimonio vno, e dos, e mas los que pidiesen, e menester fuesen. Testigos que a esto fueron presentes Juan de Montarco, e Alfonso de Prado, e Pero Sanchez notario, e Pedro de Calatayud, e Diego Morales Vecinos de Griñon, e Juan Gonzalez Alcalde en Cuvas, e Andres Ferrandes Vecinos de Cuvas, e Rodrigo Alfonso Clerigo Capellan en Humanes. Lo qual todo susodicho paso ante Juan Gonzalez de Roa, e Pero Sanchez de Humanes, e Juan Ferrandes Carrillo, e Benito Ferrandes de Cuvas notarios, que lo dimos vna vez signado.

(8r-11v)

E despues de lo susodicho en el dicho Logar Cuvas en veinte, y vn dias del dicho mes de Marzo del dicho año, estando presente la dicha Ynes moza niña de edad de doze a trece años poco mas, o menos, que tenia su mano suelta, e sana segun que la ende mostrò en presencia de nos los dichos Juan Gonzalez de Roa, e Benito Ferrandez Notarios, e de los testigos de yuso escriptos, parescio presente Fernand Alfonso Racionero en la Yglesia de Toledo, e Clerigo Cura en el dicho Logar Cuvas, e dijo, e pregunto a la dicha moza encargandole la conciencia, e mucho amonestandola que dijiese la verdad, e non dijiese en contrario, que dijiese si lo contenido en el dicho Instrumento suso contenido, lo qual le fue repetido todo, si avia pasado todo como dicho es de suso. La qual dicha Ynes dijo: que ciertamente como Dios es verdad, que assi avia pasado todo segun que por ella era dicho, e que ella assi lo avia entendido, e dicho como suso dicho es. E luego el dicho Ferrnand Alfonso dijo: Que pues ella avia dicho, que la dicha su mano no se avia a desatar de la dicha señal fasta que tornase de Guadalupe, que como, o por que no fue assi? E la dicha Ynes dijo, que por cierto ella assi lo avia entendido, por que quando ella fue en Guadalupe, que el Prior, e frayles, e el Alcalde dende que la cerraron [cataron], e vieron la dicha mano, e que la avian provado a abrirla, y que no podian creer sino que estava nacido [sic] assi. E que la avian puesto ante el Altar mayor de la dicha Yglesia del Monasterio de la dicha Guadalupe, e que le preguntaron, que la imagen mas baxa que esta en el dicho Altar mayor de Guadalupe, si era, o semejava a aquella que la avia aparescido? E que la dicha Ynes que dijiera que no era aquella, ni le parescia a aquella. E que luego, que le mostraron la imagen de Santa Maria, que està mas alta en el dicho Altar de Guadalupe, que es vna pequeña. E la dicha Ynes dijo: Que ciertamente aquella mesma era. E que fue dicho a la dicha Ynes, que la dicha pequeña imagen, que non esta toda cobierta de oro, ni la cara assi tan reluciente como la dicha Ynes decia. E la dicha Ynes dijo: Que por cierto que ella que la veia assi muy blanca, e assi covierta de oro como aca le avia aparescido, e que ciertamente aquella mesma era. E que despues que los dichos frayles, que avian metido a la dicha Ynes en una Camara, e que la cerraron por de fuera, e que quedò la moza alli encerrada. E que despues entraron [a cavo de hora, que tornaron] alla los dichos frayles, y el Alcalde del Logar, e otros con ellos. E que quando ellos entraron a do estava la dicha moza, que le dijeron, que mostrase la dicha mano. E que quando saco su mano para la mostrar, que la fallaron sana. E el dicho Ferrand Alfonso le pregunto: Que si le aparescio la Virgen, o otra cosa, o si le ficieron alguna cosa para que gela despegasen? E la dicha Ynes dijo: Que ni vio cosa, ni la ficieron melecina, ni otra cosa, salvo que ni vio, ni supo como, ni en que manera, que se fallo su mano suelta, e que assi se vinieron. E que quando llegaron acerca de aqui, que la dicha Ynes dis, que se adelantò de los que con ella venian, e que se fue a fazer Oracion al dicho logar donde le fue dada la señal dicha, e que como llegò al dicho logar en faciendo alli su Oracion, que le aparecio alli la dicha Señora Virgen. E que la dicha Ynes, que le dijo: Señora vuestra merced me dijo, que la mano no se me abriria fasta que tornase aqui, por que no fue assi? E dis que la dicha Señora Virgen Maria, que le dijo: tu no lo entendiste con la gran priesa, que toviste de me preguntar, que yo a esso te embie a la mi Casa de Guadalupe que quando alla fueses, que ende se te desataria. E dis que la dicha Ynes estonces que dijo: Señora plega vos de dar otra señal por que me crean, que no me quieren creer lo que digo de vuestra parte? E que la dicha Señora que dijo: Yo bien lo creo esso. Y non cures fija, que yo los darè tal señal, que aunque lo quieran creer que no puedan, que bienaventurados son los que lo vian, y lo creian, e que luego le desaparecio.

E que esto que fue quando ella fue venida de Guadalupe, que fue el Miercoles, que agora passò en la tarde, que se contaron diez, y nueve dias del dicho mes de Marzo, quando la dicha Señora le avia dicho lo que dicho es esta postrimera vez. E el dicho Ferrnan Alonso le pregunto: Que si la dicha Señora Virgen Santa Maria si le avia dicho que señal daria, o quando? E que la dicha Ynes dijo: Que non le dijo, ni sabia, que es lo que la dicha Señora queria facer. E de esto en como passò el dicho Ferrnand Alonso pidiolo por testimonio signado vno, dos, e mas los que demandados nos fuesen a nos los dichos Juan Gonzalez, e Benito Ferrandes Notarios. Testigos que fueron presentes Gonzalo Martin, Racionero en la Santa Yglesia de Toledo, e Cura de Fuenlabrada, e Gonzalo Ferrandes Mantero, e Pero Sanchez de Ledesma Vecinos de Toledo, e Rodrigo de la Quadra, e Rodrigo de Medina Escuderos del Señor Luis de la Cerda, e Juan Gonzalez de Calleja Berrueco, e Bartolome Sanchez, e Juan Ferrandes Calahorro Vecinos de Cuvas.

E yo el dicho Juan Gonzalez de Roa Escrivano, e Notario publico por las Autoridades Apostolicas, e de nuestro Señor el Rey fui presente a todo lo que dicho es con los dichos Notarios, y con los dichos testigos segun, e en la manera que dicho es.

E por ruego, e peticion del dicho Ferrnand Alonso, e de los demas susodichos este publico Instrumento fize segun que ante los dichos Notarios, e ante mi paso, e de suso se face mencion que va escripto en estas cinco fojas de papel con esta en que va mi signo. E en fondon de cada plana va fecha vna rubrica de mi nombre. E por ende fis aqui mi signo a tal. En Testimonio de Verdad. JUAN GONZALEZ de ROA NOTARIO.

(25r-31r) Diocesan investigation, Cubas, April 23, 1449; testimony of Inés

E la dicha Ynes fija de Alfonso Martinez Vecina de Cuvas jurada, e preguntada, que es lo que save, e vido en la dicha razon acerca de lo en el dicho testimonio, e por su dicho de ella de antes depuesto contenido para el juramento, que fizo preguntada por el primer articulo en el dicho testimonio contenido conviene a saver de lo que dijo, que vido el dicho dia Lunes, que se contaron tres dias de Marzo que proximo paso.

E luego la dicha Ynes dijo, e depuso assi propiamente por su voca sin desvariar ninguna cosa las mismas palabras substanciales del fecho segun que en el dicho testimonio se contiene que ella avia depuesto.

E preguntada mas por los dichos Señores Jueces, que quien estava ay con la dicha Ynes al tiempo, que el dicho dia Lunes dis que le aparescio la dicha Señora Virgen Maria.

E la dicha Ynes respondio, e dijo, que non estava ay ninguno, pero dijo que vio que estavan dos Pastorcillos, que guardavan Ovejas contra de vn tiro de vallesta de ella, los quales eran Perico fijo de Alfonso Ferrandes, e Pasqual fijo del Callejano.

Preguntada si vido que los dichos Pastorcillos miravan hacia donde decia la dicha Ynes que con la dicha Señora hablava.

E dijo que ellos estavan merendando, pero que non paro mientes si la miraban.

Preguntada si ella quando dice que se fue la Virgen Maria de cavo ella, si ovo miedo de lo que assi avia visto, dijo, que quando se partio de ella, que como no la vido, que ovo miedo.

Preguntada si traya fermosos olores,

dijo, que no olio nada.

Preguntada si la dicha Señora traya corona en la caveza?

dijo que gela non vido.

Preguntada que traya en la caveza, e que era la ropa que traya vestida?

Dijo que la vido que resplandescia el su rostro, e que tenia vna como saya vestida, e abrochada por delante, e que era blanca como la nieve, e vna toca en la caveza.

Preguntada si la toca era blanca.

Dijo que no, que todo le parescio de oro la toca, e la saya.

Preguntada si traya cinta cenida?

Dijo que gela non vido.

Preguntada si traya sortijas en las manos?

Dijo que gelas non vido, salvo que las manos traya blancas como la nieve.

Preguntada si traya chapines?

Dijo que non traya sino zapatas de oro.

Preguntada si traian puntos las zapatas?

Dijo que non que sin puntos le parescio que eran.

Preguntada si quando se partio de ella la Virgen Maria, e dice que ovo miedo, si fue facia los dichos Pastorcillos, o que fizo?

Dijo que alli se quedo, e cenò pan, e agua.

Preguntada que fizo dende fasta la tarde esse dia?

Dijo que guardo sus puercos, e torno a decir ciento, e cinquenta Ave Marias con sus pater nostes, que solia decir, e otras Oraciones.

Preguntada si savia el Ave Maria, e el Pater noster?

Dijo qual le ficieron ay decir los dichos Jueces ante ellos, e lo dijo simplemente.

Preguntada que Oraciones otras savia?

Dijo que otras dos las quales dijo ay, e eran de buenas palabras, e santas de devocion, la vna de la Virgen Maria, y la otra quasi del Pater noster.

E preguntada que si ese dia dijo a alguno algo de lo que avia visto?

E dijo que ese dia viniendose a la dicha Cuvas con los puercos, que guardava, que se vino con los Pastorcillos, e que por el camino que les dijo, si avian visto algo, e que le dijeron que non. E que esta les dijo: No vistes oy a medio dia aquella muger, que vino a mi quando estavedes merendando? E que le dijeron non, por que lo dices? E que les dijo: Vino a mi vna muger muy fermosa, e me pregunto si ayunava los dias de Santa Maria. E yo dijele que si. E que ellos le dijeron no vimos nada quiza seria alguna mondaria. E que ella que les dijo, no se quien se era, e que ellos no se curaron, e se fueron con su ganado.

Preguntada por el segundo Articulo en el dicho testimonio contenido conviene a saver de lo que la dicha Ynes depone que vido el dia Martes siguiente por diversos modos, por ver si desvariava de lo que antes avia dicho la dicha Ynes, no desvario palabra alguna de ello: mas las mismas palabras que avia dicho primero contenidas en el dicho testimonio, aquellas torno, e dijo. E preguntada mas por los dichos Jueces que esse dia Martes, que traya vestida la Virgen Maria?

Dijo que de la manera que la vido el dia antes, la vido esse dia.

Preguntada si traya la Virgen Maria en la ropa falda?

Dijo que non, que redonda la traya la saya.

Preguntada por el tercero Articulo en el dicho testimonio contenido conviene a saver de lo que la dicha Ynes depuso que vido el dicho dia Viernes siguiente por diversos modos para ver si excedie de la forma que de antes avia dicho la dicha Ynes en el dicho testimonio se contiene sin mudar substancia alguna de como paresce lo avia dicho. E preguntada mas si avia miedo quando veya a la dicha Señora?

Dijo, que quando la veya a sobre hora que avia miedo, pero des que la fablava que no avia temor. E des que se iba de cavo de ella, que asi mismo avia temor.

Preguntada, que quanto estava de ella la Virgen Maria?

Dijo que un poco estava desviada de ella.

Preguntada si estava en pie, o de rrodillas?

Dijo que amas a dos estavan en pie.

Preguntada aquel dia quando a ella vino, que hora era?

Dijo que seria medio dia.

Preguntada que si avia comido esse dia?

Dijo que non, por que ayunava esse dia.

Preguntada en el quarto articulo en el dicho testimonio contenido conviene a saver de lo que la dicha Ynes depuso que vido el dicho dia Domingo siguiente por diversos modos para ver si excedia de la forma que de antes avia dicho la dicha Ynes, dijo delante los dichos Jueces al tanto como se contiene que dijo en el dicho testimonio, sin mudar palabra ninguna de como primero paresce que lo dijo. Preguntada mas por los dichos Jueces si aquel dia Domingo quando dice que la llamo la Virgen Maria, e le dijo, levantate fija: si venia como de antes la avia visto?

Dijo que si.

Preguntada si venia calzada, o descalza?

Dijo que descalza venia.

Preguntada, que si entonces ovo miedo della mas que las otras veces?

Dijo que si.

Preguntada que si le fablo otras palabras demas de las que se contienen en el dicho testimonio que le dijo.

Dijo que quando la dicha Ynes se levanto, e le dijo a la Virgen Maria: dame Señora señal que no me quieren creer. Entonces le respondiera la dicha Señora: Yo bien lo creo esso.

Preguntada si quando la llamo la Virgen Maria la primera vez si la vido?

Dijo que non.

Preguntada si a la segunda vez que la llamo, si la vido:

Dijo que entonces la vido.

Preguntada si venia andando por el camino la Virgen Maria, o como la vido?

Dijo que la vido en el camino queda en pie a do aora esta una Cruz puesta.

Preguntada, que que tan lejos la vido de si?

Dijo, que contra echadura de vn tejo della. E que la dicha Señora estovo queda, e que la dicha Ynes se fue para ella.

Preguntada si anduvo con ella,

dijo, que como se llego a la dicha Señora, luego comenzò a andar, e la dicha Ynes con ella.

Preguntada si le parescio el andar, o en el acatamiento, e forma de ella muger?

Dijo que si.

Preguntada si ovo miedo de ella?

Dijo, que si.

Preguntada si la voz tenia gorda, o delgada?

Dijo que delgada mucho fermosa.

Preguntada si venia vestida como las otras vezes?

Dijo que si.

Preguntada si quando iva fasta do finco la Cruz, si iva corriendo, o paso a paso?

Dijo que no iva corriendo, sino como a pasito: pero dijo que llegaron en un trote, e que no save como fueron tan ayna llegadas.

Preguntada, que si vido que dejase pisadas la dicha Señora por do iva?

Dijo que non.

Preguntada que si vido, que dejase pisadas donde llegaron?

Dijo que alli donde llegaron, e finco la Cruz la Virgen Maria estava vn arenalejo, e que le parescio, que alli quedo vna forma de pisadas chiquitas llanas.

Preguntada si yendo ella con la dicha Señora por aquel camino, si le fablo algo la dicha Señora, o ella a la dicha Señora?

Dijo que non.

Preguntada, que por que non la fablo algo?

Dijo, que nunca la pudo fablar nada, que parescia que no llegava los pies a tierra.

Preguntada si quando la dicha Señora le tomò la Cruz, por que logar, o pie de ella la tomo?

Dijo que un poco bajo acerca de la mitad del grandor della. La qual dicha Cruz le mostraron ay los dichos Señores Jueces, e ella lo señalo quasi el logar que deponie.

Preguntada si quando se la tomò la Virgen Maria, con que mano se la tomo?

Dijo que con la derecha.

Preguntada, que como la finco en la tierra?

Dijo, que non fizo sino ponerla assi quedo, e se finco en el suelo quantia de un palmo, e medio, e que assi gela dejo a la dicha Ynes, e le dijo, tenla aqui fasta que la Procesion allegue.

Preguntada, que facia que parte se fue la Virgen Maria, o que camino llevava.

Dijo, que como estovo con ella un poquito, que se arredredo de ella un poco, e luego se desaparescio.

Preguntada, con gran diligencia por las otras preguntas, e articulos en el dicho testimonio contenidas para ver si desvariava de lo que avia dicho en el dicho testimonio la dicha Ynes todavia por vna forma lo tornò a decir como en el dicho testimonio parece que lo avia dicho. Preguntada, si quando la mirava a la Virgen Maria, si la podia bien mirar?

Dijo que tanto resplandecie, que lo quitava la vista de los ojos, e que aquel dia que la veye, que no veyeyo [sic] tam bien como de antes.

Preguntada que la imagen que le mostraron en Guadalupe los frayles de alla, que a quien parecie?

Dijo que le parescio a la Virgen Maria, que aca avia visto, e assi de aquella vestidura misma.

Preguntada, si le parescie que estava viva?

Dijo que si.

Preguntada si los ojos tenia abiertos?

Dijo que si.

Preguntada si la fablo algo?

Dijo que non.

Preguntada si en tanto que la dicha Ynes alli la vido, si la mirava la Virgen Maria?

Dijo que si.

Preguntada que tanto la estovo mirando?

Dijo que en casi todo ese dia mientras alli estubo.

Preguntada si quando le cerrò la mano nuestra Señora, si le quedò dolor en ella?

Dijo, que fasta el cobdo.

Preguntada, si le dolie mucho?

Dijo, que no le dolie mucho, sino que le parescie el brazo que tenia seco.

Preguntada, si quando despues se le abrio la mano, si se le quito el dolor?

Dijo que si.

E para el juramento que fizo esta era la verdad, e deste fecho no savia mas.

4. Guadalupe. AHN Clero Codice 48 B, fols 5v-8v, written or transcribed c. 1400-1440 (see above Ch. 1, note 71).

. . . fasta que passaron a un rrio que llaman guadaluppe & fallaron ay vnas muy grandes montañas & en estas montañas fizieron vna cueua aquestos santos clerigos a manera de sepulcro & çercaron aquesta cueua con muy grandes piedras & pusieron dentro la ymajen de nuestra señora santa maria & con ella vna canpanilla & vna carta en la qual carta estaua escripto como aquella ymajen de santa maria fuera enbiada de rroma a sant leandre arçobispo de seuilla con otras rreliquias que le enbiara el doctor sant gregorio. E desque la ouieron puesto cobrieronla con vnas piedras grandes & echaron su tierra ençima & fueronse. E en tierra de almaraz dexaron eso mesmo soterrada la cruz & fueronse fuyendo a las montañas de castilla la vieja.
. . . . plego al señor dios de esforçar los coraçones de los christianos para que tornassen a cobrar las tierras que auian

perdido. E asi fue que cobraron mucha tierra de aquella que
poseyan ya los moros. E por abreuiar contarnos hemos del noble
rrey don alfonso el qual gano a los moros gran partida de castilla
// ouo con ellos muy grandes batallas & en espeçial la que ouo
en las nauas de tolosa donde fue ensalçada la santa cruz del
nuestro señor iesu christo. E de alli los abatio en tal manera que
nunca alçaron cabeça & de esta uez gano a ubeda & a baeça &
a otros lugares munchos guadalquiuir ayuso & por la sierra
morena. [About six words are crossed out.] durmio en paz &
nuestro señor dios leuo la su alma a la su santa gloria. E rreyno
en españa su nieto el rrey don ferrnando el qual gano la muy
noble cibdat de seuilla & otros munchos lugares & durmio en
paz. & nuestro señor dios leuo la su anima al su santo rreyno
   E rreyno su fijo don alfonso el qual gano las algeziras & murio
sobre gibraltar. En el tiempo que aqueste rrey don alfonso rrey-
naua en españa aparesçio nuestra señora la virgen santa maria
a un pastor en las montañas de guadaluppe en aquesta manera.
Andauan vnos pastores guardando sus vacas çerca de vn lugar
que llaman halia en vna defessa que se llama oy en dia la defessa
de guadaluppe. E en aquesta defessa andauan aquestos sobre-
dichos pastores guardando sus vacas. E vno dellos fallo menos
vna vaca de las suyas & apartosse para la buscar por espaçio de
tres dias. & non la fallando metiosse en las montañas grandes
que estauan el rrio arriba & apartosse a vnos grandes rrobledales
& alli vido estar su vaca muerta çerca de vna fuente pequeña.
E el pastor desque vio su vaca muerta allegosse a ella: & fue
muy marauillado por quanto non estaua mordida de lobos nin
ferida de otra cosa & saco su cochillo de la vayna para la dessollar
& abriendola por el pecho a manera de cruz segund es costumbre
de dessollar en essa ora se leuanto aquella vaca & el muy espantado tirosse afuera.
   E la vaca estuuo queda & en esa ora le aparesçio nuestra
señora la virgen santa maria & dixo a este pastor. non ayas
myedo ca yo so la madre de dios por la qual alcanço la humanal
generaçion rredenpçion. toma tu vaca & uete & ponla con las
otras. ca de aquesta vaca avras otras munchas en memoria de
aqueste aparesçimiento que aqui se aparesçi. & desque la pu-
sieres con las otras vacas yras a tu tierra & diras a los clerigos

& a las otras gentes que vengan aqui a este lugar donde te
aparesçi. & que cauen aqui & fallaran vna ymajen mia. E [word
crossed out, desque added] nuestra señora le dixo estas cosas
[seven words crossed out] se contienen en este mesmo capitulo.
& en esta ora desaparesçio [two words crossed out]
& el pastor tomo su vaca & fue con ella & pusola con las otras
& conto a sus conpañeros todas las cosas que le auian acaesçido.
& sus conpañeros fazian burla del. & el pastor rrespondio &
dixo. Amigos non tengades en poco aquestas cosas. ca sinon
queredes creer a mi. creed a aquella señal que trahe en los pechos
la vaca & ellos veyendo la señal que traya en los pechos la dicha
vaca a manera de cruz creyeronlo.

E el despidiosse de sus conpañeros & fuese para su tierra. E
sabed que por doquier que yua contaua a todos quantos fallaua
este miraglo que le auia contesçido. E sabed que este pastor que
era natural de caceres & ay tenia muger & fijos & des que llego
a su casa fallo a su muger llorando & el dixo a su muger por
que lloras. & ella rrespondio. vuestro fijo es muerto. & el dixo
non ayas cuydado ni llores ca yo lo prometo a santa maria de
guadaluppe que ella me lo dara viuo & sano & yo gelo prometo
para seruidor de su casa. E en esa ora se leuanto el moço biuo
& sano & dixo a su padre. Señor padre aguisad & vamos para
santa maria de guadaluppe & quantos estauan alli fueron ma-
rauillados & creyeron todas las cosas que dezia del aparesçimiento
de nuestra señora santa maria.

E este pastor llego a los clerigos & dixoles. Señores sabed que
me aparesçio santa maria en vnas montañas çerca del rrio de
guadaluppe & mandome que uos dixiesse que fuessedes alli
donde me aparesçio. & que cauasedes en aquel mesmo lugar
donde me ella aparesçio & que fallaredes ay vna ymajen suya
& que la sacaredes de alli & que le fiziesedes vna casa. E mandome mas que dixiesse que a los que touiessen cargo de su casa.
que diessen a comer a todos los pobres que a ella viniessen vna
vez al dia. E dixome mas que faria venir a esta su casa munchas
gentes de munchas partes por muchos miraglos que faria por
todas las partes Ansi por mar como por tierra. E dixome mas
que alli en aquella grand montaña se faria vn grand pueblo.
& desque oyeron los clerigos & las otras gentes aquestas cosas.

pusierenlo luego por obra & andudieron su camino fasta aquel lugar donde aparesçio nuestra señora santa maria. E en esa ora que llegaron comensçaron a cauar en aquel mesmo lugar donde el pastor les mostro que le aparesçiera santa maria. E ellos cauando en aquel mesmo lugar fallaron vna cueua a manera de sepulcro. & sacaron la ymajen de nuestra señora santa maria & vna canpanilla que estaua con ella & la piedra sobre que estaua asentada & deuedes saber que todas las otras piedras que estauan alderredor todas las quebrantaron & las leuaron por rreliquias & en esa ora le edificaron vna casa muy pequeña de piedras secas & de palos berdes & cubrieronla de corchas. ca sabed que auia çerca asaz de alcornoques. E sabed que vinieron con aquestas gentes munchos enfermos de diuersas enfermedades. & en la ora que llegauan a la ymajen de santa maria luego cobrauan salud de todas sus enfermedades & yuanse para sus tierras loando a dios & a la su bendita madre por los grandes miraglos & marauillas que auia fecho & quedose el pastor por guardador con su muger & sus fijos & su linaje por seruidores de santa maria.

E asi como fueron manifiestos estos miraglos por toda españa venian de todas las partes muy munchas gentes a uisitar esta ymajen a reuerençia de santa maria por los munchos miraglos & marauillas que por ellos fazia.

5. Navas de Zarzuela, now Navas de San Antonio (Segovia), 1455. Parish archive, Legajo 4, Numero 3, "Testimonio de la Aparicion de S Ant°. y Papeles tocantes a su Capilla, y Capp^{nia}.," a transcript made in 1737 (see above Ch. 1, note 75). I have eliminated the double ss and double tt forms, and excess capital letters.

Este es un traslado vien y fielmente sacado de un testimonio signado de escrivano publico escripto en pergamino signado y firmado de mi Martin Gomez escrivano de el rei de ziertos milagros que Dios nuestro Señor quiso mostrar al tiempo que se comenzo a fundar la Cofradia de San Antonio de padua de las navas que se prinzipio su casa donde aora esta su tenor del

qual de verbo ad verbum es este que se sigue—En las Navas de
Zarzuela, Aldea de la Ziudad de Segovia: viernes quatro de
agosto año de mill y quatrozientos y zinquenta y zinco en presenzia de mi Martin Gomez Vezino de el dicho lugar e escrivano
y notario publico de el rei nuestro Señor en la su corte y en
todos los sus reinos e señorios y de los testigos de yuso scriptos,
estando en unas casas donde morava Juan Gonzalez de Havila
Vezino de el dicho lugar parezio presente Luis Gonzalez peraile
Vezino de el dicho lugar e Juan su hijo y de la otra parte ziertos
ofiziales perailes Vezinos de el dicho lugar a los quales el havia
rogado que se juntasen alli de parte de Dios y de el Señor San
Antonio

e luego llegados los dichos ofiziales dijo el dicho Luis Gonzales
que vien saven que el a dicho e amonestado al pueblo que hagan
e ordenen una cofradia a onor de el Señor San Antonio y que
fiziesen una casa donde el estuviese en la yglesuela camino de
Segovia asomante al monte de Sancho lo qual le havia dicho
Juan su hixo tres vezes de parte de el Vienaventurado San Antonio y por quanto se le havia aparezido que io nunca se lo havia
creido hasta que otra vez me lo torno a requerir de parte de Dios
y de el Bendito San Antonio que lo dijese al dicho pueblo que
hiziesen la dicha cofradia y casa y que si la fiziesen que verian
algunos milagros de los que a el se encomendasen.

E luego el dicho Luis Gonzalez dixo a su hijo Juan dijese a
los que estaban presentes e ante mi el presente escrivano en que
manera o como se le havia aparecido San Antonio y dijo el dicho
Juan que estando yo un dia en la yglesia de el dicho lugar yendo
a leer vi a un ombre en havito de fraile y llamome y dixo ben
aca niño di a los de este lugar que fagan una yglesia a la yglesuela
camino de Segovia como va deste lugar a Segovia asomante al
monte de Sancho. e nunca bi mas al fraile e luego dende a poco
vino Anton Garzia sacristan mi hamigo y dijele lo que me havia
dicho el fraile y luego mi hamigo dixome que callase sino que
me açotaria y no ose dezir nada ha ninguno salvo ha mi madre
y a mi padre e dijome que mentia

dende en diez y seis del mes y año dicho dijo el dicho Juan
yendo io a tañer al Ave Maria vi al dicho fraile y llamome y
yo obe miedo, y dijome di niño hiziste lo que te mande e yo

dije no se que me mandaste. Yo te mande que dijeses al pueblo
hiziesen una yglesia y cofradia y respondi sois vos el que me
lo mandasteis si pues dijelo ha mi hamigo y a mi padre y ame-
nazome que me feriria e dijeron que callase e yo queriendome
partir que era noche para casa de mi padre me dixo di a los de
este pueblo que crean lo que les dijeres y no le vi mas e fuime
a casa de mi padre e puseme al fuego y dijome mi padre que
havia que no dezia nada y dije ha mi padre que havia venido
a mi el fraile de el otro dia y que me dijera dijese a los de el
pueblo le fiziesen una yglesia a la iglesuela e cofradia e mi padre
dixo no dijese nada o que me feriria y que mentia e otro dia
fuime a la yglesia y dijelo al dicho mi hamigo y dijo que mentia
y que alguna fantasma era que me aparezia y que si lo dezia a
el o a otro me hazotaria e yo no lo oze dezir a nadie.

  y otro dia me ynvio mi padre a la deesa del enzinar por una
borrica y andandola a vuscar vi venir al fraile y eche a fuir de
miedo y el me llamo y dijo niño ven aca non fuias e non pude
mas fuir y vinose para mi y dijo di niño porque no as dicho lo
que te mande y dije ya lo e dicho a mi padre y a mi amigo e
me amenazaron e mandaron que no dijese nada que era alguna
fantasma—y luego dijo cata que te mando digas a los de este
pueblo que me fagan una yglesia y confradia porque todos se
juntasen a fazer mi yglesia y luego ybame io y tornome a dezir
di a los de ese pueblo que io soi San Antonio y es mi voluntad
que me fagan una yglesia donde tengo dicho e ordenen la cofradia. y vine a mi padre y contele lo que havia havido:

  E luego dixo el dicho Luis Gonzalez que presente estava que
verdad era todo lo que su hijo dezia e que lo havia dicho e no
lo havia creido por ende que rogava a los dichos ofiziales pues
halli estavan que fuesen en ordenar e fazer con los de el pueblo
como fiziesen lo susodicho y quando el pueblo no quisiese que
ellos ordenasen la cofradia a servizio de Señor San Antonio

  e luego dijeron los dichos ofiziales que ellos querian comenzar
a ordenar la dicha cofradia e tener manera con el Señor Obispo
para que se hiziese la dicha cofradia e yglesia con protestazion
que hazian de hazer relazion al pueblo y luego estando en esto
hizieron clamores y dijeron por el lugar que fuesen a enterrar
la mujer de Antonio Fernandez de mazarias e luego el dicho

Luis Gonzalez por lo que su hixo havia dicho devotamente en presenzia de mi el dicho escrivano y testigos dichos y de los ofiziales yinco las rodillas en tierra y dixo: O Señor San Antonio yo te ruego que ruegues a mi Señor Christo por su amor aquella mujer por quien doblan sea resuzitada y de haqui prometo en su nomvre la mortaja suia de la llevar a la yglesia.

e luego partimos para la yglesia a acompañar la cruz para traer la dicha difunta y entrando con la cruz donde estava la difunta en ese punto avrio los ojos y alzo la caveza y dijo O Señor Santo bendito sea tu santo nomvre que me a vuelto de la muerte a la vida—y luego el dicho Luis Gonsales dixo O Señor San Antonio bendito sea tu nomvre que has mostrado este milagro—e luego a grandes vozes dixo lo que su hijo havia dicho ante toda la gente.

e luego los que lo oieron dieron grazias a Dios y a Señor San Antonio y prometieron fundar la dicha casa e cofradia para su servizio e luego el dicho Luis Gonsales dijo ha mi el dicho escrivano lo diese por testimonio y lo que avia visto y havia pasado y havia dicho Juan su hijo para publicarlo al Señor Rei e a otros Obispos en todos los lugares en tal manera que haga fee

e despues de esto otro dia siguiente veinte y ocho del dicho mes y año se junto el pueblo e ordenaron una prozesion devotamente y fueron al lugar donde dezia el niño y todos aiuntados en el dicho lugar donde se havia de edificar la dicha casa en presenzia de mi el dicho escrivano y testigos hizieron boto de hazer la dicha yglesia y luego hordenaron una cofradia a onra de Señor San Antonio.

y despues de esto diez de Septiembre año dicho estando en casa de Anton Garzia, yierno de Juan Gonzales estando su muger enferma de una nazida, y teniendola por muerta e su marido con gran devozion la prometio a San Antonio y a terzero dia se levanto de la cama. e luego su marido lo pidio por testimonio

testigos a todo ello Sancho Gonzales y Juan Gonzalez de Havila yierno de Pedro Sanz errero y Vernabe Sanz cojedor e Gomez Garzia tundidor e Anton Garzia sacristan y Diego Sanz Diez texedor Vezinos de el dicho lugar. e yo el dicho Martin Gomez escrivano y notario fui presente a lo susodicho con los

dichos testigos a pedimento de los dichos Luis Gonzales e de
Juan su hijo lo fize escrivir en tres foxas de pergamino y devajo
sellado de mi ruvrica y por enzima tres resgos de tinta con esta
en que va este mi signo: en testimonio de verdad Martin Gomez.
fecho e sacado fue este traslado de el dicho testimonio orijinal
en las Navas de Zarzuela en diez de maio de mill e quinientos
e veinte y zinco años testigos presentes Franzisco Martinez Cura
theniente e Pablo de Arevalo e Matias Garzia Vezinos de el
dicho lugar de las Navas e yo Christoval Hasenxo escrivano de
las Navas de Su Majestad e su Notario publico en la su corte
y en todos los sus Reinos e señorios por ruego de Franzisco de
Bernardo rezetor de la dicha hermita en testimonio saque de el
original este tanto el qual va zierto e por ende fize haqui este
mi signo tal.
Xptoval Asenxo = Escrivano.

6. Escalona (Segovia), c. 1490. Excerpts from 1617 "Interrogatorio" in parish archive (see above Ch. 1, note 86).

[*2v: The first question of the questionnaire, or interrogatorio*]
Primeramente sean preguntados si saven o tienen noticia o
an oydo descir a sus antepassados que tanto abra que se aparecio
la uirgen santisima madre de dios que dicen de la cruz deste
lugar y en que forma y a quien y como se apareçio y en que
sitio digan lo que supieren e ouieren oydo descir a sus antepassados y moyores [sic]——

[*18r-21v: The reply of María Herranz to the first question,
October 23, 1617*]
A la primera pregunta del interrogatorio dixo este testigo que
oyo descir a madalena goncalez suegra desta testigo y madre de
joan herrero su marido muchas y muy dibersas ueçes la qual
era una muger de grandisimo entendimiento y memoria que en
uida de sancho herrero su suegro de la dicha madalena goncalez
y aguelo del dicho joan herrero marido desta testigo tubo el
dicho Sancho Herrero una criada que se llamaua joana la qual
era muy birtuosa y muy umilde temerossa de dios y que uibia

con mucho recato y temor de dios a la qual en xamas mientras
que biuio con el dicho sancho herrero nunca la bieron jurar ni
maldeçir ni a la jente ni al ganado por ninguna ocasion y enoxo
que la hiciessen con ser una cassa de muchisimo trafago de xente
y ganados

y que la muger del dicho sancho herrero suegra de la dicha
madalena goncalez inuio un ssauado a coxer un costal de cardos
a la dicha criada para que comiessen las mulas de su amo quando
uiniesen de arar y la dicha criada fue por ellas a las tierras de
carramaxuelos termino deste lugar descalona y auiendo cojido
un aldada se la aparecio nuestra señora la madre de dios muy
rresplandeciente y rreluciente y la dicha moza como la uio tomo
mucho pabor y miedo y se turbo y la madre de dios la dixo que
aces hixa

y la moca rrespondio senora coxo estos cardos

la madre de dios la dixo corre hixa y be y di a tus amos que
ablen al cura y al concexo que alli adonde esta la cruz del sendero
del prado agan un hermita en mi nonbre que se llame santa
maria de la cruz la qual sera mucha debocion y consuelo y
anparo para toda la cristiandad y mientras mas mas en los tiempos uenideros

y la moca rrespondio señora coxere el costal de cardos y luego
ire y lo dire

y la uirgen nuestra señora la dixo anda uete que ya el costal
esta lleno y la desaparecio al punto la uirgen madre de dios

la moca fue al costal y le allo uien lleno de cardos de lo qual
quedo mas turbada y dandola esfuerco nuestra señora tomo su
costal y se fue en cassa de su amo sancho herrero y el ama como
la uio benir tan presto espantosse y dixo a la criada como es
pusible que tan presto as abreuiado con los cardos no lo entiendo

la criada dixo tia uino la madre de dios a mi una senora muy
rreluciente hermosa y rresplandeciente y me yncho el costal
porque como no ouiesse cojido mas de una aldada quando uino,
a mi me dixo que ya estaua lleno que me uiniesse y que os
dixese a bos y a mi tio que adonde estaua la cruz del prado se
aga una hermita en su nombre que se llame santa maria de la
cruz la qual a de ser de mucha debocion y consuelo para todos
los cristianos y mientras mas mas en los tienpos benideros

el ama se admiro de lo que la moca decia y la dixo calla asta
que benga tu amo que no esta en cassa y dicirselo emos entramas,
y que en uiniendo el marido y amo de la dicha moca se lo
contaron ama y moca el casso como subcedio y el dicho sancho
herrero hico burla de ello y las rrino por que lo decian y las
mando que no lo dixessen ni lo hechassen de la boca
    y a cabo de otros dos o tres dias los dichos sancho herrero y
su muger suegros de la dicha madalena goncalez ynuiaron a la
dicha joana su criada a escardar a un rrubial que tenian en la
graneruela bien çerca de donde estaua la cruz adonde nuestra
señora mando que se la hiçiesse la hermita y enuiaron con la
dicha moca a un criado de cassa que se llamaua bartolome y
estando escardando la dicha joana uio uenir cara ellos por el
prado arriua a la uirgen madre de dios en la misma forma que
la auia aparecido los dias antes y encima della uenian grande
multitud de paxaros muy hermossos y la uirgen madre de dios
llego asta la cruz dicha y se arrodillo y abraco con la misma cruz
y la moca dixo al dicho moco bartolome bartolome mira a la
senora que uino a mi estotro dia que uiene al por el prado muy
rreluciente y encima della mucha ynfinidad de paxaros y a alle-
gado a la cruz del prado y se a arrodillado y abracado con ella
y el moco aunque mas miraua no podia uer ninguna cosa
    y la madre de dios dixo a la dicha joana que porque no auia
dicho a su amo lo que la mando y la moca rrespondio que ya
lo auia dicho y no la auian querido creer y la madre de dios la
mando que boluiesse a deçirlo a sus amos que hiciesen la hermita
adonde tiene dicho porque es boluntad de su hixo y suya porque
a de ser gran consuelo y anparo para la cristiandad
    y la moca fue en cassa de sus amos y se lo dixo y el dicho
sancho herrero no lo quisso creer y se lo rretraxo a la moça y
la llamo loca y necia y que no lo dixese ni lo sacasse de la uoca
que se artarian de rreir de ella y ansi la moça callo,
    y otro dia, por mandado, de los dichos sus amos, la dicha
moça y el dicho moço fueron, a escardar, al dicho rrubial, y
andando escardando la dicha joana, bio benir a la madre de dios
muy luciente ermosa y rresplandeciente y con la multitud de
aues y paxaros encima della y dixo al dicho moço ay bartolome
que la señora que a uenido a mi estotros dias biene por el prado

y se arrodilla y abraca con la cruz que esta alli mirala mirala y el moco aunque mas miraba no bio nada sino es unos pa-xaruellos rrebolear encima de la misma cruz y la madre de dios uino a la moça y la dixo que por que no auia hecho lo que la auia mandado y la moca dixo señora yo ya lo dixe mas no me creen

y la madre de dios dixo ya lo sse mas agora te creeran y luego con sus dedos la madre de dios toco a la dicha joana y se la pegaron los lauios de la boca uno con otro y la madre de dios la mando que fuesse en cassa de sus amos de la manera que eestaua y seria creida para que se hiciese la dicha hermita

y la dicha moca fue en cassa de los dichos sus amos muda y no pudo ablar ni descir palabra sino es por señas y el amo hico llamar a los clerigos y contoles el casso como la moca se lo auia contado y se xunto el concexo y todos los del pueblo acudieron a uer la moca y se acordo que otro dia por la mañana se fuese en proçesion asta la dicha cruz del prado

y fueron la clerecia y todo el pueblo en procesion asta la dicha cruz otro dia y llebaron a la dicha moca en ella pegados los lauios de la boca y con un par de mulas senalaron el sito adonde se auia de acer la hermita

y se boluieron con la dicha procesion a la iglessia y dixeron missa del espiritu santo y en acabando de desçir yte misa es se las despego a la dicha joana la uoca y arroxo dos o tres bocados de agua y luego ablo y comenco de alauar a dios y a su bendita madre y conto todo el casso a desde el principio asta el fin de todo lo subcedido y el moco bartolome conto todo lo que la moca le auia dicho quando bia a nuestra señora y que todo el pueblo que estaua junto a este subçesso y milagro alabo a dios y a su bendita madre

y que luego se hico la dicha hermita y se puso altar con ymagen de nuestra señora la madre de dios y en el mismo altar se pusso y pinto y estanpo este milagro de la manera que se apareçio la rreyna del çielo a la dicha joana como oy dia se be pintado en el mismo altar i con el mismo rrubial adonde escar-dauan

y desde aquel dia pusieron los clerigos por nombre a la dicha joana que se llamasse joana de la cruz por el dicho aparecimiento y anssi se llamo y la pussieron por hermitaña en la misma hermita y toda la jente la tocaua a la rropa por deuocion y la cortauan dello y lo lleuauan por rreliquias porque la tenian por santa

y esto es lo que dixo que saue y lo que oyo deçir y contar a la dicha madalena goncalez su suegra y lo mismo oyo deçir y de la misma manera a muchas perssonas uiexas hombres y mugeres uecinos que fueron deste lugar y esto a ssido siempre y lo es publico y notorio y publica boz y fama y esto rrespondio desta pregunta——

[*Juana de la Cruz, Ermitaña (pp. 37-38 of manuscript Libro de Milagros, 1618-, in parish archive).*]

La primera hermitaña que ubo en la santa hermita de la cruz fue Juana criada de sancho herrero: como atras queda dicho elexida por la boca santisima de la madre de dios: no se sabe el tienpo que lo fue: porque la tradicion que ay es que en los aparecimientos que la birguen santisima la yco la mando que no se casase o que perseberase birgem: lo uno u lotro aunque no ay claridad qual de las dos cossas la mando guardar y que despues en el tienpo questubo rrecoxida en la ermita se la comencaron a llegar algunas malas conpañias de mugeres y binieron a engañalla y a usar de muchas comidas que acian dentro de la dicha ermita y bayles y otras cosas no licitas ni decentes al estado de hermitaña ni al que se debia de tener al santo lugar en que estaba rrecoxida y con las malas conpanias se bino a destraher la dicha Juana y a casarse en tierra de quellar no se sabe donde ni en que lugar de cierto aunque yo e oydo decir que fue en los yañez: mas no para testificarlo por cossa cierta tanbien e oydo contar a personas biexas que la dicha Juana despues de casada muy de ordinario benia a bisitar muchas beces entrel año la dicha ermita y en cada bez que benia acariciaba mucho a todas las personas que la bisitaban y los contaba todo lo sucedido en los aparecimientos con mucho contento y alegria y les encargaba mucho la debocion de la hermita y que de contino asta que murio contynuo el benir muchas beces y muy de hordinario en cada un año a bisitar la dicha santa hermita.

[*Description of painting (Interrogatorio, 91v-92r)*]

al lado del euangelio en el mismo rretablo esta pintado de pincel antiguo un milagro que la uirgen maria obro con una

moca y esta en la forma siguiente = La madre de dios esta
pintada con una saya de oro y manto acul arrodillada y abracada
a una cruz dorada y del clabo de los pies de la cruz sale un
letrero que da buelta por cima de la corona y espaldas de la
uirgen que dice en letras muy antiguas y grandes desta manera
salbe crux preciosa que in corpore xpi, dedicata est et ex menbris
eyus tan quam margaritis = y luego por el otro lado de la cruz
esta un rretrato de una moca bestida de colorada al traxe antiguo
el cabello rrubio y tendido sin tocadura y esta incada de rrodillas
adorando la cruz y a la uirgen y a las rrodillas de la dicha moca
esta pintado un rrubial muy berde con çinco taxones =

   yten en la peana del dicho rretablo ay un letrero de letra muy
anti̦ua negra que dice = este rretablo se hico el año de mill
y quatroçientos y nouenta y nueue años siendo cura lugarte-
niente garcia goncalez por el honrrado garçia del rrio y ma-
yordomo martin fernandez a honor y rreberencia de nuestra senora y rreberencia a la cruz =

7. El Miracle (Lleida), 1458. Text compiled by Cebrià Baraut
(*Santa Maria del Milacre*, Montserrat, 1962, 163-170) from
two sources: A. Archive of El Miracle, Llibre calendari de totas
les terras y proprietats de esta casa del Miracle (seventeenth c.),
f. 9-15. B. Parish archive, La Curriu (J. Viladrich, *Memoria
histórico-descriptiva de la Imagen y Santuario de Nuestra
Señora del Milagro de Riner* (Lérida, Imprenta Mariana, 1898,
144-153) (see above Ch. 2, note 7). Words in parentheses are
found only in B.

   I. Noverint universi, quod die octavo mensis augusti, anno
a nativitate Domini millesimo quadringentessimo quinquagesimo octavo, coram honorabile Jacobo Vilar, rectore ecclesiarum
de Perecamps et de Torradenagó ac officiali ville Celsone, pro
reverendo domino Patriarcha Alexandrinensi et Urgellensi Epis-
copo, personaliter invento in rectoria de Torradenagó, com-
paruerunt honorabiles Bernardus Vilar, et Guillelmus de Fontestar consules ville Celsone, Franciscus de Viladecans, et Petrus
del Estany Josà, jurati castri de Riner, et Petrus Sorribes Sancti

Justi de Ardévol, qui dictis nominibus verbo dixerunt dicto honorabili officiali: Com sie pervengut a notícia nostra que un gran miracle se's seguit en la parròchia de Sant Martí de Riner, que us pregam y requirim que us plàcia bé[1] y diligentment pendre informació, per saber-ne plenament[2] la veritat, que si així com se diu no pot ésser sinó[3] algun gran misteri, perquè pus ne som tant prop, si us serà plasent anem là hon se's seguit per veure'n la veritat. Quibus sic instatis et requisitis, confestim dictus honorabilis officialis, una cum praenominatis consulibus et juratis recto tramite ierunt ad dictam parochiam et locum, et receperunt informationem super requisitis et denuntiatis in modum sequentem.

[*Jaume Cirosa*]

Jacobus Cirosa, filius Joannis Cirosa termini castri de Riner, interrogatus medio juramento.viii°. mensis augusti, anno a nativitate Domini millesimo quadringentesimo quinquagesimo octavo, coram honorabile Bernardo Vilar et Guillelmo de Fontestar, consulibus ville Celsone, et Jacobus Cirosa filius Joannis Cirosa mansi de la Cirosa, termini castri de Riner, deponens in posse discreti Jacobi Vilar, presbiteri et officialis in officialatu dicte ville Celsone, et interrogatus dicere veritatem in et super his quibus interrogabitur.

Et primo fuit interrogatus, si ell testimoni deposant a vista ninguna visió en aquestos dies passats. E dix ell que hoc, que dijous.

Item fuit interrogatus ell deposant, e què vehé. E dix ell deposant, que dijous pus prop passat, que comptavem tres de agost, en la hora de vespres que ja la hombra passave los torrents, ell deposant vehé una creatura semblant a un infant bell e ros, la qual portave una manteta vermella vestida a son semblant. E més, dix, portave a son parer una creu en lo coll molt bella.

Interrogatus, si ell deposant podia albirar quina creu era. E ell deposant dix, que li semblave tal com una que n'ha en lo altar de sant Sebastià a Riner.

Item fuit interrogatus, com ell deposant vehé aquella visió

---

[1] venir B   [2] planament A
[3] sens B

semblant a un infant, si ell deposant lo vehé estar denpeus o aguinollat. E dix ell deposant, que aguinollat.

Item fuit interrogatus, si ell deposant podie albirar que fos infant o infanta. E dix ell deposant, que li semblava infanta.

Item fuit interrogatus, per quina rahó li semblave infanta. E dix ell deposant, que per tant com tenie los cabells molt larchs així com a dona, e rossos.

Item fuit interrogatus, si ell deposant se acostà molt a ella. E dix ell deposant que hoc, a dos passos.

Interrogatus, si ell deposant vehé la dita infanta abans que se acostàs a ella. E dix ell deposant, que no la avie vista, sinó que així com volia girar una ovella que anàs ab les altres, ell deposant esdevingué en la dita infanta.

Item fuit interrogatus, si ell deposant li dix res a la dita infanta abans que la infanta a ell. E dix ell deposant, que no.

Item fuit interrogatus, si com ell deposant agué vista la dita infanta, si la dita infanta parlà a ell. E dix ell deposant, que hoc.

Item fuit interrogatus, e què li dix. E dix ell deposant que li dix: Digues al poble que fasse proffessons, e que les fassen devociosament, e que's confessen e que's convertesquen e que's tornen a la part de Déu, e que si'u fan, Déu los ho relevarà.[4]

Item fuit interrogatus, si la dita infanta li dix, que us relevare[5] Déu, si fegen tals coses. E dix ell deposant, que no li dix.

Item fui interrogatus, si la dita infanta li dix alre. E dix ell deposant que hoc, dient-li: Digues-los que si no'u volen creure, mon fill los ho farà creure.

Item fuit interrogatus, si la dita infanta li dix alre. E dix ell deposant que hoc, que li dix: No'y ha infant de quatre anys avant que no trosege lo meu fill.

Item fuit interrogatus, si li dix alre. E dix ell deposant, que no li dix alre, sinó que's levà (denpeus) e donà-li la creu en mà esquerra de ell deposant e besà-li la dreta a ell deposant.

Item fuit interrogatus, si la dita infanta li féu altre. E dix ell deposant que no, sinó que se'n anà per un camí la via de Torradenagó.

Item fuit interrogatus, si ell deposant parà esment, aprés que

----

[4] revelara A   [5] revelara A

la dita infanta se fou partida de ell, a hon ne anà e si desparés.[6]
E dix que no sab, sinó que vehé que tingué la dita via.

Item fuit interrogatus ell deposant, en quin loch vehé la dita
infanta. E dix que en un prat que's anomene lo prat de la Basa
Dòria.

Item fuit interrogatus, si ell deposant sab quants ans ha. E
dix ell deposant que no sab, sinó que son pare e sa mare dien
que ha de nou en deu anys.

Item fuit interrogatus, si ell deposant porie mostrar lo loch
ahont ha vista la infanta. E dix ell deposant que hoc, bé'u mos-
trare si hi pogués anar, mas que la malaltia lo congoxave tant
que'l feye exir de seny, e que no'y poguere anar, mas que ya
ho avie amostrat a son pare e a sa mare.

Item fuit interrogatus ell deposant, què feye al prat quant
vehé la dita infanta. E dix ell deposant, que gordave lo bestiar.
E com ja a dit, e volen girar la ovella que anàs ab les altres, ell
vehé la infanta.

Item fuit interrogatus, si hi avie ningú ab ell. E dix ell deposant que no, sinó lo bestiar.

Item fuit interrogatus, si ell deposant lo avie pregat ningú
que digués aquelles coses que damunt ha dites. E dix ell deposant
que no, sinó la verge Maria, que li dix que'u digués al poble.

Item fuit interrogatus, si ell deposant vehé ningú estar ab la
dita infanta. E dix ell deposant que no, negú.

Item fuit interrogatus, si la dita infanta tenie res en lo cap.
E dix ell deposant que no, sinó en cabells.

Item fuit interrogatus, quines vestidures vestie la dita infanta.
E dix que no li vehé vestir altres vestidures, sinó una manteta
vermella.

Item fuit interrogatus, si ell deposant parlà may ningun mot
a la dita infanta. E dix que no, sinó que la escoltà.

Item fuit interrogatus, si és estat induït per ningú. E dix que
no.

Fuit sibi lectum et perseveravit.

[Joan Cirosa]

Die jovis, decima mensis Augusti, anno predicto, hora quasi

---

[6] despres B

meridie vel inde circa, Joannes Cirosa mansi de la Cirosa termini castri de Riner, testis citatus per venerabilem Bernardum Montaner, locum (tenens) baiuli dicti termini de Riner, interrogatus in posse dicti honorabilis officialis, instantibus et requirentibus Francisco Viladecants et Petro Estany et Bernardo Rovira et Jacobo Miquel, proceribus et juratis dicti castri, et interrogatus dicere omnimmodam veritatem in et super quibus infrascriptis interrogabitur.

Et primo fuit interrogatus, si ell testimoni sab ni ha oyt que ninguna visió sie apareguda a son fill Jaumet quoddam, en dies passats. E dix ell deposant e testimoni sobre les dites coses, açò és a saber, que dijous pus prop passat, que's comptave tres del dit mes de Agost, en la matinada després que fonch levat, ell testimoni deslibera de anar a Vilaseca, del dit castell (de Riner), per aiudar lo que pogués a soterrar una infanta que se avie morta. E així ell testimoni anà a dit mas, e no tornà en sa casa [que] en lo enfoscant, que apenes veje anar com fou arribat en sa casa. E com fou allà, troba la muller de dit Vilaseca plorant e dient-li que per amor de Déu anàs fins a sant Just, e que digués an En Pere dels Ots[7] que li aportàs les medicines que avie fetes per altra minyonasa que tenie malalta. E si lo dit Pere no les podie portar, que ell testimoni les hi portàs. E encontinent ell testimoni, vist lo necessari, prestament anà al dit Pere dels Ots,[8] lo qual no troba, sinó sa muller, la qual no li volgué donar les dites medicines dient no sabie que's ere. Mas com son marit fos vingut, que ella lo'y dirie.[9] E així ell testimoni se'n tornà la via del dit mas de Vilaseca per fer relació dels dits affés. E com fonch prop casa sua d'ell testimoni, en un comellar de forment que'y avie per a segar, estigué maravellat com no troba allí sa muller e son fill lo major, que segassen dit forment com los agués dit jo dematí. E així partin-se del dit comellar tirà devers casa sua d'ell testimoni. E com fonch un tros luny del comellar la via de sa casa, encontrà sa muller e lo dit son fill que venien a segar portant una sistella, hon avie pa, vi e altres coses. E així avent rahons sobre lo dit forment, ell testimoni dix que ere

---

[7] horts B   [8] horts B
[9] darie B

cansat e que volie beurer, pus tenen pa e vi que beguéssem, e
així ho férem; e que aprés aver begut, ell testimoni tirà la via
del mas de Vilaseca per tornar resposte de ço que avien tramés,
dient-los com no avie pogudes aver les dites medicines. E com
fou al dit mas de Vilaseca aver retuda[10] sa resposta, Na Vilaseca
lo pregà molt que s'estigués aquí ab ella, e ell testimoni dix-li
que no'u podia fer per rahó de cert accident que li sol venir, e
no volguere que en loch de fer-los-ne pler ne aguessen aver
enuig, mas que irie can Vivet e que'l pregarie que'y vingués,
e així ho feu; lo qual Vivet, jo així le'n pregàs, no'y volgué
anar. E ell testimoni vehent açò encara deliberà tornar al dit
mas de Vilaseca, e així anant e pensant en si matex, sentí trepijar
una mula, e així sentint lo trepig, ell retirant[11] en si mateix vehé
venir en Vilaseca marit de la dita dona, e dix com anave a casa
sua per tenir companya a sa muller, mes pus que ell ere vingut,
el testimoni se'n tornarie a sa casa e que li perdonàs. E així, a
fi de moltes rehons, ell testimoni s'en tornà a casa sua. E com
fonch a sa casa, ere ya quasi foscant que apenes veje anar; e
com fonch a casa arribat, ell testimoni trobà la muller e sos fills
que avien ya encortat lo bestiar, e en continent li contaren lo
cas que'ls ere seguit.

Interrogatus, quin cas li comptaren que'ls ere seguit. E dix
ell testimoni que lo dit son fill lo major li dix unes semblans
paraules: Adés a hora quasi de vespres que s'ombraven bé los
solans, yo anava a les mules que eren al prat de la Bassa Dòria.[12]
(E com fuy prop de la dita bassa) en un disopte me trobí davant
mi una persona semblant a un bell infant, ab una manteta vermella, aguinollada, ab les mans iuntes envers lo cel, ab una bella
creu que tenie en les mans. E com jo la viu, soptosament perdí
quasi la vista e fuy en mi matex molt regirat, e així volent fugir,
costeregí a mes vàries[13] de la dita persona. E com fuy un petit
luny, ella cridà dient-me: O fill fes ensà. E jo lavors oynt açò,
se meté en mi molt major por pensant me vingessen devers mi,
e doní fort a fugir no sabent hont me'n anava, que tot lo món
me semblave barranchs. E la dita cosa tot temps me parlave,

[10] rebuda B
[12] bassa de oria B
[11] returant B
[13] mos vejazes B

mas yo era tant espaordit que no entenia que's deje, sinó que
entreoí que dix: Digues al poble. E fugint pus fort, ella tostemps
parlant, entreoí que dix semmanes e altre no poguí compendre.
E com fuy un tros luny jo'm regonaguí e cobrí esfors, e
meníment les dites mules allà hon ma mare segave.

Interrogatus ell testimoni, si sab ni ha oyt a dir si sa mare
li dix res aprés que fonch vengut a ella. E dix ell testimoni que
ha oyt a dir a sa muller que li dix, digues que has feyt, ne com
vens així, ni com has estat tant, com lo vés tant mudat de
manera[14] e ab la cara regirada. E lo dit fill li respòs, no res,
volent dissimular dits affés. E de fet ella tant lo interrogà, que
lo fill li dix lo que li havia esdevingut en la manera sobredita.

Interrogatus, si ell testimoni sab ni ha oyt a dir que son fill
lo menor haye vista la dita visió. E dix ell testimoni, que hoc.

Interrogatus, a qui ho ha oyt dir. E dix que al dit son fill
menor matex.

Interrogatus, què li dix lo dit son fill menor a ell testimoni.
E ell testimoni dix, que lo dit dia de dijous, hora quasi com los
solants se ombraven, hora baixa, lo dit son fill, volent menar
lo bestiar a casa e tocant lo dit bestiar, encontrà lo dit infant,
que tenie una manteta vermella, ab cabells bells e rossos, sense
res al cap, ab una bella creu que tenie en les mans, aguinollada,
semblant la dita creu a una que'n ha a Riner en lo altar de sant
Sebastià, e levàs dempeus, e acostàs a ell e meté-li la creu en
la mà esquerra e besà-li la dreta. E aprés levà-li la dita creu e
dié-li: Digues a ton pare e a ta mare, que diguen al poble que's
confessen e que's peniden e que fassen professons devociosament, sinó no's valrie res, e que si açò fegen Déu los ho rele-
varie,[15] no dient què ni què (no). E que li dix, mas no'm creuran.
Mas digues-los que mon fill los ho farà creure; que no'y ha tant
xich ni tant gran, de quatre anys avant, que no trosege lo meu
fill. E així partiren, e que la infanta se meté la creu al coll ben
alta, e ab les mans juntes tirà la via de Torradenagó, e passà a
unes roques prop la alzinera Dòria.[16]

Interrogatus, si ell testimoni sab que lo dit fill sie estat may

[14] de manera gran B   [15] revelarie A
[16] de oria B

en ninguna vila. E dix ell testimoni, que may no fou en vila ni enlloch, sinó a Riner, que anave alguns diumenges per a oyr missa.

Interrogatus ell testimoni, quina vida tenia lo dit son fill, ni si sabia que sabés negunes oracions. E dix que la sua vida era gordar lo bestiar e que no sabie sinó lo Pater e la Ave Maria, e que aquell li feyen dir tots dies,[17] e que may no'l oy jurar de Déu a l'un ni a l'altre.

Interrogatus, si aprés de aquest cas ell coneix que lo dit son fill menor donàs millor rahó de sí matex que de abans. E dix que sempre[18] donà prou[19] bona rahó de sí matex.

Interrogatus, si sab que son fill acostumàs de dir falcies. E (dix) que no li recorde que may li'n digués.

Interrogatus, si ell testimoni sab que lo dit son fill menor, lo qual es mort, fos sa lo dia que vehé la dita visió. E dix que hoc, sa e alegre.

Interrogatus, de quin mal es mort. E dix que de glànola que tenie en la exelera[20] dreta.

Interrogatus, quant morí. E dix que vuy (dia) e any damunt dits.

Interrogatus, quant li vení lo dit mal. E dix que dilluns prop passat.

Generaliter autem fuit sibi lectum et perseveravit.

[Constança, wife of Joan Cirosa]

Dicta die, domina Constantia, uxor dicti Joannis Cirosa, testis citata, jurata et interrogata de mandato et instantia predictorum dicere veritatem.

Et primo fuit interrogata, si ella testis a oyt dir a son fill lo major que en dies passats hage vista ninguna visió ni hage trobat ninguna cosa. E dix ella testis, que dijous pus prop passat lo dit son fill major li vench a la segada dient-li que avie trobat una belle cosa, semblant a un bell infant, als pradets prop la Bassa Dòria, aguinollada en cap de una riba, ab una bella creu que tenie en les mans, ab una manteta vermella que tocave en terra, en cabells bells e rossos; no li demanà si eren larchs o curts. E

---

[17] cada dia B
[18] tot temps B
[19] molt B
[20] exeleta A

ella testis dix-li, garda que digues veritat, per tres vegades; que li dix, que si veritat dius, jo'u iré cercar per veurer si la trobarie, e lo dit fadrí refermant dix, certament així és. E ella testis coneixie en la sua cara que estave mudat e que la cosa devie ésser veritat. E deliberà anar-hi, mas[21] no s'i gosà acostar per por que's meté en ella testis, sinó de luny que mirave lo dit loch, mas no'y vehé res. E sorti-li una lebre de prop los peus, e així se'n tornà a la segada, hon avie llexat son fill ab un altre fill menor, dienti-li, no'y he trobat res. E lavors lo fill menor dix jaquiu'y anar a mi, que jo'u iré a cercar; e així encontinent y anà, mas en aquella hora no y trobà res. E tornassen al bestiar.

Interrogata, si ella testis ha oyt dir pus al major. E dix que hoc, que la dita cosa li parlava molt dolçament, mas què ell no'u gosave escoltar, sinó que entreoy que deye que fessen professons, e altres coses dix que li deje, mas no'u gosave escoltar, tant ere espantat.

Interrogata, si li dix altre. E dix ella que no.

Interrogata, si sab ni ha oyt a dir que son fill lo menor hage trobat la dita cosa, ni què ha trobat. E dix ella testis, açò saber, que lo dit son fill menor lo dit dia de dijous, a hora baixa que lo sol se enramave, dix avie trobada la dita cosa, semblant a un bell infant, prop la bassa Dòria, assats prop de là hon l'altre fill major dix l'avie trobada. E que tenie vestida una bella manteta vermelle, ab cabells bells e rossos, ab une creu que tenie en les mans, aguinollada, semblant-li de edat de un infant molt petit, e acostant-se a ell[22] li meté la creu en la mà esquerra e besà-li la dreta, e aprés tornassen la dita creu. E dix-li: Digues a ton pare e a ta mare, que diguen al poble que's confessen e que's tornen a la part de Déu, è que fassen professons devociosament, sinó no'ls valdrie res; e si no t'en volen creure, digues que lo meu fill los ho farà creure. E que així, ab les mans juntes, ella se partí del dit minyó, tirant la via de la alzinera Dòria envers Torradenagó. E més dix, que li dix, que no'y avie tant xich ni tant gran, que de quatre anys avant no troseyàs lo seu fill.

Interrogata, si sab quants anys avie lo dit son fill major e menor. E dix que devie aver entorn deu anys.

[21] e may B [22] ella B

Interrogata, si acostumave de dir falcies lo dit son fill. E dix que no.

Generaliter autem fuit sibi lectum et perseveravit.

[*Celidoni Cirosa*]

Dicta die Celidonius Cirosa, filius dicti Joannis Cirosa, testis et deponens, citatus, juratus et interrogatus de mandato et instantibus predictis dicere veritatem.

Et primo fuit interrogatus, quina visió és aquella que's²³ diu qu'ell ha vista en dies passats. E dix ell testimoni, açò saber, que dijous prop passat, dia sobre dit, passades vespres que los solans se ombraven, ell deposant e testimoni anà a les mules que eren prop la Bassa Dòria, e com fonch prop la Bassa en un pradet que a desús, lo qual diu que mostrarie, en un desopte ell testimoni esdevingué davant una cosa, semblant a un bell infant, prop d'ell a tres passos, la qual estave aguinollada ab les mans juntes envers lo cel, ab una bella creu que tenie en les mans, semblant a son parer a una que n'a a Riner en lo altar de sant Sebastià, ab Nostre Senyor que ere crucificat, e vestie²⁴ una manteta vermella fort gallarda que li tocave en terra, així com estave aguinollada, tot entorn d'ella. E encontinent que ell testimoni la vehé se més por en ell, e tornà arrere dos o tres passos costerejant a la mà dreta. E en açò ella li parlà e dix-li: O fill fe't ensà, e digues al poble; e no'u escolti pus per por, ans fugí fort e ella tostemps parlave. E com ell testimoni fonch un trosset luny, sentí que ella dix semmanes, e no'n oy pus, ans se'n tornà a segar tot espaordit e mudat. E així contà lo dit cas a sa mare, la qual y anà de continent e no hi trobà res.

Interrogatus, si li parie molt gran. E dix que de grandària de un infant de dos o tres anys a son parer.

Interrogatus, si pogué albirar si ere home o dona. E dix que no sabie ni sab si's tenie res al cap, tanta por se meté en ell que no'u pogué albirar.

Interrogatus, quants anys ha ell testimoni. E dix que entorn devuit anys.

Interrogatus, si sab pus. E dix que no.

Generaliter autem fuit sibi lectum et perseveravit.

---

²³ que A   ²⁴ vestida ab A

[*Pere dels Ots*]

Dicta die et anno Petrus dels Ots, [25] parrochiae Sancti Justi termini castri de Ardevol, testis citatus juratus et interrogatus dicere veritatem.

Et primo fuit interrogatus, quin cas és aquell que's diu que li ha esdevingut ara en dies passats asén prop la Cirosa. E dix ell testimoni, que dimarts pus passat ell testimoni venie de Fornell de Riner, que ere anat per visitar un fadrí que'y ere malalt de glànola. E així com se'n tornave a sa casa devers Sant Just, com fonch prop un llaurat del mas de Vilaseca, en un gran ginebrar que'y ha prop lo camí general que va dels Estanys a Cardona, per molt que ell se esforçàs en sí mateix, ell no podia anar de aquí avant; e ell senyant-se, en sí matex pensave que podia ésser allò, com no's sentís nengun mal en sa persona, e així pensant se aseguè prop un raboll que'y avie. E sient així, ell testimoni sentí una veu que li dix: com estàs així? Perquè no vas a la Cirosa per un infant que'y ha malalt e recitar-t'a les paraules que l'a dites la Verge Maria. E ell testimoni oynt açò, estet girant-se dessà e dellà mirant si vere ningú, tota la persona li tremolà, e levàs denpeus e no vehé negú. E encara volent-se esforsar de tirar la dita via de sant Just e no pogué may passar avant. E ell testimoni vehent açò e pensant en la dita veu, deslliberà anar a la Cirosa, pensant que açò ere qualque mysteri, e així ell hi anà: e com fonch a la dita casa, trobà na Estanya la vella e na Lordella. E digueren-li com un minyó que li deyen Jaumet estave malalt e que's duptaven lo mal no li fos vengut per una visió que avie vista. E així ell testimoni hi entrà en la cambra per veure'l. E interrogat sobre la dita visió e què avie vist, e lo dit fadrí dix-lo-li tot de mot a mot, així com damunt és contengut. E com testimoni l'agués largament interrogat, dix-li si la Verge Maria li avie dit en quin dia farien dites professons. E dix que lo dit fadrí dix-li, no m'ho ha dit. E de aquí avant no ne agué pus resposta.

Interrogatus, si ell testimoni avie propòsit de anar a la Cirosa abans sentís la dita veu. E dix que no, ni jamés hi pensà.

Interrogatus, si ell testimoni avie oyt dir res may a negú de la dita visió abans que anàs a la Cirosa. E dix que no.

[25] orts B

Interrogatus, com se'n tornà si agué nengun empaig en son
camí. E dix que no.
Generaliter fuit sibi lectum et perseveravit.

[*Visit to Site*]

Et uno eodem contextu, non divertendo ad alios actus, dictus
Celidonius Cirosa una mecum Petro Cerda presbitero et scrip-
tore huiusmodi processus, presentibus etiam dicto regente ba-
juliam et proceribus prenarratis²⁶ et venerabilibus Guillermo²⁷
de Fontestar mercatore, Jacobo Torrentallar, Antonio Torrentallar villae Celsone, et in presentia etiam plurimorum aliorum
hominum hic presentium, dictus Celidonius designavit occula-
riter dictum locum ubi predicta vidit, qui locus est et se tenet
cum vico generali, quo tenditur de loco de Su ad villam Celsone,
satis prope locum Dòria predictum, in quodam prato diversis
herbagiis ornato, inter alia erant due matae de ginebres.

Laus Deo Optimo Maximo

[In A:]

Copia huismondi, in his sex foliis papirii huius formae, aliena
manu fideliter scripta, sumpta et extracta fuit a suo vero originali
in aerario beatae Mariae Virginis de Miraculo invento et bene
custodito, receptum per discretum Petrum Cerdà, presbiterum
et scriptorem reverendi officialis Celsone olim, et cum dicto
originale fideliter de verbo ad verbum comprobatum per me
Josephum Jordana presbiterum, sacrae theologiae doctorem, re-
sidentem in domo beatae Mariae Virginis de Miraculo, aucto-
ritate Apostolica nottarium publicum et dicto nomine regentem
scripturas publicas dicti archivi, et eidem copiae scribi feci, et
ut in juditium et extra juditium ab omnibus plene impendatur
fides, hic me subscribo et meum quo utor in publicis et clau-
dendis instrumentis apono Signum.

8. Jafre (Girona), 1460. From the manuscript book "Confraria
del Roser 1622" in parish archive and the original in ADG Sec.
C, no. 16, lligall 71, courtesy Da. Maruja Arnau i Guerola (see
above Ch. 2, note 11). My paragraphs.

---

²⁶ prenominatis B   ²⁷ Gabrielle

Informatio recepta super nona. . . . (illegible) demostrato fonte virtuoso in loco de Jafre—Año 1461.

Ad perpetuam rei memoriam.

[*Miquel Castelló*]

Die martis decima February Anno Domini millesimo qua-dringentesimo sexagesimo primo en civitate Gerunde juravit et deposuit testis sequens. Michael Castelló parrochiae de Jaffero testis denuntiatus juratus dixit que en veritat esta que en lo mes de novembre prop passat ell testimoni llauraura un seu camp qui es apellat camp del bosch de la dita parrochia de Jaffer e llaurant vench a ell testimoni un home de mija talla vestit de roba de palmella fins a mija cama e calsat de calses de palmella e sabates burelles ab bonet de dita color de palmella que portaua en son cap e una canija en la ma de llarch al parer dell testimoni[1] de XX fins a 23 anys sens fil de barba, e, com fou prop de ell testimoni demana a ell testimoni com auia nom, e ell testimoni dixli que auia nom Miquel Castelló, e apres lo dit home dir a ell testimoni quantes creus hi auia en entreforchs de camins a Jaffer, e ell testimoni dixit que no auia sino una, e llavors lo dit home dix a ell testimoni quen mathes una en so del seu si podra, sino en altre loc en entreforcs de camí;

apres dix a ell testis tals o semblants paraules: lous pos en carrec de la vostra anima que digau al poble de Jaffer que aquella font qui es al camí quan hom va a Colomes qui fa bassa que esta ben closa e tinguda en estima car aquexa aygua ahuia gran virtut e per ço com hi uien llauades bugades li auien feta perdre la virtut pero que si la tencauen e la tenien en stima que la dita font cobreria sa virtut

e llavors ell testis dix que si ell o dehia a la gent que nol creurien, e llavors lo dit home dix a ell testis que si farien car aqui se morria un albat tantost e que axo lo poria dar per senyal e llavors lo creurien e ell testimoni dix al dit home de qui seria lo dit albat e lo dit home dix a ell testimoni que tantost ho sabria e llavors lo dit home se partà dell e sen anà via de Colomes vora de Ter. Axi e perdre de veure que nos sabe ques feu,

---

[1] In Camós this line reads, "una caña en la mano, de largo, según pareció al dicho, de ocho palmos, ..."

e apres ell testimoni ana a la vila de Jaffer e com fou a casa sua senti ver tocar los senys per un albat den Bernat Dolça parayre de Jaffre qui solament era mort en dita parrochia e ell testis ana a mossen Joan Ballester prevere de Jaffer e dix li totes les dites coses les quals ell dit Ballester denuncia lo diumenge següent a la trona de la isglesia de Jaffre a la gent de la dita parrochia e fou lo dit cas en divendres e apres veu ell testis que molta gent hi ve per algunes malalties e gorexen segons havia dit ell testimoni.

Fuit sibi lectum et perseveravit.

[*Bernat Guillen*]

Jovis XII mensis et anni deposuit et juravit testis sequens: Honorabilis Bernardus Guillermus de Jaffero, miles, in parrochia de Jaffero domiciliatus testis monitus iuratus et interrogatus dicere et deponere quam sciat veritatem in et super his de quibus inferius, fuit interrogatus si ell testis ho ohit dir que en la dita parrochia de Jaffero se sia trobada una font i sia bona a ningunes malalties e que gent hi hage devocio ne hi vingan a la dita font per portansen per malalties gorir,

et dixit que en veritat sia que aqui en la dita parrochia de Jaffer ha una font al camí que va a Colomes la qual es molt apropiada a moltes malalties e ha vist ell testis que divendres prop passat ha que tres setmanes que a ell testis vench gran mal e dolor de costat e fou molt spantat que ell testimoni se tingue per mort e demana li fos donat a beure de la aygua de dita font, e tantost li fou donat de la dita aygua que ell testis ne begue tres o quatre tassades se conegue lo cor molt clar e apres se feu cobrir be, e sua molt e fou gorit per grasia de Deu perfectament e creu ell testis que Nostre Senyor Deu ab mija de la dita aygua la gorit car ell testis no pensaua scapar del dit mal

e axi matex a vist ell dit testis segons dix que an Miquel Trobat de Jaffer abans que ell testimoni se ajagues per lo dit mal vench gran mal de coll en tal manera que aquell vehe lo tenia per mort com ja tenia lo coll molt gros rombayaua e donaren li a beure de la aygua de la dita font e posi a poch millora entant que ara per grasia de Deu es ben gorit e sa,

e mes dix interrogatus que lo en Gaspar Costa de Ullastret ha dit a ell testis que a Monells auia haudes VII persones que

auian beguda de la aygua de la dita font la qual ell testimoni
la auia tramesa a les VII persones auien mal de costat e mal de
coll que tots eren gorits sino una dona vella quis era morta

e axi a hoit dir ell testis que un sclau den Caramany que era
malalt que jal tenien per mort e donaren de la dita aygua e es
gorit e que lo dit Caramany a offert lexarlos dos mesos a Jaffre
per ajudar a fer la capella a la dita font si si fa.

E veu ell testis que son ajut esdeve que en un jorn hi venen
sobre cent persones e tot jor hi ha moltes persones car sobre la
dita font han posada una caxeta que tot jorn troben sis sous, e
haja montat calque jorn a vuyt sous y sis diners lo jorn, e veure
que las dites gents ab barrals carabasses, botes e miges botes sen
portan e si ranten ab gran devocio e ha ohit dir ell testis pu-
blicament que quasi tots quans ne beuen gorexen de totes malalties e que es molt apropiada a mal de ulls.

Fuit sibi lectum et perseveravit.

9. El Torn (Girona), 1483. Parchment in shrine archive, probably contemporaneous, as per photograph in Constans, *Historia
de Santa María de Collell* (Santuario del Collell, 1954).

Die iouis tricesima mensis Nouembris Anno a natiuitate domini Millesimo quadrigentesimo Octauagesimo Tertio Michael
noguer parrochianus parrochie Sancti Andree de Turno Ge-
rundensis diocesis dixit et denunciauit ut inferius continetur Et
prime dix e denuncia que dissapta prop passat que teniem vint
e sinch de Octubra predit ague vuyt jorns que era la festa de
mossen Sant luch venint ell testimoni denunciant de cassa hora
baxa del seny del perdo E passant per la capella de la verge Maria
del collell vingue en deuocio a ell testimoni denunciant que fahes
oratio a la porta de la sglesia la qual staua tanchada ab clau e
que tochas la oratio del perdo E agenollat qui fo a la porta de
la capella fahent ça oratio y aquella hauer feta segons deu li
hauia administrat volentse leuar senti e hoy ell testimoni denunciant dins la dita capella grans plants y grans plors de vna
Infanta pocheta E axi ell testimoni denunciant stigue molt torbat
e admirat del dits plants y plors e volentse leuar per anar tochar

lo perdo las portas de dita capella que com dit es stauan tanchadas ab clau se obriran miraculosament

E stant ell agenollat e aquellas ubertas ell testimoni denunciant vahe dins dita capella deuant ell testimoni denunciant tres o quatra passos dins aquella vna bellissima infanta de edat de set en vuyt anys tota vestida de vestidures blanchas com la neu la qual continuament se treballaua ab las mans batent e juntas clamant e demanant merçe a Jesu xpist y aquell ssupplicant que fos de ça merce y pietat que volgues hauer merce y pietat y misericordia del pobla seu cridant molt alt ab veu molt dolça la qual infanta vista e hoyda per ell denunciant com dalt a dit stant ell testimoni tostemps agenollat ell denunciant volentse fforçar e se fforça e cobra lo animo que tenia quasi spantat e dix interrogant a la dita Infanta per vnas tals o semblants paraulas O dolça creatura vullas me dir y denunciar quin es lo trebayll tan fort que tu tens

E per la dita infanta li fo respost com se segueix O fill meu pos te en carrech de la tua anima que tu vullas posar en carrech de las animas dels obres de las parrochias del torn de milleras y del salent y de Sant Miquel de campmaior que posen en carrech de las animas dels curats que vullan demanar al pobla que vullan pagar be los delmas e tots los drets de la sglesia e altras cosas que tingan amagadament o manifesta que no sian llurs que las vullan restituhir y tornar en aquells de qui son dins spay de trenta jorns que be sera mester e ben colra lo sant dimenga

E per la segona se vullan separar y guardar de jurar de deu E pagar vullan las charitats acustumadas per llurs passats lexadas e instithuidas

Aximateix ma posau en carrech de la anima dels obres qui son o per temps seran que si vehen hun peccat en las ditas lo vullan castigar

y ditas aquestas paraulas e manadas per la dita infanta a ell testimoni denunciant que aquell las denuncias com dal a dit la dita Infanta se torna a complanyer e complanyentse dix e mana a ell testimoni denunciant stant agenolat com dalt ha dit ab las paraulas seguents que li posa en carrech de la sua anima que ell denunciant degues posar en carrech de las animas de aquells

obres demunt dits que dins spay de trenta dias aguessen tret y
relevat lo interdit que es en aquesta cambra e apres aquell tret
de dita cambra mana fer proffessons a ditas quatra parrochias
y a totas las altras qui entendra si vullan que tots diuendras
ffassan proffessons ab tot lo pobla aiustat y en deju vullan venir
en aquesta mia cambra y fer aquell be que deu llurs administrara

E mes dix y li mana la dita Infanta que totas las cosas demunt
ditas volgues denunciar al Reuerendissimo Senyor Bisba de
Gerona o a son vicari que vulla fer relleuar y remoura dit entradit
mes y posat en la dita sua cambra E aço sots carrech de la anima
sua y aquell hagues fet traura dins spay dels trenta dias demunt
dits

E seguidas totas las paraulas y cosas demunt ditas per la dita
Infanta a ell denunciant tal la dita Infanta li desaparech que ell
testimoni no vahe res pus sino que las ditas portas de la dita
capella miraculosament se tornaron cloura y tanchar ab clau
com miraculosament se eran ubertas restant ell testimoni agenolat en la porta de la dita capella haunt se era agenollat per fer
ça oratio e en aço ell testimoni denunciant se leua en peus e sen
ana a casa sua E totas las ditas cosas demunt designadas y descritas odi y denunciadas per lo descarrech de la anima sua y per
lo carrech quen te o denuncia ara de present a vosaltres mos-
senyors de vicaris del Reuerendissimo Senyor Bisba

Interrogat ell testimoni denunciant aquestas cosas si demana
a dita infanta que diu que vahe ella qui era et dixit que ell
testimoni denunciant demana a dita infanta que li plagues dir
ella qui era y la dita Infanta li respos que ella era la verge maria

Interrogat ell testimoni denunciant com la infanta li desaparech si ell testimoni resta desaconsolat ni desconfortat y dix
ell testimoni resta molt aconsolat com la Infanta li fo desapa-
reguda

Interrogat si li demana y reuella a ell testimoni denunciant
que nostro Senyor deu volgues donar alguna punitio al pobla
y dix que si que la dita infanta li dix que si lo pobla nos conuertia
que donaria grans mortaldats de glanolas per la terra

Interrogat si ell testimoni denunciant te memoria que la dita
Infanta li haia ditas altras cosas sino las demunt ditas o descritas

et dix ell testimoni denunciant que no altras cosas sino las demunt ditas descritas y continuadas
Fuit sibi lectum et perseuerauit

10. Pinós (Lleida), 1507. N. Camós, *Iardin de Maria* (1657)
383-384.

Queda autenticada esta marauilla en vn auto que tiene de ella
el archiuo de la Iglesia Collegiata de San Vicente de Cardona,
el qual tomò Iuan Noguès, Notario Publico de Cardona, y Escriuano de dicho Monasterio: y despues fue hecho dèl, vn tra-
sumpto (que està en su Capilla) por Geronimo Alsina, y Iuan
Torrebruna, Notarios Publicos con Autoridad Apostolica, y Re-
gia, de Cardona, y es del tenor siguiente, y con el mismo len-
guage.
Dijous que tenim sinch de Setembre del any 1507, per mossen
Balle de Cardona, è lo venerable mossen Iuan Piñet, Official per
lo Reuerent señor Bisbe de Vrgel ensemps ab lo honrat en Iofre
Marti, Consul en lo present any de dita Vila, fonch presa la
seguent deposicio en la Parroquia de Matamargò, del señer en
Bernat cases de dita Parroquia, en è per la forma seguent. E
primo fou interrogat lo demunt dit Bernat Cases com ni quina
era estada la visio, ò aparicio que segons fama li ere estada feta,
è que digues veritat, que asso no era cosa de burles.
E ell dit Bernat Cases responent dix semblants paraules, que
dimecres qui teniam lo primer de Setembre, dia de Sant Gil, a
les set hores, ò entre set è vuit de mati el parti de la casa per
anar a la via de Biosca per veure vna sua tia, è partit tira son
cami la volta de la Verge Maria de pinos, è arribat ali volent fer
oracio trobà les portes tencades de manera que noy pogue entrar,
è axi ell pres lo cami derrera la Capella la volta de la cisterna
per tirar son cami, è com fou al canto de la Iglesia, a la part de
Tremontana deuant dita cisterna, li aparegue subitament ab vna
remor quasi de vn tro somort vna dona tota vestida de vermell,
de que ell se espantà molt. E ella li dix: No hajes por bon hom,
haont vas? E ell li dix, que anaue la volta de Biosca per veure

vna sua tia. E ella li demana don era. E ell dix que de la volta
de Matamargò: è ella li dix: Diges, quin temps y ha a Cardona?
E ell respon. Señora de la pesta be, que dies ha no ni ha mort
ningun; pero ay algunes febres de que ni moren molts. E ella
li dix. E per los veynats, dix aquest: Señora ara començan. E
ella li dix: Bon hom jot man que tu vajes a Cardona, è que
digues a los Iurats, que temps era que ells se recordauen de
aquesta Capella, è que ara la hauian mesa en oblit: empero que
ells diguessen a tots los castells, ço es Ardeuol, y Riner, Castelltallat, è altres Parroquies entorn de dita Capella, que entre
. tots se disponguessen en hauer vn bon Preuere. E que fes la
seruitut ques pertañy a dita Capella, è al seruey de Deu, com
se acostumaue, è ell los haurie misericordia. E ell respon, è dix:
Señora no men creuran. E ella dix: Ve, è si no te volen creure
lexels estar. E dit asso de continent ella desaparegue: e no vè
cosa ninguna, ni persona del mon.

Interrogat quina dona era, ni quina cara tenie, dix que no la
pogue compenre, ni may los seus vlls la gozaren afigurar.

E interrogat perque li dix Señora, ni qui pensaue que ere, dix
que en opinio sua, pensaue que ere la Verge Maria.

E interrogat dels articles de la Fè Catolica los confessà com
a Cathilich Christia. Exortat, è iurat per mossen official, que en
virtut de aquells articles que ell hauie confessats creure digues
veritat si allo que auie deposat passaue axi en esser visio, è sino
que aquells fossen en condemnatio de la sua anima.

E ell respos, è dix, que tots fossen en condemnatio de la sua
anima, si axi no ere com demunt hauie deposat.

11. Sant Aniol (Girona), 1618. N. Camós, *Iardin de Maria*
(1657) 101-102. The original document was probably in Catalan.

Entre los muchos portentos que obra el Cielo por esta Imagen
fue notable aquel que sucedio à Maria Torrent de la Parroquia
de san Aniol: como ella misma depuso por dos vezes, que fueron
la vna a los 8 de Deziembre del año 1618. delante del R. miguel
carrer natural de Olote, y residente en esta casa (siendo ma-

yorales los honorables Antonio Collell Mir, Raphael Coll, Antonio Aulet, y Emanuel Seol, todos desta Parroquia) y de muchas otras personas congregadas en su Iglesia: y la otra a los 28 de Iulio del año 1629. delante de los Reuerendos Bartholome Seol Retor de san Aniol, y de Esteuan Mas Bernat Clerigo de Besalu, y residente entonces en dicha casa: de Iuan Torrent Marido suyo: y otras muchas personas honradas, y dignas de fe. Esta sigunda deposicion hizo conformandose con la primera, como consta en lo que esta escrito en la misma Iglesia, donde se contiene lo siguiente.

Dia de todos Santos del año 1618 partio de la casa, y Quinta de la Parroquia de san Aniol, Baronia de Santapau del presente Obispado de Girona, dicha Maria Torrent muger de Iuan Torrent jornalero de dicha Parroquia, y fuesse a la de san Miguel de Lacot (de donde era natural, y tenia enterrados sus padres) con intento de hazer recitar responsos por la almas dellos, y de quien tenia obligaciones; por lo qual trahia seys dineros. Llegando en fin à dicha Parroquia, hallò el Retor ocupado, y por esto no se atreuio a dezirle nada. Boluiose por esso muy triste y a la que llego al llano de camias, haziendose ya de noche, encomendose muy de veras a la Virgen de los Arcos, suplicandole fuesse seruida de ampararla, y fauorecerla en aquello que mas le conuenia para el bien de su alma. Yua con esta disposicion rezandole su Rosario, y al cabo de poco tiempo le aparecio vna muger muy hermosa, galan, y bella, vestida de blanco: la qual le hablo, diziendole: Buena muger venid aca, no tengays miedo, ni os espanteys, que vos venis de la Parroquia de Lacot de donde soys natural, y traheys seys dineros por hazer cuitar [sic] responsos por aquellos que teneys obligacion, y no los haueys podido hazer recitar, y assi agora hareys dezir psalmos. De aqui le fue diziendo que no lleuasse ropa de color en todo vn año sino blanca, que no flastomasse las criaturas que Dios le hauia encomendado, que todos los dias por espacio de vn año recitasse el Rosario a N.S. antes de hazer otra cosa, si le era possible, y tenia ocasion, que procurasse à cumplir los votos que hauia echo à N.S. del Collell, y de los Arcos con mucha diligencia, y lo mas presto que pudiesse, que dixesse a la gente de san Aniol que no flastomassen, ni jurassen de Dios, que el quedaua muy agrauiado, que mirassen mucho, y tuuiessen mucha cuenta en que no se leuantassen falssos testimonios vnos à otros, que se castigassen mucho de sus uicios: y si no lo hazian nuestro señor Dios les castigaria muy rigurosamente, que se dexassen de parcialidades, y malicias, que dixesse a los de S. Aniol que la madre de Dios de los Arcos les hauia alcançado misericordia, y perdon con su preciosissimo hijo, y que fuessen con procession a su santa Capilla, y todos los que podrian yr à pie descalço que lo hiziessen, sino el Retor: que quando fuessen a ssu Santa Capilla, dixesssen tres Padres Nuestros, y tres Aue Marias por el alma mas necessitada del Purgatorio, y despues que continuassen vn año essa deuocion, y que recitassen juntamente sinco Padres Nuestros, y sinco Aue Marias todo el año por las almas de Purgatorio en general, y diez Padres Nuestros, y Aue Marias en reuerencia de la sangre preciosa que nuestro señor Iesuchisto [sic] hauia derramado por los pecadores, y que todas las mañanas antes de hazer alguna cosa recitassen vn Rosario, y en la noche de la misma suerte.

Dicho esto despidiola con estas palabras: Buena muger andad que es muy tarde para llegar á vuestra casa. Fuesse ella, y la señora le passó por el lado, y luego la siguio vn resplandor por todo el camino que era mas aspero: y dicha Maria Torrent viò otra vez à esta señora por vna sendica abaxo que estaua sentada en vna piedra, azia la fuente del mas faja de S. Aniol, y dixo que a su rededor hauia vn grande resplandor. Llego despues dicha Torrent à casa de vn tal Font labrador de la Parroquia de san Aniol temblando, y pidiendole que tenia, y de que temblaua: respondio que la madre de Dios de los Arcos le hauia salido en tal parte, y contò todo lo que hauia passado (estando presentes la muger de dicho Font, y muchas otras personas de dicha casa) en el punto que fue llegada, y luego que huuo sucedido el caso. Todo sea para gloria de Dios, y de Maria Santissima de los Arcos.

12. La Mota del Cuervo (Cuenca), c. 1514, and El Toboso (Toledo), c. 1516. Inquisition of Cuenca ADC Inquisición, Leg. 71, num. 1039.

[*Denunciation*]

a xxviii de março de Mdxvii años

testigo

madalena muger de di*e*go de pozo vezina de santa maria de los
llanos testigo jurado en forma[?] dixo allende de lo que dicho
tiene contra otro que oyo dezir a vn juan de rabe* vezino de
la dicha villa e otras vezes de la mota que se traspone munchas
vezes e que vee a dios e a santa maria en el parayso e a los
sanctos e a los angeles e arctangeles e que si alguna persona dize
mal del que luego lo sabe e que lo dize delante de todo el pueblo
que dicho es ansi en la mota como en santa maria de los llanos
e que se acuerda este testigo que en la dicha villa de la mota
dixo el dicho juan de rabe que avia visto a nuestra señora ca-
vallera en vn asnito e quel pueblo como lo supo hizo hazer vna
procesion desde la yglesia e lleuaron vna cruz la qual lleuo el
cura de santa maria de los llanos a cuestas hasta el lugar donde
el dicho pastor avia dicho que avia visto a nuestra señora e que
avra mas de dos años que paso e que este testigo fue con el
pueblo juntamente en la dicha procesion

lo mesmo dixo su hermana deste testigo que se dize ysabel
lopez e alonso lopez vezinos del dicho testigo e juan castillo
vezino del dicho lugar aviendo jurado y estan sus dichos en lo
de villamayor en el segundo pliego de los sueltos.

[*Interrogation*]

en diez e ocho dias de hebrero de Mdxviii años

juan de rabe vezino de la mota fue mandado llamar por sus
Reveren*çi*as a la sala estando preso en las carçeles deste sancto
ofiçio por su mandado e syendo del reçibido juramento en forma
por el señor ynq*uisi*dor juan yañes fue preguntado por su Reverençia como se llamava dixo que se llama juan de rabe hijo
de juan de rabe e de ynes rod*r*iguez defunctos vezinos que fueron
de villaverde e de alli naturales christianos viejos de todas partes
e que no tiene mas de vna hermana que vyue en la mota que

---

* [marginal note] este pastor biue con m*arti*n sanchez e con pedro
de la calle vezinos de la mota

se llama maria de rabe que es casada con pedro garcia labrador
vezino de la dicha villa de la mota.

preguntado sy es casado o lo auia seydo dixo que no e que
es de hedad de çinquenta años poco mas o menos. preguntado
por que no se ha casado. dixo que porque no avya hallado quien
bien se hiziese. preguntado que hazienda tenia. dixo que no
tenia ninguna hazienda saluo que se mantyene de su trabajo
cavando y arando y a las vezes syendo pastor e quel año passado
antes deste hera pastor. preguntado donde ha vyuido estos años
passados. dixo que en la dicha villa de la mota y en sancta maria
de los llanos. preguntado si sabe que año es el que agora estamos
dixo que no sabe aunque sabe ques el mes de hebrero.
fue preguntado por su Reverençia sy sabia el credo y la salue
regina dixo que no. y sy sabia el pater noster y el ave maria
dixo que sy. fuele mandado que lo dixese dixo el ave maria toda.
y el pater noster todo lo mas pero no bien sabido. fue preguntado
por su Reverençia sy se ha confessado cada vn año como manda
la sancta madre yglesia. dixo que cada quaresma de cada vn año
se ha confessado en la dicha villa de la mota con el cura viejo
y que ha rescibido el sanctissimo sacramento cada que se confessava.

preguntado sy sabe los diez mandamientos y los articulos de
la fe y los siete peccados mortales y sy sabia los çinco sentydos.
dixo que no sabe nada de todo esto ni parte dello. preguntado
por su Reverençia de que se confessava pues dize que no sabe
los pecados mortales ni los diez mandamientos ni los çinco sentydos dixo que de lo quel sabia se confessava. fue preguntado
sy sobervya o enbidia o luxuria o matar algun hombre o dezirle
palabras ynjuriosas baldonandole sy es pecado a cada cosa dellas
dixo que no sabe. fuele preguntado sy el hurtar sy hera pecado.
dixo que nos guardase dios que hurtar hera muy gran peccado.

preguntado que cosas heran las que confessava pues no confessava peccados ningunos dixo que yendo este confitente a cabar
en vna vyña puede aver quatro años a sancta maria de los llanos
que hera de vn primo suyo que se dize françisco martinez solo
y llevaua vn açadon para cabar y vna bota y su pan para comer
yendo por el camino oyo vn trenuedo grande en el çielo y
estonçes dixo este que depone o valame dios del çielo raso esta
el çielo como trenueda y mirando hazia el lugar dixo que avya

oydo otro trenuedo y vyendo como estava raso dixo valame dios
ques esto y que en esto miro a sus pies y dixo que avya visto
a nuestra señora la virgen maria cabe sus pies. e que le paresçio
que hera como vna niña chiquita e que venia cavalgando en vn
borriquito chiquitico e bestida de blanco
   preguntado de color hera el borrico dixo que hera muy her-
moso que no sabe de que color hera.
   preguntado quien venia con ella dixo que no venia otra persona ninguna.
   preguntado que como sabia o quien le dixo que aquella hera
[sic] que dize hera nuestra señora. dixo que ella misma se lo
dixo. e que le avya dicho o quanta mala gente ay en este tu
lugar que no hazen syno jurar y perjurar a mi hijo e que no
bastava los hombres syno que tanbien las mugeres. y que le
fuese a dezir a todo el pueblo y al cura que tomasen la cruz y
fuessen en proçissyon hasta el sancto cabero questa en el pedernoso o hazia el pedernoso y que pusiesen vna cruz donde
avya venido i aparesçido a este confitente.
   y que asy fue luego a dezirgelo a todos. y vynieron luego con
vna cruz y la pusyeron en el mismo lugar que este confitente
los dixo que le avya aparesçido nuestra señora; y de alli fueron
al dicho sancto cabero que puede estar de alli mas de quatro
tiros de vallesta e despues que se tornaron luego al lugar en
proçessyon y que antes que fuesse a dezir al pueblo aquesto que
le avya dicho se le avya desaparesçido e que nunca mas la vydo
e que esto hera vn sabado por la mañana y que le dixo que no
lo dixiese hasta la tarde e que asy lo hizo y que no le queria
absoluer el clerigo hasta que el domingo luego lo dixo antel
pueblo en la yglesia.
   preguntado sy nuestra señora la que dize que vyo sy traya
en sus braços alguna criatura dixo que no le avya visto nada
syno como venia sentada en el borriquito.
   preguntado sy sabe que hera borrico o mulia dixo que no sabe
syno que le paresçio borrico y muy bonito. e que nunca otra
bez ninguna se le aparesçio saluo la que dicha tiene
   pero que otra vez dende a dos años se le aparesçio sanct
sevastian en los llanos de casa sola e que traya vn vestido de
pardo y con sus saetas con sangre e que traya vna corona de oro
como a manera de estrella y que hera tan alto como la meitad

deste que depone y benia solo y que hera vna mañana antes que almorzase este deponente andando con ganado de *christ*oval sanchez de la mota. y le dixo como hera sanct sevastian. y que le dixo que fuesse al toboso porque murian estonçes mucha gente de pestilençia e los dixese que hiziesen dos hermitas la vna en el çerro espartoso e que les avya mandado hazer nuestra señora que no avyan querido hazer hasta que torno aquella mortandad como antes las avya avydo como ella avya mandado. y la otra baxo de señor sanct pedro la qual esta començada a hazer y que no sabe de que sancto saluo que la del çerro espartoso les mando que fuese de señor sanct roque

Visto por sus Reverençias la confesion del dicho juan rabe e todo lo que mas devyo ver y examinar fallaron que le debian mandar e mandaron dar çiento açotes por las culpas que contra el resultan de su confesyon. los quales le mandaron dar publicamente por las calles acostumbradas desta ciudad a voz de pregonero y asy le mandan que buelua a la dicha carçel para le ynformar de lo nescessario para salud de su anima. y esto hecho que se vaya con dios donde quisiere e le mandaron que de aqui adelante no cure de andar publicando las vanidades por el confessadas por ser como son cosas de vanidad e perjudiçiales a nuestra sancta fee catolica e a las animas de las personas symples e catolicas que las oyen

fue dada esta senten*ç*ia a diez e syete dias del mes de hebrero de Mdxviii años testigos lope suarez allid e françisco de oyos portero del sancto ofiçio yo françisco ximenez notario fuy presente

13. Quintanar de la Orden (Toledo), 1523. Inquisition of Cuenca ADC Inquisición, Leg. 83, num. 1190

Processo contra françisca la braua muger de pedro garçia de la romera cardador y peynador vezino del quintanar

[*Investigation by Town Officials, October 23, 1523*]
    en la villa del quintanar en veynte e tres dias del mes de otubre de quini*e*ntos e veynte e tres años los señores alu*a*ro de

cepeda e her*n*and *muñoz* de horcajada alcaldes hordinarios en
la dicha villa por razon que dezian que françisca la brava muger
de pedro garçia de la romera vezino de la dicha villa abia dicho
e dezya que se le avie apareçido nuestra señora la virgen marya
oyeron de su ofiçio la ynformaçion syguiente

[*Witness María Fernándes*]
　　este dicho dia los dichos señores alcaldes reçibieron jur*amento*
en forma de derecho de maria fer*n*andes muger de juan mu*ñ*os
de abi*la* la qual syendo preguntado que es lo que sabe e oyo
dezir a françisca la brava muger de pedro garçia de la romera
dixo este dicho testigo que lo que sabe e oyo dezir a la dicha
françisca la brava dixo que ayer jueves junto con el pozo duçe
topo con la muger de pedro garrydo e le dixo que entrasen en
casa de juana m*art*inez y que sabryen de françisca la brava y
le preguntaryen que dizie que avye visto a nuestra señora e que
este testigo dixo [illegible word] nuestra señora y que se quedo
espantada y que no dando credito a ello ni con pensamiento de
le preguntar cosa ninguna entro en casa de la dicha juana martinez para ver sy podia cozer en un hornillo suyo y que vido
que estava alli la dicha françisca la brava
　　y que como la vido juana martinez a este testigo le dixo llegaos
en ca la de juan muños y cocaros a françisca la brava como a
visto a nuestra señora y que este testigo quando se lo oyo ovo
tanto plazer que se le saltaron las lagrymas de los ojos de plazer
e que penso en sy e se maravillo e dixo valame nuestra señora
como estan en esta villa mu*n*chas personas devotas que nunca
hazen sino rezar en espeçial la de pedro ortyz e la de villoslada
y no se le apareçe y apareçersele a esta muger que pensando en
esto le dixo a la dicha françisca la brava bienaventurada soys
vos sy tal aveys visto
　　e que estonçes le dixo la dicha françisca a este testigo por
çierto que es verdad que yo la vi y fue desta manera que ella
se levanto a orynar estando acostada y como hera noche y fazye
escuro no açertava la puerta e que como no açertava la puerta
dixo valame nuestra señora y como no fallo esta puerta y que
a estas palabras le respondie nuestra señora e dixo ella te vala
& que nuestra señora soy la que te sostiene sobre la faz de la
tierra e que le echo el braço sobre el pescueço a la dicha françisca

la brava y como estava desnuda le echo la falda de la saya que
traye nuestra señora sobre su varriga a la dicha francisca la
brava e que le dixo no ayas temor hija
    que la dicha francisca le dia [sic] valame nuestra señora sy
es algund diablo que me viene a engañar e que le torno a dezyr
no ayas temor que nuestra señora soy e que asymismo le dixo
la dicha francisca que abye tornado esta noche pasada como que
hacia la mañana e que le dixo madre de dios no me creheran
que soys vos avnque digo que os he visto y que le dixo nuestra
señora pues toma esta candela y vn pedaço de çendal y vna
piedra yman e que esto todo le dixo a la dicha francisca le brava
que abie visto e avie pasado y que es verdad que todo esto lo
oyo este testigo dezir a la dicha francisca para el juramento que
hizo
                              [signed] aluaro de cepeda alcalde

[*Witness Juana Martínez*]
    este dicho dia los dichos señores alcaldes resçibieron jura-
mento en forma de derecho de juana martinez muger de
francisco *sanchez* palomares para en el dicho caso la qual so
cargo de dicho juramento syendo preguntada en el dicho caso
dixo que lo que oyo dezir a la dicha francisca fue que ayer por
la mañana vino la dicha francisca a su casa deste testigo e le dixo
que yva a misa & que le pidio que le diese sy tenia vn cabo de
candela e que este testigo le pregunto que para que e que le dixo
que quirye confesar e que se fue la dicha francisca a misa e que
despues de que vino de misa se vino por su casa de este testigo
e que deque la vido dixo que tienes francisca que quieres confesar
    e que le dixo la dicha francisca no se no os lo dixe esta mañana
y dezyros lo he agora & que le dixo que estando acostada en
la cama y su marydo con ella la dicha noche miercoles en la
noche recordo con voluntad de hazer aguas e que se levanto e
que quiso abryr la puerta para ver que noche hazie e que como
estava muy escura la casa no podia hallar la puerta e que dixo
valame nuestra señora & que le respondio ella te vala e que
desque oyo esta palabra quiso llamar a su marydo e que le dixo
la que le avie dicho esa te vala calla calla no le recuerde no ayas
temor que yo soy nuestra señora que te vengo a visitar e acuer-
date de tal dia que mageste a tu niño e le dixyste valame nuestra

señora y que es esto no puedes callar e que la dicha françisca
a esto ovo muncho temor e dixo bienaventurada yo sy asi es
que nuestra señora me venga a visitar e que le torno a dezir
pues no temas que yo soy nuestra señora e que dixo la dicha
françisca no sea algund diablo que me venga a engañar e que
le dixo que no hera syno nuestra señora & que le dixo que
hiziese dezir çiertas tres misas para sus finados e que cogiese
tres domingos para nuestra señora de la piedad e otros tres para
nuestra señora de guadalupe e que hiziese dezir syete misas
adonde [?] destierro de nuestra señora e que le dixo que avie
de bolver jueves en la noche e que le oyo dezir oy viernes que
avie venido esta noche ya al dia e que le dio vna candela de çera
& vna piedra yman para que la mostrase e diesen credito para
ello e que todo lo suso dicho le oyo dezir este testigo a la dicha
françisca la brava & que esto es asi verdad que lo oyo so cargo
del juramento que hizo

        [signed] aluaro de cepeda alcalde

Confesion [*of Francisca la Brava to the Alcaldes of Quintanar*]
    este dicho dia los dichos señores alcaldes fueron a casa del
dicho pedro garçia de la romera donde hallaron a la dicha
françisca la brava su muger e reçibieron juramento della en
forma devida de derecho so cargo del los señores alcaldes le
mandaron e preguntaron sy es verdad que ella avia dicho e
manifestado que avie visto a nuestra señora miercoles en la
noche e jueves en la noche proximos pasados.
    la qual dixo que so cargo del juramento que hecho avia que
es verdad que ella vido a nuestra señora e que lo a dicho e
manifestado a muchas personas vezinos desta dicha villa e que
çiertamente es nuestra señora la que ella vido por que sy fuera
otra cosa no viniera como vino e que paso lo que vido desta
manera que el martes en la noche que agora paso que se contaron
veynte dias deste dicho presente mes de otubre estando en su
casa al fuego e que se queria agostar el dicho pedro garçia su
marydo ella no se quisiera acostar tan presto & que el dicho su
marydo le dixo acostemonos que tengo de madrugar a cardar
& se acosto el prymero & ella se acosto & no pudo dormir en
toda aquella noche devido en que le vino al coraçon pena que
en su cara e cuerpo no sentya mala disposiçion sino muncha

alegrya & que como estava con aquella pena de coraçon e no
podia dormir que se echo en rogatyva a nuestra señora la virgen
marya que le encaminase en lo que mas fuese saluaçion para
su anyma a su entero juyçio & con esto adormiose dende a vn
poco

r que el miercoles en la noche luego syguiente despues de
estar acostada en su cama syn pensamiento de lo de antes le
vino al coraçon el mismo dolor & pena como la primera noche
& que como estava asy rogava a nuestra señora que pues estava
con tanta pena syn saber de que que le encaminase & declarase
de que hera aquella tan grande pena que tenia en su coraçon e
que estando en esta rogatyva se durmio

& que recordo haza media noche r que estando acostada y su
marydo junto con ella se levanto syn saber que estoviese en su
libre poder y quiso hazer aguas desnuda e en carnes que no
tenia sobre ella cosa ninguna saluo vn cofya sobre su cabeça
& que estava como trasportada que no tenia notiçia ni pensamiento que estava en este mundo sino en el otro & quiso llegar
a la puerta de su cozyna para la abryr y como estava tan des-
atynada no la podia açertar la puerta & que ya que entro en sy
llego a la puerta & ya que la estava abryendo dixo valame
nuestra señora o yo no estoy en mi libre juyzio o estoy fuera
de seso e que asy como dixo estas palabras le respondio nuestra
señora e dixo ella te vala & que torno a dezyr valame nuestra
señora y que le torno a dezyr ella te vala e que esta declarante
quando oyo esto dixo valame nuestra señora en ryedro vaya
satanas heres algund diablo que me vienes a engañar e que le
dixo yo soy la que te tengo de valer sobre la haz de la tierra a
ty e a todo *christ*iano

e que fue estonçes esta declarante a llamar a su marydo e dixo
pe para lo llamar e nunca pudo acabar de dezillo e que le dixo
nuestra señora hija ninguna cuenta tenga*des* no de mal susto
a su marydo e que se llego a ella e le echo a esta declarante su
manto ençima de su barryga como estava desnuda & que estonçes le dixo que fuese a confesar & que comulgase antes que
lo dixese a persona ninguna e que hiziese dezir tres misas vna
por su madre e otra por su suegro e otra por su suegra & que
dixese que hiziesen vna proçesion donde el capitan de los pe-

cadores y la justiçia de la villa dixesen a vna cruz e la pregonasen
por esta villa que fuesen todos & que los que no fuesen que los
prendasen porque se acordasen de la proçisyon que se hazia &
que despues de hecha la proçision fuesen a nuestra señora de
la piedad e dixesen alli misa e se encomendasen todos en ella
& que todo lo suso dicho fue lo que supo el dicho dia miercoles
en la noche

yten dixo que oy dicho dia viernes por la mañana vn poco
antes que amaneçiese estandose en la cama sola le torno el dolor
segund que de primero e que se encomendo en nuestra señora
que le revelase aquella pena e la encaminase en su juizio y se
levanto y se sygno y santyguo y abryo la puerta de su cozyna
y en abryendola vido a nuestra señora que estava junto con la
dicha puerta y con grande conpañia de angeles e a reçibie tanto
gozo e plazer en ver tantos angeles con tantas candelas
ençendidas que se cayo en el suelo con pauor cozida e que le
dixo que abie treynta & tantos dias que andava fuera de su casa
bendita rogando a su hijo precioso que nos enbiase salud para
nuestros cuerpos e salvaçion para nuestras almas e que estonçes
dixo ay madre mia madre que no me creeran e que estonçes le
dio vna candela atada en vn trapo e vna piedra yman lo qual
todo le dio al cura desta villa e que luego se desapareçio della

e que ensigida fue esta declarante a vna vezina suya muger
de fernando ximeno e le dixo amiga beni aca e que le dixo entra
e que le torno a dezyr beni aca syquito que no he gana de entrar
e salio con ella e que esta declarante torno a ver a nuestra señora
e se la mostrava diziendole catalda alli no la bedo e que la dicha
su vezina no la pudo ver e que la vido un hijo pequeño que traye
la dicha su vezina muger del dicho fernando ximeno e que asi
se desapareçio e se fue y que todo esto es asy la verdad que paso
e vido y es verdad so cargo del juramento que hizo

[signed] aluaro de cepeda alcalde

la qual dicha ynformaçion de suso contenida los dichos señores
alcaldes ovieron de las personas de suso contenidas por ante mi
juan garçia verdejo escrivano publico en la dicha villa la qual
va escrito en tres fojas de papel con esta en que va mi fyrma
e va oryginalmente lo qual di por mandamiento que me fue

notificado para ello de los señores ynquisidores e porque es
verdad que la dicha ynformaçion paso ante mi e no dixeron ni
pusyeron los testigos ni la dicha françisca la brava otra cosa
ninguna mas de lo que de suso va escrito lo di fyrmado de mi
nombre

[signed] Juan garçia de verdejo escrivano

[*Investigation by the Inquisition of Cuenca in Belmonte.*
First Interrogation of Francisca la Brava, Nov. 21, 1523]

En la villa de belmonte a veynte e vn dias del mes de nouienbre
de mill e quinientos e veynte e tress años ante el Reverendo
señor licençiado mariana Inquisidor y en presençia de mi pedro
de vranga notario paresçio françisca la braua muger de pedro
garçia de la romera vezino del quintanar que fue çitada e llamada
por mandamiento de su Reverençia e paresçida su Reverençia
resçibio della juramento en forma deuida de derecho sobre la
señal de la cruz e de los santos ebangelios so cargo del qual
prometio de dezir verdad. E su Reverençia le mando leer e por
mi el dicho notario le fue leydo su confesion que ante los alcaldes
de la dicha billa del quintanar hizo sobre que nuestra señora se
le abia apareçido. E asi leyda la dicha confesyon segund e como
de suso se contiene a la letra. la dicha françisca la braua dixo
ser verdad lo contenido en la dicha su confesyon segund e como
lo tenia dicho e declarado e le ha sido leydo e que en ello se
afirmaua e afirmo e ratificaua e ratifico & que no consta otra
cosa so cargo del juramento que tenia fecho

Syendo preguntada dixo que su padre se dezia alonso brauo
que no sabe si es biuo o defunto e que no sabe como se dezia
su madre porque no la conosçio e quel dicho su padre quando
biuia en el quintanar hera pastor e que es christiana vieja de
todas partes e que es natural del corral de caracuel e ha biuido
desde pequeña en el quintanar donde biue al presente e que ha
biuido alli con alonsso lopez de horcajada e despues con anton
de la mota vn año e que despues estubo con pedro brauo su tio
hasta que se caso e desposo e caso con el dicho su marido e que
sera de hedad de xxv años

fue preguntada sy esta quaresma proxima pasada se confesso

e comulgo e con quien. dixo que sy e que la confeso e comulgo
gallardo cura del quintanar

fue preguntada sy todos los domingos & fiestas oye la misa
mayor continuamente. dixo que sy eçepto algunas vezes que
dexa de yr por sus hijos e por el mal *tien*po

fue preguntada de la dotrina christiana dixo el abe maria y
el pater nostre y el credo en lo qual herro algunas palabras y
la salue regina synose e santiguose. no supo el anima christo
ni sabe otras ningunas oraçiones mas de que al tienpo que se
va a acostar dize la oraçion sy*guiente*. encomiendo a dios padre
e a santa maria madre e a la *san*ta magestad e a la flor (?) que
en ella esta e a senor sant bernaldo que en rroma esta enterrado
que me libre e me guarde de todos los pecados bacteados e por
batear que ni en la bida no me acusen ni en la muerte no me
engañen. encomiendo en aquella sacratisima virgen e madre de
dios bienaventurada ni sabe otras deboçiones e que ayuna la
mitad de las quaresmas e las bigilias e algunas que otro tenporas

fue preguntada que que dia o noche y a que ora se le apareçio
nuestra señora y de que manera la primera vez. dixo que se le
apareçio la primera vez el miercoles en la noche ouo quatro
semanas a media noche despues que abian cantando los gallos e
que se le apareçio como muger cubijado vn manto blanco y tocas
blancas y que no le bido las sayas que traya

fue preguntada que de que tamaño y de que color hera y sy
quando la hablo estaua en pie o asentada y con que compañia
venia. dixo que hera pequeña de estatura y de color morena e
que quando la hablo estaua en pie e que estonçes no traya
conpaña ninguna que hera la primera vez e desque la hablo hizo
grand resplandor e claridad

fue preguntada que palabras le dixo la que dize que le apareçio
nuestra señora y esta con*fitente* a ella y sy ouo temor y que
diga e declare todo lo que con ella passo. dixo que pronunçio
las palabras que tiene dichas en la confesion que hizo ante los
alcaldes e que al prinçipio ouo temor

fue preguntada sy quando se bolvio a acostar a la cama sy
recordo a su marido e le conto lo que abia pasado o a quien lo
dixo primero. dixo que no recordo a su marido ni gelo dixo y
que al primero que lo dixo fue a su cura porque se confesso

fue preguntada que quando lo dixo al cura. dixo que gelo dixo otro dia juebes syguiente con el qual se confesso e comulgo el dicho dia y le dixo como la noche antes abia visto a nuestra señora

fue preguntada sy al tienpo que dize que se le apareçio nuestra señora si ouo algund ruydo y si hazia escuro o claro y sy estaua dormia [sic] o entre sueños dixo que no ouo ruydo ninguno y que hazia claro como de dia y que no estaua dormida syno despierta e que su casa no tiene corral ninguno

fue preguntada sy otras noches antes de aquella se a acostunbrado a leuantar a hazer aguas o a otra cosa. dixo que no eçepto quando esta preñada

fue preguntada sy quando dize que se leuantaua de noche estando preñada si salia fuera del palaçio donde duerme a hazer aguas. dixo que no porque dentro tiene vn tiesto para hazer aguas e que aquella noche despues que abia hecho aguas se salio y abrio la puerta y se paro al hunbral della para ber que tienpo hazia

fue preguntada sy ella salio a la calle e sy aquella que dize que hera nuestra señora sy entro en su casa y palaçio y la abraço o dio paz o sy la derribo en el suelo o que le hizo. dixo que no salio a la calle syno al hunbral y que nuestra señora se llego a esta testigo al hunbral de la puerta y no entro mas adentro y que le echo el braço por el pescueço que le *derribo* a el albanega de la cabeça y que no la derribo en el suelo y le dixo que se confesase y comulgase y que hiziese dezir tress myssas y que hiziesen la procesion que dicha tiene e dezir la misa acabada la procesion como lo tiene declarado en su confesyon

fue preguntada que por espacio de que tanto tienpo estouieron asy juntas. dixo que muy poco estouieron que seria parte de bna hora no sabe quanto mas de que hera poco y que esta declarante no hablaua

fue preguntada sy al tienpo que se partio la que dize nuestra señora que que le dixo o que hizo. dixo que acabado que le dixo lo que declaro en su confesyon asy se deshaspareçio y que no dixo a su marido nada de aquello porque nuestra señora no le dio lugar para que gelo dixiese antes la mando que se confesase e comulgase

fue preguntada que de que tamaño y estatura le apareçio la
que dize nuestra señora y que si benia descalça o que calçado
y bestidos traya. dixo que se le apareçio del tamaño de vna
criatura de quatro años e que como traya manto blanco como
vn papel y tocas blancas no vido que vestidos traya ni si traya
calçado o venia descalça ni le vido corona syno sus tocas blancas
ni le daua lugar para ello

fue preguntada sy olia bien o que holor traya consygo y aquel
resplandor que dize si hera de la luna. dixo que no le dio lugar
a que la oliese sus olores e que el resplandor no hera de la luna
syno del que traya consygo e que las tocas no sabe de que heran
mas de que heran blancas

fue preguntada sy quando dize que paso lo suso dicho si estaua
adormida trasportada o entre sueños o estaua despierta y en su
libre poder y juyzio. dixo que estaua despierta y en su libre
poder y juyzio como agora esta y no estaua adormida ni entre
sueños ni trasportada y que bien se acuerda de todo lo que dicho
tiene. E que la segunda vez se le apareçio nuestra señora como
dicho tiene en su confesyon viernes en amaneçe no amaneçe
çercada de angeles

preguntada que que tal le apareçio aquella que dize nuestra
señora estonçes y con que bestidos e que otras cosas traya. dixo
que ya lo tiene dicho en su confesyon e que aquello mismo dize
agora y que le pregunto que si abia mandado hazer lo que le
abia dicho y que esta confitente respondio que si abia dicho pero
que no la creyan y que al tienpo que se yba nuestra señora esta
confitente dixo ay madre mia que no me creeran y estonçes le
dio nuestra señora vna candela con vna piedra yman dentro en
vn trapo labrado y que le dixo cata ay porque te crean y asy se
desapareçio y nunca mas la vido ni se le ha apareçido y que
luego esta confitente dio las dichas candelas e piedra al cura y
el cura lo tomo y lo metio en el seno

fue preguntada que que tales heran los angeles que dize que
benian con nuestra señora sy heran grandes o pequeños y que
bestidos trayan y sy trayan alguna musyca o candelas o antorchas en las manos o si trayan alas o syn ellas. o si estauan en
el suelo y andauan o estauan en el ayre o si cantauan o que
bestidos trayan y sy hablauan algo. dixo que no tubo habilidad

para saber que tales heran mas de que acompañauan a nuestra
señora al tienpo que subia al çielo e que heran pequeños e que
no vido si benian vestidos ni calçados ni tubo abilidad para ello
e que no trayan alas ni musica ni cantauan ni candelas e que
no los bido syno al tienpo que nuestra señora se subia al çielo
ni podria mas declarar dellos. E que esta segunda vez su marido
no estaua en casa que ya se hera ydo a trabajar.
   a lo qual fuy presente yo el dicho notario

[*Inquisition. Witness Pedro García de la Romera, Husband of
Francisca la Brava, Nov. 21, 1523*]
   En belmonte a xxi de nouienbre de Mdxxiii años antel Reverendo señor licençiado mariana Inquisidor
   pedro garçia de la romera cardador a dicha villa del quintanar
testigo jurado so *cargo* e syendo preguntado dixo que es verdad
que es marido de françisca la braua e que es casado e belado con
ella a ley e a bendiçion
   fue preguntado sy sabe que la dicha su muger aya dicho que
nuestra señora se le apareçio e como e de que manera y quantas
vezes y donde que declare todo lo que sobre esto ha bisto e oydo
dezir.
   dixo que abra vn mes poco mas como que vn juebes o biernes
antes que amaneçiese estandose este testigo vestiendo para yr
a trabajar en su ofiçio y estando la dicha françisca su muger en
la cama le començo a dezir muncho bien aveys tenido en vuestra
casa pedro garçia y este testigo le pregunto como y ella le dixo
que se abia leuantado aquella noche y que abia ydo a la puerta
a hazer aguas y que como abia ydo y abrio la puerta dixo valame
nuestra señora y que nuestra señora le abia respondido essa te
vala. y que le dixo que yba desnuda en carnes y que nuestra
señora la avia cubijado con su manto y que no sabia sy estaua
en su libre poder ni sy no. E que este testigo le dixo que no
dixiese nada de aquellas cosas y con tanto se fue a trabajar y
que esta vez fue la primera vez que la dicha su muger dize que
se le apareçio nuestra señora.
   e que otro dia syguiente la dicha su muger dixo asymismo
a este testigo que se le avia tornado apareçer nuestra señora
aquel dia y gelo conto a la noche y que al tienpo que se yba

nuestra señora le abia dicho que no seria creyda e que le abia
dado vna candela y vna piedra e que abia visto a nuestra señora
benir blanca como vna paloma las rodillas chorreando sangre i
que no abia entrado en su cassa munchos dias abia rogando a
nuestro senor por los pecadores y que le abia mandado dezir
tress misas y que dixese la dicha su muger que hiziese proce-
syones e que venia con nuestra señora munchos angeles y que
benian todos de blanco. e que tanbien le dixo la dicha su muger
que en saliendo la puerta le abia echado nuestra señora el braço
sobre el pescueço e que ella le abia besado la mano a nuestra
señora e que este testigo le dezia e dixo que no dixiese ninguna
cosa de aquello

yten dixo que en el dicho tienpo andres fernandez labrador
vezino del quintanar vino a este testigo e le dixo que castigase
a la dicha su muger porque le podria subçeder mal dello porque
andaua deziendo que se le avia apareçido nuestra señora e que
abia venido con tanboriles o tronpetas e que lo mismo le dixo
tanbien juan pintado vezino del quintanar

yten dixo que la dicha su muger françisca dixo a este testigo
que le abia dicho nuestra señora quando se le abia apareçido que
anduviese a pedir syete domingos para nuestra señorà de guadalupe con la baçina en la yglesia e que aquella primera noche
que lo suso dicho le dixo la dicha su muger este testigo no la
syntio leuantarse de la cama ni que se boluiese a acostar

[Inquisition. Witness Alonso Fernández Gajardo, Parish Priest
of Quintanar de la Orden, Nov. 26, 1523]
en belmonte a xxvi de nouienbre de Mdxxiii años antel Reverendo señor licençiado mariana Inquisidor

alonso fernandez gajardo cura de la yglesia de la villa del
quintanar testigo jurado so cargo fue preguntado sy conosçe a
françisca la braua muger de pedro garçia de la romera vezina
del quintanar e que diga e declare que es lo que sabe e ha oydo
dezir sobre que dize la dicha françisca que se le apareçio nuestra
señora.

dixo que conosçe a la dicha françisca la braua de seys o syete
años a esta parte de bista habla y conversaçion e que lo que sabe
deste caso es que abra vn mes poco mas o menos que la dicha

françisca fue a casa deste testigo que estaua a la sazon rezando y le dixo que ella se hallaua dichosa o bienaventurada que a vna mugar pecadora como ella se le abia apareçido nuestra señora y este testigo le dixo yo no os dixe ayer que callasedes vuestra boca y no dixiesedes essas cossas que el diablo seria que os queria engañar y entonçes la dicha françisca dixo a este testigo pues señor pues que me escurio que nuestra señora se me apareçio veys aqui lo que me dio y le mostro y dio vna candelica y vn poco de piedra negra enbuelta en panezico pequeño de lienço labrado un poco. lo qual presento luego ante su Reverençia y este testigo como tomo lo suso dicho dixo a la dicha françisca otras palabras de reprehensyon e que no dixiese nada de aquello que el diablo seria que le engañaria y asy se fue estonçes.

e que dende a tress o quatro dias un domingo de mañana vyno a casa deste testigo pedro garçia marido de la dicha françisca e le dixo senor por amor de dios que vays a mi casa porque mi muger se ha salido de casa y esta sentada a la puerta enclabijadas las manos y no quiere hablar ni la podemos hazer entrar en cassa

y este testigo se leuanto de la cama y fue alla y hizo meter dentro en su casa a la dicha françisca y le desenclabijo las manos y en todo esto no hablo la dicha françisca y este testigo le dixo munchos exenplos de la sagrada escriptura deziendole que aquello que se le avia pareçido no seria syno el diablo y ya que se queria yr le dixo que se encomendase a nuestra señora e que ella la ayudaria y a esto dixo la dicha françisca ella me remedie y a ella me encomiendo y que asy se fue este testigo y que estauan presentes a esto çiertas mugeres e que despues aca este testigo no la ha hablado y que ha oydo dezir munchas que dizen que ha dicho la dicha françisca a algunos personas pero que este testigo no sabe mas

fue preguntado sy la dicha françisca es christiana vieja de todas partes e dixo que de lo que este testigo sabe y ha oydo dezir que es christiana bieja de todas partes

fue preguntado sy la dicha françisca va a misa todos los domingos & fiestas de guardar y otros dias y se confiessa e comulga en los tienpos que la yglesia manda y haze las otras cosas que buen christiano deve hazer y esta bien famada dellas. dixo que

continuamente la vee yr muchos domingos e otros dias a missa
e que desde syete años a esta parte continamente la ha confessado
este testigo cada año e no ha dexado de confesarse ninguno e
que esta tenido por buena christiana y esta bien ynfamada dello
    fue preguntado sy la dicha françisca sabe que es persona
cuerda y sy algun tienpo ha sydo endemoniada o sospechosa
dello. dixo que la dicha françisca a lo que della ha alcançado es
persona cuerda e no sabe que aya sido endemoniada
    fue preguntado sy este declarante ha creydo que nuestra
señora se le apareçio a la dicha françisca. dixo que no que antes
como dicho tiene la repr*e*hendia de lo que dezia porque lo tenia
por liuiandad
    fue preguntado sy sabe o ha oydo dezir la cabsa porque la
dicha françisca ha dicho e publicado que se le hapareçio nuestra
señora dixo que no la sabe mas de quanto ha pensado entre sy
si lo abra ensoñado o la abra enganado el diablo
    fue preguntado que pues que esto ha tenido por liuiandad
como dize que porque no la ha venido a manifestar ante su
Reverençia pues que la examinaçion desto perteneçia a la jurisdiçion deste santo ofiçio como cura del dicho lugar pues por este
tenia mas obligaçion. dixo que bien vee que hera obligado a
manifestar pero que de estar como esta enfermo lo ha dexado
de venir a dezir
    fue preguntado sy antes de lo suso dicho supo o oyo como
se leyo en la yglesia del quintanar la c*arta* de edicto. dixo que
oyo leer la dicha carta con todas sus censuras desdel prinçipio
hasta el fin
    fuele dicho que pues que conoçe este caso perteneçia a la
jurisdiçion deste santo ofiçio y oyo la dicha carta de hedito que
porque no lo manifesto o enbio a manifestar por vna via o por
otra mayormente siendo cura e pastor del dicho lugar. dixo que
este testigo escriuio a su Reverençia con el cura del touoso al
qual dio la carta para que la truxiese en que le escriuia haziendole
saber el dicho casso
    fue preguntado sy fue publico e notorio en la villa del quin-
tanar e su comarca lo que la dicha françisca ha dicho e publicado
que nuestra señora se le avia apareçido. dixo que sy porque se
supo en toda la villa y en la comarca

[*Inquisition. Witness Alvaro de Cepeda, Alcalde, Nov.* 26, 1523]

En belmonte a xxvi de nouienbre de Mdxxiii años antel dicho
señor licençiado mariana Inquisidor paresçio aluaro de çepeda
alcalde e bezino del quintanar que fue llamado por mandamiento
del qual su Reverençia reçibio juramento en forma so cargo de
lo qual le pregunto sy conosçio a françisca la braua vezina del
quintanar e de que tienpo a esta parte. dixo que la conosçia de
doze años a esta parte de bista habla e conversaçion

fue preguntado que diga e declare que es lo que sabe e ha
oydo dezir sobre lo que la dicha françisca ha dicho e publicado
que nuestra señora se le apareçio. dixo que lo que sabe del dicho
caso es que este testigo como alcalde de la dicha villa del quintanar resçibio ynformaçion sobre ello e la confesion de la dicha
françisca la qual todo se mando traer ante su Reverençia e que
a aquello se refiere porque este testigo no sabe otra cosa ninguna
e que ha oydo dezir que a la dicha françisca la braua la besauan
y abraçauan munchas mugeres y que de su casa llebauan çiertas
piedreziellas e tierra de donde ella dezia que se abia sentado
nuestra señora e que este testigo vido yr algunas mugeres a su
casa y oydo dezir que abia ydo e yban munchas *mu*geres de la
dicha villa del quintanar e de otras partes a oyrle dezir como
se le abia paresçido nuestra señora a la dicha françisca e lo que
mas dezia sobre ello e que venian mugeres del touosso a ello
e que lo suso dicho fue muy publico e notorio en la dicha billa
e en su comarca

fue preguntado que si sabe o ha oydo dezir que cabsa le mouio
a la dicha françisca a dezir e publicar lo suso dicho. dixo que no
sabe la cabsa porque se mouio e que este testigo lo tiene por
liuiandad e falsedad e mentira que nuestra señora se le apareçiese
e que cree que fue el diablo sy alguna cosa se le apareçio

fue preguntado sy sabe que la dicha françisca es christiana
vieja y si esta y*n*famada de buena christiana en su bida. dixo
que de parte de padre sabe que es christiana vieja e de la madre
no sabe nin caso [?] de la confitente en la pregunta e que ha
oydo dezir que sabe bien echar pullas

fue preguntado que pues lo que la dicha françisca publico ha
tenido por falsedad e mentira e vee que hera cosa en detrimento
de nuestra *santa* fe catholica y diminuiçion de su abtoridad y

que la examinaçion dello perteneçia a la jurisdiçion deste santo
ofiçio que porque como tal alcalde no la denunçio e remetio ante
su Reverençia. dixo que es verdad que este testigo y su conpañero alcaldes del quintanar viendo que lo suso dicho hera
publico resçibieron como dicho ha ynformaçion sobre ello e lo
enbiaron al licençiado de lillo a ocaña para que les dixiese su
pareçer sobre ello y que el dicho licençiado les enbio su dezir
que no proçediesen en aquello sino que amedentrasen a la dicha
françisca que no dixiese nada de aquello y que este pareçer no
selo enbio por escripto syno con pedro de billanueba procurador
del confitente con quien enbiaron la dicha ynformaçion y gelo
dixo de palabra y que si les enbiara a dezir que hera cosa que
tocaua a este santo ofiçio que este testigo lo denunçiara e re-
mitiera a este santo ofiçio e que si por ynadvertençia y
negligençia ha caydo en alguna dexcomunion o pena que pide
misericordia e absoluçion.

[*Inquisition. Witness Hernand Muñoz de Horcajada, Alcalde,
Nov. 26, 1523*]
    En la dicha billa este dicho dia antel dicho señor Inquisidor
paresçio hernand muñoz de horcajada alcalde del quintanar e
abiendo jurado en forma e syendo preguntado sobre lo suso
dicho dixo que no sabe mas de la dicha françisca la braua de lo
contenido en la ynformaçion que este testigo e çepeda alcaldes
del quintanar resçibieron sobre ello. mas de que ha oydo dezir
que munchas mugeres yban a casa de la dicha françisca a oyrle
lo que dezia de como nuestra señora se le abia apareçido e que
la besauan la boca e los ojos e los oydos e que llebauan de su
cassa piedra y tierra de la parte donde dezian que se le avia
pareçido nuestra señora e que a este testigo le pareçio mal aquello
que dezia la dicha françisca dezian porque lo tenia por burla e
no por çierto ni verdadero.
    E que este testigo ha quatorze años que conosçe a la dicha
françisca de bista habla e conversaçion e que la ha tenido e tiene
por christiana vieja e que es muger cuerda i no loca avnque es
algo engueydilla y liuiana y burlona y ristadora e que no sabe
la cabsa que le mouio a dezir lo suso dicho e que es muger pobre
    fue preguntado que pues tenia por falsedad lo suso dicho que

porque no lo remitio ante su Reverençia pues vee q*u*el
conosçimiento dello perteneçe a este santo ofiçio. dixo que enbiaron la ynformaçion a vn letrado el qual les enbio a dezir que
no curase dello syno que dixiesen a la muger que no dixiese mas
de aquello que abia dicho e que si les enbiaron a dezir que lo
remitiesen al santo ofiçio que tanbien lo hizieran y que sy por
la negligençia yncurrio en alguna pena o sentencia de exco-
munion pide pen*itenci*a e absoluçion.

[*Inquisition. Second Interrogation of Francisca la Brava, Nov.
28, 1523*]
En la dicha billa de belmonte a veynte e ocho dias del mes
de nouienbre de mill e quinientos e veynte e tress años el Reverendo señor licençiado mariana Inquisidor en presençia de mi
el dicho notario mando paresçer ante sy a la dicha françisca la
braua e paresçida su Reverençia so cargo del juramento que tiene
fecho la pregunto que si despues que publico como se la abia
aparecido nuestra señora concurrieron e benieron a su casa
munchas personas e le besauan los ojos e la boca e otras partes
diziendo que benditos fuesen ojos que ouiesan visto nuestra
señora e se llebauan de la tierra e piedras donde esta declarante
dezia que se abia aparecido nuestra señora.
dixo que benieron munchas mugeres a su casa vn dia que fue
ayer viernes como çinco semanas e que tanbien vino alli miguel
tgrado [?] e que la de juan de billanueba llego su rostro con el
desta confitente e le dixo que bendita fuese cara que tal cosa avia
visto e que otra ninguna persona la besso e que es verdad que
las dichas mugeres lleuaron de la piedra donde esta confitente
dixo que se avia alli paresçido nuestra señora que hera junto al
hunbral de la casa de su puerta donde estaua la dicha piedra e
que truxieron un niño de la de alonso de yepes çeçionario e le
hizieron besar en la dicha piedra e luego sano de las çeçiones
que tenia. e que esta confitente dixo que veya que venia entre
los angeles que benian con nuestra señora vn hijo suyo que se
le abia fallecido hecho angel
fue preguntada que sy quando la primera vez dio notiçia e
parte de lo suso dicho a alonso fernandez gajardo cura del quintanar sy le mando que callase su boca e no dixiese cosa ninguna

dello a ninguna persona porque hera cosa de liuiandad e burla. dixo que es verdad que el dicho cura le dixo que callase e no dixiese nada que si nuestra señora hera quel se echaria en rogatiua para que tornase a ella y esto fue la primera vez. e despues desto lo dixo & manifesto esta declarante a algunas personas e que antes que se confesase con el cura que no lo dixo a persona ninguna

fueronle mostradas la candela & piedra con el pañezico vn poco labrado que dize que la dio nuestra señora para que lo reconoçiese. dixo que es verdad que nuestra señora le dio las dichas candela e piedra con el pañezico e que reconoçio ser aquello mismo que le fue mostrado

fue preguntada que pues que esto que ha dicho e publicado que nuestra señora se le apareçio es falsedad e mentira como es publico e notorio que que es la cabsa porque lo ha dicho e publicado e ha afirmado e afirma con las otras cosas que en su confesyon dize. dixo que es verdad lo que dicho tiene e que sienpre tendra en su coraçon que fue nuestra señora la que se le apareçio

fuele leydo y dicho a la letra todo el dicho & deposiçion que su marido pedro garçia dixo & depuso en xxi deste presente mes ante su Reverençia e preguntada sobre el sy aquello es verdad. dixo que es verdad todo lo que el dicho su marido dize que esta confitente le dixo e que ella gelo dixo como lo dize

fue preguntada que pues que dixo que nuestra señora no sabia sy benia calçada o descalça que como dixo a su marido que benia chorreando sangre las rodillas e porque se ha querido perjurar. dixo que la primera vez que vido a nuestra señora no sabe sy benia calçada o descalça e que la segunda vez que bien vido que benia chorreando sangre sus rodillas & sus rostros e que estonçes le dixo que abia treynta y tantos dias que no entraua en su casa rogando a nuestro senor por salud para nuestros cuerpos y saluaçion para nuestras anymas

fueronle tornadas a leer e fueron leydas todas sus confesiones a la letra e dichole que ya vee la variaçiones e contradiçiones dellas e como en munchas cosas se contradize e perjura. por ende su Reverençia dixo que la amonestaua e amonesto de parte de dios nuestro señor e de su bendita madre nuestra señora la

virgen maria que diga e manifieste la verdad e no se perjure ni
condene su anima e que diga e declare que es la cabsa que la
mouia a dezir e publicar que nuestra señora se le apareçio pa-
resçiendo claramente ser falsedad. E que si asy lo hiziere e la
verdad dixiere que con ella se vsara de misericordia. donde no
que la administrara justiçia y la mandara castigar conforme a
derecho. dixo que dize lo que dicho tiene antes de agora

E luego su Reverençia mando pareçer ante sy al dicho pedro
garçia de la romera y presente al dicha su muger les dixo que
been sy quiere concluyr con sus confesiones para que determyne
esta cabsa o si quieren seguir su justiçia que aquella les guardara.
E luego la dicha françisca la braua con consejo e pareçer del
dicho su marido dixo que concluya e concluyo con sus confesyones e no tiene ni quiere mas dezir porque ellos no quieren
pleito.

A lo que fuy presente yo el dicho pedro vranga notario

[*Inquisition. Sentence, Nov. 28, 1523*]

Bisto el presente processo por nos los Inquisidores deste obispado de Cuenca e las confesyones de la dicha françisca la braua
e ynformaçion de testimonio que contra ella ay resçibida de
nuestro ofiçio e como por toda consta la dicha françisca ser en
muncha culpa de aver grauemente delinquido contra nuestra santa
fee catholica en aver publicado e afirmado como nuestra señora
se le apareçio por dos vezes segund y de la manera y forma que
en las dichas sus confesyones dize e afirma siendo todo burleria
e falsedad e como de las dichas en sus confesyones e ynformaçion
de todo claramente se colige demas de averse claramente per-
jurado en muchas cosas dellas e por lo qual puesto que de rigor
de derecho nos podieramos con ella aver mas rigorosamente por
aver sydo lo suso dicho muy publico y escandalosso a los fieles
christianos por los aver atraydo e ynduzido a que creyesen ser
verdad lo que dezia e publicaua siendo todo vanidad e liuiandad
pero attentas algunas justas cabsas que nos mueben para mitigar
el rigor fallamos que para que a la dicha françisca la braua sea
castigo e a otros exenplo de no cometer semejantes cossas que
la debemos condenar e condenamos en pena de lo suso dicho
a que sea apuesta en vn asno y le sean dados çient açotes pu-

blicamente por las calles acostumbradas desta villa de belmonte
desnuda del medio cuerpo arriba e otros tantos en la villa del
quintanar de la manera que como dicho es. E que de aqui adelante
no diga ni afirme en publico ni en secreto dire ni yndirete las
cosas que dichas tiene en sus confesyones sobre lo suso dicho
so pena que se procedera contra ella como contra ynpenitente
y como contra persona que no tiene ni syente bien lo que tiene
e cree nuestra santa fee catholica e asi lo pronunçiamos e manda*mos* por esta nuestra sentencia nuestros escriptos e por ellos
[signed] yo licenç*iado* [illegible]

    dada & pronunçiada fue esta sentençia por el Reverendo señor
licençiado mariana Inquisidor que en ella firmo su nombre en
belmonte a xxviii de nouienbre de mill e quinientos e veynte
e tress años en absençia de la dicha françisca la braua. a lo qual
fueron presentes por testigos pedro barela portero deste santo
ofiçio e pedro martin de mariana criado del dicho señor Inquisidor e yo pedro de vranga notario que fuy presente
    Este dicho dia luego yncontinente yo el dicho notario notifique
la dicha sentençia a la dicha françisca la braua en su persona e
se executo en ella quanto a los vnos açotes testigos los susos
dichos e yo el suso dicho notario

Index

Words in Spanish Texts Referring to Ailments, Attire, and Emotions

Library of Congress Cataloging in Publication Data

Christian, William A., 1944-
  Apparitions in late Medieval and Renaissance Spain.

  Includes index.
  1. Visions.   2. Apparitions.   3. Mary, Blessed
Virgin, Saint—Apparitions and miracles (Modern)—
Spain.   4. Spain—Religious life and customs.   I. Title.
BV5091.V6C48   248.2   80-8541
ISBN 0-691-05326-X   AACR2